藩の無理非道
慢がならぬ！
十四万石
ら
せう！

小林正樹 監督作品

3.8.78

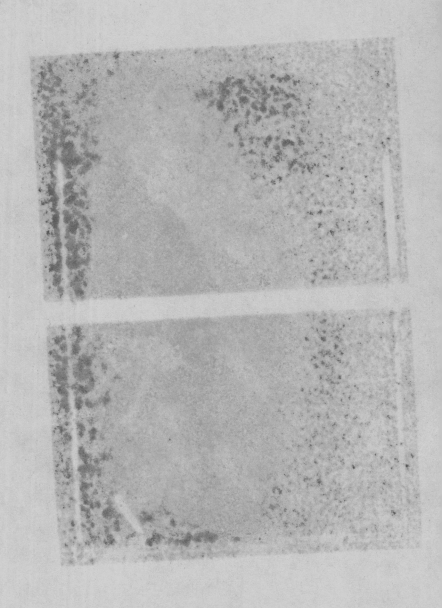

JAPANESE FILM DIRECTORS

JAPANESE

FILM DIRECTORS

Audie Bock

Preface by **Donald Richie**

Published for the Japan Society, New York
by **KODANSHA INTERNATIONAL LTD.,** Tokyo, New York & San Francisco

Publication of this book was assisted by a grant from The Japan Foundation

Distributed in the United States by Kodansha International/USA, Ltd. through Harper & Row,
Publishers, Inc., 10 East 53rd Street, New York, New York 10022. In Canada by Fitzhenry &
Whiteside Ltd., 150 Lesmill Road, Don Mills, Ontario M3B 2T6. In Mexico and Central
America by Harla S.A. de C.V., Apartado 30–456, Mexico 4, D.F. In South America, by Harper
& Row, International Department. In the United Kingdom by Phaidon Press Ltd., Littlegate
House, St. Ebbe's Street, Oxford OX1 1SQ. In Europe by Boxerbooks, Inc., Limmatstrasse 111,
8031 Zurich. In Australia and New Zealand by Bookwise (Australia) Pty. Ltd., 104–8 Sussex
Street, Sydney 2000. In the Far East by Toppan Company (S) Pte. Ltd., No. 38, Liu Fang Road,
Jurong, Singapore 22.

CONTENTS

for Masatoshi Ohba

FOREWORD

It has been my good fortune to have played leading roles in the films of more than half the directors discussed in Miss Bock's book. Each director I have worked with is a very different personality—ranging from morose Mikio Naruse to exuberant Masahiro Shinoda—and my experience with each of them has been a challenge to me as an actor, whether playing a samurai, a businessman, a student or a gangster. From conversations with Miss Bock over several years, I have learned that she has not only a deep interest in Japanese cinema and Japanese culture, but an ability to see and evaluate in a way that only "international eyes" can. At the same time her excellent command of the Japanese language, her years of experience in Japan and her clear insight make her the equal of the best Japanese critics. She has selected the most important representatives of each age of Japanese film history, and I am certain that her contribution to the appreciation of these great artists will be valuable to people all over the world for many years to come.

Tatsuya Nakadai
1978

centuries ago by the Kabuki theater: a chilling ghost story for summer, a serious literary adaptation for New Year's and the like. Here is where the remakes appear, the tried and true, the copies of the monuments of the national art constructed by Kurosawa, Naruse and other masters of the past. Here is where a whole bygone mode of expression assumes the appellation "classic."

This is the moment for the film archivist and film historian to step in, as indeed they have done. In the last several years not only has the Tokyo National Museum of Modern Art Film Center sponsored a large number of retrospective showings of classic Japanese films, but the Japan Film Library Council has organized an annual series that circulates among archives, museums and specialized organizations abroad, many of which also organize Japanese film series independently. In the course of these activities "new" old films long thought to be lost forever are being rediscovered and preserved—two spectacular recent finds in Japan, for example, are Mizoguchi's *The Straits of Love and Hate* (*Aienkyo*, 1937) and Teinosuke Kinugasa's best film, the 1926 avant-garde *A Page Out of Order* (*Kurutta Ippeiji*, released under the title *A Page of Madness* in the U.S.). The felicitous outcome of such efforts is that the classic masterpieces of the Japanese cinema are becoming better known abroad as well as at home as more and more old films are reintroduced and put into 16 mm. distribution for easy access. So it is that the works of Ozu have become well known abroad only in the last few years, early films of Kurosawa and Mizoguchi are being distributed for the first time, and there is hope for more exposure in the near future to such neglected masters as Mikio Naruse and Shohei Imamura. Now the achievements of these directors can be seen and evaluated instead of merely tantalizing us as passages in books. Consequently, a clear reassessment of the expressive quality of the Japanese film with a historian's view to the selection of landmarks can now be attempted, and such is the purpose of this book.

The ten directors whose works are treated here represent the most consistently high achievements of Japanese cinematic art from each of three significant eras. The first "golden age" of Japanese film occurred in the 1930s, when the Great Depression widened the gulf between the rich and the rest, and the Japanese as an audience began to display their preference for films about "people like you and me." Kenji Mizoguchi distinguished himself with films that decried the exploitation of the poor, especially women, the tragic theme he would pursue for life. Yasujiro Ozu and Mikio Naruse perfected the *shomin-geki*, a genre showing the realistic problems of life in the lower-middle classes, Ozu emphasizing acceptance and Naruse defeat. After the Pacific War, the work of these three pioneers would reach still greater heights in the second golden age of the 1950s, when higher production values and greater artistic control allowed them to refine their individual cinematic styles.

A second generation of humanists, with faster pacing and more action for the new age, emerged from the moral chaos after the war. With the introduction of Akira Kurosawa's *Rashomon* (1950) at the Venice Film Festival, Japanese cinema embarked on a relationship with the rest of the world. While exoticism became an export issue, Kon Ichikawa, Keisuke Kinoshita and Masaki Kobayashi joined Kurosawa in exploring ethical values and the social forces that thwart them, today and in the past, as well as the aesthetic form of the film.

By 1960, however, a new mood overtook the cinema. It is as yet too soon to determine if the 1960s are the last golden age of Japanese film, but what is certain is that, as in France, a newer generation brought new content and a new form to the art. Nagisa Oshima, Masahiro Shinoda and Shohei Imamura all turned their backs on what now seemed to be the naive universal humanism of the past and searched for the essence of Japaneseness. Oshima found political despair, Shinoda an aesthetic sado-masochism, and Imamura the power of the irrational mythic consciousness. In the 1960s, sex, violence, anti-narrativity and self-referentialism assumed roles never before seen in the Japanese film, and these three directors have proved best at employing all these elements as expressive means in their aesthetic statements.

By introducing the works of these ten directors with greater thoroughness than has been undertaken in a single volume before, I hope to convey some of the feeling of the times in which they have worked, as well as a familiarity with the individuals themselves. The complete annotated filmographies provide reference material heretofore unavailable, and a detailed discussion of one representative work in each chapter attempts to point the way to thematic and technical qualities meriting further study. All of the living directors have graciously spent some hours with me, and I have tried in the course of analyzing their work to let them speak for themselves as well by incorporating parts of these conversations. While there is no substitute for the act of viewing, my hope is that this book will be of some use to all who admire the art of the Japanese film.

In researching and writing this manuscript I have been aided and encouraged by many friends in both the U.S. and Japan. I am indebted to Donald Richie whose books on the subject and direct introductions brought me to work in the field of Japanese cinema in 1970. To Sheldon Renan, producer of "The Japanese Film" Public Broadcasting Service television series, I am beholden for the original suggestion and encouragement to write. I am also grateful for the aid of Mari Eijima, Peter Grilli, Robert Ruenitz and David MacEachron of the Japan Society of New York.

Numerous representatives of film organizations have been most generous with their facilities and time: Kazuto Ohira of Toho International in New York; Daniel Tanner and Linda Artel of the Pacific Film Archive at the University of California Berkeley; Kiyotsugu Kurosu of Shochiku Films of America in Los Angeles, and Charles Silver of the Museum of Modern Art in New York. Joseph L. Anderson of WGBH Television in Boston shared his knowledge with me and lent me his Japanese-language reference materials. Film critic Leonard Schrader lent me translated materials on Naruse. At Harvard University, professors John Rosenfield, Howard Hibbett, Vladimir Petric and Alfred Guzzetti, as well as my students, have been patient and responsive, while Ellen P. Wiese gave me the first encouragement.

I could have done nothing without the aid of Mrs. Kashiko Kawakita of the Japan Film Library Council and the Council staff, including Akira Shimizu, Toshimi Aoyama, Ayako Kabasawa and Yumiko Ichikawa. I thank Yukinobu Toba, Masatoshi Ohba, Sadamu Maruo and Masayoshi Tsukada of the Tokyo National Museum of Modern Art Film Center for countless screenings, research materials and introductions.

I am grateful to Shinichiro Sekido and Sanezumi Fujimoto of Toho in Tokyo for screenings and introductions. At Shochiku in Tokyo Shinji Serada provided screenings and introductions, and Satoshi Funahashi and Yoshitaro Nomura took me to location shooting. Kazuko Kawakita of the Shibata Organization was most generous with information, screenings and introductions. Yoichi Matsue of Atelier 41, Inc., gave me research materials, film stills and access to Akira Kurosawa. Kiichi Ichikawa of Filmor Enterprises introduced me Kon Ichikawa, who showed me studio shooting.

Tadao Sato and his wife gave me voluminous research materials, friendly guidance and introductions. Matsuo Kishi, Nei Kawarabata and Yoshio Shirai also provided invaluable information, and Koichi Hasegawa of the *Yomiuri Shimbun* and Mitsu Ono of the *Mainichi Shimbun* provided material from their archives. Kiyomi Kawano of *Agora* magazine and Mitsuyoshi Gunji helped me read Japanese names and difficult passages. Kihachi Okamoto and his wife have been close friends and informants; Tatsuya Nakadai and his wife have also been most helpful, as has Hideko Takamine. Above all, the directors whose works are treated in this book have given their time and the most essential information on themselves.

Japanese names are treated western style, with the surname last. All translations are my own except where otherwise noted.

Most of the directors' comments in the filmographies are based on interviews published in *Kinema Jumpo* magazine. Stills, except where otherwise noted, are courtesy of the Japan Film Library Council, Tokyo.

Audie Bock
Somerville, 1978

16

Filmography Key: Abbreviations and Circulation

*	recommended film.
pr	production company, distributor listed last.
sc	scriptwriter.
ph	cinematographer (unless otherwise indicated, black-and-white, flat photography).
KJ #	annual poll of Japan's "Best Ten" films taken by *Kinema Jumpo* magazine. 1941–42 *KJ* awards replaced by Nihon Eiga Zasshi Kyokai (Japan Film Magazine Association; designated NEZK) "Best Ten." 1943–45, no "Best Ten" awards given.
FC	Tokyo National Museum of Modern Art Film Center, 3–7–6, Kyobashi, Chuo-ku, Tokyo. Non-circulating 35 and 16 mm. unsubtitled prints; screenings by application.
JS	Japan Society Inc., 333 East 47th Street, New York, N.Y. 10017. Subtitled 35 mm. prints; non-theatrical circulation through Toho International Inc.
ME	Matsuda Eigasha, 3–18–8 Towa, Adachi-ku, Tokyo. Unsubtitled 35 and 16 mm. prints; screenings by application.
MOMA	New York Museum of Modern Art, 11 West 53rd Street, New York, N.Y. 10019. Non-circulating subtitled and unsubtitled 35 and 16 mm. prints; screenings by application.
PFA	Pacific Film Archive, University Art Museum, University of California Berkeley, 2625 Durant Ave., Berkeley, CA 94720. Subtitled 35 mm. prints; non-theatrical circulation through Shochiku Films of America (PFA/SH) and Toho International Inc. (PFA/TO); screenings on premises by application.
SH	Shochiku Films of America, 3860 Crenshaw Blvd., Suite 102, Los Angeles, CA 90008. Subtitled 35 mm. prints; theatrical circulation.
TO	Toho International Inc., 1501 Broadway, Suite 2005, New York, N.Y. 10036. Subtitled 35 mm. prints; theatrical circulation.

Distributors of subtitled 16 mm. prints in the U.S.

AB	Audio Brandon/CCM, 34 MacQuesten Parkway South, Mount Vernon, N.Y. 10550.
FI	Film Images, 17 West 60th Street, New York, N.Y. 10021.
GR	Grove Press, 53 East 11th Street, New York, N.Y. 10003.
JA	Janus Films, 745 Fifth Avenue, New York, N.Y. 10003.
NL	New Line Cinema, 853 Broadway, 16th fl., New York, N.Y. 10003.
NY	New Yorker Films, 43 West 61st Street, New York, N.Y. 10023.
TW	Twyman Films Inc., 329 Salem Ave., Box 605, Dayton, Ohio 45401.
Note	In the case of old films released in the U.S. under a title varying significantly from a literal translation of the original Japanese title, the release title follows the literal translation, which is also preferred in the text.

1 THE EARLY MASTERS

The cinema of Japan developed close on the heels of movies in the west, but due to peculiar national tastes, such as the persistence of the narrator (*benshi* or *katsuben*) even into the sound era, it was slower in surpassing the function of mere illustration for a storyteller. The young Japanese film industry, absorbing technical innovations and national styles from all over the world, preserved until the mid-1920s a certain insularity of approach. Japanese films were influenced largely by the Kabuki theater in the period realm and the Shimpa theater ("New School" tragedies of contemporary but fast becoming past contemporary life). The wonders from abroad were given separate treatment—German, French, Italian, U.S. and, finally in the 1930s, Russian films were all shown only in special theaters that never showed Japanese productions. While the foreign cinema went avant-garde, Japan tended to look back.

Directors who are known today as the most Japanese were the ones who began incorporating foreign influences to create a more contemporary domestic cinema. Kenji Mizoguchi in the early 1920s drew on German expressionism; Yasujiro Ozu in the late 1920s copied American films. But by the time the sound era was approaching, they were developing a synthesis that would be purely their own. When they were belatedly joined by Mikio Naruse in 1930, and all three looked to contemporary Japanese life for their subject matter, they became the major creators of the first golden age of Japanese cinema. We have known the work of these three master directors almost exclusively through their postwar works, but in recent years the rediscovery, restoration and preservation of many of their films from the 1930s has revealed another era of achievement previously known only through books.

The Great Depression in Japan, like the 1950s, saw the formation and dissolution of a great number of film production companies, the revolutionary technical introduction of sound—like the revolution of the wide screen in the fifties—and along with such innovations, a great mobility for directors. The social and political tone of the film world, where many began as uneducated, often impoverished adventurers, was heavily influenced by the proletarian movement, as witnessed in the rise of the leftist "tendency film" (*keiko eiga*) genre. Although Mizoguchi was the only one of the three directors representing this generation who admitted to making a real tendency film, the lost 1931 *And Yet They Go*, most of their works of the early thirties are marked by a focus on lowerclass life and problems.

But during this era the Japanese film world, while producing a phenomenal number of films per year and absorbing a wide variety of influences from all over the world, had little view to exporting the domestic product. Only Naruse's top domestic prize winner, *Wife! Be Like a Rose!* (1935), was shown in New York. Gradually, with the rise of militarism and the descent into war in China in 1937, most freedom of expression and any concern for showing Japanese features in the west were lost until well after the end of the Pacific War.

The war was a rude shock for the film industry, as it was for all the arts in Japan. "National policy" promotion of the war effort became the only justification for producing paintings, literature or films. Mizoguchi took the opportunity to embark on the making of elaborate period films, pursuing the historical "Japanese spirit." Ozu and Naruse went on making contemporary dramas like the 1942 *There Was a Father* and the 1939 *The Whole Family Works* that look entirely unlike what we know as propaganda until Ozu was drafted and Naruse succumbed to making his first (lost) period film in 1945.

For these first generation directors, the immediate postwar period was perhaps a worse shock. The U.S. Occupation seemed to be trying to change the very fabric of Japanese daily life, from which they drew their subject matter. None of them could deal effectively with a policy that not only forbade period films as potential promoters of feudal values, but actually required kissing scenes as an expression of democracy, according to film historian Tadao Sato. It was not until the end of the 1940s that they began to retrieve their strength and find their own voices again.

The reconstruction era brought new stimulus in the form of a new generation of filmmakers who rose up to compete. Japanese cinema saw its second golden age in the decade of the 1950s as the older generation responded to the challenge by refining their product to its most delicate. Mizoguchi created his finest period films, and Ozu and Naruse returned to their perennial concern: relationships in the family.

During this era television had not yet perfected its stranglehold on information and entertainment, and for the average person the movies were still the major easily accessible art form. Office worker, laborer and housewife alike still entered the darkened theater with expectations of the marvelous. One could relish seeing one's own everyday beliefs and experiences ennobled in the films of Ozu; one could decry the injustices of a feudal heritage with Mizoguchi's spirited but defeated heroines; one could share in the lonely determination of Naruse's heroines to make it on their own.

With such reliable clientele and such cheap postwar labor, this was the era of the big budget film. Mizoguchi could make period films the extravagance of which could never be equaled today, and Ozu could demand tens of retakes of a single line of dialogue, and produce only one film or less per year, without incurring the wrath of financiers. In short, the director was king. He had the two greatest luxuries in the business: time and money. He could spend months, sometimes years working over the scenario with his scriptwriter, he could tell the photographer what to do, he could have whole sets torn down and rebuilt on the spot if they did not please him, and far from today's method of selecting the director for a particular star, the actors of the golden age hungered after a chance to appear in the films of these men. It was only Naruse who continued to let himself be controlled by the studio.

In the west, the year 1951 brought sudden enlightenment. The Japanese film, long absent from the international scene, reemerged triumphant with Akira Kurosawa's Venice Film Festival Grand Prix winner *Rashomon*. This sensation occasioned an overnight demand for Japanese films, and a number of directors saw some of their works sent abroad. These included Mikio Naruse, Tadashi Imai, Teinosuke Kinugasa, Heinosuke Gosho, Kaneto Shindo and others, but the critical attention focused on Kurosawa and Mizoguchi, who began winning prize after prize at Venice. Interest was so great that a debate ensued over the "montage" style of Kurosawa as opposed to the "mise-en-scène" style of Mizoguchi. The French critics, led by film theorist André Bazin and budding directors Jean-Luc Godard and Jacques Rivette, became strong partisans of the personalism and musicality they saw in Mizoguchi, to the extent that Godard, praising Mizoguchi in *Arts* in 1958, called Kurosawa a second-rate director. In retrospect such tirades must be seen as a reflection of the political-artistic stance of this avant-garde group that sought to construct a new aesthetic of the cinema, and Bazin himself attempted to soften the invectives in a *Cahiers du cinéma* review of *Ikiru* in 1958 by calling attention to the universality of Kurosawa's themes and the challenge of his ethical message. However, to this day Mizoguchi remains the god of Japanese film to the French, who have difficulty finding flaws in even his mediocre works, while Kurosawa retains a greater appeal for the action- and ethics-oriented audiences of Britain and the United States.

A thorough introduction of Ozu's work in the west came only later, due to the Japanese reluctance to export a product they felt could only be understood by Japanese. Here the nationalist sentiment proved misguided, for Ozu has assumed his place as one of the three most appreciated Japanese directors in the occident. The enlightened critical analyses of Donald Richie (*Ozu: His Life and Films*, 1974) and scenarist Paul Schrader (*Transcendental Style in Film: Ozu, Bresson, Dreyer*, 1972) have undoubtedly contributed to a deeper understanding of his contemporary drama of everyday life.

Naruse still suffers today from the same neglect, for in Japan he is often named by such noted critics as Akira Iwasaki, alongside Ozu, as "the most Japanese director." His determined, independent women have been fleetingly introduced abroad with *Mother* (1952) in France and *When a Woman Ascends the Stairs* (1960) in New York shortly after its release and in the 1975 PBS television series. The Japan Society of New York has also put on a small retrospective of his works; and the Japan Film Library Council together with the Japan Foundation often includes Naruse films in the annual retrospectives it circulates worldwide, but generally he remains unknown outside Japan as well as among the young generation of contemporary Japanese. A large but incomplete posthumous retrospective in Tokyo in 1970 did much to restore his status in Japan, but despite Joan Mellen's discussion of his work in her 1976 *The Waves at Genji's Door*, none of his films have become accessible in 16 mm. in the United States.

Mizoguchi, Ozu and Naruse are by no means the only great directors from the first generation of the Japanese cinema. But they are the only ones whose achievements spanned the two golden ages with equal prowess. Despite periodic slumps, longest in Naruse's case, these three produced first-rate works throughout remarkably lengthy careers—Mizoguchi for 33 years, Ozu for 35, and Naruse for an amazing 37 years. That their creations could appeal to two entirely different generations of filmgoers separated by the incomprehensible trauma of the Pacific War in Japan, and to a public all over the world today, attests to the magnitude of their artistry.

KENJI MIZOGUCHI

●*Taki no Shiraito, the Water Magician (Taki no Shiraito),* 1933, Tokihiko Okada and Irie Tanaka

● *Osaka Elegy (Naniwa Erejii)*, 1936. Eitaro Shindo, Isuzu Yamada and Hara Kensaku

● *Sisters of the Gion (Gion no Shimai)*, 1936. Isuzu Yamada

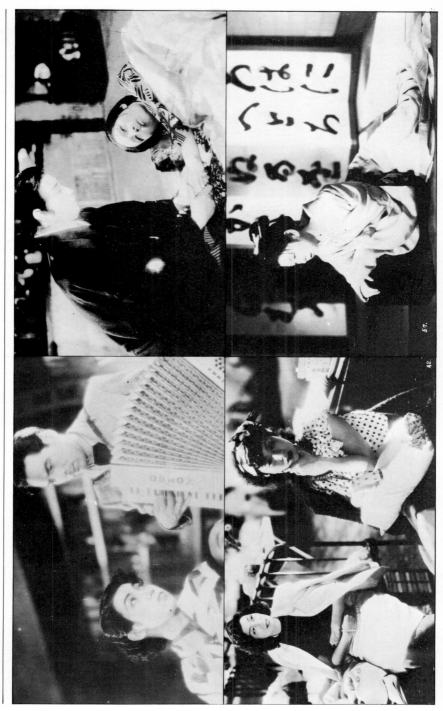

●The Straits of Love and Hate (Aienkyo), 1937. Chieko Takehisa (left), and Taizo Fukami

●Women of the Night (Yoru no Onnatachi), 1948, Sanae Takasugi and Kinuyo Tanaka

●The Story of the Last Chrysanthemum (Zangiku Monogatari), 1939, Shotaro Hanayagi and Kakuko Mori

●The Life of Oharu (Saikaku Ichidai Onna), 1952, Kinuyo Tanaka

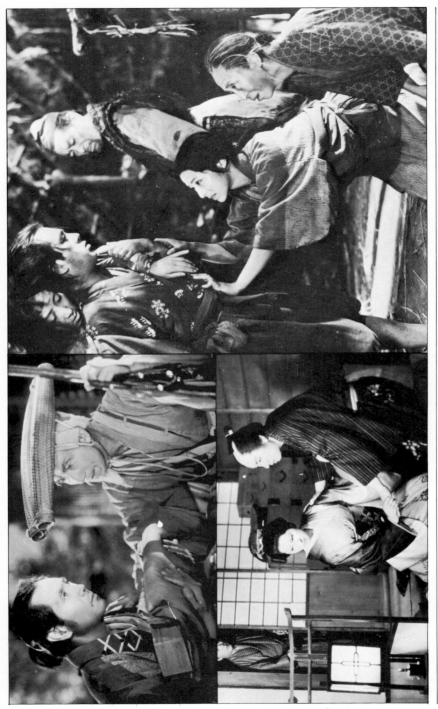

●Ugetsu (Ugetsu Monogatari), 1953, Sugisaku Aoyama and Masayuki Mori

●A Story from Chikamatsu (Chikamatsu Monogatari), 1954, Kyoko Kagawa (center) and Kazuo Hasegawa

●Sansho the Bailiff (Sansho Dayu), 1954, Takako Tachibana, Kisho Hanayagi, Kyoko Kagawa (kneeling, center)

YASUJIRO OZU

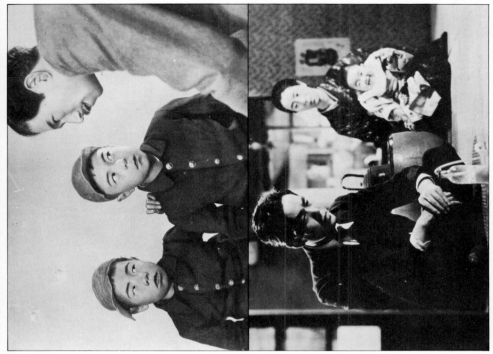

● *I Was Born, But...* (*Umarete wa Mita Keredo*), 1932, Tomio Aoki, Shoichi Kofujita and Tatsuo Saito

● *The Only Son* (*Hitori Musuko*), 1936, Shinichi Himori and Mitsuko Yoshikawa

●*There Was a Father (Chichi Ariki)*, 1942, Shuji Sano and Chishu Ryu

●*Early Summer (Bakushu)*, 1951, Setsuko Hara and Kuniko Miyake

●*Late Spring (Banshun)*, 1949, Chishu Ryu, Haruko Sugimura and Setsuko Hara

●*Tokyo Story (Tokyo Monogatari)*, 1953, Setsuko Hara and Chishu Ryu

●*Floating Weeds (Ukigusa)*, 1959, Hiroshi Kawaguchi and Ganjiro Nakamura

●*Late Autumn (Akibiyori)*, 1960, Setsuko Hara and Yoko Tsukasa

● *An Autumn Afternoon (Samma no Aji)*, 1962. Shinichiro Mikami, Shima Iwashita, Keiji Sata, and Chishu Ryu

MIKIO NARUSE

● *Wife! Be Like a Rose! (Tsuma yo Bara no Yo ni)*, 1935, Kaoru Ito (left) and Sachiko Chiba

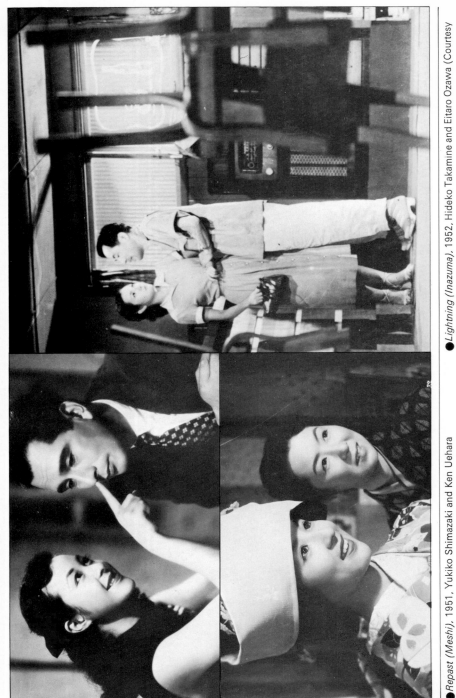

● *Repast (Meshi),* 1951, Yukiko Shimazaki and Ken Uehara
● *Mother (Okasan),* 1952, Kyoko Kagawa and Kinuyo Tanaka

● *Lightning (Inazuma),* 1952, Hideko Takamine and Eitaro Ozawa (Courtesy of Kihachi Okamoto.)

● *Sound of the Mountain (Yama no Oto)*, 1954, So Yamamura and Setsuko Hara (Courtesy of Kihachi Okamoto.)

● *Late Chrysanthemums (Bangiku)*, 1954, Ken Uehara and Haruko Sugimura (Courtesy of Kihachi Okamoto.)

● *Wife (Tsuma)*, 1953, Mieko Takamine and Ken Uehara (Courtesy of Kihachi Okamoto.)

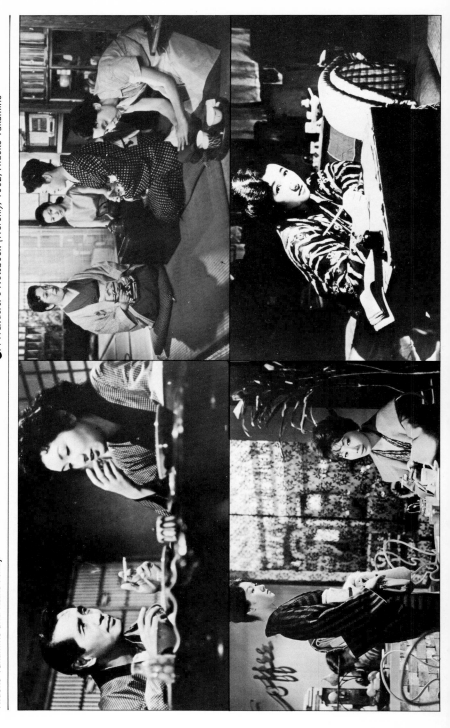

●Floating Clouds (Ukigumo), 1955, Masayuki Mori and Hideko Takamine
●When a Woman Ascends the Stairs (Onna ga Kaidan o Agaru Toki), 1960, Hideko Takamine and Keiko Awaji
●Flowing (Nagareru), 1956, Sumiko Kurishima, Hideko Takamine, Isuzu Yamada and Kinuyo Tanaka
●A Wanderer's Notebook (Horoki), 1962, Hideko Takamine

KENJI MIZOGUCHI

1898—1956

An exceptional nature, haunted by his own image. He was driven, unswerving in his search to create his ideal work.

—Akira Kurosawa

from "L'Empereur" interview in *Cahiers du Cinéma* No. 182, 1966

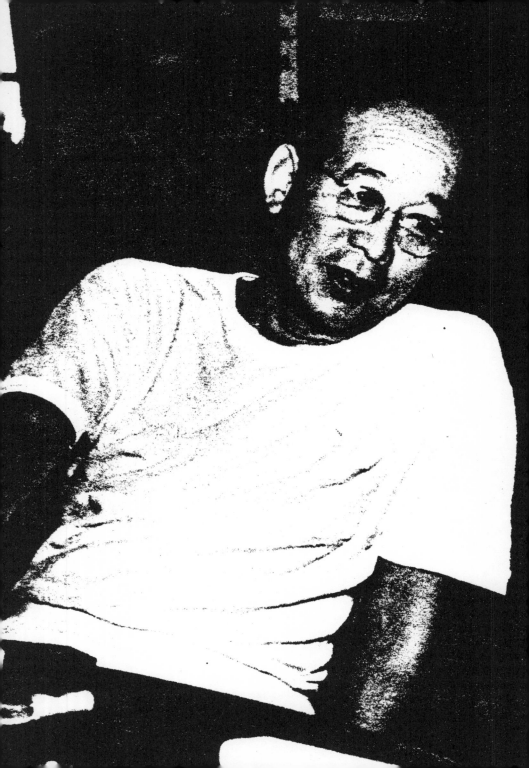

As evasive as he was redoubtable, Kenji Mizoguchi has left behind him not only some of the most pictorially exquisite films in the world, but lingering questions about the relationship between his personal life and ideals and these haunting masterpieces. One of the earliest Japanese filmmakers, with a directing career that began in 1923, at the time of his death in 1956 he had made 85 films of which only 30 are extant today. His works from 1952 on made him one of the first Japanese directors to be reckoned with internationally.

After *The Life of Oharu* won him the International Director's Prize at the 1952 Venice Film Festival, "Mizo" became an idol of the incipient French New Wave. Young critics such as Jacques Rivette adored Mizoguchi for his mastery of mise-en-scène,[1] Jean-Luc Godard eulogized his elegance, metaphysics and instinct as a director,[2] Philippe Sablon admired his scorn for logical exposition and the laws of drama and his preference for a more painterly or musical structure.[3] These qualities in fact emerge in those post-1952 works of Mizoguchi that were winning prizes year after year at Venice—*Oharu* was followed by *Ugetsu* in 1953 and *Sansho the Bailiff* in 1954—and for the avant-gardist French his films constituted symbols of purity and personalism that rendered Mizoguchi a hero and the haplessly logical, more montage-oriented Kurosawa a villain (Godard unabashedly dismissed Kurosawa as "second-rate").[4] There were even suggestions by the influential André Bazin that Mizoguchi represented a more authentic Japaneseness, while Kurosawa was quite obviously influenced by the west,[5] as was Mizoguchi.

The juxtaposition of Kurosawa and Mizoguchi in the *mise-en-scène* over montage battle cry of the New Wave undoubtedly had a political value in the imbroglios of developing a new aesthetic at the time. But the standoff is an artificial one when one considers Kurosawa's reverence for Mizoguchi and his avowed indebtedness to his methods. The most obvious influence Kurosawa has felt is Mizoguchi's unflinching realism in the application of the past to the present, the portrayal of personal drama in a broad and fully detailed historical milieu. Even today he muses on the model of directorial perfectionism and individualism that Mizoguchi, referred to by many who worked with him as the "demon," set for him to follow.[6] It was, after all, Kurosawa who said, ". . . in the death of Mizoguchi, Japanese film lost its truest creator."[7]

Kurosawa has also pointed out the fact that the realms handled best by Mizoguchi were those concerning the merchant class and women,[8] subject matter glossed over by the New Wave French and one of the sources of Mizoguchi riddles. Fluid camera movement, superb long-shot, long-take photography and intricate use of sound and framing provide a veneer of aestheticism to an ambivalent attitude toward women and an enigmatic political stance toward oppression, poverty, and even the Japanese family. In following Mizoguchi's career one finds disturbing reversals of affiliation, a consistent love of novelty, and an attitude of mixed adulation, pity and fear toward women. The keys to some of these problems lie embedded in the vicissitudes of his personal life.

Poverty, Painting, Poetry, Film

Mizoguchi was born in Tokyo in 1898, middle child of a roofer-carpenter of rather distinguished lineage. His father was an erratic, alternately stubborn and kindly dreamer of the type portrayed as the heroine's father in Mizo's 1936 *Osaka Elegy*.[9] His mother was the daughter of not very successful dealers in Chinese herbal medicine. The family was poor at the outset, but their situation became desperate when Kenji's father tried to make a killing in selling raincoats to the military during the 1904–05 Russo-Japanese War. By the time he had borrowed money, set up a factory and produced the coats, the brief war had ended and the family was forced to move. Since there was not enough food for the entire family, Kenji's older sister Suzu was given up for adoption at the age of 14. Her foster parents sold her a few years later to a geisha house, but she had the rare good fortune of finding a wealthy aristocratic patron who not only redeemed her and provided her with a house and income, but later married her when his wife died. Mizoguchi bitterly resented his father all his life for the treatment of the women in his family[10] (his mother, whom he loved dearly, and who saw to the family's needs throughout his father's caprices, died when he was 17), yet he himself later became fully dependent on his sister without the slightest compunction.

Before completing elementary school Kenji was also sent away to live as an apprentice in cold northern Iwate Prefecture with relatives who owned a pharmacy. There he was able to finish his primary education, and in 1912 he returned to Tokyo hoping to attend middle school. There were an additional two or three adopted children to feed at home, and his father refused permission. Soon after, his father began to suffer from rheumatism, and it was Suzu who came not only to support the whole family but to get Kenji his first job. At 15 he became apprentice to a textile designer of *yukata*, light summer kimonos.

Evidently it was through this apprenticeship, and another immediately following it in the same work, that Mizoguchi began to develop a love of painting. A year later he entered the Aohashi Western Painting Research Institute run by Seiki Kuroda, the first importer of European oil painting techniques of the French plein-airist school. It is the aesthetics of these early days that marks the shimmering landscapes of Mizoguchi's latest films. Through the Aohashi Institute Mizoguchi not only came to relish taunting schoolgirls by showing his nude sketches to them, but also to appreciate western opera, operetta and dance revues, for which productions the institute did stage design.[11] But he soon realized, as Akira Kurosawa would many years later, that he would not be able to make a living from painting.

Suzu again aided her brother in finding employment as an illustrator for a progressive newspaper in the southwestern port city of Kobe. After a very short abortive attempt of one day to go into porcelain design in Nagoya following another introduction by his sister he seemed to settle into newspaper work fairly happily.[12] He made a relatively good salary for the time, and busied himself with publishing his own poems. He would later claim to be more interested in literature than in painting, and put his own poetry on a par with that of the illustrious Takuboku Ishikawa.[13] The quality of his own work aside, a deep love of literature, both western and Japanese, marked his poor but leisurely life from his art school days. He felt a special affinity for Kyoka Izumi, whose work would be the basis for his lost 1929 *Nihombashi* and 1934 *Downfall of Osen*, set in neighborhoods where he lived, Hongo and Kanda, and he also devoured the poetic, brooding Soseki Natsume, the melodramatic Koyo Ozaki, and the lover of unadorned femininity, Kafu Nagai. These Japanese authors were supplemented with extensive reading of Tolstoy, Zola and Maupassant.[14] Nevertheless, Mizoguchi soon tired of his work in Kobe, and after a year returned to Tokyo because of acute homesickness.

He moved in with his disconcerted sister and showed no signs of seeking employment. But he began to see a teacher of the *biwa,* Japanese lute, and became acquainted with one of the students, a movie actor from the Nikkatsu company. The impressionable and erratic 20-year-old Mizoguchi soon succumbed to the glamorous lure of the budding film industry, and after visits to the studio fancied that he too could become an actor. This never happened, but he did have his actor friend introduce him to the rising director Osamu Wakayama, and he was hired as an assistant director in 1922.

Novelty Lover

By 1923 Mizoguchi became a full-fledged director because one of Nikkatsu's oldest directors walked out with the actors of female roles who struck the company in 1922. In a desperate flurry, the oldest major film studio in Japan, established in 1912, began to realize that to keep its audience it had not only to begin using actresses, but to move away from its standard Shimpa tragedy material—slow-moving melodramas portraying middle-class Meiji Period (1868–1912) life in opposition to the period dramas of the Kabuki stage. Apparently no one knew what Mizoguchi was up to, for his first film was a denunciation of economic class differences that was completely foreign to either film or stage at the time. Labeled as a "puro-ide" (proletarian ideology) piece, there was so little left of it when the censors finished that continuity had to be fabricated with *biwa* music.[15]

This film, long since lost along with all but two that Mizoguchi made in his most prolific years before 1930, marks the debut of a director who appeared fully committed to the left as well as to new inspirations and new techniques. Although Mizo later had so many confrontations with police and censors that he became utterly paranoid about authority figures,[16] his commitment to the left would prove shallow. But his commitment to new art would be borne out immediately and consistently throughout his career. Mizo overturned Shimpa apolitical conventions in his first film, and he also attacked—whether through inexperience or intention is not known—film conventions in the personage of the narrator. Neglecting the script that was always produced for the off-screen live narrator (*katsuben* or *benshi*), the 25-year-old Mizoguchi made flagrant use of intertitles, even for dialogue, and the narrators protested to the company.[17]

Mizoguchi's enthusiasm for novelty was even more pronounced in his 1923 *Blood and Soul,* which made use of the exaggerated sets, make-up and shadows of German expressionist films such as *The Cabinet of Dr. Caligari,* which had been released in Japan in 1921. He was also using French and American sources for his stories at this time, launching an Arsene Lupin fad with *813* and the beginnings of his flair for atmospheric settings with *Foggy Harbor,* based on O'Neill's *Anna Christie.*

In 1923 the Great Kanto Earthquake devastated Tokyo and the surrounding areas. Mizoguchi rushed into the ruins with a camera crew and filmed all he saw. His documentary footage was sent to America,[18] but he also used the event to produce a feature called *In the Ruins* before the whole contemporary drama staff of Nikkatsu's Mukojima studios was sent to Kyoto.

In Kyoto Mizoguchi entered his first slump—the fact that in 1953 he could remember few of the films he made in 1924 and 1925 may well be an indication of their poor quality. He spent his free time drinking and frequenting the Gion and Pontocho geisha districts. He had been rebuffed by a geisha in Tokyo and was leading a relatively celibate life until he fell in love with a Kyoto waitress and began living with her in 1925. This relationship lasted only two months before the woman came after him with a razor and slashed his back in a widely publicized jealousy scene. Years later when he first showed his scar to his screen-writer Yoshikata Yoda, he admonished, "Yoda, women are terrifying."[19] The raging jealous woman would be part of the realism of Mizoguchi's later films, notably in the 1946 *Utamaro and His Five Women*, which Yoda wrote using Mizo as the real-life model for Utamaro.[20] Mizoguchi forgave his mistress, however, and quit work to go to Tokyo and find her. They were reconciled, and he lived off her income as a maid in a Japanese inn until an acquaintance warned him he was wasting his life. He returned to Kyoto and pursued his filmmaking with a vitality that had been lacking prior to his encounter with the animal viciousness of a ne-glected woman. His lost film, the 1926 *Paper Doll's Whisper of Spring*, which was set in his native downtown Tokyo and showed the miserable life of the working poor, marks the moment of "my own direction beginning to be set."[21] The mistress he left behind in Tokyo disappeared into prostitution.

From his first film Mizo had shown a sympathy for the poor that irked the censors. In 1929, however, he burst into the full-fledged leftist "ten-dency film" (*keiko eiga*) fad begun that year with *Metropolitan Symphony*. Before drastic censorship, this lost film, based on the work of several proletarian writers, contained scenes in which the benevolent rich make pigs of themselves in a slum area where they go to exhort and chastise the unemployed.[22] Summoned by the police, a cowering Mizoguchi begged the company to look after his new wife, a former dance-hall girl, but he received only an order to show the poor as more cheerful: this he meekly set about doing. The "tendency" films decrying the living conditions of the poor, however, were squelched almost as soon as the movement began, due to the rise of fascist militarism, and Mizoguchi's last in the genre, the lost 1931 *And Yet They Go* would bring him back to the subject matter that was so much a part of his life: the woman who runs away with a man who then deserts her, leaving her with no means of livelihood but prostitution.

By 1932 Mizoguchi had reluctantly become involved in making a piece of militarist propaganda, *The Dawn of Manchukuo and Mongolia*. Such works are a great disappointment to those who would like to see him as the champion of the left, but his so-called proletarian films themselves reveal a political ambiguity rather than a commitment. Questioned on why he went into the "tendency" genre he said it was simply because he was a full-blooded Tokyoite and therefore a lover of novelty, but there may also have been considerable influence from his own poverty-stricken past and his association with leftist writers and theater people in Kobe and Osaka.[23] Mizoguchi's remarks were always flippant, bragging or whining, but no matter what his "tendency" motivation was, his forays into proletarianism laid the groundwork for a more fully developed, far more poignant social realism in his great mid-1930s works about oppressed women.

Feminism

Mizoguchi falls within the strong tradition of "feminists" in Japanese film, literature and drama.[24] However, this English loan word has nuances in Japan that differ considerably from its western usage. Aside from its predictable meaning, "proponent of women's rights, equality or libera- tion," it has a second, more popular usage: "a man who is indulgent toward women; a worshiper of women." In the arts such men with a marked fascination with women are epitomized by one of Mizoguchi's favorite writers, Kafu Nagai (1879–1959), whose portrayals of the downtrodden women of the prostitutes' quarters are among the most famous in Japanese literature. However, these finely drawn portraits, in Mizoguchi's case as well as Kafu's, do not necessarily imply a political concern with the improvement of women's status in society. The fasci- nation becomes an end in itself.

In this respect Mizoguchi's feminine portraits reveal inherent con- tradictions, as does the Japanese use of the word "feminist" and the direc- tor's attitude toward the women in his own life. His hatred for his father is hardly vindicated by his behavior toward Suzu, who continued to give him money until well after he had become a director at Nikkatsu. He neg- lected his Kyoto mistress, protected her from the police after she tried to murder him, quit work to look for her, lived off her when he found her and finally abandoned her to prostitution. He went through complex machinations to secure his wife, who was still married to someone else, and proceeded to neglect her. She in turn refused to cook for him at unusual hours, allowed him not a penny of his own salary, and was occasionally dragged around by the hair by Mizo during bursts of sadistic vengeance.[25] When she went insane in 1941 due to "hereditary syphilis" in Mizoguchi's words, he had her institutionalized for the rest of her life. After the Pacific War, he took his wife's widowed sister and her two daughters into his home out of pity. He lived with his sister-in-law as a wife, but proposed marriage to his leading actress, Kinuyo Tanaka, around 1947. She refused him and from 1953 on would have nothing further to do with him because he tried to prevent her from directing her first film. In short, Mizo was "unusual in the extent to which he suffered at the hands of women. He hated women; he was contemptuous of women. On the other hand, when he fell in love, it was with the sincerity of a little boy."[26] All of the admiration, exploitation, fear and pity con- cerning women shown in his life would find expression in his films.

In the mid-1930s Mizoguchi reached a peak of what has been dubbed social realism through his deepening portrayals of women on the screen. The two types of heroines he developed during this period would reappear in slightly varying incarnations throughout his films to the end of his life. His reason for selecting the social and psychological position of women as the prevailing theme of his work may be seen as a logical progression from the concerns of his late 1920s to the early 1930s "tendency" films, for "He had long thought that after Communism solved the class problem, what would remain would be the problem of male-female relationships."[27] Nevertheless, the story content of his films shows not a positive call for active revolution on the part of women, but a bleak condemnation to the status quo. What his two types of heroine have in common is a singular pathos—the fate of the long-suffering ideal woman is as grim as that of the spiteful rebel. It has been suggested that Mizoguchi himself was too deeply implicated in the psycho-social system that ensured the oppression of women to be able to cast them as revolutionaries, and that his life work consisted rather of the "purification of a national resentment" regarding women's tragic role.[28]

Mizoguchi's ideal woman is the one who can love. This love consists, however, of a selfless devotion to a man in the traditional Japanese sense. She becomes the spiritual guide, the moral and often financial support for a husband, lover, brother or son. The prototype of his self-sacrificing ideal is Taki, the heroine of the 1933 *Taki no Shiraito, the Water Magician.* Her pride of self-realization consists of her ability to ensure her lover's worldly and moral success, and his financial and spiritual dependence on her is her proof of his love. She is driven to the point of stealing and inadvertent murder in order to keep her promise of financial provision for him, and the reward for her perseverance appears in her chance to see him dressed in his judicial robes, handing down the just verdict that condemns her. Her eyes shine with pride and admiration at the image of his achievement, and never does she for a moment blame him for the cruel judgment. We do not actually see her forgive him for doing what the law demands, but her devotion is compensated by the guilt that drives him to commit suicide.

Taki's relationship with her lover expresses a value system that remains very much a part of Japanese life. Not only is she the feminine ideal of the Meiji and Taisho periods (1868–1926), when speedily modernizing Japan subscribed to the democratic theory that anyone can get ahead by subordinating women's achievements to the worldly success of their men,[29] but she represents the classic mother-son interaction in which the parent shows her suffering to induce guilt on the part of the child who is absolved only by achieving and fulfilling the mother's expectations.[30] The fact that Taki and her lover resemble a mother-son relationship more than an egalitarian male-female love relationship in the western sense reveals the lingering cultural definition of love in Japan as dependence, entailing a man's expectations of continual indulgence, forgiveness and encouragement by a woman.[31] In Mizoguchi's own life the model who most obviously corresponds to the image of Taki is his older sister Suzu, but a generous lacing of his uncomplaining mother may well be part of this saintly ideal.

The women who embody Mizoguchi's ideal often live in a time too far in the past to be role models for today, a quirk of which Mizoguchi seems to have been aware. He once said of himself that he portrayed "what should not be possible as if it should be possible,"[32] a statement that most aptly describes the virtues of his period heroines. Otoku, the devoted maid in his 1939 *Story of the Last Chrysanthemum,* is, like Taki, a Meiji Period woman. She loses all for the sake of her man's success on the Kabuki stage, sees him through years of hardship, and dies alone at the moment he fulfills her hopes for him. Mizoguchi felt that he was saying what he really wanted to say in this picture[33] made when suppression of free speech was already the rule. His wartime goal would be the celebration of the Japanese virtues of self-sacrifice and dedication, expressed not only in the revenge and suicide of *The Loyal 47 Ronin,* but also in his four-film cycle on performing artists beginning with *The Story of the Last Chrysanthemum.*

Mizoguchi's ideal postwar women show the same self-sacrificing characteristics, but they move yet farther into the past while developing a spiritual power to transcend their physical suffering. Oharu, the court lady in *The Life of Oharu* who declines into prostitution because she once allows herself to love a man beneath her station, moves out of our view, not living comfortably in a temple and prattling glibly to a couple of curious young men as in Saikaku's original late seventeenth-century story, but alone and homeless, reciting sutras from door to door with a begging bowl. The seriousness of Mizoguchi's treatment of Oharu's ever intensifying social decline, poverty and humiliation leaves no doubt in the spectator's mind that her final rejection of worldly concerns is total and sincere. Behind the flippant amorality of Saikaku's fiction, Mizoguchi read his own deep resignation. Oharu blames no one for her fate; she prays for all humanity.

Miyagi, the murdered wife in *Ugetsu* (1953), lives on despite death in her sixteenth-century setting. When her deluded husband has returned to fulfill her ideal, her voice encourages him, her spirit turns his potter's wheel. Anju, the devoted sister in the eleventh-century world of *Sansho the Bailiff* (1954), commits suicide to help her brother escape from their slave compound. Their aristocratic mother, after years of forced labor as a prostitute, crippled and blind, rejoices at reunion with her son, whose return to humanitarian values was brought about by a supernatural summons from her spirit. But the most remote feminine ideal is Mizo-guchi's last and most maudlin, *Princess Yang Kwei Fei* (1955). The eighth-century Chinese scullery maid turned imperial concubine molds herself into the distracted ruler's image of perfection, and then walks calmly to her death to save his life. The voice of her dead spirit remains to reassure the broken, powerless emperor of a love that transcends death.

In all of these paragon portayals, the vision of society remains the same. The dramatic form is tragic, and spiritual success brings death and worldly defeat. Even in the 1954 *Story from Chikamatsu,* where love is the only goal, the lovers must die for their adultery according to the feudal code. The society of every age is pictured as vicious, greedy, un-feeling. Worldly ambitions, though often encouraged by women for their men, bring spiritual loss if they are fulfilled. All ideals are envisioned in societies where the basic problems of economic class structure, abusive power and avarice have not been solved.

The other side of the paragon is the rebel. She is often a prostitute or geisha or similar social outcast, and most often a contemporary woman. She resents the abuses of fathers, employers, and men who buy her and leave her, and attempts to lash back. But her solitary, proud, spiteful opposition does nothing to change the system, and in fact she usually subscribes to its corrupt values, using seduction, deceit and financial exploitation as her methods for revenge. She has nothing spiritual with which to replace the consuming love relationship, and in rejecting it she condemns herself to a life of self-seeking bitterness. She often appears with a meek woman counterpart who underscores the unviability of either stance in the modern world.

Ayako, the innocent switchboard operator of the 1936 *Osaka Elegy,* seeks the financial help of her poor boyfriend. Rejected, she turns to exploiting the system that exploits her. By letting herself be set up as a mistress she attains financial security, but loses love, and in the end is cast out onto the street by her apprehended patron, her horrified boy-friend, and her ashamed family.

Omocha (literally "toy"), the modern geisha in *Sisters of the Gion* (1936), resents the way men treat women as objects and mocks her older sister's devotion to a bankrupt former patron. Setting out to beat men at their own game, she deceives and ruins a sincere young store clerk and has his employer provide her with what she wants: money, pretty clothes and fancy restaurant meals. But as surely as her sister's old patron returns to his wife and a new business opportunity, the clerk takes revenge on Omocha, and she ends up in a hospital bed decrying the insti-tution of geisha while her abandoned sister sits sobbing at her side.

Women like Omocha and her sister reappear in Mizoguchi's postwar films about prostitutes and geisha from the 1946 *Utamaro and His Five Women* to the 1948 *Women of the Night,* the 1953 *Gion Festival Music* and his last work, the 1956 *Street of Shame.* In this last film, Yasumi, the callous young woman who steals men from and lends money at usurious rates to her fellow-prostitutes, is as spiritually defeated in her economic success as Hanae, the middle-aged woman who sells her body to provide for her family, is admirable in her honest, devoted poverty.

In Mizoguchi's life these vivacious, volatile, condemned women were the geisha and prostitutes of Kyoto's Pontocho and Gion, Tokyo's Tamanoi and Ueno, of Osaka and every other city in which he dallied. They were also his razor-wielding mistress and the wife who went insane. These and the enduring spirit mother-sister ideals were what he knew best, and his lack of understanding for any other type of woman is best shown in his own work. The accusation that he did not really grasp the new postwar humanism proves itself in the similarity of the prostitute's dismal fate in the 1948 *Women of the Night* to that in his 1931 *And Yet They Go.*[34] His attempts to portray feminist movement heroines like Sumako Matsui (*The Love of Sumako the Actress,* 1947) and Hideko Kageyama (*My Love Burns,* 1949) show them as confident and good only as long as they have a man to whom they can devote themselves. They end by discovering they are "only women." Perhaps the most ironic of his portraits of successful women is the severe, pedantic, lonely heroine of the 1946 *Victory of Women* who shows precious little that is attractive in her encouragement of others to follow her lead.

Yet there is one heroine who retains both love and moral courage in life. Fumi, the country stage entertainer of the recently rediscovered 1937 *Straits of Love and Hate,* survives male abuse, poverty and the temptation to sell out. When the wealthy student who abandoned her with a child asks her to come back to him years later, she decides to stay with her stage partner, the man who has been her moral support through the years. She grabs the baby away from his indolent, proud father and the grandfather who has accused her of avarice in returning, realizing that the advantages her son would receive in their rich home are not worth the humiliation she would have to endure. The last shot shows her back on the stage doing comic skits with the partner who had stepped back to let her do what was best for her, and we are assured that her son will grow up poor but with people who love him and each other. One cannot help but wonder if, had the war not intervened—by the following year Mizoguchi was already making propaganda films—the director might not have developed this more positive view of love and high ethical standards into a truly modern feminism.

The "Demon" at Work

During the course of his long career Mizoguchi formulated a style peculiarly his own and an authoritarian perfectionism that both terrorized and
rewarded his staff. He bounced from company to company and back
and forth between Tokyo and Kyoto looking for total artistic control.
When a company forced him to make something he hated, such as the
1938 military propaganda film *Song of the Camp,* he would leave. When
he had a project he wanted to do, such as *The Life of Oharu,* which was
planned in 1949, and the company would not accept it, he would leave.
In this way he worked with seven different production companies in his
lifetime, often following the relocation of his friends, producer Masaichi
Nagata, who became president of the Daiei company, for which Mizo
made most of his late films, and Matsutaro Kawaguchi, an elementary
school friend who over the years would provide scripts, original stories
and a place to work when he became a studio head.

A crucial aspect of Mizoguchi's creativity was his close relationship
with scriptwriters, notably Yoshikata Yoda, who was responsible for
virtually all of his extant masterpieces from the 1936 *Osaka Elegy* on.
Together they would forge out the eloquently literary scripts that drew
on such a wide variety of sources. It was Yoda who at the beginning of
his career wanted to do Maupassant, Molière, and above all Junichiro
Tanizaki, his favorite author (he would do Tanizaki in the 1951 *Miss Oyu,*
and though Mizoguchi had already done Maupassant in the 1935 *Oyuki
the Madonna,* a Maupassant story would figure into the ideas for Yoda's
Ugetsu script in 1953). It was Mizoguchi who forced him to read Kafu
Nagai and Saikaku, the ribald portraitist of the feudal period merchant
class and demimonde.[35] Yoda has written with deep affection, close to
adoration, of the blustering tyrant who trained him, and the character
that emerges is both a petulant child and a visionary genius. "He never
told me anything concrete about the scenario. He simply said, 'This is
no good.'"[36] Mizoguchi would rant, rave, insult and reject until he got
what he wanted from Yoda, which was a synesthetic essence of humanity:
". . . you must put the odor of the human body into images . . .
describe for me the implacable, the egoistic, the sensual, the cruel . . .
there are nothing but disgusting people in this world."[37] Yoda's first script
for *Osaka Elegy* was returned to him more than ten times for revision, but
when the film was completed he felt elation and appreciation for Mizo's
strictness. Later in his career the director would take to writing out his
criticisms of the script in letters, leaving an enlightening record of a
visual perfectionist who constantly guided Yoda's dialogue away from
banality, sentimentality and commentary on the action and toward a
language of poetry, drama and. above all, emotion.[38] Yet Mizoguchi's

perfectionism regarding dialogue characterization, a perfectionism that carried over into art direction, acting and cinematography, created problems with the very emotion it sought to create.

Mizoguchi's famous "one-scene, one-shot" technique was facilitated largely through his demand for completely detailed sets. He began employing the long take as early as 1930 in the lost *Mistress of a Foreigner,* supposedly influenced by King Vidor's 1929 *Hallelujah!* and the theories of his friend psychologist Kojiro Naito,[39] but the mark of Joseph von Sternberg's moving camera technique is unmistakable in films such as the 1937 *Straits of Love and Hate,* which plagiarizes the hero's entry into the smoky, crowded bar in the 1928 *Docks of New York.* In 1936 a reverent Mizo dragged a grumbling Sternberg to see one of his own films in Kyoto, only to have him disown it because of the poor condition of the print.[40] The long-take style became fully established as Mizoguchi's own, however, through his association with art director Hiroshi Mizutani who worked with him for 20 years beginning from the lost 1933 *Gion Festival.* From 1939, with *The Story of the Last Chrysanthemum,* Mizutani did not only the detailed, massive sets for Mizoguchi's films, but also the costumes, for he found the courage to tell the director that his interpretation of Meji period clothing was inaccurate.[41] Through his art directors and other period specialists summoned to consult on his films, Mizoguchi developed the overwhelming atmosphere of his films. His passion for "exact size replica," which became an important element of his films beginning with the 1941–42 *The Loyal 47 Ronin,*[42] assumed an intensity that nearly dwarfs the human dramas taking place in these marvelous environmental constructions.

As with his scripts, never once, according to Mizutani, did the director give a specific order for his sets, but relied totally on his art director to create a full atmosphere appropriate to the delivery of the actors' lines. His method was to demand the complete performance of a particular scene, and in order not to interrupt the emotional continuity, he would follow the actors relentlessly with the camera. While he never gave instructions to actors either—a method Kurosawa later claimed is the only way to train them properly[43]—he would demand acting that "broke the barriers of the frame. Cutting and composing the frame were the staff's responsibilities, and a drama played with attention paid to the width of the frame was 'no good.'"[44] This centrifugal force applied to the edges of the frame would be a rallying cry of the New Wave French, and Mizo's long-take, moving camera one of the models for development of their hand-held camera techniques.

One of the finest examples of Mizoguchi's dramatic continuity in the long take appears in the otherwise uninspiring 1951 *Miss Oyu,* for which Mizutani designed the sets. It is a 5-minute-45-second take showing the highest emotional moment of the story: the young wife is accusing her husband of having married her solely to be near her more attractive older sister. The actors move through three rooms and seven different positions, away from each other and back together again three times, rising and sitting, as the wife finally breaks into sobs and falls prostrate to the floor while her husband stands helplessly by with his back to the camera. The scene illustrates not only his weakness, but a point Mizutani has made about all of Mizoguchi's highly emotional moments: "On the set the staff were often moved to tears, but when the scene became a filmed image no one could cry."[45] The effect of Mizoguchi's insistence on the long or medium shot, long-take method is to endistance the viewer from deep emotional involvement in the action. Kurosawa has said that Mizoguchi's camera movement serves to "animate a static composition that could become monotonous . . . the actors are fixed and the camera moves for them."[46] By the standards of fast action in Kurosawa's films, Mizoguchi's are by comparison indeed slow, but certainly not static. They move at the pace of the merchant class rather than samurai life, and the camera moves to incorporate all of the details in the surroundings of that life, the atmosphere itself, contemporary or historical, assuming its own effect on the drama and the spectator. In explaining why he rejected closeups, Mizoguchi said, "It is enough that there be a lyrical ambience in the whole of the film,"[47] and this is what his technique achieves.

Ugetsu

The inspiration for the 1953 film that best expresses Mizoguchi's elegant lyricism was, as with the majority of his works, literary. Two stories from Akinari Ueda's 1776 collection of the supernatural, *Ugetsu Monogatari* (*Tales of the Rainy Moon*), and a Maupassant character study, *La Décoration* (*How He Got the Legion of Honor*), form the basis of a film that becomes completely Mizoguchi's own. The spirit of Maupassant emerges not only in the story of Tobei (Eitaro Ozawa), the farmer who so aspires to the glories of samurai status that he neglects his wife, but in the vanity and greed of the main character, Genjuro the potter (Masayuki Mori). Mizoguchi's own recurrent themes appear in the fate of the two men's wives, Miyagi (Kinuyo Tanaka), who is murdered and becomes the spiritual guide of the reawakened Genjuro at the end, and the abandoned Ohama (Mitsuko Miura), who sinks to surviving by prostitution after being raped while searching for her husband. Throughout the film, a fidelity to the eeriness of Akinari resides in the tension between illusion and reality, while a transcendent environmental lyricism informs *Ugetsu* with a value beyond the pathos of human drama.

As in many of Mizoguchi's late films, including *Sansho the Bailiff, Princess Yang Kwei Fei, The Woman of the Rumor* and *A Story from Chikamatsu, Ugetsu* takes a circular form, beginning and ending with a landscape that places all of the human events and emotions of the narrative in the subsuming context of nature. The camera travels from fields and woods to alight on the dwelling where Genjuro and his family are busying themselves with making pottery, and the narrative begins. Closing the film, the camera moves away from the little boy offering rice at Miyagi's grave near the same dwelling to rise again to the woods and fields, where a farmer can be seen at work in the distance. Like a classic Chinese ink painting with a tiny human figure dwarfed by towering mountains, the endings of these violent dramas restore a sense of proportion to human affairs: people are barely significant entities that live, work, love, suffer and die within the greater immutable order. These enclosing moments of Zen-like space remove the viewer from the exhausting human passions and remind him of his role as spectator at a performance and as contemplator of life.

The presentation of the supernatural enhances the transcendental quality of the opening and closing shots. Mizoguchi's original impulse to do the film with surrealistic decor "à la Dali"[48] was never realized, and instead he and Yoda brought the supernatural into the narrative structure, using devices that resemble the classical Japanese Noh drama. The mist-enshrouded trip by boat across Lake Biwa, during which the protagonists encounter a dying boatman, was invented by Mizoguchi with a view to preparing the mysterious atmosphere that would dominate the whole central dream interlude of Genjuro's love affair with the phantom Lady Wakasa (Machiko Kyo). As in the structure of Noh, the entry into the supernatural is a journey, corresponding to the *jo* (introduction) section of a play. The central emotional event of the Noh, *ha* (destruction), is the protagonist's recollection or dream presented in stylized form, cor-responding to Genjuro's entire experience with Wakasa, and her danced expression of her own feelings. In Noh the protagonist finally reveals his true identity, often as a ghost or demon, in the most dramatic *kyu* (fast) movement of the play. In *Ugetsu* Wakasa is gradually exposed as a vengeful ghost in the dangerous love affair, and Miyagi also proves to have only a spiritual presence at the end of the film. Together with these structural devices, however, lighting and camerawork lend a haunt-ing air to *Ugetsu*.

The dream setting of Wakasa's mansion appears first as an isolated, dilapidated residence of the type sheltering neglected beauties in *The Tale of Genji,* the entrance choked by weeds and shrubbery, the walls cracked and crumbling. Genjuro sits waiting for the Lady to emerge from the inner depths of the house, and as a servant lights the oil lamps, the walls are transformed into well-kept opulence; the potter falls deeper under the unearthly spell. He drinks and converses with the lovely Wakasa, who flatters him for his humble pottery and completes his final enthrallment. When she sings and dances her love for Genjuro, coquettish looks embellishing her stately Noh-like movements, the voice of her dead father joins in with a muffled, rumbling recitation that seems to emanate from the warrior's helmet displayed in the room. We the audience by now accept these manifestations of the supernatural along with the spellbound potter because they are so subtle—no superimposed transparent phantoms, no dissolves and fades, no Dali-influenced decor calls attention to the otherworldliness of Genjuro's experience. All is kept in a supreme tension through affective lighting, sourceless sound and realistic sets combined with the corporeality of the forms of Wakasa and her nurse. Even when Genjuro has had a Sanskrit incantation inscribed on his back by a Buddhist priest to thwart the demon's powers, it is only through gradual, shot-by-shot alterations in Kyo's makeup that her demonic nature is revealed. Then rather than make her disappear through photographic tricks, Mizoguchi moves the camera away from her, following Genjuro's frenzied sword slashing from behind as she and her maid retreat into the darkness of the mansion's interior and he falls exhausted into the garden.

An equally delicate cinematic assertion of the supernatural within the real carries though the remainder of the film and Genjuro's return to his country home. The camera follows him through the dark house, passing the cold hearth as he leaves the house through the back door. The camera pans back to the right along the interior wall, following the sound of his voice as he calls for Miyagi outside, and as the hearth comes into view a second time in the same shot, it burns brightly. Miyagi, whom the audience knows to be dead, sits cooking supper and welcomes Genjuro as he reappears at the front door. Everything in the scene looks perfectly real, but since we have seen it empty and dark and then fully inhabited within a single take of a few seconds, the effect is one of tremendous shock, much greater shock than if the transformation had been effected through a montage.

Characteristically for late Mizoguchi, the abandoned wife forgives immediately, refusing even to listen to apologies and excuses, in a departure from the original, where she demands to know all and then states, ". . . you should know that a woman could die of yearning, and a man can never know her agony."[49] Miyagi's supernatural, forgiving presence remains even after her dawn disappearance in a further departure from the original story. In the last scenes Genjuro resumes his work at the wheel, and when Miyagi's voice assures him "Now at last you have become the man I wanted you to be," she speaks as the completely fulfilled woman.

In a setup recalling one of the earliest shots in the film, Genjuro sits in profile at his wheel fashioning a pot; to the right is the pump that Miyagi had operated to drive the wheel; it stands still but the wheel spins. The fusion of the real and the supernatural culminates in this final scene, and we accept the life-in-death of Miyagi that exists in Genjuro's mind because of a cinematic presentation that is at once startling and unobtrusive.

Mizoguchi's sought-after lyrical ambience permeates the whole film through the treatment of the human drama in environmental long shot, but it assumes its greatest strength when it moves away from the human beings altogether. This occurs not only in the opening and closing coda of the film, but in the midst of Genjuro's delusion. The camera travels through the woods to fix on a medium long shot of Genjuro and Wakasa cavorting at a sumptuous outdoor hotspring bath. Wakasa coyly teases the enraptured Genjuro, and as she makes a movement to disrobe and join him in the water, the camera moves off again through the woods. As it travels it turns downward to the barren ripples of the ground, a dissolve occurs, the ground shifts slightly, and the camera momentarily edges past the circular grooves of a raked gravel Zen garden, rises, and shows the couple disporting themselves in a distant picnic on a lawn. Not only has time passed through the dissolve (in the original story Genjuro fails to return to his native village for seven years), but the viewer has passed through an unpeopled space that brings to mind emptiness and the transiency of human life. This moment of emptiness is of the sort that would be more frequently exploited by Mizoguchi's younger contemporary and friend, Yasujiro Ozu, but it is used for the same effect. Opposing Ozu's montage details of, for example, the famous stone and gravel Ryoanji Zen garden in the 1949 *Late Spring*, Mizoguchi skims his camera over the Zen symbol as part of the larger landscape of which the characters in the story are unaware. It is the spectator alone who feels the silent, transcendental reality between and beyond the drama of mortals on the screen, and *Ugetsu* becomes one of Mizoguchi's most profound statements on the delusions of ambition, vanity, eroticism and the achievement of even so simple a goal as domestic tranquility. (In the original script, the would-be samurai Tobei never returns to his wife, but the production company would not allow such a bleak ending.)[50] *Ugetsu* is the "chronicle of a dream disappointed, of a hope deceived,"[51] and the suggestion of the beyond in the lyricism of nature surrounding the tragic mortals in a small aesthetic redemption from their fate.

International Mizo

By the time Mizoguchi, Yoshikata Yoda and Kinuyo Tanaka were taking *Ugetsu* to the Venice Film Festival in 1953, the director's life had passed through astounding metamorphoses of faith. The man who made leftist tendency films in 1931 and lost his younger brother in 1938 to the militarists' suppression of Communism[52] became a member of the Cabinet Film Committee in 1940 and published statements on the role of film in promoting the nationalistic spirit.[53] The man who traveled to China in 1943 for the purpose of making an army propaganda film, who attempted to carry a sword and demanded to be treated as a general,[54] in the same year the war ended became head of the Shochiku studio's first labor union which he inaugurated with the opening speech, "From now on I will give the orders. I expect you to be prepared to receive them."[55] By 1946 he was devising arguments to persuade the U.S. Occupation authorities to let him make a period film, which was forbidden as a glorification of feudal values. He was successful; his film portrayed the late eighteenth-century woodblock printmaker Utamaro as an artist of the people, a libertarian democrat who despised the samurai class and the police oppressors. The author of the original story was outraged at Mizoguchi's betrayal of the purely erotic, libertine spirit in his work's faithfulness to Utamaro's time.[56]

An analysis of Mizoguchi's political behavior shows simply that he never understood politics. He used his various positions of political authority to make the films he wanted to make, and if blame is to be cast, it must fall upon those who were foolish enough to grant authority to a political innocent. His direction was set well before the war and never changed: he wanted to make "real" period films true to the spirit of particular eras, as he said in a speech offending many in 1949,[57] and he wanted to make films about women, especially prostitutes. He succeeded in doing both in the postwar era, but not without opposition. When the period film he had fought to make about the Saikaku court lady who declines into prostitution at last won him the Director's Prize at Venice in 1952, after placing only ninth in the Best Ten at home, Mizoguchi's reaction was spiteful: "It seems that the Japanese do not understand movies."[58] His success at Venice would give him new energy and inspiration in his last years.

Though his political views may have lacked sophistication and commitment, Mizoguchi's late films are suffused with a view of life that transcends politics. Even his ambivalent view of women and their oppression becomes acceptable because all is cast in an aestheticism bespeaking the ephemeral quality of human suffering. The heroines of Mizoguchi's films of the 1950s all rush headlong into destruction or death, but the beauty of his presentation of their tragedies takes the viewer beyond, to the Zen garden of *Ugetsu*, to the voice of the guardian spirit of *Princess Yang Kwei Fei*, to the quiet ripples in the lake where Anju has drowned herself in *Sansho the Bailiff*, to the smiles on the lovers' faces as they ride to their crucifixion in *A Story from Chikamatsu*. In 1953 Mizoguchi took a votive image of the thirteenth-century Buddhist saint Nichiren with him to Venice. He prayed to win, swearing he could not return to Japan unless he did.[59] He had become, in his own inimitable capricious fashion, a follower of the Nichiren sect, as his detested father had done after the trauma of the 1923 Great Kanto Earthquake.[60] Mizo's discovery of the Japanese faith that would give him personal solace coincided with his portrayal of his first transcending woman, Oharu, who unsuccessfully seeks refuge from men and the bitter world in a Buddhist nunnery, and in the end becomes a solitary, sutra-chanting itinerant nun. It coincided also with his debut as an international director, for his late, pictorially exquisite, contemplative tragedies were those that made him the New Wave darling. It also may well have coincided with the onset of the leukemia that would take his life in the midst of rewriting the script for his first postwar comedy, *Osaka Monogatari*, in 1956. In 1954 with *A Story from Chikamatsu*, Mizoguchi ceased to be a demon of perfectionism;[61] the picture was finished in 28 days. A lover of novelty, worshiper and hater of women, inventor of authentic period films and fully played emotion in a distanced, lyrical long take, whimsical in politics and love, Mizoguchi died a devout Buddhist.

Notes

[1] Jacques Rivette, "Mizoguchi vu d'ici" (Mizoguchi Viewed from Here), *Cahiers du cinéma* (Paris), No. 81, 1958, p. 28.

[2] Jean-Luc Godard, "L'Art de Mizoguchi Kenji," *Art* (Paris), No. 656, 1958.

[3] Philippe Sablon, "Plus de lumière" (More Light), *Cahiers du cinéma*, No. 78, 1957, p. 50.

[4] Godard, *op. cit.*

[5] André Bazin, "Petit journal du cinéma : Vivre" (Review of *Ikiru*), *Cahiers du cinéma*, No. 69, 1957.

[6] Author's interview with Akira Kurosawa, May 1977.

[7] Donald Richie, *The Films of Akira Kurosawa* (Berkeley and Los Angeles : University of California Press, 1973), p. 97.

[8] *Ibid.*, p. 97.

[9] Matsuo Kishi, *Jinbutsu: Nihon eiga shi I* (Personalities : Japanese Film History, vol. 1) (Tokyo : Daviddosha, 1970), p. 573.

[10] Kaneto Shindo, *Aru eiga kantoku no shogai* (The Life of a Film Director) (Tokyo : Iwanami Shoten, 1976), p. 88.

[11] Kishi, *op. cit.*, pp. 573–74.

[12] *Ibid.*, p. 574.

[13] Shindo, *op. cit.*, p. 86.

[14] Kishi, *op. cit.*, p. 574.

[15] *Ibid.*, p. 579.

[16] "Mizoguchi Kenji no hyogen o sasaeta mono" (Support for Kenji Mizoguchi's Expression : Masahiro Shinoda interview with Hiroshi Mizutani), *Kikan Film* (Film Journal, Tokyo), No. 3, 1969, p. 156.

[17] Kishi, *op. cit.*, p. 579.

[18] *Ibid.*, p. 581.

[19] *Ibid.*, p. 588.

[20] Yoshikata Yoda, "Souvenirs sur Mizoguchi" (Memories of Mizoguchi), *Cahiers du cinéma*, No. 174, 1966, p. 66.

[21] "Mizoguchi Kenji : Jisaku o kataru" (Kenji Mizoguchi Talks about His Films), *Kinema Jumpo* (Tokyo), No. 80, 1953, p. 49.

[22] Kishi, *op. cit.*, p. 594.

[23] *Ibid.*, p. 595.

[24] Tadao Sato, *Nihon eiga shiso shi* (History of the Intellectual Currents in Japanese Film) (Tokyo : Sanichi Shobo, 1970), p. 17.

[25] Kishi, *op. cit.*, p. 611.

[26] *Ibid.*, p. 610.

[27] *Ibid.*, p. 603.

[28] Tadao Sato, "Mizoguchi-eiga no onna" (The Women in Mizoguchi's Films), *FC* (Tokyo National Museum of Modern Art Film Center), No. 16, 1973, p. 7.

[29] *Ibid.*, p. 6.

[30] *See* George A. DeVos, *Socialization for Achievement* (Berkeley and Los Angeles : University of California Press, 1974).

[31] *See* Takeo Doi, *The Anatomy of Dependence* (New York and Tokyo : Kodansha International Ltd., 1973).

[32] Masahiro Shinoda, "Mizoguchi Kenji kara toku hanarete" (Far away from Kenji Mizoguchi), *Kikan Film* (Tokyo), No. 3, 1969, p. 154.

[33] "Mizoguchi Kenji : Jisaku o kataru," *op. cit.*, p. 52.

[34] Yoshikata Yoda, *Mizoguchi Kenji no hito to geijutsu* (Kenji Mizoguchi : The Man and His Art) (Tokyo : Tabata Shoten, 1970), p. 170.

[35] Yoda, "Souvenirs sur Mizoguchi," *op. cit.*, No. 169, 1965, p. 37.

[36] *Ibid.*, p. 37.

37 *Ibid.*, p. 37.
38 Yoda, "Souvenirs sur Mizoguchi," *op. cit.*, No. 192, 1967, p. 56.
39 Kishi, *op. cit.*, p. 601.
40 *Ibid.*, p. 603.
41 "Mizoguchi Kenji no hyogen o sasaeta mono," *op. cit.*, p. 156.
42 Kishi, *op. cit.*, p. 609.
43 Interview with Akira Kurosawa, May 1977.
44 "Mizoguchi Kenji no hyogen o sasaeta mono," *op. cit.*, p. 158.
45 *Ibid.*, p. 158.
46 "L'Empereur" (The Emperor: Interview with Akira Kurosawa by Yoshio Shirai, Hayao Shibata and Koichi Yamada), *Cahiers du cinéma*, No. 182, 1966, p. 76.
47 Yoda, "Souvenirs sur Mizoguchi," *op. cit.*, No. 169, 1965, p. 34.
48 Yoda, "Souvenirs sur Mizoguchi," *op. cit.*, No. 192, 1967, p. 55.
49 Akinari Ueda, *Ugetsu Monogatari: Tales of Moonlight and Rain*, transl. by Leon Zolbrod (Tokyo: Charles Tuttle, 1977), p. 128.
50 Yoda, "Souvenirs sur Mizoguchi," *op. cit.*, No. 192, 1967, p. 60.
51 *Ibid.*, p. 60.
52 Kishi, *op. cit.*, p. 607.
53 *Ibid.*, pp. 608–9.
54 Yoda, "Souvenirs sur Mizoguchi" *op. cit.*, No. 181, 1966, p. 52.
55 Yoda, *Mizoguchi Kenji no hito to geijutsu, op. cit.*, p. 131.
56 Kishi, *op. cit.*, p. 619.
57 *Ibid.*, p. 619.
58 *Ibid.*, p. 623.
59 Yoda, *Mizoguchi Kenji no hito to geijutsu, op. cit.*, pp. 269–70.
60 Kishi, *op. cit.*, p. 606.
61 *Ibid.*, p. 627.

KENJI MIZOGUCHI: FILMOGRAPHY

1923 *The Resurrection of Love (Ai ni Yomigaeru Hi)*
pr: Nikkatsu (Mukojima); sc: Osamu Wakayama; ph: Toshimitsu Kosaka; cast: Kaichi Yamamoto, Kiyoshi Mori, Kasuke Koizumi et al. Melodrama scripted by the director who got Mizoguchi his job with Nikkatsu. An apprentice potter falls in love with his teacher's beautiful daughter, but she commits double suicide with another man, and the apprentice ends up with her ugly older sister. The devastatingly realistic portrayal of the life of the poor was too much for the censors, and what remained of the film was strung together with *biwa* (lute) accompaniment. (No extant prints, negative or script.)

Hometown (Furusato)
pr: Nikkatsu (Mukojima); sc: Mizoguchi; ph: Tomozo Iwamura; cast: Kaichi Yamamoto, Takeo Oguri, Mitsuaki Minami et al. Featured the *oyama* (actor who plays female roles) Oguri, though women were already acting in films. By 1953 Mizoguchi had forgotten what it was about. (No extant prints, negative or script.)

The Dream Path of Youth (Seishun no Yumeji)
pr: Nikkatsu (Mukojima); orig. story: Suenori Ozono; sc: Mizoguchi; ph: Hiroshi Watanabe; cast: Yoshio Miyajima, Yoneko Sakai et al. By 1953 Mizoguchi had forgotten what this film was about. (No extant prints, negative or script.)

City of Desire (Joen no Chimata)
pr: Nikkatsu (Mukojima); sc: Mizoguchi; ph: Hiroshi Watanabe and Toshimitsu Kosaka; cast: Mitsuaki Minami, Takeo Oguri et al. Melodrama about a geisha who is rejected by a soldier and, after drinking poison, dances to death. Mizoguchi remembered only that Oguri was in the film. (No extant prints, negative or script.)

Failure's Song Is Sad (Haizan no Uta wa Kanashi)
pr: Nikkatsu (Mukojima); orig. story: Aimi Hata; sc: Mizoguchi; ph: Junichiro Aoshima; cast: Toyosaku Yoshida, Haruko Sawamura et al. Melodrama about a girl from a fishing village who falls in love with a student tourist despite her step-father's admonitions. The boy gets her pregnant and abandons her. First film with which Mizoguchi achieved a reputation as a new director; this heroine said to be the prototype for many of his later female characterizations. (No extant prints, negative or script.)

813: The Adventures of Arsène Lupin (813)
pr: Nikkatsu (Mukojima); orig. story: Maurice Leblanc; sc: Soichiro Tanaka; ph: Toshimitsu Kosaka; cast: Mitsuaki Minami, Tsuruko Segawa et al. Detective story based on the popular French novel character. (No extant prints, negative or script.)

Foggy Harbor (Kiri no Minato)
pr: Nikkatsu (Mukojima); orig. play: Eugene O'Neill; sc: Soichiro Tanaka; ph: Junichiro Aoshima; cast: Haruko Sawamura, Eijiro Mori, Kaichi Yamamoto

et al. Based on the 1921 play *Anna Christie*, which takes place in a 24-hour period, this is a melodramatic love story about a girl and a sailor who commits a murder of moral retribution and gives himself up. Praised for its psychological portrayals, also showed Mizoguchi's first atmospheric settings, beautiful soft-focus blue photography of rain and fog scenes, for which he gave full credit to his new cameraman Aoshima. (No extant prints, negative or script.)

Blood and Soul (*Chi to Rei*)
pr: Nikkatsu (Mukojima);orig. story: Ernst Hoffmann, translated by Kokuseki Oizumi; sc: Mizoguchi; ph: Junichiro Aoshima; cast: Chiyoko Eguchi, Ryotaro Mizushima et al. Mizoguchi called this an Expressionist film, and it is said to have shown the influence especially of *Das Kabinett des Dr. Caligari* and *Von Morgen bis Mitternacht*. Based on the 1819 story *Das Fräulein von Scuderi*, this is another detective film with many humorous mishaps as various people try to steal a jewel. Earned Mizoguchi the reputation of a novelty lover. (No extant prints, negative or script.)

The Night (*Yoru*)
pr: Nikkatsu (Mukojima); orig. sc: Mizoguchi; ph: Junichiro Aoshima; cast: Koichi Katsuragi, Yoneko Sakai et al. Two independent stories, both comedies of irony. A thief breaks into a house, but befriends the child who is home while the parents are out. They return, and also become friends with the thief, and tell him about a man who is trying to run off with a neighbor's wife. The thief finds the man and robs him. In the second story a woman goes to see her ex-husband, but her new husband becomes suspicious, chases and kills her. (No extant prints, negative or script.)

In the Ruins (*Haikyo no Naka*)
pr: Nikkatsu (Mukojima); orig. sc: Hanabishi Kawamura; ph: Toshimitsu Kosaka; cast: Kaichi Yamamoto, Kasuke Koizumi et al. About the Great Kanto Earthquake, which occurred on September 1, 1923. Lovers who have been separated meet again in a temple because of the earthquake and reminisce. After completing this and a documentary filmed in the actual earthquake and fire ruins, Mizoguchi moved with the whole contemporary drama division to Nikkatsu's Kyoto "Daishogun" studios. (No extant prints, negative or script.)

1924 ### The Song of the Mountain Pass (*Toge no Uta*)
pr: Nikkatsu (Daishogun); orig. play: Lady Gregory; sc: Mizoguchi; ph: Toshimitsu Kosaka; cast: Kaichi Yamamoto, Yutaka Mimasu et al. A woman who has committed a crime returns with her child to her husband, who forgives her but not the son who left home. The boy commits suicide on the train tracks. Mizoguchi remembered this as a foreign story. It was begun within three days after arrival in Kyoto. (No extant prints, negative or script.)

The Sad Idiot (*Kanashiki Hakuchi*)
pr: Nikkatsu (Daishogun); orig. idea: Mizoguchi; sc: Tatsuro Takashima; ph: Shohei Iwaida; cast: Kasuke Koizumi, Yoneko Sakai et al. About a

demented man who finds out the woman he has been lavishing all his money on has a lover. He kills her lover and sets out after her. As in the first film a crazed man is the central character. Mizoguchi recalled that this film was also an adaptation of a foreign story, and not very good. (No extant prints, negative or script.)

The Queen of Modern Times (Gendai no Joo)
pr: Nikkatsu (Daishogun); orig. sc: Minoru Murata; ph: Seiichi Uchida; cast: Yoneko Sakai, Mitsuaki Minami et al. Script by Mizoguchi's greatest rival. Up to this time Mizoguchi had been writing his own scenarios. He was assigned an actress and ordered to make a film, but he could not recall the content in 1953. (No extant prints, negative or script.)

Women Are Strong (Josei wa Tsuyoshi)
pr: Nikkatsu (Daishogun); orig. sc: Nikkatsu Literature Division; ph: Seiichi Uchida; cast: Yoneko Sakai, Yutaka Mimasu et al. Based on a Shimpa play which in turn was based on current events. (No extant prints, negative or script.)

This Dusty World (Jinkyo)
pr: Nikkatsu (Daishogun); orig. story: Kaoru Osanai; sc: Soichiro Tanaka; ph: Seiichi Uchida; cast: Demmei Suzuki, Eiji Takagi, Kumeko Urabe et al. Another foreign adaptation, according to Mizoguchi's recollections, shot on location in the mountains, climbing up and down daily for a week. He remembered it as an interesting film (No extant prints, negative or script.)

Turkeys in a Row (Shichimencho no Yukue)
pr: Nikkatsu (Daishogun); sc: Shuichi Hatamoto; ph: Seiichi Uchida; cast: Yutaka Mimasu, Hiroshi Inagaki et al. Based on a children's comedy about a stolen diamond, and starring Inagaki who would become a great director himself. Mizoguchi remembered it as an adaptation of an American detective novel. (No extant prints, negative or script.)

A Chronicle of May Rain (Samidare Zoshi)
pr: Nikkatsu (Daishogun); orig. story: Koju Yokoyama; ph: Seiichi Uchida; cast: Utako Suzuki, Teruko Katsura, Kasuke Koizumi et al. Adapted from a Shimpa play about the love of a geisha and a Buddhist monk. Mizoguchi recalled being criticized for the subject matter. (No extant prints, negative or script.)

No Money, No Fight (Musen Fusen)
pr: Nikkatsu (Daishogun); orig. comic strip: Ippei Okamoto; sc: Shuichi Hatamoto; ph: Seiichi Uchida; cast: Kaichi Yamamoto, Kumeko Urabe et al. Satire on war, based on Okamoto's comic strip about a Chinese soldier who would only fight if paid. Released unscathed in the big cities, but censorship shelved it till the following year elsewhere. (No extant prints, negative or script.)

A Woman of Pleasure (Kanraku no Onna)
pr: Nikkatsu (Daishogun); orig. idea: Mizoguchi; sc: Shuichi Hatamoto; ph:

Sai Uchida; cast: Kaichi Yamamoto, Yutaka Mimasu, Yoneko Sakai et al. Mizoguchi had no recollection of this film. (No extant prints, negative or script.)

Death at Dawn (*Akatsuki no Shi*)

pr: Nikkatsu (Daishogun); orig. sc: Matsuo Ito; ph: Seiichi Uchida; cast: Ryotaro Mizushima, Kasuke Koizumi et al. Mizoguchi entered a slump around this time and recalled only that after *No Money, No Fight* he had to make program-filler-type films. (No extant prints, negative or script.)

1925   ### Queen of the Circus (*Kyokubadan no Joo*)

pr: Nikkatsu (Daishogun); orig. story: Tatsuro Takashima; sc: Shuichi Hatamoto; ph: Sai Uchida; cast: Demmei Suzuki, Kumeko Urabe et al. Mizoguchi could not even remember who starred in this film. (No extant prints or negative.)

Out of College (*Gakuso o Idete*)

pr: Nikkatsu (Daishogun); orig. story: Masanobu Nomura; sc: Mizoguchi; ph: Tatsuyuki Yokota; cast: Mitsuaki Minami, Aiko Takashima et al. In 1953 Mizoguchi thought he might not have made this film —indeed the title sounds more like Ozu. (No extant prints, negative or script.)

The White Lily Laments (*Shirayuri wa Nageku*)

pr: Nikkatsu (Daishogun); orig. story: John Galsworthy; translation, sc: Ryunosuke Shimizu; ph: Tatsuyuki Yokota; cast: Yoshiko Okada, Iyokichi Kondo et al. Mizoguchi remembered only who wrote the script. (No extant prints, negative or script.)

The Earth Smiles (*Daichi wa Hohoemu*)

pr: Nikkatsu (Daishogun); orig. story: Momosuke Yoshida; sc: Shuichi Hatamoto; ph: Tatsuyuki Yokota; cast: Eiji Nakano, Yoko Umemura, Eiji Takagi et al. Three-part melodrama, second and third parts directed by Osamu Wakayama and Kensaku Suzuki. Shot on location in Japan and Korea. Melodrama about a son who steals his father's money, and the involvement of everyone around them. Based on a prize-winning story in the *Asahi Shimbun* newspaper. (No extant prints, negative or script.)

Shining in the Red Sunset (*Akai Yuhi ni Terasarete*)

pr: Nikkatsu (Daishogun); orig. story: Takeshi Nagasaki; sc: Shuichi Hatamoto; ph: Tatsuyuki Yokota; cast: Eiji Nakano, Mitsuaki Minami et al. Spy story set in Manchuria. Mizoguchi recalled that war was approaching (in China) at the time. Shooting was stopped after three days due to the fight between Mizoguchi and the woman he lived with, and the film was finished by Genjiro Saegusa. (No extant prints, negative or script.)

The Song of Home (*Furusato no Uta*)

pr: Nikkatsu (Daishogun); orig. story: Choji Matsui; sc: Ryunosuke Shimizu; ph: Tatsuyuki Yokota; cast: Shigeru Kito, Mineko Tsuji et al. Mizoguchi said this script was assigned by the Ministry of Education to encourage rice production. Tragedy about a farm boy and girl attracted by the big city and a carriage driver who becomes a farmer to help the people. (FC)

The Human Being (Ningen)
pr: Nikkatsu (Daishogun); orig. story: Zentaro Suzuki; sc: Shuichi Hatamoto; cast: Yoshiko Okada, Eiji Nakano et al. Based on a prize-winning novel about a young man with dreams of greatness who comes to the capital. Things go badly for him and he drifts to Nagasaki, then Osaka, and finally finds a rich man's daughter to marry. But he is too ashamed of his past and returns to his home town. (No extant prints, negative or script.)

Street Sketches (Gaijo no Suketchi)
pr: Nikkatsu (Daishogun); planned by Nikkatsu's Shingeki drama department; ph: Tatsuyuki Yokota; cast: Yasunaga Higashibojo, Yoshiko Okada et al. Omnibus film of episodes by four directors. Mizoguchi's part is about a man who tries to commit suicide in a restaurant, but someone else drinks his poison. (No extant prints, negative or script.)

1926   ### General Nogi and Kuma-san (Nogi Taisho to Kuma-san)
pr: Nikkatsu (Daishogun); cast: Kaichi Yamamoto, Kasuke Koizumi, Kumeko Urabe et al. Mizoguchi recalled that this film about the Russo-Japanese war hero and his wife who comitted suicide when the Emperor Meiji died was popular at the time. (No extant prints, negative or script.)

The Copper Coin King (Doka O)
pr: Nikkatsu (Daishogun); orig. idea: Mizoguchi; ph: Saburo Isayama; cast: Enji Sato, Kayoko Saijo et al. Mizoguchi recalled this as a foreign detective story. Action thriller about a boy and his girl friend who come into the possession of a strange coin. (No extant prints, negative or script.)

A Paper Doll's Whisper of Spring (Kaminingyo Haru no Sasayaki)
pr: Nikkatsu (Daishogun); orig. story: Eizo Tanaka; ph: Tatsuyuki Yokota; cast: Yoko Umemura, Tokihiko Okada, Koji Shima et al. Melodrama of the lower-middle classes. The daughter of a merchant family was to marry a craftsman, but since her family is on the decline—her father is a playboy and her brother has left home—she remains single, writing her lover's name on the paper dolls she makes. Her father dies of a stroke and the craftsman goes bankrupt. Mizoguchi felt his direction was established with this film. *KJ #7.* (No extant prints or negative; script extant.)

My Fault, New Version (Shin Ono ga Tsumi)
pr: Nikkatsu (Daishogun); orig. story: Yuho Kikuchi; sc: Shuichi Hatamoto; ph: Matao Matsuzawa; cast: Komako Sunada, Eiji Takagi et al. Based on a 1908 film by Yoshizo Chiba, a Shimpa drama. Mizoguchi said he was ordered to make a film for Sunada, and regretted the results. (No extant prints, negative or script.)

The Passion of a Woman Teacher (Kyoren no Onna Shisho)
pr: Nikkatsu (Daishogun); orig. sc: Matsutaro Kawaguchi; ph: Tatsuyuki Yokota; cast: Yoneko Sakai, Eiji Nakano, Yoshiko Okada et al. Ghost story about a singing teacher who has an affair with a shamisen player, resulting in the loss of all of her pupils but one. The teacher develops a sore on her face, and the pupil begins to dislike her and runs off with a girl pupil. The teacher dies, but

her ghost haunts the young couple and makes the boy kill the girl. He then dies struck by lightning. Reputed to have been one of Mizoguchi's first films about a tenacious woman of the sort he knew so well. First scenario by his elementary school classmate. (No extant prints, negative or script.)

The Boy of the Sea (*Kaikoku Danji*)

pr: Nikkatsu (Daishogun); orig. idea: Kajiro Yamamoto; sc: Akira Takeda; cast: Tsunemi Hirose, Komako Sunada et al. Hirose was a new face fresh from maritime academy, and Mizoguchi was ordered to make a film for him. The plot involves a boy who enters a fishery from maritime school, wins the boss's daughter and goes on to get rid of the bad guys and become a success. (No extant prints, negative or script.)

Money (*Kane*)

pr: Nikkatsu (Daishogun); orig. idea: Mizoguchi; sc: Akira Takeda and Shuichi Hatamoto; ph: Tatsuyuki Yokota; cast: Kasuke Koizumi, Yoshiko Tokugawa et al. Comedy about a poor but cheerful sushi-shop boy's payday. (No extant prints, negative or script.)

1927 The Imperial Grace (*Ko-on*)

pr: Nikkatsu (Daishogun); orig. sc: Shuichi Hatamoto; ph: Tatsuyuki Yokota; cast: Harue Ichikawa, Mitsuaki Minami et al. An army request. A widow raises her two sons alone, and the younger goes off to the Russo-Japanese war, while the older goes astray. The soldier comes home disabled but decorated and reprimands his brother. Mizoguchi said the army censored "unwarlike" scenes of a disabled veteran playing a harmonica and selling medicine. (No extant prints, negative or script.)

The Cuckoo (*Jihi Shincho*)

pr: Nikkatsu (Daishogun); orig. story: Kan Kikuchi; sc: Shuichi Hatamoto; ph: Tatsuyuki Yokota; cast: Mitsuyo Hara, Eiji Nakano, Tokihiko Okada, Shizue Natsukawa et al. Melodrama of revenge. A girl has two suitors, one of whom becomes a lawyer, while the other, whom she marries, gets involved in corruption. The lawyer has the husband jailed and saves the wife, but she never forgives him, and he dies a bachelor. Mizoguchi called this a vehicle for Hara. *KJ* #7. (No extant prints, negative or script.)

1928 A Man's Life (*Hito no Issho*)

pr: Nikkatsu (Daishogun); orig. story: Ippei Okamoto; sc: Shuichi Hatamoto; ph: Tatsuyuki Yokota; cast: Kasuke Koizumi et al. Another film based on Okamoto's cartoon characters. Mizoguchi recalled making at least three of these, and being told they were "Russian comedies." (No extant prints, negative or script.)

1929 Nihombashi (*Nihombashi*)

pr: Nikkatsu (Uzumasa); orig. story: Kyoka Izumi; sc: Mizoguchi; ph: Tatsuyuki Yokota; cast: Tokihiko Okada, Yoko Umemura, Shizue Natsukawa et al. Love tragedy set in the geisha world, centering around a young man searching for his sister, who disappeared after putting him through school by being a mistress. He falls in love with a geisha whose former patron is on the decline, amid fires, suicide attempts, partings and reunions. Mizoguchi was rather proud of the fact that he wrote this adaptation of one of his favorite authors himself. (No extant prints, negative or script.)

Tokyo March (*Tokyo Koshinkyoku*)

pr: Nikkatsu (Uzumasa); orig. story: Kan Kikuchi; sc: Chieo Kimura; ph: Tatsuyuki Yokota; cast: Shizue Natsukawa, Takako Irie, Isamu Kosugi et al. Mizoguchi recalled this was a great hit, with a record made to promote it. The illegitimate daughter of a wealthy man becomes a geisha and is further abused by the men who flock around her beauty. Suggestion of social criticism. (Incomplete print at ME.)

The Morning Sun Shines (*Asahi wa Kagayaku*)

pr: Nikkatsu (Uzumasa); codirected by Seiichi Ina; sc: Chieo Kimura; orig. idea: Osaka *Asahi Shimbun*; ph: Tatsuyuki Yokota; cast: Eiji Nakano, Takako Irie et al. Promotional film made for the tenth anniversary of the founding of the *Asahi Shimbun* newspaper, centering on the life of two new reporters who are friends. (No extant prints, negative or script.)

Metropolitan Symphony (*Tokai Kokyogaku*)

pr: Nikkatsu (Uzumasa); orig. stories: Teppei Kataoka, Rokuro Asahara, Fusao Hayashi and Saburo Okada; sc: Shuichi Hatamoto and Tadashi Kobayashi; ph: Tatsuyuki Yokota; cast: Isamu Kosugi, Eiji Takagi, Reiji Hitotsugi, Shizue Natsukawa, Takako Irie et al. Told to make "another *Tokyo March*," Mizoguchi made his first full-fledged "tendency film," neglecting to tell the company it was based on the work of leftist authors. A poor boy laborer and a girl who has been played with and dropped by a rich man get together and decide to seek revenge against capitalists. Mizoguchi had another run-in with the police over this film, and 2,000 feet were cut before it was released. *KJ* #10. (No extant prints, negative or script.)

1930   ### Home Town (*Furusato*)

pr: Nikkatsu (Uzumasa); orig. sc: Iwao Mori, Toshi Kisaragi, Shuichi Hatamoto and Tadashi Kobayashi; ph: Tatsuyuki Yokota and Yoshio Mineo; cast: Yoshie Fujiwara, Shizue Natsukawa, Isamu Kosugi et al. Talkie. A down and out singer marries the scrubwoman who has been kind to him. But when a friend's efforts finally bring him success, he becomes decadent in high society. He realizes his error end comes home in the end. Mizoguchi's first talkie, hampered by many technical difficulties. Stars Fujiwara, the first great opera singer in Japan. (FC)

Mistress of a Foreigner (*Tojin Okichi*)

pr: Nikkatsu (Uzumasa); orig. story: Gisaburo Juichiya; sc: Shuichi Hatamoto; ph: Tatsuyuki Yokota; cast: Yoko Umemura, Kaichi Yamamoto, Koji Shima et al. Based on a serialized newspaper story about a girl from a poor Shimoda family who is trained in traditional arts in the mid-nineteenth century. She becomes a geisha and then, against her will, the mistress of the American consul, Townsend Harris, who forces her lover to give her up. Reputed to prefigure the tragic heroine of *Story of the Last Chrysanthemum*. (No extant prints, negative or script.)

1931   *And Yet They Go (Shikamo Karera wa Yuku)*
    pr: Nikkatsu (Uzumasa); orig. story: Chiaki Shimomura; sc: Shuichi Hatamoto;
    ph: Tatsuyuki Yokota; cast: Yoko Umemura et al. Mizoguchi himself called
    this a "tendency film" about the miserable life of prostitutes in Tokyo's
    Tamanoi district. The story focuses on one girl who is repeatedly deceived by
    men, and gradually becomes stronger as a result. (No extant prints, negative
    or script.)

1932   *The Man of the Moment (Toki no Ujigami)*
    pr: Nikkatsu (Uzumasa); orig. play: Kan Kikuchi; sc: Shuichi Hatamoto and
    Tadashi Kobayashi; ph: Tatsuyuki Yokota; cast: Koji Shima, Shizue Natsu-
    kawa et al. Comedy about two quarreling couples who get mixed up. Mizo-
    guchi said he frequented Kikuchi because of the many pretty girls at his
    house and the money he gave him. (No extant prints, negative or script.)

    The Dawn of Manchukuo and Mongolia (Mammo Kenkoku no Reimei)
    pr: Irie Prod./Nakano Prod./Shinko; orig. story: Otokichi Mikami and Sanjugo
    Naoki; sc: Shinko Kinema Scenario Division; ph: Junichiro Aoshima and
    Yoshio Nakayama; cast: Takako Irie, Eiji Nakano et al. Shot on location, pro-
    paganda film eulogizing the government's expansionist policies. Melodrama
    set during the Manchurian Incident. (No extant prints, negative or script.)

1933   **Taki no Shiraito, the Water Magician (Taki no Shiraito)*
    pr: Irie Prod.; orig. story: Kyoka Izumi; sc: Yasunaga Higashibojo, Shinji
    Masuda and Kennosuke Tateoka; ph: Shigeru Miki; cast: Takako Irie, Tokihiko
    Okada, Suzuko Taki, Ichiro Sugai et al. Silent. Heavy but beautifully photo-
    graphed melodrama about a girl water magician who falls in love with
    a poor student and puts him through school. Later she is driven to murder
    a usurer, is tried and found guilty by her lover, now a judge. She is given
    capital punishment; he commits suicide. *KJ* #2. (ME, MOMA)

    Gion Festival (Gion Matsuri)
    pr: Shinko (Kyoto); orig. story: Matsutaro Kawaguchi; sc: Mizoguchi; ph:
    Minoru Miki; cast: Shizuko Mori, Tokihiko Okada et al. Silent. Another
    heavy melodrama about a merchant's daughter who falls in love with one of
    her father's employees. The business fails and the young man tries to get the
    girl married off to a rich man to save her family. But the rich man's mistress
    kills the young man. Made in less than three weeks to coincide with summer
    festival time, and not Mizoguchi's own choice, but a company order. *KJ* #9.
    (No extant prints, negative or script.)

    The Jimpu Group (Jimpuren)
    pr: Irie Prod./Shinko; orig. story: Gisaburo Juichiya; sc: Mizoguchi; ph:
    Minoru Miki; cast: Takako Irie, Ryunosuke Tsukigata et al. Meiji era story
    about the revolt of a group of samurai who have lost their privileges, seen
    through the eyes of a beautiful water magician. Another film that Mizoguchi
    was told to make. *KJ* #10. (No extant prints, negative or script.)

1934   *The Mountain Pass of Love and Hate (Aizo Toge)*
    pr: Nikkatsu (Tamagawa); orig. story: Matsutaro Kawaguchi; sc: Tatsunosuke

Takashima and Kawaguchi; ph: Tatsuyuki Yokota; cast: Isuzu Yamada, Daijiro Natsukawa, Demmei Suzuki et al. Meiji melodrama about the love of a Liberal Party supporter and an itinerant actress who meet at a mountain pass. (No extant prints, negative or script.)

The Downfall of Osen (Orizuru Osen)

pr: Daiichi Eiga; orig. story: Kyoka Izumi; sc: Tatsunosuke Takashima; ph: Shigeto Miki; cast: Isuzu Yamada, Daijiro Natsukawa et al. Another story about the life of prostitutes, a subject which Mizoguchi liked but felt he did not capture adequately in this film. (FC; negative at Shochiku, Tokyo.)

1935   ### Oyuki the Madonna (Maria no Oyuki)

pr: Daiichi Eiga; orig. story: Guy de Maupassant, adapted by Matsutaro Kawaguchi; sc: Tatsunosuke Takashima; ph: Shigeto Miki; cast: Isuzu Yamada, Komako Hara, Daijiro Natsukawa et al. Based on *Boule de Suif*, a story about a prostitute with a heart of gold, Mizoguchi made it a period drama set during the Satsuma clan rebellion, near the end of the feudal age. (FC; negative at Shochiku, Tokyo.)

Poppy (Gubijinso)

pr: Daiichi Eiga; orig. story: Soseki Natsume; sc: Daisuke Ito; ph: Minoru Miki; cast: Kuniko Miyake, Ichiro Tsukida, Chiyoko Okura et al. A proud woman, rejected by a man whose engagement she breaks up, ends by committing suicide. (FC; negative at Shochiku, Tokyo.)

1936   ### *Osaka Elegy (Naniwa Ereji)

pr: Daiichi Eiga; orig. idea: Mizoguchi; sc: Yoshikata Yoda; ph: Minoru Miki; cast: Isuzu Yamada, Eitaro Shindo, Kensaku Hara, Benkei Shiganoya et al. First film about modern women, first work with Yoda, and the beginning of true realism. A young telephone operator is ruined because of an innocent need for money. Her boss takes advantage of her, his wife takes it out on the girl's family, and her fiancé stands helplessly by. *KJ* #3. (FC, MOMA, AB)

*Sisters of the Gion (Gion no Shimai)

pr: Daiichi Eiga; orig. idea: Mizoguchi; sc: Yoshikata Yoda; ph: Minoru Miki; cast: Isuzu Yamada, Yoko Umemura, Benkei Shiganoya, Eitaro Shindo et al. Realistic look at the glamorous world of traditional geisha in Kyoto's Gion district. The older sister is strict and traditional, while the younger is modern and opportunistic, going from man to man for money. *KJ* #1. (FC, MOMA, AB)

1937   ### *The Straits of Love and Hate (Aienkyo)

pr: Shinko (Tokyo); orig. story: Matsutaro Kawaguchi; sc: Yoshikata Yoda; ph: Minoru Miki; cast: Fumiko Yamaji, Şeizaburo Kawazu, Masao Shimizu et al. Continued pursuit of realism focusing on women. A girl who works at a hot spring hotel falls in love and runs off to Tokyo with her lover. The boy's father takes him back, and she is left with a baby. She joins a traveling theater troupe and meets her lover again. His father opposes their reunion, and she returns to the troupe and the poor stage partner she really loves. *KJ* #3. (FC; Nishihara Collection, Tokyo.)

1938   *Ah, My Home Town (Aa Furusato)*
pr: Shinko (Tokyo); orig. story: Hideo Koide; sc: Yoshikata Yoda; ph: Junichiro Aoshima; cast: Fumiko Yamaji, Masao Shimizu, Seiichi Kato et al. Mizoguchi wanted to show a woman's resistance to the pressures created when big business moves into a small town. A man who is struggling to manage a hotspring hotel tries to force his daughter to marry a rich man, but she waits for her student fiancé to return from America. He does and marries someone else. The girl and her father go back to Tokyo. *KJ* #9. (No extant prints or negative; script extant.)

The Song of the Camp (Roei no Uta)
pr: Shinko (Tokyo); orig. sc: Shuichi Hatamoto; ph: Junichiro Aoshima; cast: Fumiko Yamaji, Akira Matsudaira, Seizaburo Kawazu et al. Mizoguchi was forced to direct this film and resented this so much that he resigned. Based on a battle song. (No extant prints, negative or script.)

1939   **The Story of the Last Chrysanthemum (Zangiku Monogatari)*
pr: Shochiku (Kyoto); orig. story: Shofu Muramatsu, planned by Matsutaro Kawaguchi; sc: Yoshikata Yoda; ph: Shigeto Miki; music: Senji Ito; cast: Kakuko Mori, Shotaro Hanayagi, Yoko Umemura, Gonjuro Kawarazaki et al. Sentimental tragedy set in the Meiji era. A spoiled young actor from an important Kabuki family learns from the maid that he must work harder to perfect his art. He leaves home to join a provincial troupe and lives in terrible hardship. His family at last takes him back, after he has made a name for himself, but the faithful maid, whom he has always loved, dies. Powerful insight into the ruthless snobbery of the Kabuki world. Mizoguchi felt he finally came into his own with this film, as he was allowed to do what he wanted. *KJ* #2. (FC, AB)

1940   *The Woman of Osaka (Naniwa Onna)*
pr: Shochiku (Kyoto); orig. idea: Mizoguchi; sc: Yoshikata Yoda; ph: Shigeto Miki; music: Senji Ito; cast: Kotaro Bando, Kinuyo Tanaka, Ryotaro Kawanami et al. Rivalries in the world of the Osaka Bunraku puppet theater. Excellent character delineation of a domineering, aggressive wife who comes to realize her own faults. *KJ* #4. (No extant prints, negative or script.)

1941   *The Life of an Actor (Geido Ichidai Otoko)*
pr: Shochiku (Kyoto); orig. story: Matsutaro Kawaguchi; sc: Yoshikata Yoda; ph: Kohei Sugiyama; music: Senji Ito; cast: Senjaku Nakamura, Yoshiko Nakamura, Kokichi Takada, Minosuke Bando, Yoko Umemura et al. Another story of the Kabuki world, this time about the life of Ganjiro Nakamura and played by his son, Senjaku. Born as the illegitimate son of a Kabuki actor, he is encouraged to become an actor. After his first successful stage appearance, he and his mother go to look for his father, but find that he has died of an illness. NEZK #4. (No extant prints, negative or script.)

*The Loyal 47 Ronin I-II (Genroku Chushingura I-II)
pr: Shochiku Koa Eiga; orig. story: Seika Mayama; sc: Kenichiro Hara and Yoshikata Yoda; ph: Kohei Sugiyama; music: Shiro Fukai; cast: Utaemon

Ichikawa, Isamu Kosugi, Mieko Takamine, members of Zenshinza theater troupe et al. A two-part extravaganza Mizoguchi was forced to make because of the outbreak of the war and the demand from above for films glorifying feudal loyalty and self-sacrifice, but at least his version is based on the historical incident instead of the Kabuki play. Part II: NEZK #7. (FC, AB)

1944   *Three Generations of Danjuro (Danjuro Sandai)*
pr: Shochiku; orig. sc: Matsutaro Kawaguchi; ph: Shigeto Miki; cast: Kotaro Bando, Kinuyo Tanaka, Gonjuro Kawarazaki et al. Another that Mizoguchi was forced to make, about a famous Kabuki family. (No extant prints, negative or script.)

Musashi Miyamoto (Miyamoto Musashi)
pr: Shochiku; orig. story: Kan Kikuchi; sc: Matsutaro Kawaguchi; ph: Shigeto Miki; cast: Gonjuro Kawarazaki, Kinuyo Tanaka, Kanemon Nakamura et al. Mizoguchi said he made films like this (about a famous feudal swordsman) to keep from getting drafted, but despite the feudal ethics message, the portrayal of Musashi's girl admirer comes out well. (FC)

1945   *The Famous Sword Bijomaru (Meito Bijomaru)*
pr: Shochiku; orig. sc: Matsutaro Kawaguchi; ph: Haruo Takeno; cast: Eijiro Yanagi, Shotaro Hanayagi, Isuzu Yamada et al. Same type of subject matter as the above, focusing on the wife of the swordsmith. (FC, ME)

Victory Song (Hisshoka)
pr: Shochiku; codir: Mizoguchi, Masahiro Makino, Hiroshi Shimizu; orig. sc: Matsuo Kishi and Shimizu. Omnibus film ordered by the propaganda office to encourage a fight to the bitter end. Mizoguchi remarked on Kishi's script about a railroad snow removal laborer that he had not succeeded in showing the collective work spirit of the nation. Kishi agreed and shooting began. The film was lambasted by the critics. (No extant prints, negative or script.)

1946   *The Victory of Women (Josei no Shori)*
pr: Shochiku (Ofuna); orig. sc: Kogo Noda and Kaneto Shindo; ph: Toshio Ubukata; music: Kyoka Asai; cast: Kinuyo Tanaka, Michiko Kuwano, Mitsuko Miura et al. Assimilation of U.S. Occupation ideas on female emancipation in a story about professional women in the law courts. Pedantic, static film in which it is hard to see what the heroine gains in her lonely victory. (FC; negative at Shochiku, Tokyo.)

*Utamaro and His Five Women (Utamaro o Meguru Gonin no Onna)
pr: Shochiku (Kyoto); orig. story: Kanji Kunieda; sc: Yoshikata Yoda; ph: Shigeto Miki; music: Hisato Osawa; cast: Minosuke Bando, Kinuyo Tanaka et al. A story about government censorship and jealous women, based on the life of early nineteenth-century woodblock print artist Utamaro Kitagawa. Mizoguchi personally appealed to Occupation authorities to let him make a period drama, and with this film he emerged from his wartime slump. *KJ* #7. (FC, NY)

1947   *The Love of Sumako the Actress (Joyu Sumako no Koi)*
pr: Shochiku (Kyoto); orig. story: Hideo Nagata; sc: Yoshikata Yoda; ph: Shigeto Miki; music: Hisato Osawa; cast: Kinuyo Tanaka, So Yamamura, Kikue Mori, Chieko Higashiyama et al. Though this film about the first modern stage actress was commercially successful, even Mizoguchi did not feel it was as good as Teinosuke Kinugasa's version of the same year. (FC; negative at Shochiku, Tokyo.)

1948   **Women of the Night (Yoru no Onnatachi)*
pr: Shochiku (Kyoto); orig. story: Eijiro Hisaita; sc: Yoshikata Yoda; ph: Kohei Sugiyama; music: Hisato Osawa; cast: Kinuyo Tanaka, Sanae Takasugi, Mitsuo Nagata et al. Excellent portrayal of the postwar scene and women's pathos and bitterness through a story about an Osaka streetwalker. *KJ #3*. (FC, AB)

1949   *My Love Burns (Waga Koi wa Moenu)*
pr: Shochiku (Kyoto); orig. idea: Kogo Noda; sc: Yoshikata Yoda and Kaneto Shindo; ph: Kohei Sugiyama; music: Senji Ito; cast: Kinuyo Tanaka, Mitsuko Mito, Eitaro Ozawa et al. About a woman who was one of the more famous in the postwar women's movement, Hideko Kageyama. From a provincial aristocratic family, she goes to Tokyo for a man who turns out to be a government spy. Eventually she marries a man in a democratic movement, but is disillusioned, leaves him, and decides to dedicate her life to women's rights. (FC; negative at Shochiku, Tokyo.)

1950   **A Picture of Madame Yuki (Yuki Fujin Ezu)*
pr: Takimura Prod./Shin Toho; orig. story: Seiichi Funahashi; sc: Yoshikata Yoda and Kazuro Funahashi; ph: Joji Ohara; music: Fumio Hayasaka; cast: Michiyo Kogure, Eijiro Yanagi, Yoshiko Kuga, Ken Uehara et al. Set in Atami, the seaside hot spring resort close to Tokyo, shows the decline of a provincial aristocratic family and a woman's dissatisfaction with her marriage to a playboy husband. Though Mizoguchi wasn't satisfied with this film, it is a beautiful treatment of a proud and delicate woman threatened by insensitivity and financial collapse around her. (FC; negative at Kokusai Hoei, Tokyo.)

1951   *Miss Oyu (Oyu-sama)*
pr: Daiei (Kyoto); orig. story: Junichiro Tanizaki; sc: Yoshikata Yoda; ph: Kazuo Miyagawa; music: Fumio Hayasaka; cast: Kinuyo Tanaka, Nobuko Otowa, Yuji Hori et al. Based on *Ashikari* (The Reaper of Rushes), a film with which Mizoguchi was not satisfied, and which makes the widow who is loved by her sister's husband appear a much more selfless person than in the original. (FC; negative at Daiei, Tokyo.)

Lady Musashino (Musashino Fujin)
pr: Toho; orig. story: Shohei Ooka; sc: Yoshikata Yoda; ph: Masao Tamai; music: Fumio Hayasaka; cast: Kinuyo Tanaka, Masayuki Mori, So Yamamura, Yukiko Todoroki et al. Melodrama about the wife of a university professor living in the Tokyo suburbs. Mizoguchi tried to do something along

the lines of *A Picture of Madame Yuki* but felt that he failed. (FC; negative at Toho, Tokyo.)

1952 *The Life of Oharu (Saikaku Ichidai Onna)*
pr: Shin Toho; orig. story: Saikaku Ihara; sc: Yoshikata Yoda; ph: Yoshimi Hirano; music: Ichiro Saito; cast: Kinuyo Tanaka, Hisako Yamane, Toshiro Mifune, Yuriko Hamada et al. Another story of the life of a prostitute, based on the work of a seventeenth-century writer. Oharu declines gradually from court lady to cheap prostitute as she is victimized by men for money and sex. Told in flashbacks, with beautiful photography. *KJ* #9; Venice Film Festival International Prize. (FC, NY)

1953 *Ugetsu (Ugetsu Monogatari)*
pr: Daiei; orig. stories: Akinari Ueda; sc: Matsutaro Kawaguchi and Yoshikata Yoda; ph: Kazuo Miyagawa; music: Fumio Hayasaka; cast: Machiko Kyo, Mitsuko Mito, Kinuyo Tanaka, Masayuki Mori, Sakae Ozawa et al. Beautifully eerie story of a sixteenth-century potter, his fascination with and near death at the hands of a lovely ghost. Mizoguchi wanted to make the ending more bitter than the company would allow. *KJ* #3; Venice Film Festival San Marco Silver Lion; Italian Critics Award.`(FC, JA)

Gion Festival Music (Gion Bayashi)
pr: Daiei; orig. story: Matsutaro Kawaguchi; sc: Yoshikata Yoda; ph: Kazuo Miyagawa; music: Ichiro Saito; cast: Michiyo Kogure, Ayako Wakao, Seizaburo Kawazu, Eitaro Shindo et al. Remake of the 1936 *Sisters of the Gion,* but set in postwar Japan. Again Mizoguchi complained that the company changed the script, and the film indeed has an unfinished feeling. *KJ* #9. (FC; negative at Daiei, Tokyo.)

1954 *Sansho the Bailiff/The Bailiff (Sansho Dayu)*
pr: Daiei; orig. story: Ogai Mori; sc: Fuji Yahiro and Yoshikata Yoda; ph: Kazuo Miyagawa; music: Fumio Hayasaka; cast: Kinuyo Tanaka, Kisho Hanayagi, Kyoko Kagawa, Eitaro Shindo, Masao Shimizu et al. Romantic ideals contrasted with brutal reality. An eleventh-century aristocratic family is broken up by politics, and then further by slave traders. The son struggles to live by his father's ideals of compassion and equality, and finally succeeds for a moment in the end, only to give up his new political power. Lovely atmospheric settings. *KJ* #9; Venice Film Festival San Marco Silver Lion. (FC, AB)

The Woman of the Rumor (Uwasa no Onna)
pr: Daiei (Kyoto); orig. sc: Yoshikata Yoda and Masashige Narusawa; ph: Kazuo Miyagawa; music: Toshiro Mayuzumi; cast: Kinuyo Tanaka, Yoshiko Kuga, Tomoemon Otani, Eitaro Shindo et al. About the life of a woman who runs a geisha house in Kyoto's Shimabara district. Melodrama as she realizes her lover prefers her proper pianist daughter, but the portrayal of the geisha's life compensates somewhat. (FC; negative at Daiei, Tokyo.)

A Story from Chikamatsu/Crucified Lovers (Chikamatsu Monogatari)
pr: Daiei; orig. play: Monzaemon Chikamatsu, adapted by Matsutaro Kawa-

guchi; sc: Yoshikata Yoda; ph: Kazuo Miyagawa; music: Fumio Hayasaka; cast: Kazuo Hasegawa, Kyoko Kagawa, Yoko Minamida, Eitaro Shindo et al. Based on the seventeenth-century play, "The Almanac-Maker's Tale." A woman of the merchant class unjustly accused of adultery escapes with her supposed partner in crime, a servant. They are eventually caught and executed, but not before they realize that they really are in love. Strongly anti-feudal film focusing on the woman's status, with superb photography. *KJ #5.* (FC, NL)

1955   *The Princess Yang Kwei-fei (Yokihi)*
pr: Run-Run Shaw/Daiei; orig. sc: Matsutaro Kawaguchi, Masashige Narusawa and Yoshikata Yoda; ph (color): Kohei Sugiyama; music: Fumio Hayasaka; cast: Machiko Kyo, Masayuki Mori, So Yamamura, Eitaro Shindo, Sakae Ozawa et al. The famous story of the concubine who caused the downfall of an eighth-century Chinese emperor. But Mizoguchi has her sacrifice her own life to save the emperor. His first color film, shot on location in Hong Kong. Decorative, contrived atmosphere. (FC, NY)

New Tales of the Taira Clan (Shin Heike Monogatari)
pr: Daiei; sc: Yoshikata Yoda, Masashige Narusawa and Hisaichi Tsuji; orig. novel: Eiji Yoshikawa; ph (color): Kazuo Miyagawa; music: Fumio Hayasaka; cast: Raizo Ichikawa, Yoshiko Kuga, Naritoshi Hayashi, Michiyo Kogure et al. Almost a period spectacular; not quite Mizoguchi's element. Conflict between the decadent court and the exploited but rising warrior class at the end of the twelfth century. (FC, NL)

1956   *Street of Shame (Akasen Chitai)*
pr: Daiei; orig. sc: Masashige Narusawa; ph: Kazuo Miyagawa; music: Toshiro Mayuzumi; cast: Machiko Kyo, Ayako Wakao, Aiko Mimasu, Michiyo Kogure et al. Mizoguchi's last film, on one of his favorite subjects: prostitutes. Sensitive treatment of the hardships of several prostitutes and the reasons they are what they are —trying to send children to school, supporting unemployed husbands, trying to get fathers out of prison, and so on. Social consciousness with some shallow and some excellent character portrayal, and very irritating music. (FC, MOMA, JA)

YASUJIRO OZU

1903—63

*I portray what should not be possible as if it
should be possible, but Ozu portrays
what should be possible as if it were possible,
and that is much more difficult.*

—Kenji Mizoguchi

from Masahiro Shinoda, "Mizoguchi Kenji kara toku hanarete," in *Kikan Film* No. 3, 1969

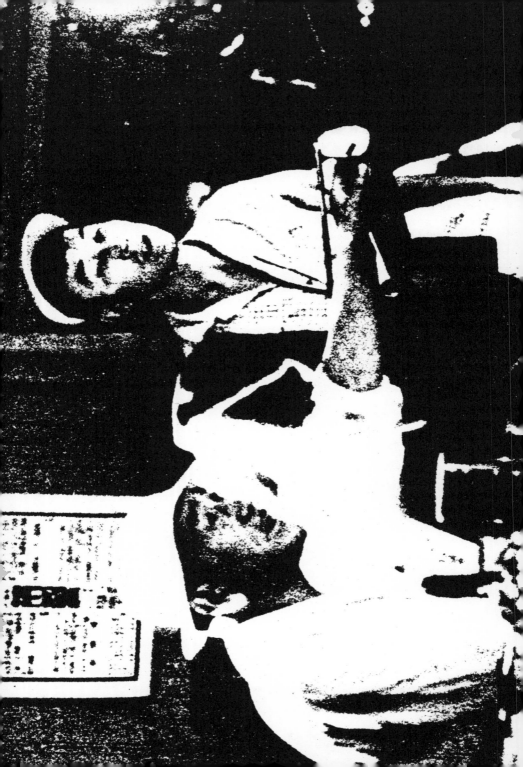

Time and again we have been assured that the Japanese, always conscious of their national identity, consider Yasujiro Ozu "the most Japanese" of Japanese film directors.[1] It was apparently this conviction that prevented his films from being shown abroad, for while the works of the first filmmaker elected to the Japanese Academy of Art were winning numerous awards at home, they were jealously guarded for exclusively Japanese audiences throughout the 1950s, "one of the canons of the Japanese business world being that the West cannot hope to appreciate anything 'truly Japanese.' "[2] Happily, such contentions have since had the opportunity to be proved wrong. Ozu, the artist of life as it is, has in the 1970s attained the international appreciation his universality deserves.

The subject matter of the Ozu film is what faces all of us born of man and woman and going on to produce offspring of our own: the family. Japanese terms such as *shomin-geki*, the drama of humor and pathos in lower-middle-class life, or *home drama*, a loan word now pejoratively equivalent to soap opera, may be applied to Ozu's works and create an illusion of peculiar Japaneseness, but in fact behind the words are the problems we all face in a life cycle. They are the struggles of self-definition, of individual freedom, of disappointed expectations, of the impossibility of communication, of separation and loss brought about by the inevitable passages of marriage and death.

Over the years of his lengthy filmmaking career, from 1927 to 1962, Ozu honed, pared down, refined his form to a spare essence allied with the devastatingly simple, everyday problems his characters face. Just as the situations and the people themselves became archetypes, the cinematic technique became a reduction to present, linear time, to sequences based on a "primitive cinema" format of long-shot, medium-shot, closeup, and back again, to camera and editing work that rejects movement and all that smacks of virtuosity. What remains after all the pruning is an anti-dramatic, slow-paced, and deeply moving revelation of character that fulfills the Mies van der Rohe maxim "Less is more."

Yet there is so composed, so restrained, so reduced a quality to Ozu's ennoblement of the everyday world of the middle-class family that toward the end of his career opposition to his style arose with the Japanese New Wave. Ozu's message, his only solution to the problem of living, had been acceptance. In this resignation to things as they are, for which he was labeled a traditionalist, or simply "old-fashioned,"[3] the younger generation of Japanese filmmakers found reason to rebel, much as do the young in Ozu's films. He was even heard to grumble that he had to make big box-office films to clean up after the irresponsible amusements of the young directors,[4] but the positivism of youth did not stop crying out for a larger world and a social consciousness. Ozu's world, the world of the human condition of fallibility, disillusionment, gentle humor and transiency, fell into disrepute with the new generation, who always, Ozu knew, had to find out for themselves.

We are fortunate in approaching the world of Ozu that his life and films have been so thoroughly documented. At present, 31 of his 53 films are preserved; some recently found prewar works were put into international circulation. For many films, of which no prints or negatives have been resuscitated from the Shochiku company's vaults, scripts are extant. The fastidious habit in which Ozu and his scriptwriter Kogo Noda indulged of keeping a diary has also provided a source of immense value in determining the process of his filmmaking. But the most burning theoretical questions, such as why he used his peculiar low camera angle, remain problems for speculation by others.

Movie Mania

Ozu was born in the old Fukagawa district of Tokyo in 1903, second son of five children of a fertilizer merchant whose ancestral home was in the city of Matsuzaka in Mie Prefecture. When Yasujiro was in his fourth year of elementary school, after the birth of his youngest sister, his father sent the whole family back to Matsuzaka for the children's education. From 1913 to 1923, Ozu lived apart from his father, developing his famous unruliness and close attachment to his mother, who would remain by his side for life.

At school in Matsuzaka Ozu was never an avid student, achieving a reputation instead for drinking, displaying a photograph of an actress on his desk, and writing a love letter to a boy in a lower class.[5] All of these activities were frowned upon by the school administration, and Ozu was expelled from the dormitory and told to commute from home with a passbook in which his mother and teachers had to stamp him in and out. He quickly took to stealing the family seal and coming and going as he pleased.

Cleverness in skirting restrictions and requirements stayed with him through his first long stint in the army reserves, when he feigned tuberculosis for nearly a year in the hospital by "dipping the thermometer in warm water and coughing."[6] Ozu would never submit to authority unless it was for the sake of doing what he wanted to do, and he would always get others to do what he wanted—such as building ceilings on sets for the first time to accommodate his low camera angle.[7] As his letter-writing approach to the boy at school may indicate, however, he also remained shy in matters of the heart. In later life he occasionally had friends arrange meetings with women in whom he was interested, only to crack a joke and walk away.[8] The result was that the director who specialized in the most delicate nuances of family relationships never had a family of his own.

In middle school Ozu's interests were strictly extracurricular. He spoke of a precocious love for contemporary fiction, including the works of Junichiro Tanizaki and Ryunosuke Akutagawa,[9] and a still greater love for movies, all of which were foreign films. He ran away to Tsu and Nagoya to see movies, wrote fan letters to film narrators in Kobe, and talked to his friends about Pearl White, Lillian Gish and William S. Hart[10] (who gets a mention in the joking dialogue of the 1949 *Late Spring*). He seems to have been proud of the fact that when he was supposed to be taking the entrance examination for the Kobe Higher Commercial School he was actually in a movie theater watching Rex Ingram's 1922 *Prisoner of Zenda*.[11]

After a year's unemployment followed by a year as an assistant teacher in a tiny village a few kilometers from Matsuzaka, Ozu returned with the rest of his family to Tokyo in 1923. Despite the opposition of his father, he was determined to enter the dubious profession of filmmaking and secured an introduction to the Shochiku company, which had just been founded in 1920. He was hired, although the executives were amazed that he had seen only about three Japanese films during his youth as a movie buff,[12] and he became an assistant cameraman.

Looking for relations between Ozu's life experience and the content of his films, such as one finds with Mizoguchi, critics are forced to speculate and stretch. College, office and marital life, none of which Ozu experienced, are the subjects of many of his films; army life never appears, and provincial life, such as he lived in Matsuzaka, only rarely. His mother, from whom he received inordinate affectionate indulgence all his life,[13] would seem to have been far more patient and tolerant than his film mothers, and the businessman and stern patriarch, from whom he lived apart during his adolescence, could not easily have provided a model for his sometimes comically gruff but always loving celluloid fathers. One must conclude that Ozu from the very beginning approached film as an art of fiction from which a realism was to be distilled. His inspiration, like the flickering foreign images populating the world of his youth, came from outside his own life, from his mind and the lives of others observed to perfection with that mind.

From "Nonsense" to Social Realism

At Shochiku's Kamata studios in Tokyo, Ozu began as third assistant to cameraman Hiroshi Sakai, cinematographer for the films of Kiyohiko Ushihara (1897–). This formidable director had written the script for the highly experimental 1921 *Souls on the Road* (*Rojo no Reikon*), and would later go to Hollywood to study filmmaking under Charlie Chaplin. Ozu apparently pestered him with questions about what the cinema of "the coming generation" should be like, according to Sakai, who since forgot what the answer was, if any.[14]

This eager young man was obviously on his way to directing. In 1926 he persuaded "nonsense" comedy director Tadamoto Okubo (1894–) to make him his assistant, a job he filled until his own debut a year later. Okubo was apparently relaxed, generous and undistinguished, specializing in films that were strung-together risqué gags. The advent of sound finished him as a director, and none of his early films remain extant. If any influence from him is to be found in Ozu's work it may lie in his nearly but not quite vulgar humor—such devices as the little boys' farting game in the 1959 *Ohayo* and the patriarch rising from his deathbed to rush to the toilet in the 1961 *End of Summer*. Yet in Ozu's hands even these touches assume a fitting position in the overall design of everyday life, whereas the gags in Okubo's films were aimed at shock value.

In any case, Ozu denied receiving any influence from anyone, although he did admit to seeing large numbers of Japanese films after entering Shochiku in order to study his seniors' techniques and make up for the lacuna in his cinematic education. He insisted that he "then formulated my own directing style in my own head, proceeding without any unnecessary imitation of others. . . . For me there was no such thing as a teacher. I have relied entirely on my own strength."[15]

Ozu was appointed to the low-prestige period film section as a director in 1927. Although he wanted to film his own scripts from the beginning, he went ahead and did *Sword of Penitence*, based on a George Fitzmaurice film, with a script by Kogo Noda, who in later years would be coscenarist for all of his great postwar films. Called up into the army reserves before shooting was completed, Ozu later saw the film in a movie theater, but felt that he hardly wanted to call it his own.[16] It would be his only period film.

For several years Ozu trained himself through the vehicle of nonsense comedies, turning out films at a frenetic rate, sometimes in as little as five days. Already he was gathering the staff who would stay with him to refine his expression: coscenarists Noda, Akira Fushimi and Tadao Ikeda; cameraman Hideo Shigehara, whose assistant Yuharu Atsuta would later replace him; actors Chishu Ryu, Takeshi Sakamoto and Choko Iida. He thought deeply about film grammar and from the beginning worked toward paring down his cinematic means. He tried using a dissolve in only one film in his entire life, the lost 1930 *Life of an Office Worker*, found it uninteresting and rejected it.[17] By the 1932 *I Was Born, But . . .*, he began to reject fade transitions, finding them, like dissolves, not to be essentials of film grammar, but rather "attributes of the camera."[18] He was also finding that his stories were developed in the course of a night's eating and drinking with his coscenarist Fushimi, and that he could shoot without having the continuity all written in advance because he could foresee successive shots while filming.[19] Some of these practices were of course necessitated by the pressure to make three to ten films a year, but they indicate a stylistic direction for Ozu nonetheless. His stories would always remain utterly simple and his continuity specific to the single shot, following a basic tempo of conversation rather than action.

The content of Ozu's films of the 1930s has been hailed as "consummate realism."[20] In this age when proletarian literature was at its most flourishing, and Mizoguchi and others began making leftist "tendency films" about the injustices of the class structure, Ozu's subjects were all lower-middle-class ordinary people. Poverty is part of their existence, as are class differences, but the Ozu message of acceptance is already clear. Later critics who have upbraided Ozu for his desertion of the lower classes in the postwar era have neatly overlooked the fact that the problems faced by his protagonists have remained the same. The late Shiro Kido, who was head of the Kamata studios when Ozu began directing, characterized Ozu in the era when the bourgeoisie were being portrayed as losers and fools and the poor as intolerably miserable: "His world lay half-way between. Although it had been the foundation of Shochiku's style from the beginning to treat the little man with good will, Ozu neither showed his life as desperate, nor did he see it as perennially cheerful. In some instances it was through cheerfulness that he discovered the truth of life in the little man, and the flavor of his films came to be the grappling with that [truth]."[21] These little men were the protagonists of a genre reaching far beyond the scope of the nonsense comedies with which Ozu began. The *shomin-geki* (drama of the common people) or film about "people like you and me" was "highly regarded for its honesty. It may have somewhat overplayed hardship, but at least it did not gloss over life's real difficulties. Ozu's refusal to give either himself or his audience an easy way out found a natural form in the *shomin-geki*. . . ."[22] In the thirties the little man was caught in the Great Depression; in the fifties he was not. Ozu's concern with life's difficulties in both periods went beyond socio-economic conditions to the metaphysical realm of expectation, disillusionment and acceptance in the family situation.

His first critical and commercial success from the silent era, *I Was Born, But. . .*, illustrates Ozu's dominant theme. Two small brothers insist their father is great and beat up his boss's son to prove it. They find their father's attitude of obsequiousness following the incident intolerable, and go on a hunger strike. But in the end they come to accept the fact that he is simply an employee and will never be the boss. They see him off cheerfully in the morning as he climbs into the boss's car, and the implication is that despite their resistance they will end up fulfilling their parents' apprehensions and leading "the same kind of sorry lives that we have."

There are clear distinctions between the haves and the have-nots in this picture, but neither side is painted more indulgently than the other. The father, who smokes cigarettes while body-building and flags immediately, is just as ridiculous as the indolent boss playing with his movie camera behind the closed office door marked "private." Neither is the "great man" the children are fighting about.

I Was Born, But. . . adds cinematic commentary on life's doldrums to the central parent-child conflict. A tracking shot of a line of school children marching in physical education drill cuts to a tracking shot of the same speed and direction down a line of office workers at their desks, all yawning. Ozu would later dispense with such associative editing, camera movement and cutting on motion, but here the message is quite amusing: the institutions that absorb most of us, the school and the office, impose a meaningless regimentation regardless of socioeconomic status. This commentary encapsulates what Ozu said the film as a whole did, it started with children and ends with adults and became very dark in the process.[23]

The following year, 1933, Ozu made another silent film—he was waiting for his cameraman Shigehara to get ready to do talkies—with a Depression mood, using the same child star who had appeared in *I Was Born, But.* . . , Tomio Aoki. *Passing Fancy* also focuses on the parent-child relationship and the disappointment of expectations. A widower who works in a brewery falls in love with a young girl who has lost her job and comes into the neighborhood looking for work. The man's son sees that the girl is in love with his father's younger friend, who treats her rudely to give the father the advantage. A gang of children confronts the boy directly: "I've got news—this boy's dad is stupid. He can't read, doesn't go to work and spends all his time in the restaurant" (where the girl has become a waitress). In shame and anger the boy destroys a potted plant in the empty house. When his father comes home they fight, and in a sudden realization the father allows the boy to pommel him with blows and then apologizes to him. The next day the boy nearly dies after eating too many sweets bought with the fifty sen his father gives him. The father, now fully reawakened, decides to go to work in far-off Hokkaido to pay the medical expenses, but when he thinks about his son he jumps ship, and happily repeating one of his son's jokes to himself, swims to shore.

Economic difficulties are ever present in the story of *Passing Fancy*, and the setting is a poor neighborhood—not without Ozu's hallmark, laundry on clotheslines and somber gas tanks. But the story could take place at any economic level, for it concerns a threat to the harmony of a parent-child relationship. The boy has nothing against the young woman, but he cannot bear to see his father make a fool of himself. Through the boy's tantrum and subsequent illness, the father recognizes that his son is the most important relationship in his life, and he chooses insurmountable debt rather than separation from the boy he loves. Unlike the later films, *Passing Fancy* ends with the restoration of the parent-child relationship instead of its dissolution, but the cost is heavy in economic terms. Even so, it is one of Ozu's most cheerful observations of life's difficulties.

One of his darkest expressions of the problem of separation and disappointed expectations appears in Ozu's first talkie, *The Only Son* (1936). A country widow who has sold everything and works in a spinning mill to put her son through university goes to visit him in Tokyo. He greets her warmly, shows her around, and then takes her to his home, where she meets the wife and baby her son has never told her about. The surprised mother accepts it all without complaint until her son expresses the feeling that he has failed her: he is nothing but a poor elementary schoolteacher. She chastises him for his lack of spirit, telling him that he is still young and must keep trying; after all, she herself never gave up. The couple borrow money to show her a good time, and she returns to the country where, too old to work in the spinning mill, she now labors as a scrubwoman. At the end of the film she reports to the woman who works with her, "My son's really made good. And he's found a good wife. . . now I can die in peace."

The socio-economic conditions contributing to the son's sense of failure are the Depression and the overcrowding in Tokyo, but the real problem is a personal one. The mother's need is that the son feel some sense of accomplishment and not give up. She says she may even be happier that he is not a big success; she is ready to accept him if he can accept himself, and she is able to find her own consolation in the fact that her daughter-in-law really is a good person. When the mother sends an encouraging letter with some money for the baby, the son promises himself that he will resume his studies, get ahead, and have her come back. The son continues to struggle against his disillusionment, but as in later Ozu films such as *Late Spring* (1949) and *Tokyo Story* (1953), the older generation finds the words to encourage the young and the strength to accept the disparity between expectation and reality. The mother prepares herself to face death; there is already a newer generation to follow, and the "Old Black Joe" theme music reinforces her peace with herself.

The Human Order

Ozu's development consisted of a refinement of the problems of life through archetypal situations and characters. Even in a wartime film such as the 1941 *There Was a Father,* the problem is separation of father and son, as in *Passing Fancy.* In the 1959 *Ohayo* the family faces difficulties because of the disparity between the logic of the adult world and the world of children, as in *I Was Born, But. . . .* In *Tokyo Story* parents face disappointment in their children similar to that shown in *The Only Son.*

The characters, though their economic circumstances may differ, are enmeshed in the same kinds of familial relationships. Their worlds are always the same enclosed circle: everyone knows everyone else who appears, everyone likes everyone else. There are no heroes and no villains, no great successes and no abject failures—everyone is ordinary. All who are not members of the immediate family in question are neighbors, school friends, war buddies, teachers, work colleagues or long-patronized eating and drinking establishment owners. In *Late Spring,* for example, even the bartender at the father's favorite haunt in Tokyo has known the daughter since she was a little girl.

Fathers, typically played by Chishu Ryu, are usually gruff, kindly, and introverted. They are lovers of alcohol, mah-jongg, and theatrical entertainments as much as literature and natural scenery. They often work in an office, but rarely appear to be absorbed in what they do there. Their shortcomings usually consist in a failure to observe the feelings of their children. Mothers, typically played by Kuniko Miyake, are gentle, devoted, hardworking, and more apt to voice opinions and feelings than their husbands. Daughters, typically played by Setsuko Hara, and later Yoko Tsukasa and Shima Iwashita, are solicitous, modest, often employed, but reluctant to be separated permanently from their parents. Children are generally either very small boys or adults about to be married. The adolescent rebel, as in *Tokyo Twilight* (1957), the unfaithful husband, as in *Early Spring* (1956), and the thoroughly dissatisfied wife, as in *The Flavor of Green Tea over Rice* (1952), are all exceptions to the rule.

Stereotyping is so extreme that it extends even to names. Favorite surnames are Hirayama, which occurs in six films, Sugiyama, in four; Sasaki, in three; and Kitagawa, in three. Favorite men's names are Shukichi, which occurs in five films, and Koichi, which occurs in three. Women are named Shige in six films, Akiko in six, Setsuko in five, Aya or Ayako in five, and Noriko in four. Norikos and Ayas are often juxtaposed as types, with Noriko the traditional daughter and Aya her modern friend, as in *Late Spring.*

The core relationship among these ordinary people of the Ozu film is that between parent and child, in his late works often that type of dependence described as *amae*, a presumption on the indulgence of another, exemplified by a baby's behavior toward its mother.[24] Or, as two parents in *There Was a Father* state it, in a formulation that does not sound so foreign to western ears, "One's child is a child no matter how old." The manifestation of dependence takes the place of a mature love shared by equals, and creates a feeling of comfortable belonging. The greatest threat to this indulgent well-being becomes separation, the impossibility of showing dependence, a kind of forced maturation.

Ozu portrays the rupture of *amae* most often through the marriage of a daughter, although father-son relationships undergo separation stresses in *Passing Fancy* and *There Was a Father*, and mother and son accept his loss of dependence in *The Only Son*. Facing separation becomes the crisis of the film, most poignant in situations involving a single parent and child. Marriage is thus not seen as an attractive prospect by daughters—one daughter in *Late Spring* describes it as "life's graveyard"—because it entails a transition to responsible adulthood. They must look forward to managing a household and bearing their own children. For the parents who are to lose the daughters, the marriage means not only the loss of a comforting dependent—as the parents in *Tokyo Story* observe, "A married daughter is like a stranger"—but the necessity of facing the end of their own lives with the termination of their responsibility toward the daughter. (The word for marrying off a daughter, *katazukeru*, also means "to finish, settle, clean up or dispose of.") Accepting the loss of dependence becomes the crucial means to continuing their own lives, and the only consolation Ozu offers is the propriety of so doing.

The rightness of severing the dependence bond is stated most clearly in the lecture the father gives his daughter in *Late Spring* when she makes one last appeal to him to let her stay at his side because she can imagine no greater happiness: "You're wrong. That's not how it is. . . . For you life is beginning now; for me it's almost over. This is the order of the history of human life." He goes on to tell her she must work to build happiness with her husband over the years, a speech very similar to what the father tells the daughter at the end of *Equinox Flower* (1958). The mother in *Late Autumn* (1960) likewise encourages her daughter to marry, and assures her that she herself will not be lonely, but in accepting the human order, the parents always in the end come to feel their isolation.

These occasions, inevitable in the human cycle, become times of assessment for Ozu characters, and the irrationality of the dialogue serves to reveal the full pathos of the human condition. In *Early Summer* (1951), aging parents who know they will move away to the country when their last daughter is married off, try valiantly to see their life in positive terms. When the decision has at last been made, the father announces, "Koichi has two children, and Noriko is about to marry. This may be our happiest time." The mother resists: "No, I think we can be happier." At the end of the film they sit alone watching a bridal procession pass through the fields where they now reside. They wonder how their own newlywed daughter is getting along, and their earlier conversation resumes as the father consoles himself, "Our family is scattered, but we have it better than most. We shouldn't want too much or there's no end to it. . . ." Again his wife objects, "But we were really happy." The last line of the film is her husband's noncommittal "Mmm." He will neither agree nor disagree, but the surprise is that his wife's view of happiness has suddenly become past tense, confirming the earliest view voiced with the frankness of the young by their daughter's friend, "Happiness is only a hope, like the night before the horse race." The parents in their continuing evaluation of their lives show that happiness is an elusive thing in the final analysis. Nothing has happened except what was supposed to happen, yet somehow satisfaction is lacking.

The structure of these stories of separations occasioned by the human order denies plot and drama. Ozu was "not simply bored by plot. He actively disliked it."[25] Speaking of the construction of one of his last films, *Late Autumn,* Ozu revealed that he had been trying since 1941 to do away with all elements of drama in order to allow a character's personality and presence to emerge fully, to create an air of sadness without making people cry, to make them, rather, "feel life." Eliciting sorrow and happiness through drama, he maintained, was "easy," but after all only an "explanation" that smothered the basic truth of character and life.[26] This plotless cinema of archetypal families meeting inevitable situations has been described as a transcendental style that proceeds from the commonplace to a recognition of disparity, to a resolution that consists in stasis.[27] The commonplace, however, represents not boredom and a lack of emotion, but a sense of security in carrying out forms. In everyday interactions Ozu's characters are extraordinarily polite, seeking to show consideration for others at all times. Disparity emerges not in an alienation from nature, but in a recognition that nature—human order— disappoints and separates. Stasis involves an acceptance of the human order, not much consolation, but a way of going on.

Ozu has often been compared to one of his own favorite writers, Naoya Shiga (1883–1971), whose works fall into the classification of *watakushi-shosetsu* or "first-person novel," a fictional form that relies heavily on autobiographical material. Both men treated family problems as their chief subject matter, and both focused especially on parent-child relationships.[28] But far more important is their shared rejection of "the undoubted convenience of story, plot and conventional dialogue."[29] Attention to the minutiae of interaction and the acceptance of the irrationality of human behavior characterize the style of both, who "prefer the simple and the natural to the striking and unusual," and Ozu, like Shiga, "eschewing ornament and exaggeration, orders the elements of ordinary experience until their beauty becomes manifest."[30] Ozu, although he never used the autobiographical "self-mining" method that finally drove Shiga into silence on completion of his only novel, *Anya Koro* (*A Dark Night's Passing*), shared the writer's power to portray the human condition as an overwhelming irrational order in which "life and death are viewed as two moments of the same natural cycle, one inexorably bringing on the other."[31] Absorbed in the ordinary and accepting its illogic, the acceptance of self is the noblest aim toward which the characters of Shiga and Ozu strive. Ozu, however, removed from himself in a way Shiga was not, achieved through his cinematic technique a philosophical reflection that the writer he so admired lacked.

Looking Up and Beyond

Dialogue is of primary importance in Ozu's construction; it was the first element he approached. Ozu and Noda conceived of the characterizations with particular actors in mind, and talked through each role until it was completely familiar to them. The dialogue script in this way achieved satisfactory form and balance before any actual writing began.[32] The slender story line of each film thus became a vehicle for character revelation. Subjectivity becomes a major element of the method because while the dialogue may give the characters moments to indulge in nostalgia, no narration or flashback ever interrupts the flow of present time.

Just as the time frame is limited by conversational flow, the geographic area in which the characters reveal themselves is circumscribed to archetypes. The home, the office, the tea salon, the restaurant or bar are the places in which the plain but deeply illuminating conversations occur. Even the types of dialogue may be controlled according to locale: domestic arrangements at home, reminiscence and social concerns in restaurants, nostalgia and expressions of disillusionment in bars.[33] These locations are always clean, evenly lighted, and though the names may change, the architectural layouts, like the character types and situations, recur from film to film. Even when specific locations such as the sights of Kyoto (*Late Spring*), Tokyo (*Tokyo Story, The Only Son*), Kamakura (*Late Spring*) or Atami (*Tokyo Story*) appear, their scenic value is entirely subordinated to the conversations and feelings of the characters. In *Late Spring,* Ozu never gives us the famous view out over the city from the veranda of Kiyomizu Temple, but shoots inward toward the characters taking in the view. In both *The Only Son* and *Tokyo Story* the only townscapes we see are nondescript buildings from behind the car's fender or through the tour bus window. When the daughter-in-law in *Tokyo Story* shows the elderly parents the various parts of the city where their children live from atop a department store, we never see what they see because the camera is looking up toward them, not down over the city.

Dialogue formulated, settings determined, Ozu next set about placing objects on the set before putting any actors into it. He was notorious for demanding that furniture, teapots, cups, vases be moved one or two centimeters this way or that until he got exactly the composifion he wanted, whether it maintained continuity from shot to shot and satisfied logic or not. Masahiro Shinoda, who was later to become a director, assisting Ozu on *Tokyo Twilight* in 1958, finally asked why a cushion was placed on the floor where no one was to sit. Ozu made him look through the viewfinder and pointed out to him, when he said he saw only what was there, that the tatami floor-mat borders all radiated from that spot.[34] Ozu wanted to cover up what he found visually distracting from the exchange between characters. He would always shoot a set straight on, with sliding doors open the same distance. In opposition to Mizoguchi, Ozu then subordinated time and environment to dialogue and character. As a result, editing became the least interesting aspect of filmmaking for Ozu.

He was no less demanding when it came to directing the actors on the set. Rather than seeking the active, emotional outpourings Mizoguchi required, Ozu wanted characters to be so controlled that the acting had to be flat, and enormous concentration devoted to how a teacup was raised to the lips and then set down. Chishu Ryu, the archetypal Ozu father, reported failing to achieve a desired effect after more than two dozen attempts in one instance.[35] Ozu would allow no one to dominate a scene, demanding equal flatness from all. Director Shohei Imamura, who assisted Ozu on several films in the fifties, finally asked to be moved elsewhere because he could not tolerate the wooden, formalized acting that Ozu required.[36] Like the stories, the settings, and the events, if the acting became individualized and special, Ozu's balance would be upset. Every expression of shock or grief had to be delivered with the same control as the good-mornings, good-bys and thank-yous. Movements appear at times so ritualized as to be dance-like, as characters sit side by side on a slightly staggered diagonal and face the camera as they talk to each other.

Ritualization and reduction of form in Ozu's films extends to the sequence structure. His pattern follows the primitive system of long establishing shot (or sign, such as "Restaurant Takikawa"), medium shot to carry movement of characters and conversation, closeup exchange of the A-B-A-B angle reverse-angle type for intimate dialogue, and back to medium and long shot to close the sequence. The camera almost never moves; when it does in late Ozu films, the effect is extremely jarring.

In the extreme formalization of Ozu's technique, however, there is one striking device that serves not only to destroy conventional Hollywood continuity and point of view, but ennoble the ordinary. Never do we look down on his characters. Even in an exchange of dialogue closeups where one person is looking down on the other, as in the blocking of the conversation between Noriko and Aya in Aya's room in *Late Spring*, the camera angle on both is low. Noriko sits looking up to the standing Aya, but the camera looks up on Noriko's face, rejecting Aya's point of view. We are thus prevented from identifying with Aya and are forced into an inhuman point of view on Noriko. This consistent low camera angle is not "the eye level of a Japanese seated on a tatami floor, the position in daily life from which he can appreciate the Japanese house in the most relaxed natural mood."[37] In medium shot it averages about 40 cm. or $1\frac{1}{2}$ feet off the floor, but whether it is a view from the end of a hallway or a voyeuristic shot from below the arm of a chair or a view of a character lying down on the floor, it is always looking up. Masahiro Shinoda has called it the point of view of a small deity observing human action,[38] because it is lower than the eye level of a seated human being. Its effect on the audience is to force to assume a viewpoint of reverence, even in face-to-face dialogue, toward ordinary people. Its power is not one of contemplation but of involuntary veneration, and as such it is one of the most prescriptive elements of Ozu's style of celebrating the everyday.

As different as Ozu's system is from Mizoguchi's traveling camera shooting in ever-changing angles, it allows the same implications of space and environment transcending human presence. Sets are usually empty but for a few frames before the characters enter, and remain empty after they leave. In employing the set like a curtainless stage Ozu allows for implication of transitoriness in the human condition. Allied with the other aspects of ritual in Ozu's techniques, it reinforces the feeling that we are watching a representative life cycle.

Extending space yet farther beyond the human presence are Ozu's still-life punctuations. Shots of water tanks, smokestacks and laundry fluttering on backyard clotheslines recur in all of his films. They are emotional rest-stops, outside of the point of view of any character in the story and reminders of mundane continuity at the same time as they remind of human transiency. These objects, held in view for varying lengths of time, take on varying meanings depending on their placement

in the chronology of the film, and according to editor Yoshiyasu Hamamura, Ozu had a peculiar emotional gauge for measuring their proper
duration. He would come into the editing room with a stopwatch, and
without looking at the image itself but staring off somewhere else, would
press the switch at an intuitively determined interval.[39] The triumph of
this method can be seen in the emotion absorbed and brought under
control by the shot of a vase in the corner of the inn room where father
and daughter have their last private conversation in *Late Spring;* the
shot lasts about eight to ten seconds. The quality of life cycle is further
enhanced by still-life shots, which always begin and end Ozu's films.
Late Spring starts with a series of shots of the Kita-Kamakura train
station, the wooded hills of the region, a temple roof and garden, and only
then takes us indoors to meet the characters in the story. At the end of
the film when the daughter is married and the father sits alone, head
bent as he stops in the middle of peeling a *nashi* (pear-apple), Ozu
does not leave us with the violins rising on his pathetic figure, but cuts
to the empty seashore and a final detail of the gentle waves before
fading out. These empty shots of nature, man-made artifacts and buildings, and even small objects like the vase in its dark alcove are not symbols in the western sense, but vehicles for the transcendent, ineffable
quality of life that takes us outside of mere human emotion.

Tokyo Story

Ranked with *Late Spring* and *Early Summer* as the best of Ozu's postwar
films,[40] *Tokyo Story* is the darkest of the three. The plots of all can be
summarized in a sentence or two, but the main event of *Tokyo Story* is
a death, while the other two films deal with marriages. These events are
part of the same natural cycle, however, and all three films show ordinary
people trying to evaluate and cope with the inevitable separations and
disappointments of life.

An elderly couple, Shukichi (Chishu Ryu) and Tomi (Chieko Higashiyama) Hirayama, set off from their home in the southern port town of
Onomichi to visit their married children in Tokyo. Their eldest son
Koichi (So Yamamura), a busy doctor, is unable to show them around,
and their eldest daughter Shige (Haruko Sugimura) is overwhelmed
with the operation of her beauty shop. Only their widowed daughter-
in-law Noriko (Setsuko Hara) takes a day off from work to show them the
sights. The older children send them to Atami hot springs, but they come
back early, and Noriko puts Tomi up for the night in her small apartment,
while Shukichi visits with old acquaintances and comes back to Shige's
late, drunk, and with a drunken friend in tow. The parents leave, stopping
to visit another son, Keizo (Shiro Osaka) in Osaka, where Tomi is briefly

taken ill. A few days later the children receive word from Onomichi that she is critically ill, and they arrive in time to witness her death. Shukichi expresses his thanks to all, especially Noriko, who remains after the others leave. The youngest daughter Kyoko (Kyoko Kagawa), a school-teacher who should marry soon, is the only companion left for Shukichi after Noriko returns to Tokyo.

Ozu said of *Tokyo Story* that he had tried, through parents and their grown-up children, to portray the destruction of the Japanese family system.[41] The film can be interpreted in this way, since in former times it would have been common practice for parents to live with the oldest son and his family, but *Tokyo Story* is about much more than this social issue. Like *The Only Son* it deals with parents' disappointment in their children; like *Early Summer* it deals with the transiency of life and the attempt of people facing the end of life to see their experience as happy. In broadest terms, it is about attempts and failures at the protection of feelings, others' and one's own.

The dialogue of *Tokyo Story* constitutes a monument of simplicity in contemporary Japanese literature and reveals the disparities inherent in living. The parents immediately realize they are a burden to their children. They never complain, but do their best to smooth things over, helping with household chores, babysitting their grandchildren, and obediently going to Atami when the children want to be rid of them. But together, they begin to talk of disappointment. Their first night in Tokyo they remark upon the poor neighborhood in which their doctor son resides. But it is in the course of Shukichi's conversation with friends in a bar that his disappointment finds its true focus. First he states, "I was under the impression that my son was doing better than he is. Then I found he's only a little neighborhood doctor."[42] He makes the typical excuse for his son that the times have changed, and chides himself for his own hopes, asserting that "we can't expect too much from our children." Finally he senses that it is not his son's socio-economic status that disappoints him: "My son has really changed. But it can't be helped. There really are too many people in Tokyo." His friend picks up and rounds out the suggestion of insensitivity: "I suppose I should be happy. Nowadays some young men would kill their parents without a thought. Mine at least wouldn't do that."

On their way back to Onomichi the old couple verbalize all their disil-lusionment and seek to console themselves:

Shukichi: Some grandparents seem to like their grandchildren better than their own children. What about you?
Tomi: And you?
Shukichi: Well, I think I like my children better.
Tomi: Yes, that's true.

Shukichi:　But I'm surprised how children change. Shige, now—she used to be much nicer before. A married daughter's a stranger.

Tomi:　Koichi's changed too. He used to be such a nice boy.

Shukichi:　No, children don't live up to their parents' expectations. But if you are greedy there's no end to it. Let's think that they are better than most.

Tomi:　They are certainly better than average. We are fortunate.

Shukichi:　Yes, fortunate. We should consider ourselves lucky.

Tomi:　Yes, we are very lucky.

The logical contradictions run rampant in this exchange, but true to life, and the repetitions at the end strike a note of self-cajolery. They are at last able to admit to themselves that their children are not nice people, and yet they want to consider themselves fortunate. They do not mention Noriko, whose considerate, warm behavior underlines the coldness of their own children. But when Shukichi tells her at his wife's death that she has treated them better than their own blood have done, Noriko too has an illogical response to an access of emotion. She denies that she is a nice person by claiming that she no longer thinks about her dead husband all the time. She even defends the behavior of the others to an angry and hurt Kyoko, saying that all children drift away from their parents and build their own lives and suggesting that she herself may become that way. The two young women, Kyoko with a pained expression and Noriko smiling cheerfully, agree on the theme of almost every Ozu film: "Isn't life disappointing? . . . Yes, it is."

Ozu also stated that of all his films, *Tokyo Story* tended most strongly toward melodrama.[43] Yet nothing in this film smacks of the easy sentiment that characterizes melodrama. A simple proverb expresses the children's failure: "Be kind to your parents while they are alive. . . filial piety cannot reach beyond the grave," and the Osaka son repeats it to himself in chagrin at the funeral. But the children all feel they have done right by their parents, and all, including Keizo, rush back to their own lives as soon as they can. Recognition of life's disappointments and people's coldness is shared only by Shukichi, Noriko and Kyoko, who are not crushed by it but strive to accept it.

Formality pervades *Tokyo Story* in framing and construction as well as in speech and gesture. The elderly parents, always models of politeness even when telling their children not to bother coming to Onomichi even if something should happen to one of them, are shown in medium shot together in most of their conversations. They sit side by side and move in unison. When they rise from sitting on the sea wall at Atami and Tomi fails to get up at the same time as Shukichi, doubled over with a slight stroke that foreshadows her death, the effect is one of the most visually disturbing in the film. But we are not present at the moment of her death, and we accept the tears poured out by Shige as a sudden recognition of the transiency of life rather than the expression of intimate grief. Ozu eschews melodrama in the music as well, which never takes over a scene, but fades in and out over transitions from sequence to sequence, lending an air of the flow of life without wrenching emotion.

The deepest reflection on life comes in the most impersonal moments of the film, when Ozu inserts the beyond. Shots of Onomichi harbor, a stone lantern overlooking the bay, small boats with put-putting motors, begin and end the film with the circularity of the life cycle. The neighbor woman greets the couple as they prepare to depart on their trip, and returns to comment on Shukichi's loneliness in the same camera setup at the end. The familiar still-life punctuations provide moments of quiet reflection during the course of the story: laundry on clotheslines, smokestacks in Tokyo, the temple and cemetery in Onomichi. In the last scene when the father is left alone, in a profile medium shot, seated in his home, the sound of the harbor boats dominates: life outside goes on. We see a boat and the rooftops of Onomichi, then a closer shot of the boat, removing us entirely from the characters of this particular life cycle.

Target for Iconoclasts

The severity and circumscription of such films as *Tokyo Story* seem to us to be marvels of understating yet clearly expressing the intrinsic sorrow of human life. Toward the end of his career Ozu's films such as *An Autumn Afternoon* (1962), about a widower arranging the marriage of his daughter, became yet more elegiac, imbued throughout with a subtle sadness, and his only message to the end remained one of acceptance. He never lost his humorous touches, such as the woman from Kyoto in *Equinox Flower* who rushes to the toilet whenever she becomes excited, but even the jokes and gags in late Ozu have a sharply ironic edge to them, often centering on aging. Ozu never, to the very end, condescended to offer palliatives for the pain of living, and in this uncompromising attitude lay his strength as a director.

Ozu would be the object of criticism by the new generation of the 1960s. They would rebel, as Imamura did, against the rigidity of his form. They would rebel, as Oshima did, against the acceptance of things as they are, seeking the redress of social evils. They would bring all levels of society into their films, and they would show the passions, vulgarities and cruelties that Ozu had rejected in favor of mundanity. They believed that rebellious youth was their contribution to film culture, that people do not try to protect each other's feelings, and that widescreen and hand-held cameras would open up the closed, static world of the Ozu film.

Yet Ozu's inalienable truths of human life and the limited cinematic means with which he showed their emotional facets could not be completely rejected. His last words to Shiro Kido, who came to see him in the hospital where he lay dying of cancer, may be interpreted as defiance against the New Wave, "Mr. President, it is after all the home drama, isn't it?"[44] And indeed, Ozu's message of graceful resignation, couched in his spare but eloquent form, proved to be universal, not particular. His films are shown all over the world today to highly appreciative audiences. His films in the end came to be respected by such New Wave directors as Masahiro Shinoda, who learned from him a severity of attention to detail and a value placed on the director's own space in the film.

Ozu's films are not for those seeking utopian solutions. He never made claims for the possibility of romantic love, worldly success, or even human communication. Only acceptance, never happiness, was open to his characters, no matter what social class they belonged to. In avoiding virtuoso technique as well as dramatic structure he went straight into the irrationality of character and that terrible truth: life is disappointing, isn't it?

Notes

[1]   Donald Richie, *Ozu: His Life and Films* (Berkeley and Los Angeles: University of California Press, 1974), p. xi.

[2]   Joseph L. Anderson and Donald Richie, *The Japanese Film: Art and Industry* (New York: Grove Press, 1960), p. 359.

[3]   Tadao Sato, *Ozu Yasujiro no geijutsu* (The Art of Yasujiro Ozu) (Tokyo: Asahi Shimbunsha, 1971), p. 10.

[4]   *Ibid.*, p. 10.

[5]   *Ibid.*, pp. 77–78.

[6]   *Ibid.*, p. 81.

[7]   Shiro Kido, *Nihon eiga den: Eiga seisakusha no kiroku* (The Story of the Japanese Film: A Movie Producer's Record) (Tokyo: Bungei Shunju Shinsha, 1956), p. 77.

[8]   Sato, *op. cit.*, p. 82.

[9]   Yasujiro Ozu, *Boku wa eiga no mame-kantoku* (I Am a Miniature Film Director) (Tokyo: Maki Shoten, 1953).

[10]   Sato, *op. cit.*, p. 79.

[11]   *Ibid.*, p. 80.

[12]   Ozu, *op. cit.*

[13]   Sato, *op. cit.*, p. 76.

[14]   *Ibid.*, p. 86.

[15]   Ozu, *op. cit.*

[16] Yasujiro Ozu, "Eiga no aji; Jinsei no aji" (The Flavor of Cinema; the Flavor of Life), *Kinema Jumpo* (Tokyo),special issue, Feb. 10, 1964, p. 30.

[17] *Ibid.*, p. 31.

[18] *Ibid.*, p. 32.

[19] *Ibid.*, p. 32.

[20] Sato, *op. cit.*, p. 69.

[21] Kido, *op. cit.*, p. 75.

[22] Richie, *op. cit.*, p. 207.

[23] Ozu, "Eiga no aji," *op. cit.*, p. 32.

[24] *See* Takeo Doi, *The Anatomy of Dependence* (translation of *Amae no kozo*) (Tokyo: Kodansha International Ltd., 1973).

[25] Richie, *op. cit.*, p. 25.

[26] Ozu, "Eiga no aji," *op. cit.*, p. 35.

[27] Paul Schrader, *Transcendental Style in Film: Ozu, Bresson, Dreyer* (Berkeley and Los Angeles: University of California Press, 1972), pp. 39–51.

[28] Sato, *op. cit.*, p. 44.

[29] Richie, *op. cit.*, p. 25.

[30] Francis Mathy, *Shiga Naoya* (New York: Twayne Publishers Inc., 1974), p. 125.

[31] *Ibid.*, p. 65.

[32] Richie, *op. cit.*, p. 22.

[33] Schrader, *op. cit.*, pp. 31–32.

[34] Sato, *op. cit.*, p. 59.

[35] Richie, *op. cit.*, p. 146.

[36] Rikiya Tayama, *Nihon eiga sakka-tachi: Sosaku no himitsu* (Japanese Filmmakers: Secrets of Creation) (Tokyo: Daviddosha, 1975), p. 12.

[37] Sato, *op. cit.*, p. 19.

[38] Author's interview with Masahiro Shinoda, September, 1974.

[39] Sato, *op. cit.*, p. 67.

[40] Howard S. Hibbett, ed., *Contemporary Japanese Literature* (New York: Alfred Knopf, 1977), p. 189.

[41] Ozu, "Eiga no aji," *op. cit.*, p. 35.

[42] Translations of *Tokyo Story* script by Donald Richie and Eric Klestadt, from Hibbett, *op. cit.*

[43] Ozu, "Eiga no aji," *op. cit.*, p. 35.

[44] Sato, *op. cit.*, p. 11.

YASUJIRO OZU: FILMOGRAPHY

1927   *The Sword of Penitence* (*Zange no Yaiba*)
pr: Shochiku (Kamata); orig. film: George Fitzmaurice's *Kick-In*; sc: Kogo Noda; ph: Isamu Aoki; cast: Saburo Azuma, Kunimatsu Ogawa, Eiko Atsumi, Choko Iida et al. Period drama. (No extant prints, negative or script.)

1928   *The Dreams of Youth* (*Wakodo no Yume*)
pr: Shochiku (Kamata); orig. sc: Ozu; ph: Hideo Shigehara; cast: Tatsuo Saito, Nobuko Wakaba, Hisao Yoshitani, Junko Matsui, Takeshi Sakamoto et al. Comedy about college dormitory life, based on several American films. (No extant prints, negative or script.)

  Wife Lost (*Nyobo Funshitsu*)
pr: Shochiku (Kamata); orig. idea: Ononosuke Takano; sc: Momosuke Yoshida; ph: Hideo Shigehara; cast: Tatsuo Saito, Ayako Okamura, Takeshi Sakamoto, Junko Matsui, Shigeru Ogura et al. Light comedy about marital mixups. (No extant prints, negative or script.)

  Pumpkin (*Kabocha*)
pr: Shochiku (Kamata); orig. sc: Komatsu Kitamura; ph: Hideo Shigehara; cast: Tatsuo Saito, Yurie Hinatsu, Takeshi Sakamoto, Yoko Kozakura et al. Comedy about a young man's misadventures with women. (No extant prints, negative or script.)

  A Couple on the Move (*Hikkoshi Fufu*)
pr: Shochiku (Kamata); orig. idea: Ippei Kikuchi; sc: Akira Fushimi; ph: Hideo Shigehara; cast: Atsushi Watanabe, Mitsuko Yoshikawa, Kenji Oyama, Tomoko Naniwa, Ichiro Ogushi et al. Comedy about a couple who abhor living in the same house for any length of time. (No extant prints or negative; script extant.)

  Body Beautiful (*Nikutai Bi*)
pr: Shochiku (Kamata); orig. sc: Ozu and Akira Fushimi; ph: Hideo Shigehara; cast: Tatsuo Saito, Choko Iida, Mitsuko Yoshikawa et al. Comedy about a woman painter who uses her unemployed husband as a model and fails to win recognition. When they switch roles and he paints her in the nude, he wins all the first prizes. (No extant prints or negative; script extant.)

1929   *Treasure Mountain* (*Takara no Yama*)
pr: Shochiku (Kamata); orig. idea: Ozu; sc: Akira Fushimi; ph: Hideo Shigehara; cast: Tokuji Kobayashi, Ayako Okamura, Choko Iida, Yurie Hinatsu, Tomoko Naniwa et al. Melodramatic comedy about jealousy between a traditional young geisha and a modern girl. (No extant prints or negative; script extant.)

  Days of Youth (*Wakaki Hi*)
pr: Shochiku (Kamata); orig. sc: Ozu and Akira Fushimi; ph: Hideo Shigehara; cast: Ichiro Yuki, Tatsuo Saito, Junko Matsui, Shinichi Himori et al. Student comedy about skiing. (FC; negative at Shochiku, Tokyo.)

Fighting Friends, Japanese Style (*Wasei Kenka Tomodachi*)
pr: Shochiku (Kamata); orig. sc: Kogo Noda; ph: Hideo Shigehara; cast: Atsushi Watanabe, Ichiro Yuki, Tomoko Naniwa, Hisao Yoshitani, Ichiro Takamatsu et al. Comedy about two truck drivers in love with the same woman. Modeled after Wallace Beery-Raymond Hatton comedies. (No extant prints, negative or script.)

I Graduated, But. . . (*Daigaku wa Deta Keredo*)
pr: Shochiku (Kamata); orig. idea: Hiroshi Shimizu; sc: Yoshiro Aramaki; ph: Hideo Shigehara; cast: Minoru Takada, Kinuyo Tanaka, Utako Suzuki, Kenji Oyama, Shinichi Himori et al. Social comedy about a college graduate who comes to Tokyo and cannot find a job. First his mother and then his fiancée come to live with him in his tiny room. (Incomplete print at FC, ME)

The Life of an Office Worker (*Kaisha-in Seikatsu*)
pr: Shochiku (Kamata); orig. sc: Kogo Noda; ph: Hideo Shigehara; cast: Tatsuo Saito, Mitsuko Yoshikawa, Takeshi Sakamoto, Tomio Aoki et al. Comedy about a couple looking forward to the husband's year-end bonus, only to find that he is fired because of the general depression. He looks for a new job and finds nothing until he is hired by several friends. Considered to be Ozu's first genuine *shomin-geki*. (No extant prints, negative or script.)

A Straightforward Boy (*Tokkan Kozo*)
pr: Shochiku (Kamata); orig. idea: "Chuji Nozu" (Kogo Noda, Tadamoto Okubo, Tadao Ikeda and Ozu); sc: Tadao Ikeda; ph: Ko Nomura; cast: Tatsuo Saito, Tomio Aoki, Takeshi Sakamoto et al. Social comedy centered around the child star Aoki (Tokkan Kozo). (No extant prints, negative or script.)

1930 *An Introduction to Marriage* (*Kekkon-gaku Nyumon*)
pr: Shochiku (Kamata); orig. idea: Toshio Okuma; sc: Kogo Noda; ph: Hideo Shigehara; cast: Tatsuo Saito, Sumiko Kurishima, Minoru Takada, Mitsuko Yoshikawa et al. Comedy about a husband and wife who have tired of each other. (No extant prints or negative; script extant.)

Walk Cheerfully (*Hogaraka ni Ayume*)
pr: Shochiku (Kamata); orig. idea: Hiroshi Shimizu; sc: Tadao Ikeda; ph: Hideo Shigehara; cast: Minoru Takada, Hiroko Kawasaki, Satoko Date, Takeshi Sakamoto et al. Comedy about a delinquent boy who reforms for love of a pure typist. (FC; negative at Shochiku, Tokyo.)

I Flunked, But. . . (*Rakudai wa Shita Keredo*)
pr: Shochiku (Kamata); orig. idea: Ozu; sc: Akira Fushimi; ph: Hideo Shigehara; cast: Tatsuo Saito, Ichiro Tsukita, Kinuyo Tanaka, Tomio Yokoo, Chishu Ryu et al. Satire on college life, partly based on Ozu's earlier *I Graduated, But. . .* Ryu's first big role, in a "nonsense" comedy with the message that since graduates can't get jobs in the Depression anyway, the boy who flunks is better off. (FC; negative at Shochiku, Tokyo.)

That Night's Wife (*Sono Yo no Tsuma*)
pr: Shochiku (Kamata); orig. short story: Oscar Shisugoru (phonetic); sc: Kogo Noda; ph: Hideo Shigehara; cast: Tokihiko Okada, Togo Yamamoto, Emiko Yakumo, Tatsuo Saito et al. Suspense melodrama taking place in twelve hours from 9 p.m. to 9 a.m. in which an impoverished father robs a bank to get money to pay medical expenses for his very ill son, is pursued by police and caught. (FC; negative at Shochiku, Tokyo.)

The Revengeful Spirit of Eros (*Erogami no Onryo*)
pr: Shochiku (Kamata); orig. idea: Seizaburo Ishihara; sc: Kogo Noda; ph: Hideo Shigehara; cast: Tatsuo Saito, Satoko Date, Ichiro Tsukita, Hikaru Hoshi et al. "Nonsense" comic ghost story. (No extant prints, negative or script.)

Lost Luck (*Ashi ni Sawatta Koun*)
pr: Shochiku (Kamata); orig. sc: Kogo Noda; ph: Hideo Shigehara; cast: Tatsuo Saito, Mitsuko Yoshikawa, Takeshi Sakamoto, Tomio Aoki, Ichiro Tsukita et al. Depression story about office workers and their insufficient salaries. (No extant prints or negative; script extant.)

Young Miss (*Ojosan*)
pr: Shochiku (Kamata); orig. sc: Komatsu Kitamura; ph: Hideo Shigehara; cast: Sumiko Kurishima, Tokihiko Okada, Kinuyo Tanaka, Tatsuo Saito, Togo Yamamoto et al. Light comedy about a woman journalist. *KJ* Best Ten Poll #3. (No extant prints or negative; script extant.)

1931   **The Lady and the Beard** (*Shukujo to Hige*)
pr: Shochiku (Kamata); orig. sc: Komatsu Kitamura; ph: Hideo Shigehara; cast: Tokihiko Okada, Ichiro Tsukita, Toshiko Iizuka, Hiroko Kawasaki, Choko Iida et al. "Nonsense" college comedy about a bearded *kendo* swordfighting star and his typist girlfriend, who tames him and makes him shave. (FC; negative at Shochiku, Tokyo.)

Beauty's Sorrows (*Bijin Aishu*)
pr: Shochiku (Kamata); orig. story: Henri de Regnier; sc: Tadao Ikeda; ph: Hideo Shigehara; cast: Tatsuo Saito, Tokihiko Okada, Yukiko Inoue, Sotaro Okada, Mitsuko Yoshikawa et al. Apparently inadvertent melodrama about two men who fall in love with the daughter of a famous sculptor. The playboy marries the girl, while the serious boy gets a statue. Later the girl dies and the husband wants the statue. The two men fight and both die. (No extant prints or negative; script extant.)

*Tokyo Chorus (*Tokyo no Gassho*)
pr: Shochiku (Kamata); orig. novel: Komatsu Kitamura; sc: Kogo Noda; ph: Hideo Shigehara; cast: Tokihiko Okada, Hideo Sugawara, Emiko Yakumo, Mitsuo Ichimura, Takeshi Sakamoto et al. Beginning of Ozu's *shomin-geki* dramas of humor and pathos about ordinary people. An office worker sticks up for a colleague who is fired for trivial reasons and gets fired himself. Afraid to tell his wife, he takes part-time work as a sandwich man, and is finally rescued by old school friends. *KJ* #3. (FC; negative at Shochiku, Tokyo.)

1932 *Spring Comes from the Ladies* (*Haru wa Gofujin Kara*)
pr: Shochiku (Kamata); orig. idea: "James Maki" (Ozu); sc: Tadao Ikeda and Takao Yanai; ph: Hideo Shigehara; cast: Jiro Shirota, Tatsuo Saito, Yukiko Inoue, Takeshi Sakamoto et al. College comedy in which university life is seen as a golden age without any of the problems of the real world. (No extant prints or negative; script extant.)

*I Was Born, But. . . (Umarete wa Mita Keredo)
pr: Shochiku (Kamata); orig. idea: "James Maki" (Ozu); sc: Akira Fushimi, Geibei Ibushiya; ph: Hideo Shigehara; cast: Tatsuo Saito, Hideo Sugawara, Tomio Aoki, Shoichi Kofujita et al. Two small boys learn to live with the fact that their father is not a great man, but simply a company employee. A touching, serious comedy and Ozu's first great film. *KJ* #1. (FC, NY)

Where Now Are the Dreams of Youth? (*Seishun no Yume Ima Izuko*)
pr: Shochiku (Kamata); orig. sc: Kogo Noda; ph: Hideo Shigehara; cast: Ureo Egawa, Haruo Takeda, Kinuyo Tanaka, Tatsuo Saito, Choko Iida et al. Sentimental tragedy arising from class differences as two boys who are friends in college graduate, one becoming a company president and the other his employee. (FC; negative at Shochiku, Tokyo.)

Until the Day We Meet Again (*Mata Au Hi Made*)
pr: Shochiku (Kamata); orig. sc: Kogo Noda; ph: Hideo Shigehara; cast: Joji Oka, Yoshiko Okada, Hiroko Kawasaki, Satoko Date et al. Sound, but no dialogue. Romantic melodrama about a prostitute in love with a boy whose father dislikes her. *KJ* #7. (No extant prints or negative; script extant.)

1933 *A Tokyo Woman* (*Tokyo no Onna*)
pr: Shochiku (Kamata); orig. idea: "Ernst Schwartz" (Ozu); sc: Kogo Noda and Tadao Ikeda; ph: Hideo Shigehara; cast: Yoshiko Okada, Ureo Egawa, Kinuyo Tanaka et al. Sound, but no dialogue. Melodrama about a girl who puts her younger brother through school only to have him commit suicide when he finds out she did it by working at a bar of doubtful reputation. (FC; negative at Shochiku, Tokyo.)

Dragnet Girl (*Hijosen no Onna*)
pr: Shochiku (Kamata); orig. idea: "James Maki" (Ozu); sc: Tadao Ikeda; ph: Hideo Shigehara; cast: Joji Oka, Kinuyo Tanaka, Hideo Mitsui, Sumiko Mizukubo et al. Silent. About a delinquent, something along the lines of Ozu's 1930 *Walk Cheerfully*. (No extant prints or negative; script extant.)

*Passing Fancy (*Dekigokoro*)
pr: Shochiku (Kamata); orig. idea: "James Maki" (Ozu); sc: Tadao Ikeda; ph: Shojiro Sugimoto; cast: Takeshi Sakamoto, Den Ohinata, Tomio Aoki, Nobuko Fushimi, Choko Iida et al. Silent. Subtle, beautiful film showing Ozu's new interest in the primacy of blood relations and archetypal situations. A father and son live together in an impoverished but mutually supportive relationship. The father becomes captivated by a new girl in the area, but she herself is infatuated with his younger bachelor friend. The father recognizes his folly when his son becomes deathly ill, but survives. Hoping to clear his debts, the

father sets off for a new job in a distant town, but jumps ship when he realizes he cannot leave his son. *KJ* #1. (FC, AB)

1934   *A Mother Should Be Loved (Haha o Kowazu-ya)*
pr: Shochiku (Kamata); orig. idea: Kogo Noda; sc: Tadao Ikeda and Masao Arata; ph: Isamu Aoki; cast: Den Ohinata, Junko Matsui, Mitsuko Yoshikawa, Yukichi Iwata, Hideo Mitsui et al. Silent. Family drama about the relations between two half-brothers. Good characterization but somewhat spoiled by melodrama. (No extant prints or negative; script extant.)

*A Story of Floating Weeds (Ukigusa Monogatari)
pr: Shochiku (Kamata); orig. film: George Fitzmaurice's *The Barker*; sc: Tadao Ikeda; ph: Hideo Shigehara; cast: Takeshi Sakamoto, Choko Iida, Hideo Mitsui, Emiko Yakumo, Yoshiko Tsubouchi et al. Silent. The head of a traveling theater troupe returns to a mountain village where he meets his son, now a young man, the product of a casual affair. Ozu added the vital character of the former mistress to the 1928 American circus film, and in the delineation of the older man, his jealous actress wife, the son and young girl from the troupe, he weaves a subtle story that far surpasses the original, and even his own 1959 remake. *KJ* #1. (FC, MOMA, NY)

1935   *An Innocent Maid (Hakoiri Musume)*
pr: Shochiku (Kamata); orig. story: Sanseki Shikitei; sc: Kogo Noda and Tadao Ikeda; ph: Hideo Shigehara; cast: Kinuyo Tanaka, Choko Iida, Takeshi Sakamoto, Tomio Aoki, Kenji Oyama et al. Silent. Uninspired story of how a thoughtful friend ruins a marriage. (No extant prints or negative; script extant.)

An Inn in Tokyo (Tokyo no Yado)
pr: Shochiku (Kamata); orig. sc: Tadao Ikeda and Masao Arata; ph: Hideo Shigehara; music: Senji Ito; cast: Takeshi Sakamoto, Yoshiko Okada, Choko Iida, Tomio Aoki et al. A vagrant father and his two sons find companionship with an equally poor widow and her little girl as the father looks for work. *KJ* #9. (FC; negative at Shochiku, Tokyo.)

1936   *College Is a Nice Place (Daigaku Yoi Toko)*
pr: Shochiku (Kamata); orig. idea: "James Maki" (Ozu); sc: Masao Arata; ph: Hideo Shigehara; cast: Toshiaki Konoe, Chishu Ryu, Sanae Takasugi, Tatsuo Saito, Kenji Oyama et al. Silent. Reputed to be the best of Ozu's college films, about four dormitory friends who graduate and begin a hopeless search for jobs back home. (No extant prints or negative; script extant.)

*The Only Son (Hitori Musuko)
pr: Shochiku (Kamata); orig. idea: "James Maki" (Ozu); sc: Tadao Ikeda and Masao Arata; ph: Shojiro Sugimoto; music: Senji Ito; cast: Shinichi Himori, Choko Iida, Chishu Ryu, Yoshiko Tsubouchi, Masao Hayama, Mitsuko Yoshikawa et al. Ozu's first talkie, and a very serious and moving film. A woman slaves to raise her son and send him off to college in Tokyo. Hearing nothing from him for a long time, she goes to visit him, using up all her savings and going into debt. She finds him married, with a child, and painfully poor and disillusioned with himself and life. But he borrows money to entertain his

mother, and she returns to the country where she can still feel proud of him. *KJ* #4. (FC, MOMA, AB)

1937   **What Did the Lady Forget?** *(Shukujo wa Nani o Wasuretaka)*
pr: Shochiku (Ofuna); orig. sc: "James Maki" (Ozu and Akira Fushimi) ph: Hideo Shigehara; music: Senji Ito; cast: Sumiko Kurishima, Tatsuo Saito, Michiko Kuwano, Shuji Sano, Takeshi Sakamoto et al. A spoiled, indolent bourgeois wife has her professor husband completely cowed, but when their modern niece comes to visit from Osaka the couple are finally reconciled. Biting satire on the upper classes. *KJ* #8. (FC; negative at Shochiku, Tokyo.)

1941   **The Brothers and Sisters of the Toda Family (Toda-ke no Kyodai)*
pr: Shochiku (Ofuna); orig. se: Ozu and Tadao Ikeda; ph: Yuharu Atsuta; music: Senji Ito; cast: Mieko Takamine, Shin Saburi, Hideo Fujino, Fumiko Katsuragi, Mitsuko Yoshikawa et al. Family tensions at their most subtly disturbing. A widow and her youngest daughter move in with the other married children in succession. Everywhere they are treated as burdens and eventually decide to go and live with the second son, who has settled in China. First work with cameraman Atsuta, who had assisted Shigehara from 1930 on. NEZK #1. (FC, AB)

1942   **There Was a Father (Chichi Ariki)*
pr: Shochiku (Ofuna); orig. sc: Tadao Ikeda, Takao Yanai and Ozu; ph: Yuharu Atsuta; music: Gyoichi Saiki; cast: Chishu Ryu, Shuji Sano, Mitsuko Mito, Takeshi Sakamoto, Shin Saburi et al. Remarkable film made under propaganda requirements with virtually no propaganda in it. A father who cares deeply for his son sees him through graduation from college, conscription, and finally to marrying the daughter of his own best friend. NEZK #2. (FC, MOMA, AB)

1947   **The Record of a Tenement Gentleman** *(Nagaya no Shinshi Roku)*
pr: Shochiku (Ofuna); orig. sc: Ozu and Tadao Ikeda; ph: Yuharu Atsuta; music: Ichiro Saito; cast: Chishu Ryu, Choko Iida, Takeshi Sakamoto, Reikichi Kawamura, Tomio Aoki et al. Ozu's first film on return from the war in Singapore, based on an old script of his own. A war orphan found on the streets of Tokyo is sent to live with a middle-aged woman. She finds him a nuisance at first, but grows to love him. His father is eventually found and she has to give him up, but she opens an orphanage, in a very un-Japanese ending. *KJ* #4. (FC, NY)

1948   **A Hen in the Wind** *(Kaze no Naka no Mendori)*
pr: Shochiku (Ofuna); orig. sc: Ozu and Ryosuke Saito; ph: Yuharu Atsuta; music: Senji Ito; cast: Kinuyo Tanaka, Shuji Sano, Kuniko Miyake, Chishu Ryu, Chieko Murata et al. Melodrama about a woman waiting for her husband to come home from the war. Her child falls ill and she is forced to become a prostitute to pay the medical expenses. When her husband returns she confesses to him. He knocks her down the stairs in a rage, but later apologizes. *KJ* #7. (FC; negative at Shochiku, Tokyo.)

1949   **Late Spring (Banshun)*
pr: Shochiku (Ofuna); orig. story: Kazuo Hirotsu; sc: Ozu and Kogo Noda;

ph: Yuharu Atsuta; music: Senji Ito; cast: Chishu Ryu, Setsuko Hara, Haruko Sugimura, Jun Usami, Yumeji Tsukioka et al. Beginning of the classic Ozu in which only the most ordinary things happen in a very moving way. A young woman slightly past the usual marriage age lives with her widowed father. She keeps refusing to marry until she is told that her father himself wishes to marry. Finally she gives in, and the father, who had no intention of remarrying in the first place, is left alone. *KJ* #1. (FC, NY)

1950   *The Munekata Sisters (Munekata Shimai)*
pr: Shin Toho; orig. novel: Jiro Osaragi; sc: Ozu and Kogo Noda; ph: Joji Ohara; music: Ichiro Saito; cast: Kinuyo Tanaka, Hideko Takamine, Ken Uehara, So Yamamura, Chishu Ryu et al. Ozu's first of a total of three productions outside of the Shochiku studios. Based on a newspaper serial, this story centers on the conflict between a traditional older sister and her modern younger sister. Essentially a portrait of middle-class life. *KJ* #7. (FC; negative at Toho, Tokyo.)

1951   *Early Summer (Bakushu)*
pr: Shochiku (Ofuna); orig. sc: Ozu and Kogo Noda; ph: Yuharu Atsuta; music: Senji Ito; cast: Setsuko Hara, Ichiro Sugai, Chieko Higashiyama, Chishu Ryu, Haruko Sugimura et al. Almost plotless life cycle film about three generations of one family living in Kamakura. The archetypal marriageable daughter finally resigns herself to her fate, and the grandparents, satisfied that she is taken care of, move away to the country in resignation to their own fate. *KJ* #1. (FC, AB)

1952   *The Flavor of Green Tea over Rice (Ochazuke no Aji)*
pr: Shochiku (Ofuna); orig. sc: Ozu and Kogo Noda; ph: Yuharu Atsuta; music: Ichiro Saito; cast: Shin Saburi, Michiyo Kogure, Koji Tsuruta, Keiko Tsushima, Kuniko Miyake et al. Somewhat atypically clearly defined crisis in the marital life of a middle-aged childless couple. The wife persists in scorning her husband until his job threatens to take him away, when she comes to a new appreciation of him. In a parallel substory, their out-of-town niece realizes she should marry a reliable man. (FC, NY)

1953   *Tokyo Story (Tokyo Monogatari)*
pr: Shochiku (Ofuna); orig. sc: Ozu and Kogo Noda; ph: Yuharu Atsuta; music: Takanobu Saito; cast: Chishu Ryu, Chieko Higashiyama, So Yamamura, Haruko Sugimura, Setsuko Hara et al. Ozu's most poignant statement on family relationships, their tensions, affections, and inevitable dissolutions. An elderly couple go to visit their children in Tokyo, who find them obstacles to their daily family life and decide to send them off to a hot spring resort. The only child who is genuinely affectionate toward them is their widowed daughter-in-law. When the old people return home the mother falls ill and dies, and all the shocked children assemble too late, only to rush off again to their own lives. The daughter-in-law, who stays on longest, consoles the father but gently refuses his advice to remarry. In the end he is left alone. *KJ* #2; Geijutsusai Grand Prize; London National Film Theatre Southerland Prize, 1957. (FC, NY)

1956 *Early Spring (Soshun)*
pr: Shochiku (Ofuna); orig. sc: Ozu and Kogo Noda; ph: Yuharu Atsuta; music: Takanobu Saito; cast: Ryo Ikebe, Chikage Awashima, Keiko Kishi, Chishu Ryu, Daisuke Kato et al. Marital problems again sensitively treated. A white-collar worker is bored with his job and his wife, and has an affair with the office flirt. He and his wife quarrel, but later when he accepts a transfer to the country, she goes with him to start over. *KJ* #6. (FC, NY)

1957 *Twilight in Tokyo (Tokyo Boshoku)*
pr: Shochiku (Ofuna); orig. sc: Ozu and Kogo Noda; ph: Yuharu Atsuta; music: Takanobu Saito; cast: Setsuko Hara, Isuzu Yamada, Ineko Arima, Chishu Ryu, Nobuo Nakamura et al. Dissolution of a family that verges on atypical melodrama. A father lives with his two daughters, the older having left her husband and come home with her child. The younger has an affair that ends in an abortion. The two women also find that mother, whom they thought dead, is living nearby with another man. Their shock results in the younger committing suicide and the older returning to her husband, leaving the father alone. (FC, AB)

1958 *Equinox Flower (Higanbana)*
pr: Shochiku (Kamata); orig. novel: Ton Satomi; sc: Ozu and Kogo Noda; color ph: Yuharu Atsuta; music: Takanobu Saito; cast: Shin Saburi, Kinuyo Tanaka, Ineko Arima, Keiji Sata, Chieko Naniwa et al. Open family tensions and a new shift in emphasis to representatives of the younger generation. A daughter wishes to marry a man of her own choice, and her father objects. Her mother and a friend from Kyoto sympathize, and the father is finally won over, his real objection having been only that he was not consulted. *KJ* #3; Geijutsusai Grand Prize. (FC; NY)

1959 *Ohayo (Ohayo)*
pr: Shochiku (Ofuna); orig. sc: Ozu and Kogo Noda; color ph: Yuharu Atsuta; music: Toshiro Mayuzumi; cast: Chishu Ryu, Kuniko Miyake, Yoshiko Kuga, Keiji Sata, Koji Tsuruta et al. Remake of Ozu's 1932 *I Was Born, But. . .*, centering around the parents' refusal to buy the two small sons a television. They boycott the adult world by refusing to respond to the customary daily greetings, and a neighborhood quarrel results. All is righted when the father relents and buys the TV. (FC, AB)

Floating Weeds (Ukigusa)
pr: Daiei; orig. sc: Ozu and Kogo Noda; color ph: Kazuo Miyagawa; music: Takanobu Saito; cast: Ganjiro Nakamura, Haruko Sugimura, Machiko Kyo, Ayako Wakao, Hiroshi Kawaguchi et al. Remake of Ozu's 1934 *A Story of Floating Weeds*, with an easier resignation. The head of the traveling troupe has a jealous mistress who forces a girl from the troupe on the son of the troupe leader. She ends up staying behind with the son and the troupe breaks up, with the old man and his mistress continuing on together. Beautifully photographed by Daiei cameraman Miyagawa. (FC, NY)

1960 *Late Autumn (Akibiyori)*
pr: Shochiku (Ofuna); orig. novel: Ton Satomi; sc: Ozu and Kogo Noda; color

ph: Yuharu Atsuta; music: Takanobu Saito; cast: Setsuko Hara, Yoko Tsukasa, Chishu Ryu, Mariko Okada, Keiji Sata et al. Pattern familiar from Ozu's 1949 *Late Spring*, but with a mother-daughter instead of a father-daughter relationship. An unmarried girl wishes to stay with her widowed mother until she comes to believe, mistakenly, that her mother wishes to remarry. The daughter dutifully marries, and the mother goes back to their apartment to live alone. Elegiac sadness about what is fitting. *KJ* #5. (FC, NY)

1961 *The End of Summer (Kohayagawa-ke no Aki)*
pr: Toho; orig. sc: Ozu and Kogo Noda; color ph: Asakazu Nakai; music: Toshiro Mayuzumi; cast: Ganjiro Nakamura, Setsuko Hara, Yoko Tsukasa, Michiyo Aratama, Yumi Shirakawa et al. Picture of a large Osaka merchant family that is one of Ozu's bleakest films despite many humorous touches. An elderly widower has three daughters by his wife and one by a former mistress. When he takes up again with his old mistress the daughters are all upset, but in the midst of their efforts to reform him he dies of a heart attack. (FC, NY)

1962 *An Autumn Afternoon (Samma no Aji)*
pr: Shochiku (Ofuna); orig. sc: Ozu and Kogo Noda; color ph: Yuharu Atsuta; music: Takanobu Saito; cast: Shima Iwashita, Shinichiro Mikami, Keiji Sata, Mariko Okada, Nobuo Nakamura et al. The simplest of Ozu's simple patterns, with an intensely autumnal mood. A widower arranges the marriage of his daughter and is left alone with the realization that he is growing old. *KJ* #8. (FC, MOMA, NY)

MIKIO NARUSE

1905—69

He was the most difficult director I ever worked for. He never said a word. A real nihilist.

—Tatsuya Nakadai

The third member of the triumvirate of early cinematic portraitists, Mikio Naruse approached his subjects from an angle that has much in common with both Mizoguchi and Ozu, yet he remains the most withdrawn and the most clinical, and, consequently, the one with the darkest view of life. Like Ozu, Naruse never made period films if he could help it, but concentrated on the *shomin-geki* genre showing contemporary life in the lower middle classes. His image of the inevitable trials of life was far gloomier than Ozu's, however—for Naruse communication, satisfaction, even acceptance were impossible, and all resignation retained a doubt and a bitter aftertaste.

Like Mizoguchi, Naruse saw life as a crushing fate, and it was for him too the position of women in society that best expressed the claustrophobia and resentment we feel about our lot. Yet unlike Mizoguchi, still less like Ozu, Naruse allowed no moments of stillness, no redemption through the expanse of subsuming nature, no recognition of the rightness of order. Naruse found no quasi-religious reconciliation to the sorrow of living, and in his films showed only the confirmation of what he himself said of the human condition: "From the youngest age, I have thought that the world we live in betrays us; this thought remains with me."[1]

Despite this bleak view on the part of the director, however, the determined characters of the Naruse film never give up. A stubborn dedication to their own self-respect in the face of overwhelming crassness, vulgarity and exploitation from even those who should be most sensitive and protective toward the individual lends Naruse's heroines a distinctive nobility. They never allow themselves to be swallowed up in self-sacrifice to the extent that a Mizoguchi heroine like Oharu does; if they throw themselves away for a man, like Yukiko in Naruse's best-loved film in Japan, *Floating Clouds* (1955), they do so with such a complete awareness that we cannot feel pity for them. Naruse heroines retain the dignity of evaluating their acts to the end, and the persistence of their search for happiness, despite accumulating evidence of its non-existence, becomes the terrifying statement of all of Naruse's work. His portraits of aware feminine resistance to fate complement the aware resignation in Ozu as well as the passive destruction in Mizoguchi, and this alternative view expressed in his personalized cinematic technique has secured him an equally revered position in the annals of Japanese film.

However, outside of a few select organizations in Japan such as the Tokyo National Museum of Modern Art Film Center and the Japan Film Library Council, which sponsored a retrospective in 1970, Naruse has been as neglected at home as abroad. The reasons are probably many. A major cause may be that at the time of his death in 1969, unlike Ozu and

Mizoguchi in their last years, Naruse had not been producing his best work. His peaks had been in the first half of the 1930s and the first half of the 1950s, and although two of his last films, *Stranger within a Woman* (1966) and *Scattered Clouds* (1967), captured places in the *Kinema Jumpo* magazine's annual "Best Ten" awards, the majority of his fifteen "Best Ten" ranking films were made long before. Perhaps, then, a habit of underestimating Naruse had been formed from the late fifties on.

It has also been suggested that because most film critics in Japan are men, they have not been sympathetic toward Naruse's feminine viewpoint.[2] More likely, however, they have not been sympathetic toward Naruse's negative viewpoint, as he has indeed been lambasted for portraying women as "miserable and unhappy"[3] by critics who cannot accept his belief that unhappiness is the intellectual and emotional human condition. Especially in the postwar era, it has been widely held that films should fulfill Akira Kurosawa's requirement of being "positive and constructive."[4] Neither the content nor the form of Naruse's films fulfills this prescription; they are not only pessimistic, but inconclusive and undramatic. Many may share the private opinion of the late Shiro Kido who, while publicly chastising himself for letting Naruse leave the Shochiku company in 1934,[5] nevertheless admitted to disliking the monotone pace, the absence of dramatic highs and lows that he found characteristic of Naruse's style.[6]

Another great handicap Naruse suffered in developing the reputation his work deserved may have been his own painful modesty. Hesitant to demand anything, his tendency was rather to perform obediently what was asked of him. That he lacked the assertiveness to claim his due in the way that Ozu and Mizoguchi did has undoubtedly affected his renown. While Kido remembered having to build ceilings on sets for the first time for Ozu, Naruse's long-time producer at Toho, Sanezumi Fujimoto, has nothing but praise for the quiet director for the simple reason that he never exceeded the budget.[7] In a film world placing highest value on the *auteur*, Naruse's humility makes him an embarrassment to the critic. But the modesty, taciturnity and bleak world view that won Naruse so few friends had their roots in his personal background, and the contrary, stubborn determination that pervades his films in feminine guise may very well be the reflection of the director who refused the limelight. Whatever the cause of the critical neglect, however, the rediscovery and preservation of 44 of Naruse's 88 films now affords the opportunity to review and assess his work in historical perspective and accord it the recognition it deserves throughout the world.

A Poor Boy's Poesie

Naruse was born in what is now the Wakabacho section of central Tokyo in 1905 and was named "Mikio" because it was the year of the snake (*mi*). He was the youngest of three children of an embroiderer and his wife whose impoverished life always bordered on desperation. Mikio attended elementary school in the area and graduated in 1918 with high marks. He was already a lover of literature and would have liked to go to middle school, but his family's finances would not permit it, and he entered a two-year technical school in the Tsukiji district instead.[8] Matsuo Kishi, Naruse's lifelong friend and scenarist for *Ginza Cosmetics,* the film that brought the director out of his long slump in 1950, recalls that the only thing the boy Mikio ever asked for from his family was a winter coat he saw in the window of a pawn shop for only five yen (almost $20).[9]

While at technical school, which did not interest him in the least, Mikio spent all of his free time reading books he borrowed from the library. Among his favorite authors were the poet-novelist Toson Shimazaki, and Shusei Tokuda whose *Arakure* ("Untamed") he would adapt for the screen in 1957.[10] He nevertheless graduated unscathed from the technical school in 1920, and though he wanted to go to university, he was unable to because his father died and the family suddenly became dependent on Mikio's older brother. At the age of fifteen, Mikio had no choice but to go to work, and through a friend's introduction he entered the newly established Shochiku company as a prop man at the Tokyo Kamata studios. He went to live in a room rented from relatives near the studio, and his life sank into deep loneliness: "I had to immediately become an adult; it was the darkest period of my life."[11]

He had never dreamed of becoming a film director, but prop man was undoubtedly one of the last things he wanted to be. From the end of his boyhood his story was that of a talent nearly crushed by the studio system. He joined Shochiku during the exciting youth of the film industry when almost anyone could become a director with a few months of training. Mizoguchi apprenticed only one year at Nikkatsu before succeeding to director status, and Ozu, who joined Shochiku long after Naruse, would do the same, preceding Naruse in making his own films by three years. Such was also the case with the man under whom Naruse first worked as assistant director, Yoshinobu Ikeda (1892–). When Ikeda entered Shochiku in 1920, Naruse helped him write his first script for another director, and during shooting the prop man and the assistant spent many lunch hours on location discussing literature and "poésie," a French loan word popular at the time to express lyrical qualities in many arts.[12] When Ikeda became director in 1921, he put Naruse on his staff. In 1922 Hiroshi Shimizu (1903–66) was hired as assistant to Ikeda, and Naruse too was at last promoted to the same status. Shimizu, notorious for his laziness, often criticized Naruse for working too hard but became director within two years. And so it went: Torajiro Saito (1905–) and Heinosuke Gosho (1902–) joined those entering Shochiku after Naruse but preceded him in making their own films.

In 1928 Naruse was still assistant to Ikeda, and he was without hope. He knew that Shiro Kido's system of promotion was based on script-writing ability (and so it remained for the duration of his long producing career), so he had been turning out one short comedy after another under the ironic penname "Chihan Miki"—"Miki-chan" for Mikio was Naruse's nickname around the studio, and "chi" is the first character in the name Ikeda, while "han" means "one-half." He self-deprecatingly assumed his abilities to be only half those of Ikeda. Kishi claims that the cheerful Kido simply disliked the melancholy Naruse, and may not even have bothered to read his scripts,[13] although the producer denied any such personal bias.[14] In any event, Naruse was on his way to tender his resignation in 1928 when he ran into his friend Gosho who persuaded him to hang on a little longer. The next year Naruse joined Gosho's staff, and in 1930, ten years after joining the company, he at last had his chance to direct—not a script of his own, but a slapstick comedy about tenement life written by Kido himself, the lost *Mr. and Mrs. Swordplay.*

From Slapstick to Serious Women

Working in the same company under the same demanding studio head, Naruse and Ozu necessarily had much in common in the early 1930s. Naruse never felt that slapstick was his genre, but like Ozu he had to begin with Kido's formulas requiring series of gags with sudden sad plot twists—that blend of farce and melodrama that so repelled Sergei Eisenstein in 1928 when Kido showed him Gosho's 1927 *Tricky Girl* (*Karakuri Musume*).[15] It was Ozu, in fact, who was the first to call attention to Naruse's talent, when he saw the lost *Pure Love:* "Someone who can do that well on only his second film has real directorial strength."[16] Encouraged, Naruse went on making slapstick tear-jerkers, of which the best extant example is the 1931 *Flunky, Work Hard!* Set in the same kind of new suburb, it contains the same kind of acceptance of irreversible economic class differences to be found in Ozu's *I Was Born, But . . .* , made the following year, but Naruse's protagonists are poorer, closer to the edge. Unlike the relatively secure office-worker father of the Ozu film, Naruse's insurance salesman father competes furiously and ludicrously for the attention of a wealthy prospect for a very tangible reason: to keep his family out of the poorhouse. He hides from the landlord coming to collect the rent, and he cannot afford to buy his son the toy air-plane that would keep him out of fights with the rich woman's son. The boy's injury, like the son's sickness in Ozu's 1933 *Passing Fancy,* brings the father enlightenment: his own child is more valuable than even the sale that saves the family finances. A peculiarly Naruse touch, however, appears in the nagging wife, who complains about poverty and blames her husband for it in a way Ozu wives never do.

These early blue-collar and low-status white-collar dramas by Ozu and Naruse are undoubtedly a shade subtler than the lost leftist "tendency films" by Mizoguchi of the same era. Class differences and financial woes are a realistic and integral part of the Great Depression life portray-ed, but there is no call to revolution in the Shochiku films. But by the time Naruse had completed his lost 1932 *Be Great!,* the similarities in style became too much for Kido: "Naruse, we don't need two Ozus," he said, and also prohibited any similarities to the work of Gosho, Shimizu or Yasujiro Shimazu (1897–1948), the founder of the *shomin-geki* genre in the mid-1920s.[17] Naruse was left with no recourse but to search for material from his own life.

Although he was now a full-fledged director, until he left Shochiku in 1934 Naruse was earning less than ¥100 a month (almost $360), putting him in the class of studio employees who had to line up at the pay window and get cafeteria meal tickets. The very private, alcohol-loving Naruse, however, traded his meal tickets for cigarettes and went to eat at a cheap restaurant near the studio. Here he spent much time ob-serving and conversing with the waitresses, one of whom fell in love with him. Naruse did not respond to her letters, and the unfortunate woman committed suicide, bringing down the wrath of the film world upon the director for his "cold heartlessness."[18] The incident may well have aggravated Naruse's already morose demeanor, for his life was exceed-ingly lonely—he always drank alone, at the same table, and conversa-tions with these working women was his only social life. His mother had died in 1922, and his brother and sister had as little to do with him as possible; he rented a second-floor room from a family who did pro-gressively worse in their sushi business, and every time they moved to poorer quarters, Naruse went along. The subjects of the film scripts Naruse was writing, although he was supposed to be doing Kido style comedies, thus came from among the inhabitants of the cheap bar and restaurant world, and the poor of the ever-expanding suburbs. He found he could inject gags at appropriate intervals to please Kido, and after proceeding to the next phase in the producer's system, adaptation of an original story (the lost 1932 *Motheaten Spring*), he was able to reach what he felt was a synthesis of his lyricism, slapstick and melodrama to date with the lost 1932 film *Chocolate Girl.*[19]

The best of Naruse's extant Shochiku films, however, is an original script of his own, the 1933 *Apart from You*. It presents the poor of the geisha world in a way that treats the universal problems of the woman outside of the marital familial relationship, a theme Naruse would explore until the end of his career. The widow Kikue, who must support her son, works as a geisha and gradually sees her patron desert her for younger interests, while her son, shamed by his mother's profession, becomes a delinquent. The young apprentice geisha Terugiku, who is in love with Kikue's son, was sold by her alcoholic father to support the family. The most touching moments of the film are when Teru takes the rebellious boy to see her family situation and tries to explain to him that his mother does not enjoy earning her living in the way that she does. In a rather sentimental ending, Teru succeeds in reforming the boy, establishing that he loves her too, and departing to work in the country so that her father will not sell her younger sister as a geisha as well. But the pluck of the later Naruse heroines is already there: Teru, in a way a Mizoguchi or Ozu heroine never would, speaks to her father with defiance, "The reason there's no money is because you're just playing around, isn't it?" And at the very end she utters that stubborn refrain that characterizes all Naruse's independent women who are pulling themselves back from the brink of despair: "I would be so happy if I could just die right now . . . but I'm going to live. No matter how painful it is, I won't give up." And like many a later Naruse heroine, Teru, fighting spirit notwithstanding, is caught in the web of family obligations.

Naruse would make other successful films in the thirties about independent women, notably his first talkie at the newly formed P.C.L. studios, and his first adaptation of novelist Yasunari Kawabata's work *Three Sisters with Maiden Hearts* (1935) and his very popular "Best One," *Wife! Be Like a Rose!* the same year. The latter was considered slick enough—it is a very urbane comedy about a working girl and her poetess mother trying to bring a wandering father back home—to be shown in New York, the first Japanese feature film accorded such an honor in the prewar era. But *Apart from You* remains the truest to Naruse's consistent theme, the question of living without love and in service to something else or giving in to the urge to escape all pain and responsibility in death. Its nonverbal moments are also some of the most expressive in Japanese cinema of the era: the middle-aged Kikue searching the mirror for gray hairs and discovering there are simply too many to pluck out; Kikue showing her anger over being slighted in favor of a younger woman by getting drunk in front of her patron; Teru's youngest brother accidentally smashing the bottle of sake his father has sent him to buy. Its style is a dramatic break with *Flunky, Work Hard!* and even the previous year's *Not Blood Relations,* both of which contain much camera movement and fast montage sequences. At the same time as Ozu, with *Apart from You* Naruse begins restricting his cinematic technique, avoiding camera movement, large fast action, exterior scenes. Instead, accompanying Ozu in the direction of a bare-boned style that allows the fullest characterization, he concentrates on significant objects, facial expression, and slight body movement.

Family Ties

Quiet, gloomy Naruse surprised all of his few friends in 1937 by marrying the vivacious star of *Wife! Be Like a Rose!* Sachiko Chiba.[20] His dissatisfaction with Shochiku, where he could neither earn a living wage nor make talkies, came to a head when he was forced to make the dull, sentimental *Street without End* in 1934. P.C.L. came asking for Naruse and Kido let him go, to watch him make Japan's best film the following year. Probably heartened by his successes, Naruse embarked on a marriage that also produced a child, but lasted only until 1942, when he resumed his bar and second-floor-rented-room life. Much later, he remarried very, very quietly.

Whether it was due to the strain in his marriage, as some have suggested,[21] remains uncertain, but the period of Naruse's life with Chiba coincides with a bad slump enlivened only in 1939 by *The Whole Family Works*, a *shomin-geki* in the guise of a national policy film. Naruse, like Mizoguchi, went on working into the war era and, like Mizoguchi, made a number of performing arts films, such as the 1938 *Tsuruhachi and Tsurujiro*, the lost 1940 *Traveling Actors*, a tedious 1943 *Song Lantern*, and the lost 1944 *Way of Drama*. His element, however, was the life of the working-class poor, and *The Whole Family Works* presents wartime, aside from a brief dream sequence of practice maneuvers, as a kind of intensified Depression from the viewpoint of a large impoverished family. The required patriotic slogans pasted on walls appear almost ironic, as everyone in the film is concerned with the far more immediate problem of how to eat. Tellingly, one child's education is sacrificed so that all can survive. A major achievement in Naruse's work of this period is his nearly total avoidance of national policy—the 1941 *Hideko the Bus Conductor,* Hideko Takamine's first starring picture for Naruse, is a story that could take place in any poor rural town at any time. It was not until 1945 that Naruse succumbed to making a period film for the first time, the lost *Tale of Archery at the Sanjusangendo,* which he would rather have forgotten.

The immediate postwar era was no kinder to Naruse, the U.S. Occupation demands for democratic subjects being just as annoying as the earlier propaganda requirements—he referred to it as a "noisy age."[22] It was also a time of severe internal strife at the Toho company, which had developed out of P.C.L. in 1937. In the midst of violent leftist activities, Naruse refrained from red-flag waving and simply quit the company to become a free-lancer. While he was making bad films for various companies in order to eat, he and Matsuo Kishi began work on *Ginza Cosmetics.*

Kishi's first script was very faithful to the original, so much so that Naruse was roused from his doldrums to assert that if they did not make it more realistic it would not be worth doing.[23] Kishi rewrote, embellishing with locations, characters and conversations he and Naruse knew from their own Ginza back-street bar hopping.[24] The result was a sentimental but authentically characterized story of a bar hostess widow approaching middle age with a child—recalling Kikue of the 1933 *Apart from You.* Private jokes such as the bar with its French name ("Lupin"), reference to the poetry of "Fujimura"—a misreading of "Toson" (Shimazaki), undoubtedly added to the pleasure of filming a familiar subject, and Naruse said that "it was from here, wasn't it, that somehow [things improved] . . . It seemed to suit my temperament. I seemed to have relaxed."[25]

Ginza Cosmetics reopened the territory Naruse knew he treated best: the lower economic strata and the psychology of women on their own. The demands of the family system almost invariably prove to be the factor that traps these women, often widows, into occupations that are socially frowned upon but ironically remain the only avenues of relative financial independence open to them. Without husbands, or with families to support, they are forced to work, yet there is nothing for the respectable single woman to do in Japan that does not make her prey to unsavory male advances, false promises, and continuing degradation. These women fight to maintain their dignity, for they are always proud, honest and uncompromising, but they are also painfully aware of others' expectations. The early prototypes, the two trapped geisha, Kikue and Terugiku, in *Apart From You,* find their reincarnation in the geisha of *Late Chrysanthemums* (1954) and *Flowing* (1956), the bar-hostess widows of *Ginza Cosmetics* and *When a Woman Ascends the Stairs* (1960), the poor widow trying to run a dry-cleaning establishment and support her children in *Mother* (1952), the farm widow in *Herringbone Clouds* (1958), the middle-class widows with avaricious families in *Daughters, Wives and a Mother* (1960), *Yearning* (1964) and Naruse's last film, *Scattered Clouds* (1967). Elements of the determined solitary woman also appear in the young working girls of *Lightning* (1952), *Floating Clouds* (1955), *A Wanderer's Notebook* (1962) and the contrasting sisters in *Older Brother, Younger Sister* (1953). All of these women succumb to fleeting illusions of the salvation of love, and some carry out tremendous self-sacrifices for its sake, like Yukiko in Naruse's most popular film in Japan, *Floating Clouds*, but they are never blind to its dangers as Mizoguchi's heroines are.

It is with this self-awareness that Naruse prevents his heroines from being tragic and pathetic and makes them instead contrary and stubborn. The refusal to give up in the face of emotional blankness on the part of a lover or insurmountable financial obstacles to a secure life has led Naruse's heroines to be called "egoists."[26] It is always their own limitations they are pushing, their own ideals they are testing. Yukiko in *Floating Clouds* knows her lover is fickle, weak, insensitive; Fumiko in *A Wanderer's Notebook* knows her man is so jealous of her success that their relationship cannot survive; Keiko in *When a Woman Ascends the Stairs* knows that the married banker over whom she breaks her promise of fidelity to her dead husband will not leave his wife and family for her; the middle-aged geisha in *Flowing* knows she cannot continue financially without a patron to whom her body must be sold; yet all of these women go on struggling, refusing to be defeated. "If they move even a little," Naruse said, "they quickly hit the wall."[27] This they know, yet even a woman like Mon in *Older Brother, Younger Sister*, who has been ruined and abandoned by her first lover, refuses to see herself as pathetic and fights bitterly with her brother at the very suggestion. In all of these willful women rejecting sorrow and pathos, one cannot help but see the literary boy who could not attend school because of his family's poverty, the young man who signed his consistently rejected scripts "One-Half Ikeda," and the mature director who throughout his life accepted assignments he knew he did not want to make.

However, Naruse also found films he did want to make, beginning from the same year he took up the solitary woman theme again in *Ginza Cosmetics*. Another director stepped down from the project, and Naruse was assigned to direct an adaptation of the unfinished novel Fumiko Hayashi was writing at the time of her sudden death in 1951. He liked it. The result was *Repast*, one of his finest works, the study of a childless wife in a marriage full of minute tensions and frustrations that increase day by day. Naruse would turn this theme of the dangerous moments in married life (which he later said were actually ever present)[28] into a cycle of wedded disharmony films: *Husband and Wife* (1953), *Wife* (1953), his adaptation of Yasunari Kawabata's *Sound of the Mountain* (1954), and the apparently less successful *Sudden Rain* (1956). The close reading of feminine psychology—the feeling of dissatisfaction with the man upon whom she must, society demands, be totally dependent financially and emotionally—progresses from the nonverbal associations of *Repast* (the empty rice bin, the husband's new shoes) to the open harping about money and the defiant slovenliness found in

Wife, where the kitchen contains but a single rust-covered knife. Adapting from different authors and employing different scriptwriters, Naruse's vision remains consistent: these women are all unfulfilled, embittered, but none will give up the social security of marriage. The wives in *Repast* and *Sound of the Mountain* toy with the idea of independence, but in the end return to unloving husbands. But just as Naruse's romantic single women reject the fact that happiness is an illusion, his disabused married women reject the fact that they too are condemned to perpetual dissatisfaction. Unlike Ozu's accepting protagonists and Mizoguchi's transcending heroines, Naruse's characters continue to question and to beat their heads against the wall.

The temptation exists to ascribe Naruse's abilities in portraying unhappy wives to his own marital experience. But his sensitivity to the strains of marriages goes back to a much earlier time. In the 1932 *Flunky, Work Hard!* we see the wife glaring fiercely and accusingly at her husband and saying, "I've had just about enough of this poverty," just as the protagonist of *Wife* would 21 years later. The 1935 *Wife! Be Like a Rose!,* also made before Naruse's marriage, treats the poetess mother with great humor as she constantly interrupts herself to compose poems, but the fact remains that her romantic odes are all addressed to a husband with whom she cannot stand to live. The sullen Naruse, nicknamed "Yaruse Nakio" (Mr. Disconsolate) at Toho[29] and reputed never to have agreed with anyone,[30] appears to have seen living with people as a terribly difficult thing even before he tried it.

Perhaps the greatest rediscovery Naruse made in the 1950s, which was his period of highest achievement, was the writing of Fumiko Hayashi (1904–51). This woman who was born in poverty, wandered fatherless, who worked as a waitress, who produced proletarian literature, and progressed to popular serialized depictions of downtrodden but determined women, was a true counterpart to Naruse. As early as 1934, when Shochiku promised he could do what he wanted, Naruse had chosen a Hayashi story about a café waitress and had completed the script, but his move to P.C.L. prevented its realization in film.[31] Like Naruse, Hayashi had a pessimistic view of ordinary lower and lower middle-class life that nevertheless reveals an admiration for human obstinacy and irrationality as a kind of courage in the face of meaninglessness. The Hayashi quotation with which Naruse begins *Repast* sums up the coincidence of their world views: "I cannot help but feel an excruciating love for the pitiful assiduousness of human beings, managing their lives in the midst of endless time and space." Living itself is a heroic effort, no matter how miserable the content of that life may seem. This fiercely negative view, which has been called Naruse's nihilism by not a few, pervades the six fine adaptations he was finally able to make of

Hayashi's work: *Repast, Lightning, Wife, Late Chrysanthemums, Float-ing Clouds,* and a final tribute, Hayashi's autobiography, *A Wanderer's Notebook,* in 1962. Masao Tamai, Naruse's cinematographer for many of his best films, including *Repast* and *Floating Clouds,* reported that when the director had exhausted the greater part of her work for screen adapta-tions the smile with which he lamented, "There's nothing left of Hayashi's any more, is there?" betrayed a certain loneliness,[32] as if he had truly lost a soul-mate in the writer he had never met.

A Vision of Entrapment

Naruse's creative method reflects the sullen, self-effacing, unexpectant attitude of his favorite author, and a good deal of her stubbornness as well. Although in his early days at Shochiku he wrote some fine original scenarios, such as *Flunky, Work Hard!* and *Apart from You,* by the time he had entered his late-thirties slump he was having doubts about his abilities and felt he should have had others write for him.[33] Matsuo Kishi asserts that Naruse came to believe what Akira Kurosawa and Kon Ichikawa would find about themselves in the postwar era: if he wrote an original scenario alone, the film would be too easy for him to make; the work of others provided a challenge to confront.[34]

Different scenarists describe a different Naruse. Sumie Tanaka, who says he taught her everything about scriptwriting on their two prize-winning films *Repast* and *Lightning,* portrays a terribly strict director who like Mizoguchi gave no explicit instructions at the outset, but demanded as many as three complete rewrites of the 400-page *Repast* script in the interval of only ten days, and never offered a word of thanks or praise.[35] Yoko Mizuki, on the other hand, said Naruse told her to begin writing from wherever she pleased and not to worry about the theme, and that all in all he was the easiest person in the world to work for.[36] But he had such strong objections to her script that he wanted to talk all night. He told her to rewrite all of the location scenes, and then went off and shot them while she was doing it. One suspects that the two scriptwriters' interpretation of the same director resolve to the same trait: stubbornness. Nevertheless, Mizuki divulges at least one clue to the subtlety of Naruse's scripts when she says she learned from him that although it appears unobtrusively observed, all the beauty in the flow of movement is con-scious and calculated, and that she learned from *Floating Clouds* and *Untamed* to incorporate emotional rhythm into the form of her scripts.[37] Kishi offers another clue to what Naruse taught him about the intention of the script (Mizuki's elusive "theme") which must make itself felt from about half-way through: if everything is explained from the beginning, there is no interest to the film.[38]

Naruse's purpose was unstated but clear enough, yet he constantly encountered difficulties in getting what he wanted. Like Mizoguchi, he disliked giving detailed instructions as to what a script, set or action should be. He did not, however, have Mizoguchi's capacity for throwing tantrums if the results were below his standard, and he often made do. Akira Kurosawa, who assisted Naruse on the lost 1937 *Avalanche,* recalls Naruse was working with a new art director who made sets for a crucial scene that completely swallowed the actors in uncontrollable mottled lighting. Naruse mumbled that they were impossible to film in, but he did not have the courage to tell the man so, have them redone, and go over budget and schedule.[39] When the director did complain, it was in far distant retrospect—a quarter-century after the fact, for example, he observed that P.C.L. had made only one kind of film and had to use its own contract stars, so he had felt quite constricted working there.[40] All who worked with him knew him as the man who never asked for anything, and who never praised or blamed, which made him, many agree with Kurosawa, "the hardest director of all to work under."[41]

Naruse was notorious for disliking location shooting, an idiosyncrasy in which he far exceeded Ozu or any other contemporary. Director Kihachi Okamoto, who assisted on *Floating Clouds,* remembers with what great relish Naruse, he, and a skeleton staff rushed off and completed all the location shooting before any crowds could gather or anyone who had any say in the matter knew what was happening.[42] Naruse disliked not only crowds, but scenery, weather, color, and any other background element that distracted from acting. When Okamoto says he learned a reserved cinematic style from Naruse, whom he assisted for several years, he means an actor-oriented technique that eschews environment of the full sort favored by Mizoguchi. Landscapes in Naruse films always appear incidental, unimportant, even unwillingly included in many late films such as the otherwise excellent *Daughters, Wives and a Mother* or the disastrous 1959 Hokkaido pastorale *Whistling in Kotan* during which Naruse was surprised by the northern island's fast seasonal changes and had to have leaves painted green.[43]

It was acting and close camera work that held primary importance in Naruse's closely observed characterizations. His preference for studio work, controlled low-key lightning and interiors of Japanese houses restricted movement of all kinds and emphasized the actor as conveyor of his intention. Cinematographer Tamai, whose style has been called "perfectly matched" to Naruse's content,[44] explained the director's compositions in confined Japanese houses as requiring minimal camera movement and total rejection of unusual camera angles in order to allow full concentration on the human or acting scale, which creates the rhythmic flow of the Naruse film.[45] Like Ozu, Naruse preferred character revelation through slow, almost dramaless stories, conversations shot in medium and close shots to catch the nuances of every eye movement, every slight momentary frown; but he did not employ Ozu's reverential camera angle. Naruse's angles are straight on, often three-quarters from the rear, like an "objective third-person observer,"[46] their coldness and lack of involvement perfectly coordinated with the matter-of-fact grimness of life.

This relentless camera eye and the close sets, along with the succinctness of dialogue that reveals only gradually, put a terrific responsibility on the actor. Tatsuya Nakadai, who appeared in *Untamed, When a Woman Ascends the Stairs,* and other late Naruse works, found the directors's silence intimidating: "He was the most difficult director I ever worked for. A real nihilist."[47] But again in this area, just as there were no instructions, there was no praise or blame, only a making do. Naruse consequently disliked novices or even actors new only to him. Hideko Takamine, who worked with Naruse and Keisuke Kinoshita more than any other directors (some 25 years and 17 starring roles with Naruse), became so accustomed to his method that she claims if she were told today she is to act in a Naruse film she would know exactly what to do.[48] This she knows from experience, as he never coached her acting. Like scriptwriter Mizuki, Takamine learned unconsciously what Naruse wanted, and her reward was some of the finest roles in Japanese cinema: the morose Yukiko of *Floating Clouds,* the petulant Fumiko of *A Wanderer's Notebook,* the valiant Keiko of *When a Woman Ascends the Stairs,* the determinedly pure Kiyoko of *Lightning.* The actor in the Naruse film had to create the fullness of the character entirely on his own, but also had to be careful not to overdo in the restricted Naruse world. The last wish Naruse expressed to Takamine before his death was an idea that would have epitomized his restriction: a film to be shot with only white curtain backdrops, no real sets, no exteriors, all concentration on the nuances of human movement expressing feeling carved down to the quick.[49]

With continuity fully worked out in advance (the rumor that Naruse never showed anyone the continuity before the day of shooting is groundless),[50] harmony calculated between an almost stationary camera and the actors' slightest movement, for Naruse as for Ozu, editing assumed a minor role. He nevertheless supervised his own cutting, in his later films refraining from cuts on motion, but never did he create the spiritual rest-stop of the empty room or the peaceful still-life as Ozu did. "The strange thing about Naruse," says director Masahiro Shinoda, "is that there is no space of his own in his films."[51] Everything is the character's headlong rush against the wall. Even music follows the same rules of unobtrusive punctuation in the best Naruse as in the best Ozu, and from 1952 to 1964 it is almost all composed by Ichiro Saito. It too becomes a subordinate element in the pace of human beings persisting in the miraculous ant-like management of their lives.

Lightning

In 1952 Naruse had been successful in returning to the poor working-class setting he "best understood" with *Mother*, and as a result he felt confident in selecting what he wanted to do next, a Fumiko Hayashi story starring his favorite actress, Hideko Takamine.[52] The women in *Lightning* represent the whole gamut of Naruse types, from the stubbornly dependent to the stubbornly strong, satisfying his own desire to portray women who take control of their destinies as well as what he perceived to be the audience demand for women who were weak and abused.[53] The mother who has borne four children by different fathers has no introspection about her life and simply goes on accepting the structures of dependence and obligation. Kiyoko is the one sister who tries to break away from this trap, while her half-sister Mitsuko most resembles the mother, but without the mother's courage, and the other half-sister Nuiko approaches the system from underneath, the way Shohei Imamura's women would later, using her sexuality to exploit men for money. Half-brother Kasuke remains oblivious to anyone else's problems, playing pinball, drinking beer, and allowing himself to be waited on by his solicitous mother. The coexistence of these various types within the same family leads inevitably to conflict among them, strained relations that Naruse portrays with his finely woven continuity and Sumie Tanaka's eloquently understated dialogue.

Kiyoko (Hideko Takamine), a marriageable 23-year-old, works as a bus conductor and lives with her mother Osei (Kumeko Urabe) and unemployed half-brother Kasuke (Osamu Maruyama) in poor downtown surroundings. Kiyoko's slatternly half-sister Nuiko (Chieko Murata), whose husband's business is failing, comes with a marriage proposal for her: a middle-aged baker, Goto (Sakae [Eitaro] Ozawa, Tobei in Mizoguchi's *Ugetsu*). Kiyoko remains aloof, however, realizing that Nuiko is scheming to get money out of the baker. At this moment the overweight husband of Kiyoko's other half-sister, Mitsuko (Mitsuko Miura), suddenly dies, and she is left in shocked grief but with a large life insurance compensation on the way. While the various family members concentrate on persuading Mitsuko to part with her money, a woman with a baby claiming to be the dead husband's long-time mistress appears with her own monetary demands. A doubly shocked Mitsuko refuses to acknowledge her at first, but when threatened with legal action agrees to give the woman what she asks despite Kiyoko's exhortations to keep her money for herself. The baker continues to pursue Kiyoko, but he also provides money for Nuiko to start a hotspring hotel, thus winning her away from her ineffectual husband, and becomes Mitsuko's patron when she starts a coffee shop to support herself. Kiyoko, filled with disgust at the behavior of her family and their attempts to use her as bait, moves out without leaving word to students' lodgings let by a gentle, refined widow in the suburbs. Just as she is beginning to feel at ease and to enjoy new friendship with a cultured boy and girl next door, her mother arrives complaining that Nuiko's cuckolded husband has moved in with her and Mitsuko has run away from Nuiko's jealousy over the slippery baker. Osei talks of her own responsibility as mother of the woman who deserted a debt-ridden husband, but Kiyoko angers and tells her she never should have had her four children by four fathers, that she herself never asked to be born. Osei cries over Kiyoko's bitterness, and the daughter softens before accompanying her back to the station.

The story is much what Shiro Kido criticized and lost Naruse over: it rejects plot rationality and dramatic highs and lows in favor of character-revealing day-to-day dialogue and a feeling of treading water. As inconclusive as Naruse's marriage cycle films, it deals with the same narrow, virtually static world of the home and family that Ozu portrayed, but in a very different and disapproving way. The marriageable daughter, far from reconciling herself to society's demand for her to be wed, runs away from a distasteful prospect. Instead of speaking in innocence of marriage as "life's graveyard" like an Ozu daughter, Kiyoko has experiential proof that "men are beasts" in Goto's lewd advances to her, coinciding with his seduction of both her half-sisters. Kiyoko chooses independence over the meddling of her family, the underlying message of the Naruse film being the opposite of the Ozu film: family members do not have each other's best interests at heart. Rather than showing politeness and consideration for each other, they display consistent meanness, selfishness, jealousy, intolerance, and instant susceptibility to money. Instead of comforting her bereaved daughter Mitsuko, for example, Osei asks for some of the insurance money to have a suit made for Kasuke so that he will look presentable when seeking employment.

Yet Naruse also shows that family relations are never black and white; no matter how abusive interpersonal behavior becomes, a residue of affection remains, and it is this affection, tinged by a sense of responsibility toward other human beings, that traps the individualist. This view goes beyond the bitterness of Hayashi's outlook, which is summarized in the last accusation Kiyoko hurls at her mother: "Who was it who brought me into the world in such a way that I would never be able to marry like everyone else?"[54] Hayashi's story ends with this violent resentment, and all blame for Kiyoko's feelings of claustrophobia and betrayal by life is cast upon the mother, for having had so many husbands. Naruse amplifies, softens, and adds greater breadth to the characters and their motivations, giving Kiyoko other goals in life besides the single one of a normal marriage, but nevertheless refusing to diminish the hopelessness of the overall human condition portrayed. At the end of the film mother and daughter argue, and Kiyoko says they should hurry and eat so that she can see Osei off at the station and not disturb the landlady. Osei gradually stops crying.

Osei: Up till now I thought you were my best daughter . . . you're the worst . . . making your mother cry.

Kiyoko (looking at herself in the mirror): Mama, are my eyes pretty?

Osei: How would I know?

Kiyoko (taking her bank book from the dresser): Guess how much I have here, Mama.

Osei (curious): How much? Show me.

Kiyoko (not showing her): ¥4500 . . . I had ¥7000, but I bought some pots and pans.

Osei: Really . . . ?

Kiyoko: Mama, I'll buy you a summer kimono—a cheap one on sale at the end of the season.

Both laugh.

Kiyoko: Mama, stay overnight.

Osei: No, I'll be going . . . Mitsuko may be home by now.
Sound of the piano from next door.

The street in the evening. Lightning spreads across the sky. Mother and daughter walk side by side.

Osei: She'll be back by now, I'm sure . . . Mitsuko. She's always hated thunder since she was a little girl. When it thundered she'd come and cling to me.

The piano continues to sound in Kiyoko's ears. Naruse also added humor at the very end of the film that does not appear in the published script: Osei bends down in the half light to pick up something on the street that looks like a 50-sen piece, but turns out to be a beer-bottle cap. Both women laugh, and Kiyoko is reminded that she had her father's ruby ring appraised and it had turned out to be real. Her mother looks delighted, "Really?" she says, "So your father was not a liar, you see." And the two walk into the distance together. So much reconciliation through ironic humor, gentleness and self-mockery at the end of the film almost completely mitigates the painful standoff at the end of Hayashi's story, and Naruse's characters emerge as all the more real for their self-contradiction.

Much of the atmosphere of the Naruse film resides in nonverbal effects, the telling details of confined action. One such is Mitsuko's response to her family's vulturous descent upon her for the insurance money. She slips outside into the alleyway. As she crouches in fearful isolation, shown in objectifying long shot, she hears a cat's meow. Forgetting the vicious humans around her for a moment, she calls to the cat—as if its response could offer some consolation. This device of the lonely, pressured woman finding companionship with a cat is a frequent and always effective one, appearing also in *Repast,* the very early *Apart from You,* and *Flowing,* where the comment is openly made that cats receive more attention than human beings in the middle-aged geisha's household. It is one of those devices that represent the impossibility of human comfort and communication.

Touches like the cats, the lonely sounding *chindonya* (parading costumed musicians who publicize the opening of a new small business establishment), children playing in alleyways, and sounds of street vendors' calls create the world and the mood of the Naruse film. It is the downtown atmosphere—poor, crowded, traditional—in which the director grew up and which he rediscovered in the works of Fumiko Hayashi. It is an atmosphere that comforts at the same time it imprisons the poor, the uneducated, the observers of custom and obligation. Characters like Kiyoko, in order to realize themselves, pull away from the downtown atmosphere to places where there are open spaces, and the sound of the piano replaces the sound of the shamisen and the street vendor, but the mesh of family obligations reaches out to ensnare them with habit and affection. It is their awareness of both their determination and their doom that constitutes the nearly unbearable truth of the Naruse film.

Something Personal

For 47 years Naruse worked in meek compliance with the studio system. Even when he became a free-lancer and produced some of his best work with companies other than Toho, it was only for a brief interlude in the early 1950s. He has been condemned over the years for his portrayals of unhappy women, coinciding with his own weakness in the face of production companies. He has been accused of having had no talent except for emotionalism and lyricism until he began to work with scriptwriters Mizuki and Tanaka, who are credited with injecting a postwar anti-traditional ideology into his films.[55] The uneven quality of many late Naruse films of the sixties has been attributed to producers forcing him to do the same things over and over again.[56] But in the final analysis, as Naruse always knew, the director must take responsibility for the films that bear his name.

He complained of his own inability to say no to even a bad project— but he also took these opportunities to work in unaccustomed areas, making bad films to be sure, but in so doing clarifying what he was better able to do. In his last years he did what many a prodigious creator has done and tried to break away from what he had shown he could do best. He wandered far afield into experiments with the pure melodrama (*Yearning*), the thriller (*The Stranger within a Woman*), and even the uplift of minorities (*Whistling in Kotan*). But when he did new things well, as in the former two films, it was because he cast them into his own style.

Naruse's tastes had become clear from some of his earliest works. He was drawn to literary subjects, to the world of the poor like himself, and the psychology of the single woman struggling on her own in society, often on its darker side in the bars and geisha houses. Most of his best films were not projects that were forced on him, but were his own original scenarios (*Flunky, Work Hard!, Apart from You*), projects he adored for the familiarity of their mood and subjects (*The Whole Family Works; Ginza Cosmetics; Mother*), or projects he himself initiated (*Lightning; Older Brother, Younger Sister; Sound of the Mountain; Untamed*). That he also did so well with so many projects that were not his own shows not his weakness, but his strength in turning material into his own.

For Naruse employed the two major studio restrictions, time and money, to the advantage of his style. Rejecting attention-drawing locations and elaborate sets, flashy camera movement and angles, even imaginative editing, his style narrowed in on the character in the everyday agony of life. The shift of a gaze, the burning of a photograph, a shamisen thrown to the floor, a summons to a cat require the basic component of the dramatic film, the actor, to perform with highest control and deepest understanding of the containment of pain. For Naruse all was reduction—scriptwriting movement, cinematography. Emotionalism and lyricism were always part of the Naruse style, but as the further adaptation of the *Lightning* script and the reminiscences of Naruse and his colleagues show, the defiance was with him, the refusal to accept mere pathos. Despite his compliance with studio demands, he never compromised on the lies of life and movies. There are no happy endings for Naruse, but there are incredibly enlightened defeats.

Notes

1 Joseph L. Anderson and Donald Richie, *The Japanese Film: Art and Industry* (New York: Grove Press, 1960), p. 364.

2 Conversation with Leonard Schrader, author of "Masters of the Japanese Cinema," 1975.

3 Akira Iwasaki, *Nihon eiga sakka ron* (Theories on Japanese Filmmakers) (Tokyo: Chuo Koronsha, 1958), p. 77.

4 Akira Kurosawa, "L'Empereur" (The Emperor), *Cahiers du cinéma*, No. 182, 1966, p. 7.

5 Shiro Kido, *Nihon eiga den: Eiga seisakusha no kiroku* (The Story of the Japanese Film: A Movie Producer's Record) (Tokyo: Bungei Shunjusha, 1956), p. 112.

6 Author's conversation with Shiro Kido, November 1976.

7 Author's conversation with Sanezumi Fujimoto, June 1976.

8 Matsuo Kishi, "Naruse Mikio shoden" (Short Biography of Mikio Naruse), *Naruse Mikio no tokushu* (Mikio Naruse Retrospective) (Tokyo: Tokyo National Museum of Modern Art Film Center, 1970), p. 4.

9 Author's conversation with Matsuo Kishi, April 1977.

10 *Ibid.*

11 Anderson and Richie, *op. cit.*, p. 364.

12 Kishi, *op. cit.*, p. 5.

13 Kishi conversation, *cit.*

14 Kido conversation, *cit.*

15 Anderson and Richie, *op. cit.*, p. 67.

16 Kishi, *op. cit.*, p. 5.

17 *Ibid.*, p. 6.

18 Kishi conversation, *cit.*

19 Mikio Naruse, "Eiga sakka no peesu" (A Filmmaker's Pace), *Kinema Jumpo*, No. 273, 1960, pp. 58–59.

20 Kishi conversation, *cit.*

21 Kishi, *op. cit.*, p. 9.

22 Naruse, *op. cit.*, p. 61.

23 Kishi, *op. cit.*, p. 9.

24 Kishi conversation, *cit.*

25 Naruse, *op. cit.*, p. 62.

26 Tadao Sato, *Nihon eiga shiso shi* (History of the Intellectual Currents in Japanese Film) (Tokyo: Sanichi Shobo, 1970), p. 41.

27 Anderson and Richie, *op. cit.*, p. 364.

28 Naruse, *op. cit.*, p. 63.

29 Fujimoto conversation, *cit.*

30 Kishi conversation, *cit.*

31 Naruse, *op. cit.*, p. 59.

32 Masao Tamai, "Naruse-san no omoide" (Recollections of Mr. Naruse), *Naruse Mikio tokushu, op. cit.*, p. 19.

33 Naruse, *op. cit.*, p. 60.

34 Kishi conversation, *cit.*

35 Sumie Tanaka, "Kokoro o utta otokotachi" (Men Who Struck My Heart), *Nihon Keizai Shimbun*, November 30, 1976.

36 Yoko Mizuki, "Omoidasu koto" (Remembering), *Naruse Mikio tokushu, op. cit.*, p. 17.

37 *Ibid.*, p. 18.

38 Kishi conversation, *cit.*

39 Author's conversation with Akira Kurosawa, May 1977.

40 Naruse, *op. cit.*, p. 60.

41 Kurosawa conversation, *cit.*

[42] Author's conversation with Kihachi Okamoto, August 1976.

[43] Naruse, *op. cit.*, p. 64.

[44] Kaneei Wada, *Gendai eiga koza* (Survey of Contemporary Film) (Tokyo : Sogensha, 1955), vol. 2, p. 145.

[45] Masao Tamai, "Satsuei no junjo to hoho" (The Order and Method of Cinematography), *ibid.*, p. 88.

[46] Tadao Sato, *Ozu Yasujiro no geijutsu* (The Art of Yasujiro Ozu) (Tokyo : Asahi Shimbunsha, 1971), p. 40.

[47] Author's conversation with Tatsuya Nakadai, January 1976.

[48] Author's conversation with Hideko Takamine, June 1976.

[49] Hideko Takamine, *Watashi no tosei nikki* (My Professional Diary) (Tokyo : Asahi Shimbunsha, 1976), vol. 2., p. 332.

[50] Okamoto conversation, *cit.*

[51] Author's conversation with Masahiro Shinoda, August 1976.

[52] Naruse, *op. cit.*, p. 62.

[53] *Ibid.*, p. 63.

[54] *Hayashi Fumiko shu* (Collected Works of Fumiko Hayashi) (Tokyo : Shinchosha, 1971), p. 171.

[55] Tadao Sato, *Gendai Nihon eiga* (Contemporary Japanese Films) (Tokyo : Hyoronsha, 1969), p. 31.

[56] Kishi conversation, *cit.*

MIKIO NARUSE: FILMOGRAPHY

1930 *Mr. and Mrs. Swordplay (Chambara Fufu)*
pr: Shochiku (Kamata); orig. sc: Haruo Akaho (Shiro Kido); ph: Shojiro Sugimoto; cast: Hisao Furuya, Mitsuko Yoshikawa, Tomio Aoki, Nobuko Wakaba et
al. Silent. Short slapstick comedy made at studio head Kido's command, on an
inhuman schedule. The day Naruse was given Kido's script, he completed the
casting, found the locations the next day, and then proceeded to film for 36
straight hours. He collapsed in exhaustion at the end, and his friend and
mentor, director Heinosuke Gosho, edited for him. (No extant prints, negative
or script.)

Pure Love (Junjo)
pr: Shochiku (Kamata); orig. sc: Ayame Mizushima; ph: Shojiro Sugimoto;
cast; Mitsuko Takao, Shoichi Kofujita, Haruo Takeda, Eiko Komatsu, Hatsuko Tsukioka et al. Silent. Lyrical story of the sort thought to appeal to young
girls. In 1960 Naruse felt this medium-length film was very similar to his
current style. (No extant prints, negative or script.)

Hard Times (Fukeiki Jidai)
pr: Shochiku (Kamata); orig. idea: Naruse; sc: Takao Yanai; ph: Shojiro
Sugimoto; cast: Tatsuo Saito, Tomio Aoki, Takeshi Sakamoto, Tokuji Kobayashi, Hiroko Kawasaki et al. Silent. Another slapstick comedy, not Naruse's element. (No extant prints, negative or script.)

Love Is Strength (Ai wa Chikara Da)
pr: Shochiku (Kamata); orig. sc: Takao Yanai; ph: Shojiro Sugimoto; cast:
Ichiro Yuki, Shizue Tatsuta, Hiroko Kawasaki, Teruo Mori, Haruo Takeda et
al. Melodrama that was a good script, Naruse said, but when finished it was
shelved. (No extant prints, negative or script.)

A Record of Shameless Newlyweds (Oshikiri Shinkonki)
pr: Shochiku (Kamata); orig. story: Naruse; sc: Tadao Ikeda; ph: Shojiro
Sugimoto; cast: Hisao Furuya, Mariko Aoyama, Midori Matsuba, Teruo Mori
et al. Silent. Naruse considered this a failure, showing his own weaknesses
despite Ikeda's rewrite. He was accused of copying Ozu, and the film, though
actually his third, was shelved for a long time. (No extant prints, negative or
script.)

1931 *Now Don't Get Excited (Nee Kofun Shicha Iya yo)*
pr: Shochiku (Kamata); orig. sc: Tadao Ikeda; ph: Shojiro Sugimoto; cast:
Tomio Yokoo, Eiran Yoshikawa, Junko Hara, Tokio Seki, Teruko Wakamizu
et al. Silent. Another slapstick comedy. Naruse began to fear he would never
be allowed to make good films, and hit on the idea of doing what he wanted
and inserting token gags at necessary intervals. (No extant prints, negative
or script.)

Screams from the Second Floor (Nikai no Himei)
pr: Shochiku (Kamata); orig. sc: Naruse; ph: Mitsuo Miura; cast: Hisao
Furuya, Nobuko Wakaba, Masao Hayama, Osamu Soga, Isamu Yamaguchi

et al. Silent. Naruse now began to write from his own life experience (he was a second-floor boarder over a sushi shop). This and the following were films about low-paid white collar workers in new housing developments. (No extant prints, negative or script.)

Flunky, Work Hard! (Koshiben Gambare)
pr: Shochiku (Kamata); orig. sc: Naruse; ph: Mitsuo Miura; cast: Isamu Yamaguchi, Tomoko Naniwa, Seiichi Kato, Hideo Sugawara, Tokio Seki et al. Silent. Sad comedy of contrast between rich and poor as an impoverished insurance salesman desperately tries to sell accident coverage to a wealthy woman with five children while his own uninsured child is hit by a train. (FC; negative at Shochiku, Tokyo.)

Fickleness Gets on the Train (Uwaki wa Kisha ni Notte)
pr: Shochiku (Kamata); orig. sc: Naruse; ph: Mitsuo Miura; cast: Isamu Yamaguchi, Tomoko Naniwa, Masao Hayama, Eiichi Takamatsu, Teruko Wakamizu et al. Silent. Life in the lowest echelons of salaried workers, set in a new suburban housing development. (No extant prints, negative or script.)

The Strength of a Moustache (Hige no Chikara)
pr: Shochiku (Kamata); orig. sc: Naruse; ph: Suketaro Inokai; cast: Kenichi Miyajima, Tomoko Naniwa, Tokkan Kozo (Tomio Aoki), Keinosuke Sakai, Reiko Tani et al. Silent. Another low-salaried workers' comedy with contrast between rich and poor. A boy whose father works as a chauffeur admires him because his moustache is better looking than the employer's. The jealous employer fires the father, but hires him back again when he finds a miracle hair grower. The son, however, no longer thinks his father is so great. (No extant prints, negative or script.)

Under the Neighbors' Roof (Tonari no Yane no Shita)
pr: Shochiku (Kamata); orig. sc: Yoshio Kimura; ph: Suketaro Inokai; cast: Shigeru Ogura, Tomoko Naniwa, Taeko Kiyokawa, Takeshi Sakamoto et al. Silent. Another low-salaried workers' drama. (No extant prints, negative or script.)

1932 ### *Ladies, Be Careful of Your Sleeves (Onna wa Tamoto o Goyojin)*
pr: Shochiku (Kamata); orig. sc: Naruse; ph: Suketaro Inokai; cast: Kenji Oyama, Shigeru Ogura, Einosuke Naka, Kyoko Mitsukawa et al. Silent. Slapstick comedy. (No extant prints, negative or script.)

Crying to the Blue Sky (Aozora ni Naku)
pr: Shochiku (Kamata); orig. sc: Ayame Mizushima; ph: Suketaro Inokai; cast: Hideo Sugawara, Mitsuko Takao, Tokkan Kozo (Tomio Aoki), Shoichi Nodera, Tokuji Kobayashi et al. Silent. A return to the pure lyricism of Naruse's second film, *Pure Love*, with the same scenarist. (No extant prints, negative or script.)

Be Great! (Eraku Nare)
pr: Shochiku (Kamata); orig. sc: Naruse; ph: Suketaro Inokai; cast: Shigeru Ogura, Tomoko Naniwa, Tokkan Kozo (Tomio Aoki), Reiko Tani, Masao Haya-

ma et al. Silent. Low-salaried workers' drama along the lines of Naruse's 1931 *Flunky, Work Hard!*, not a fully developed feature. (No extant prints, negative or script.)

Motheaten Spring (*Mushibameru Haru*)
pr: Shochiku (Kamata); orig. story: Kan Kikuchi; sc: Takashi Oda; ph: Suketaro Inokai; cast: Kinuko Wakamizu, Yumeko Aizome, Sumiko Mizukubo, Hideo Fujino, Utako Suzuki et al. Silent. Melodramatic love story about a middle-class family on the decline because of corruption in the father's business. The oldest daughter gives up the man she loves, the middle daughter still hopes for an easy life, and the youngest tries to become independent by finding a job. Naruse's first commercial success, and the first time he was given literary material to direct. *KJ* #6. (No extant prints, negative or script.)

Chocolate Girl (*Chokoreito Garu*)
pr: Shochiku (Kamata); orig. sc: Ryuji Nagami; ph: Suketaro Inokai; cast: Sumiko Mizukubo, Tatsuko Fuji, Tokkan Kozo (Tomio Aoki), Ichiro Yuki, Jun Arai et al. Silent. Combination of styles Naruse had practiced to date — slapstick, pure love and melodrama — and his favorite of this era, an idea suggested to him by Kogo Noda, Ozu's scenarist. A girl who works in a candy shop is invited to an upper class party by a friend who wants to pass her off as his sister. The women take an immediate dislike to her because the men are attracted. She secretly begins to fall in love with one of them, but in the end marries a man chosen by her mother. (No extant prints, negative or script.)

Not Blood Relations (*Nasanu Naka*)
pr: Shochiku (Kamata); orig. story: Shunyo Yanagawa; sc: Kogo Noda; ph: Suketaro Inokai; cast: Shinyo Nara, Yukiko Tsukuba, Yoshiko Okada, Joji Oka et al. Silent. Melodrama Naruse did not like, but appreciated that he was allowed a star cast. A young woman who went off to Hollywood to become a star returns rich and famous and sets out to find the daughter she left behind. Her brother, a gangster, helps her intimidate her ex-husband and mother-in-law, and she succeeds in wresting the girl away from the step-mother she loves. In the end, however, the movie star gives in to the child's love for the woman who has taken care of her and returns to America. (FC, negative at Shochiku, Tokyo.)

1933　### *Apart from You (*Kimi to Wakarete*)
pr: Shochiku (Kamata); orig. sc: Naruse; ph: Suketaro Inokai; cast: Mitsuko Yoshikawa, Akio Isono, Jun Arai, Sumiko Mizukubo, Tokkan Kozo (Tomio Aoki) et al. Silent. Love melodrama full of excellent character details and vignettes of the geisha world. A young girl who has been forced to become a geisha to help support her family with a lazy, drunkard father is in love with son of an older geisha. The boy is ashamed of his mother's profession and begins to run around with a rough crowd. The girl takes him to see her family in a seaside town and they have a few peaceful moments together while she urges him to mend his ways and take care of his mother. They recognize their love for each other, but the girl has to leave to find more lucrative work in

order to prevent her younger sister from becoming a geisha too. *KJ* #4. (FC; negative at Shochiku, Tokyo.)

Every Night Dreams (Yogoto no Yume)

pr: Shochiku (Kamata); orig. idea: Naruse; sc: Tadao Ikeda; ph: Suketaro Inokai; cast: Tatsuo Saito, Sumiko Kurishima, Teruko Kojima, Mitsuko Yoshi-kawa, Jun Arai et al. Silent. Melodrama about the poor, with a visual influence of von Sternberg's 1928 *The Docks of New York*. A woman with a small boy who has been deserted by her husband is forced to earn a living as harbor prostitute. One day she comes home to find her husband returned. He promises to find work so that she can give up her trade, but even with the neighbors' help he fails to come up with anything. When their son is injured the wife has to resume streetwalking to pay the medical bills, but her desperate husband tries to rob a safe. Pursued by the police, he decides everyone will be better off without him and commits suicide, leaving the wife with nothing more than the hope her son will grow strong. *KJ* #3. (FC; negative at Shochiku, Tokyo.)

A Man with a Married Woman's Hairdo (Boku no Marumage)

pr: Shochiku (Kamata); orig. sc: Ryosuke Saito; ph: Suketaro Inokai; cast: Mitsugu Fujii, Sumiko Mizukubo, Jun Arai, Shinichi Himori, Reiko Tani et al. Silent. Naruse remembered this as a not very impressive film. (No extant prints, negative or script.)

Two Eyes (Sobo)

pr: Shochiku (Kamata); orig. story: Masao Kume; sc: Takao Yanai; ph: Suketaro Inokai; cast: Kinuyo Tanaka, Yumeko Aizome, Joji Oka, Mitsugu Fujii, Yukichi Iwata et al. Silent. Melodrama in which Naruse was grateful for the chance to use a star like Tanaka. (No extant prints, negative or script.)

1934   ### Street without End (Kagirinaki Hodo)

pr: Shochiku (Kamata); orig. story: Komatsu Kitamura; sc: Tomizo Ikeda; ph: Suketaro Inokai; cast: Kimiko Nakada, Chiyoko Katori, Setsuko Shinobu, Akio Isono et al. Silent. Melodrama based on a newspaper serial about the love and marriage of a girl who works in a tea salon. No one else in the company wanted to film it, and Naruse did so only because he was promised his next film would be something he wanted to make. But Naruse left Shochiku after this because he was neither allowed to make talkies nor paid a living wage. (FC; negative at Shochiku, Tokyo.)

1935   ### *Three Sisters with Maiden Hearts (Otome-gokoro Sannin Shimai)

pr: PCL; orig. story: Yasunari Kawabata; sc: Naruse; ph: Hiroshi Suzuki; music: Kyosuke Kami; cast: Chikako Hosokawa, Masako Tsutsumi, Tatsuko Ume-zono, Osamu Takizawa, Heihachiro Okawa et al. Talkie. Melodrama with a "downtown" setting in Tokyo's Asakusa district. Three sisters are treated virtually as slaves by their mother, who seeks to make shamisen street musi-cians of them. The older sister runs off with her lover and disappears, while the middle sister does as her fearsome mother commands. One day the middle sister meets her older sister, who is looking for money to return with her husband to his home town. Their mother refuses to help, and the girl decides to enlist some of her old hoodlum friends in a badger game. The man they cheat turns out to be the youngest sister's boyfriend, and the middle sister is injured in the escape fray. Hiding her pain, she goes to the station to see her older sister off. Naruse understandably overdid the sound. (FC; dupe positive at Toho, Tokyo.)

The Actress and the Poet *(Joyu to Shijin)*
pr: PCL; orig. story: Minoru Nakano; sc: Ryuji Nagami; ph: Hiroshi Suzuki; music: Kyosuke Kami; cast: Sachiko Chiba, Hiroshi Uruki, Kamatari Fujiwara, Haruko Toda, Kimba Sanyutei et al. Talkie. Naruse referred to this as a stopgap kind of film during which he was still getting used to the problems of sound recording. (No extant prints; dupe positive at Toho, Tokyo.)

Wife! Be Like a Rose!/Kimiko *(Tsuma yo Bara no Yo ni)*
pr: PCL; orig. story: Minoru Nakano; sc: Naruse; ph: Hiroshi Suzuki; music: Noboru Ito; cast: Sadao Maruyama, Tomoko Ito, Sachiko Chiba, Yuriko Hanabusa, Setsuko Horikoshi et al. Talkie. Naruse's first great success, starring his wife to be, Chiba. A bright office girl who lives with her poetess mother wants to get married. She finds out where her father is living with his mistress in the country and decides to go and persuade him to come back home. On arrival she sees the huge family, the poverty, and the mistress' love for the father and children. The father comes to town for the wedding, but it is obvious to all that he and the mother are unsuited for each other, and he returns to his other family. *KJ* #1. (FC; positive, dupe and negative at Toho, Tokyo.)

Five Men in the Circus *(Sakasu Gonin-gumi)*
pr: PCL; orig. story: Roppa Furukawa; sc: Ryuji Nagami and Kohei Ima; ph: Hiroshi Suzuki; music: Kyosuke Kami; cast: Masako Tsutsumi, Kamatari Fujiwara, Heihachiro Okawa, Hiroshi Uruki, Tatsuko Umezono et al. Naruse remembered this as a weak film along the lines of *The Actress and the Poet*, as a kind of rest between two important works. (No extant prints; dupe positive at Toho, Tokyo.)

The Girl in the Rumor *(Uwasa no Musume)*
pr: PCL; orig. sc: Naruse; ph: Hiroshi Suzuki; music: Noboru Ito; cast: Sachiko Chiba, Ko Mihashi, Tatsuko Umezono, Kamatari Fujiwara, Heihachiro Okawa et al. Naruse's first completely original script since his 1933 *Apart from You*, and a great success that ensured his being able to make what he wanted at PCL. Complex portrayal of family relations with two step-sisters, the older a very traditional type. The younger rebels when her father brings his mistress to live with them, not knowing the woman is really her own mother. *KJ* #8. (No extant prints; dupe positive at Toho, Tokyo.)

1936　### Kumoemon Tochuken *(Tochuken Kumoemon)*
pr: PCL; orig. story: Seika Mayama; sc: Naruse; ph: Hiroshi Suzuki; music: Noboru Ito; cast: Ryunosuke Tsukigata, Chikako Hosokawa, Sachiko Chiba, Kaoru Ito, Masao Mishima et al. Project handed down from above about a Meiji era storyteller who was also a notorious roustabout. Naruse had great diffi-

culties with the actors, and the reaction to his script was that the film was about the storyteller's wife, not the man himself. Very talky and slow moving. (FC; dupe positive at Toho, Tokyo.)

The Road I Travel with You (*Kimi to Iku Michi*)
pr: PCL; orig. story: Yukiko Miyake; sc: Naruse; ph: Hiroshi Suzuki; music: Noboru Ito; cast: Heihachiro Okawa, Hideo Saeki, Masako Tsutsumi, Tamae Kiyokawa, Kamatari Fujiwara et al. Based on a play by a woman writer, Naruse remembered this as a very lukewarm film. (No extant prints; dupe positive at Toho, Tokyo.)

Morning's Tree-Lined Street (*Asa no Namikimichi*)
pr: PCL; orig. sc: Naruse; ph: Hiroshi Suzuki; music: Noboru Ito; cast: Sachiko Chiba, Heihachiro Okawa, Ranko Akagi, Hatsuko Natsume, Misao Yamaguchi et al. Recognizing that he had entered a slump at this time, Naruse complained of the uniformity of PCL and the necessity of using its contract stars. (No extant prints; dupe positive at Toho, Tokyo.)

1937   ### A Woman's Sorrows (*Nyonin Aishu*)
pr: PCL; orig. sc: Naruse and Chikao Tanaka; ph: Mitsuo Miura; music: Yoshi Eguchi; cast: Takako Irie, Hyo Kitazawa, Heihachiro Okawa, Ko Mihashi, Kaoru Ito et al. Naruse said this was also not an impressive film, and that he did not realize at the time that he should not be writing his own scripts. (No extant prints; dupe positive at Toho, Tokyo.)

Avalanche (*Nadare*)
pr: PCL; orig. story: Jiro Osaragi; sc: Naruse; asst. dirs: Akira Kurosawa and Matsuo Kishi; ph: Masaya Tachibana; music: Nobuo Iida; cast: Noboru Kiritachi, Ranko Edogawa, Hideo Saeki, Sadao Maruyama, Yuriko Hanabusa et al. Naruse considered this another failure. (No extant prints; dupe positive at Toho, Tokyo.)

Learn from Experience, Parts I, II (*Kafuku I, II*)
pr: Toho Tokyo; orig. story: Kan Kikuchi; sc: Fumio Iwasaki; ph: Mitsuo Miura; music: Takio Niki (Part I), Noboru Ito (Part II); cast: Takako Irie, Minoru Takada, Chieko Takehisa, Yumeko Aizome, Sadao Maruyama et al. Naruse lamented his inability to refuse anything he was asked to do, and described this as another failure. (No extant prints; dupe positive at Toho, Tokyo.)

1938   ### Tsuruhachi and Tsurujiro (*Tsuruhachi Tsurujiro*)
pr: Toho Tokyo; orig. story: Matsutaro Kawaguchi; sc: Naruse; ph: Takeo Ito; music: Nobuo Iida; cast: Kazuo Hasegawa, Isuzu Yamada, Kamatari Fujiwara, Heihachiro Okawa, Masao Mishima et al. Love story of competition and self-sacrifice set at the end of the Meiji era. Tsuruhachi the shamisen player and Tsurujiro the ballad singer are a professional team, but they fight continually. They split up, but Tsurujiro does not thrive on his own. They reunite, but when Tsurujiro realizes Tsuruhachi is in love, he picks a fight with her to cause a permanent break that will allow her to marry. (FC; positive and dupe at Toho, Tokyo.)

1939 **The Whole Family Works (Hataraku Ikka)*
pr: Toho; orig. story: Sunao Tokunaga; sc: Naruse; ph: Hiroshi Suzuki; music: Tadashi Ota; cast: Musei Tokugawa, Noriko Homma, Akira Ubukata, Kaoru Ito, et al. Skirting the requirements of national policy propaganda films, Naruse makes a film about the day-to-day life of the working poor. All eleven members of this printer's family are forced to work so that they can eat, including the grandparents and young children. When the oldest son wishes to quit work in order to go to school, a survival crisis ensues. (FC; dupe positive at Toho, Tokyo.)

Sincerity (Magokoro)
pr: Toho; orig. story: Yojiro Ishizaka; sc: Naruse; ph: Hiroshi Suzuki; music: Tadashi Hattori; cast: Takako Irie, Minoru Takada, Etchan, Sachiko Murase, Teruko Kato et al. Naruse called this an ordinary parent-child film. (No extant prints; dupe positive at Toho, Tokyo.)

1940 *Traveling Actors (Tabi Yakusha)*
pr: Toho; orig. story: Mushu Ui; sc: Naruse; ph: Seiichi Kitsuka; music: Fumio Hayasaka; cast: Kamatari Fujiwara, Ko Mihashi, Hisako Yamane, Taizo Fukami, Sugiko Ise et al. Pathos and comedy in the life of a family of traveling actors. Naruse liked this film and sought to emphasize the humorous aspects at a time when most films were grim, but it was heavily cut. (No extant prints; dupe positive at Toho, Tokyo.)

1941 *A Face from the Past (Natsukashi no Kao)*
pr: Toho (Kyoto); orig. sc: Naruse; ph: Seiichi Kitsuka; music: Tadashi Ota; cast: Ranko Hanai, Masaru Odaka, Soji Kiyokawa, Takashi Odaka et al. Short film about a family that sees their son in a newsreel, but the short length prevented it from attaining any critical notice. (No extant prints; dupe positive at Toho, Tokyo.)

Shanghai Moon (Shanhai no Tsuki)
pr: Toho; orig. idea: Keiji Matsuzaki; sc: Yusaku Yamagata; ph: Akira Mimura; music: Tadashi Hattori; cast: Isuzu Yamada, Den Ohinata, Heihachiro Okawa, Soji Kiyokawa, Hideo Saeki et al. The most popular star of the day, Yamada, playing a Chinese girl in a film Naruse felt was not his type of material. He resented the strictures of wartime just when he was beginning to find himself. (No extant prints; dupe positive at Toho, Tokyo.)

Hideko the Bus Conductor (Hideko no Shasho-san)
pr: Nanyo; orig. story: Masuji Ibuse; sc: Naruse; ph: Ken Azuma; music: Nobuo Iida; cast: Hideko Takamine, Keita Fujiwara, Daijiro Natsukawa, Tamae Kiyokawa, Masako Kawada et al. Sentimental comedy about a girl who takes tickets on a rickety old bus in a small country town. She helps everyone out of financial difficulties by persuading a writer from Tokyo staying in the area to write tour information, which she recites to the passengers. Caricature of the do-nothing swelled-head company president. (FC; dupe positive at Toho, Tokyo.)

1942   *Mother Never Dies (Haha wa Shinazu)*
pr: Toho; orig. story: Sensuke Kochi; sc: Katsuhito Inomata; ph: Seiichi Kitsuka; music: Tadashi Hattori; cast: Takako Irie, Ichiro Sugai, Keita Fujiwara,
Susumu Fujita, Yukiko Todoroki et al. Undistinguished film glorifying a
mother's tribulations, about which Naruse commented that he was unable
even in wartime to make films in which soldiers appeared. (No extant prints;
dupe positive at Toho, Tokyo.)

1943   *The Song Lantern (Uta Andon)*
pr: Toho; orig. story: Kyoka Izumi; sc: Mantaro Kubota; ph: Asakazu Nakai;
music: Shiro Fukai; cast: Shotaro Hanayagi, Isuzu Yamada, Kan Ishii, Masao
Murata, Eijiro Yanagi et al. Naruse escapes into the Meiji era and the traditional performing arts. A Noh actor is disowned by his father for causing the
death of an old man from shock over his rudeness. The young man becomes a
street musician and wanders for years until he is finally able to help the
daughter of the man who died, and in the process find his father's forgiveness.
(FC; dupe positive at Toho, Tokyo.)

1944   *This Happy Life (Tanoshiki Kana Jinsei)*
pr: Toho; orig. sc: Toshio Yasumi and Naruse; ph: Takeo Ito; music: Seiichi
Suzuki; cast: Kingoro Yanagiya, Hisako Yamane, Entatsu Yokoyama, Meiko
Nakamura, Tamae Kiyokawa et al. Slapstick comedy about a Jack of all trades
who moves into a small town. (FC; dupe positive at Toho, Tokyo.)

The Way of Drama (Shibaido)
pr: Toho; orig. story: Koen Hasegawa; sc: Toshio Yasumi; ph: Kinya Ogura;
music: Yasuji Kiyose; cast: Kazuo Hasegawa, Isuzu Yamada, Roppa Furukawa, Ranko Hanai, Tomosaburo Ii et al. A traditional performing arts film
along the lines of Naruse's 1943 *Song Lantern*; he enjoyed filming it. (No
extant prints; dupe positive at Toho, Tokyo.)

1945   *Until Victory Day (Shori no Hi Made)*
pr: Toho; orig. sc: Hachiro Sato; ph: Masaya Tachibana and Seiichi Kitsuka;
music: Seiichi Suzuki; cast: Roppa Furukawa, Musei Tokugawa, Hideko
Takamine, Isuzu Yamada, Kenichi Enomoto et al. A non-story made strictly
for the troops at the front. (No extant prints; dupe positive at Toho, Tokyo.)

*A Tale of Archery at the Sanjusangendo (Sanjusangendo Toshiya
Monogatari)*
pr: Toho; orig. sc: Hideo Oguni; ph: Hiroshi Suzuki; cast: Kazuo Hasegawa,
Kinuyo Tanaka, Torazo Hirosawa et al. Naruse's first period film, made in
Kyoto while Tokyo burned. He was not sure if and where it was released.
(No extant prints; dupe positive at Toho, Tokyo.)

1946   *The Descendants of Taro Urashima (Urashima Taro no Koei)*
pr: Toho; orig. sc: Ryuichiro Yagi; ph: Kazuo Yamazaki; music: Kazuo Yamada;
cast: Susumu Fujita, Hideko Takamine, Hisako Yamane, Haruko Sugimura,
Nobuo Nakamura et al. Naruse implied that this postwar democracy film, reputed to be a copy of Frank Capra's style, was content that was forced on

him in the same way his wartime films had been. (No extant prints; dupe
positive at Toho, Tokyo.)

Both You and I (Ore mo Omae mo)
pr: Toho; orig. sc: Naruse; ph: Kazuo Yamazaki; music: Noboru Ito; cast:
Entatsu Yokoyama, Achako Hanabishi, Hisako Yamane, Ichiro Sugai, Itoko
Kono et al. Another undistinguished work emphasizing the spirit of labor
unions. Naruse complained that this was an era of noisy demands. (No extant
prints; dupe positive at Toho, Tokyo.)

1947   *Four Love Stories, Part II: Even Parting is Enjoyable (Yottsu no Koi
no Monogatari, II: Wakare mo Tanoshi)*
pr: Toho; orig. sc: Hideo Oguni; ph: Seiichi Kitsuka; cast: Michiyo Kogure,
Isao Numazaki, Chieko Takehisa et al. A four-part omnibus film made by
Naruse, Shiro Toyoda, Kajiro Yamamoto and Teinosuke Kinugasa to celebrate
the complete postwar revival of Toho. Naruse's part about an older dancer and
her love for a younger man was not his own project, but one that was supposed to have been made by Yutaka Abe. (FC; dupe positive at Toho, Tokyo.)

Spring Awakens (Haru no Mezame)
pr: Toho; orig. sc: Toshio Yasumi and Naruse; ph: Shunichiro Nakao; music:
Seiichi Suzuki; cast: Yoshiko Kuga, Hiroyuki Sugi, Kazumasa Hoshino, Kazumi
Hanabusa, Haruko Sugimura et al. This and the following two films were
planned as a series, and Naruse decided to stop writing scripts alone. Turmoil
within Toho prevented the earlier realization of the projects. (No extant prints;
dupe positive at Toho, Tokyo.)

1949   *Delinquent Girl (Furyo Shojo)*
pr: Toyoko Eiga; orig. story: Taijiro Tamura; sc: Naruse; ph: Masao Tamai; music: Ryoichi Hattori; cast: Masayuki Mori, Yoshiko Kuga, Mitsuko Yoshikawa,
Akihiko Katayama, Shin Tokudaiji et al. Delinquent genre film with emphasis
on the erotic that was a commercial success. Naruse knew the material was
unsuited to him, but he had left Toho and had to work if he wanted to eat. (No
extant prints, negative or script.)

1950   *Conduct Report on Professor Ishinaka (Ishinaka Sensei Gyojoki)*
pr: Shin Toho; orig. story: Yojiro Ishizaka; sc: Ryuichiro Yagi; ph: Hiroshi
Suzuki; music: Tadashi Hattori; cast: Ryo Ikebe, Toshiro Mifune, Yoko Sugi,
Yuji Hori, Setsuko Wakayama et al. A comedy full of regional flavor that Naruse
said he enjoyed directing at last. (No extant prints; dupe positive at Toho,
Tokyo.)

The Angry Street (Ikari no Machi)
pr: Toho; orig. story: Fumio Niwa; sc: Naruse and Motosada Nishikame; ph:
Masao Tamai; music: Nobuo Iida; cast: Yasumi Hara, Yoshiko Kuga, Yuriko
Hamada, Setsuko Wakayama, Jukichi Uno et al. Melodrama of which Naruse
did not seem particularly proud. (No extant prints; dupe positive at Toho,
Tokyo.)

White Beast (*Shiroi Yaju*)

pr: Toho; orig. sc: Naruse and Motosada Nishikame; ph: Masao Tamai; music: Akira Ifukube; cast: Mitsuko Miura, So Yamamura, Noriko Sengoku, Tanie Kitabayashi, Yaeko Izumo et al. This sex film about young streetwalkers was begun while Naruse was freelancing, but the star, Miura, left for the U.S. when it was nearly finished, so completion and release were delayed. (No extant prints; dupe positive at Toho, Tokyo.)

The Battle of Roses (*Bara Gassen*)

pr: Eiga Geijutsu Kyokai/Shochiku (Kyoto); orig. story: Fumio Niwa; sc: Motosada Nishikame; ph: Haruo Takeno; music: Seiichi Suzuki; cast: Kuniko Miyake, Setsuko Wakayama, Yoko Katsuragi, Koji Tsuruta, Toru Abe et al. Melodrama adapted from a prewar serialized novel about a girl who works in a cosmetics firm and her two younger sisters. Naruse did not even particularly like the original novel, and chastised himself for not proposing better material, which Shochiku probably would have let him make. (FC; negative at Shochiku, Tokyo.)

1951   ### *Ginza Cosmetics (Ginza Gesho)*

pr: Shin Toho; orig. story: Tomoichiro Inoue; sc: Matsuo Kishi; ph: Akira Mimura; music: Seiichi Suzuki; cast: Kinuyo Tanaka, Ranko Hanai, Yuji Hori, Eijiro Tono, Eijiro Yanagi et al. Naruse finally emerges from his postwar slump with material related closely to his own life experience—the script has little to do with the original and is based largely on his and Kishi's own Ginza observations. A Ginza bar hostess approaching middle age has worked for ten years to support her child, and her ex-husband, who comes to ask for money from time to time. She tries to help the faltering bar by seeking out a rich patron, whose sexual attentions she refuses, and she begins to dream of escape when a rich young man from the country she entertains for a married friend who is deceiving her husband begins to talk of poetry. But the young man falls in love with a younger woman, and the hostess is left struggling to take care of her son. Full flavor of Naruse's trapped characters. (FC; negative at Kokusai Hoei, Tokyo.)

Dancing Girl (*Maihime*)

pr: Toho; orig. story: Yasunari Kawabata; sc: Kaneto Shindo; ph: Asakazu Nakai; music: Ichiro Saito; cast: Mieko Takamine, So Yamamura, Mariko Okada, Hiroshi Nihonyanagi, Akihiko Katayama et al. Naruse said he did not dislike this film, but felt that he was not very good at long works, and that while he liked Kawabata, this original showed the difficulty of his recent writing. (No extant prints; dupe positive at Toho, Tokyo.)

Repast (Meshi)

pr: Toho; orig. novel: Fumiko Hayashi; ed. supervision: Yasunari Kawabata; sc: Sumie Tanaka and Toshiro Ide; ph: Masao Tamai; music: Fumio Hayasaka; cast: Ken Uehara, Setsuko Hara, Yukiko Shimazaki, Yoko Sugi, Eitaro Shindo et al. Superb psychological description with a minimum of plot and a maximum of nuance, the kind of woman's film Ozu tried to make in his 1952 *Flavor of Green Tea over Rice* but could not surpass Naruse. A childless couple living in the Osaka suburbs are drifting apart. The woman dreams of escape from the dreary life of a low-salaried white-collar worker's wife, and returns to her family in Tokyo, where she hopes to find a job. In a trapped ending Naruse added to Hayashi's unfinished novel, the woman resigns herself to going back to her husband. *KJ* #2. (FC; positive and dupe at Toho, Tokyo.)

1952 *Okuni and Gohei (Okuni to Gohei)*
pr: Toho; orig. story: Junichiro Tanizaki; sc: Toshio Yasumi; ph: Kazuo Yamada; music: Ichiro Saito; cast: Michiyo Kogure, Tomoemon Otani, So Yamamura, Jun Tazaki, Eiko Miyoshi et al. Naruse's second attempt at period drama, and in his own opinion a failure, for which he blamed the company for forcing him to make. (No extant prints; dupe positive at Toho, Tokyo.)

* Mother (Okasan)
pr: Shin Toho; sc: Yoko Mizuki (based on a prizewinning story in a contest for children); ph: Hiroshi Suzuki; music: Ichiro Saito; cast: Kinuyo Tanaka, Kyoko Kagawa, Akihiko Katayama, Eiji Okada et al. The world Naruse said he understood best. A widow with three children tries to make a go of the drycleaning and dyeing business left by her husband. Told from the older daughter's viewpoint, the unfolding is sentimental, but justifiably so. *KJ* #7. (FC; negative at Kokusai Hoei, Tokyo.)

*Lightning (Inazuma)
pr: Daiei; orig. novel: Fumiko Hayashi; sc: Sumie Tanaka; ph: Shigeyoshi Mine; music: Ichiro Saito; cast: Hideko Takamine, Sakae Ozawa, Mitsuko Miura, Jun Negami, Kyoko Kagawa et al. Naruse's own project, story of a poor and weak-willed mother with four children by different fathers. The youngest, unmarried daughter refuses an unsavory marriage proposal and tries to break away from the sordidness around her, but in the end she cannot help being kind to her anxious, pathetic mother, who comes looking for her. *KJ* #2. (FC; negative at Daiei, Tokyo.)

1953 *Husband and Wife (Fufu)*
pr: Toho; orig. sc: Yoko Mizuki and Toshiro Ide; ph: Asakazu Nakai; music: Ichiro Saito; cast: Ken Uehara, Yoko Sugi, Rentaro Mikuni, Keiju Kobayashi, Kamatari Fujiwara et al. Conceived as a sequel to the 1951 *Repast*. A low-salaried white-collar worker and his wife live in a rented room and are growing tired of each other. The recently widowed landlord, a nervy, curious character, brings some distraction into their lives. (No extant prints, dupe positive at Toho, Tokyo.)

* Wife (Tsuma)
pr: Toho; orig. story: Fumiko Hayashi; sc: Toshiro Ide; ph: Masao Tamai; music: Ichiro Saito; cast: Ken Uehara, Mieko Takamine, Yatsuko Tanami, Rentaro Mikuni, Michiyo Aratama et al. With this film Naruse sought to round out his trilogy on dangerous periods of marriage, though all three films have inconclusive endings. A white-collar worker and his wife are drifting apart. Money, the wife's inability to serve her husband in the tradi-

tional way, and another woman all put strains on the relationship. When the wife realizes she may lose him, she fights desperately and unattractively to hold on. (FC; dupe positive at Toho, Tokyo.)

Older Brother, Younger Sister (Ani Imoto)
pr: Daiei; orig. story: Saisei Muroo; sc: Yoko Mizuki; ph: Shigeyoshi Mine; music: Ichiro Saito; cast: Machiko Kyo, Masayuki Mori, Yoshiko Kuga, Reisaburo Yamamoto, Eiji Funakoshi et al. Siblings grow up and grow apart, unable to protect each other or express their love for each other. A younger sister who has gone to Tokyo to work comes home pregnant by a student who has deserted her. Her rough, rowdy brother abuses her, and then beats up the student when he comes inquiring after her a year later. The youngest sister's marriage prospects are ruined as a result of her sister's misfortune, and in a last family reunion, the city sister appears to have become a streetwalker, and her brother throws her out again. (FC; negative at Daiei, Tokyo.)

1954 *Sound of the Mountain (Yama no Oto)*
pr: Toho; orig. novel: Yasunari Kawabata; sc: Yoko Mizuki; ph: Masao Tamai; music: Ichiro Saito; cast: Setsuko Hara, So Yamamura, Ken Uehara, Yatsuko Tanami, Chieko Nakakita et al. Naruse's own project, with sets designed to look like Kawabata's house, and shot in the vicinity. Story of the affection between a father and daughter-in-law, whose husband's mistress has a baby, while she herself has an abortion. It is only her father-in-law who makes the young woman persevere. KJ #6. (FC; positive and dupe at Toho, Tokyo.)

Late Chrysanthemums (Bangiku)
pr: Toho; orig. stories: Fumiko Hayashi; sc: Sumie Tanaka and Toshiro Ide; ph: Masao Tamai; music: Ichiro Saito; cast: Haruko Sugimura, Yuko Mochizuki, Chikako Hosokawa, Sadako Sawamura, Ken Uehara et al. Naruse's own project, as he was reading much of Hayashi's work at the time. Fashioned from three short stories, it returns to the sad world of the aging geisha he had touched on in his 1933 *Apart from You*. Four retired geisha find nothing but loneliness, disillusionment and continuing deceit by men in middle age. Power of the film not in plot, but eye movements, detailed actions that reveal character. KJ #7. (FC; dupe positive at Toho, Tokyo.)

1955 *Floating Clouds (Ukigumo)*
pr: Toho; orig. novel: Fumiko Hayashi; sc: Yoko Mizuki; asst. dir: Kihachi Okamoto; ph: Masao Tamai; music: Ichiro Saito; cast: Hideko Takamine, Masayuki Mori, Mariko Okada, Daisuke Kato, Chieko Nakakita et al. Naruse's most popular film, showing the problems of postwar life through the love of a young woman for a married man she met at the front in Southeast Asia during the war. She accepts every sort of humiliation at his hands —refusal to leave his wife, taking up with another mistress, and job transfers that leave her behind. Following him to a remote island, she dies before they can establish a life together. KJ #1. (FC; positive, dupe and dupe negative at Toho, Tokyo.)

The Kiss, Part III: Women's Ways (Kuchizuke, III: Onna Doshi)
pr: Toho; orig. story: Yojiro Ishizaka; sc: Zenzo Matsuyama; ph: Kazuo Yamazaki; music: Ichiro Saito; cast: Hideko Takamine, Meiko Nakamura, Keiju

Kobayashi, Ken Uehara, Hajime Izu et al. Naruse recognized this film as the beginning of another slump. Omnibus he coproduced, introducing two younger directors, Hideo Suzuki and Masanori Kakei. A doctor's childless wife finds his pretty nurse's diary and imagines a love affair from the girl's admiration for her husband. She conspires to get the girl married off, and succeeds, only to be paid for her spite by seeing the new replacement is even prettier. (PFA/TO; positive and dupe at Toho, Tokyo.)

1956 *Sudden Rain (Shu-u)*
pr: Toho; orig. story: Kunio Kishida; sc: Yoko Mizuki; ph: Masao Tamai; music: Ichiro Saito; cast: Setsuko Hara, Shuji Sano, Kyoko Kagawa, Keiju Kobayashi, Akemi Negishi et al. Episodic story of another middle-aged couple growing tired of each other in which Naruse felt he did not live up to the urbanity of the original. Hastily made for New Year's release, it contrasts this couple with some newlyweds, and further confuses their life with a relative's daughter who runs away from her husband. (Positive and dupe at Toho, Tokyo.)

A Wife's Heart (Tsuma no Kokoro)
pr: Toho; orig. sc: Toshiro Ide; ph: Masao Tamai; music: Ichiro Saito; cast: Hideko Takamine, Keiju Kobayashi, Toshiro Mifune, Yoko Sugi, Akemi Negishi et al. Feeling he had thoroughly portrayed the passive woman who is susceptible to men up through his 1955 *Floating Clouds*, Naruse wanted to show stronger women. The film is said to show total rigidity in the family system. (Positive and dupe at Toho, Tokyo.)

*Flowing (Nagareru)
pr: Toho; orig. story: Aya Koda; sc: Sumie Tanaka and Toshiro Ide; ph: Masao Tamai; music: Ichiro Saito; cast: Hideko Takamine, Isuzu Yamada, Kinuyo Tanaka, Mariko Okada, Sumiko Kurishima et al. The decline of the geisha world as observed by a meek and gentle maid in the home of a proud middle-aged geisha who fights to keep professional values against the pressure to decline into prostitution. Her daughter balks at her mother's stubbornness, and ends by taking in sewing work because her mother cannot provide for her, nor can she herself hope to make a good marriage. *KJ* #8. (FC, positive and dupe at Toho, Tokyo.)

1957 **Untamed (Arakure)*
pr: Toho; orig. story: Shusei Tokuda; sc: Yoko Mizuki; ph: Masao Tamai; music: Ichiro Saito; cast: Hideko Takamine, Ken Uehara, Masayuki Mori, Daisuke Kato, Eijiro Tono et al. Naruse wanted to make a film about a very strong woman, but complained people would only come to see abused, pathetic heroines. This heroine falls in love easily and is easily deceived. Believing she does as she pleases, in the end she is a victim of circumstance. (Positive and dupe at Toho, Tokyo.)

1958 *Anzukko (Anzukko)*
pr: Toho; orig. story: Saisei Muroo; sc: Sumie Tanaka and Naruse; ph: Masao Tamai; music: Ichiro Saito ;cast: Kyoko Kagawa, So Yamamura, Keiju Kobayashi, Daisuke Kato, Nobuo Nakamura et al. Dark psychological drama about a family unable to get along. Kyoko (nickname: Anzukko) marries a man who

was kind to her and her father during the war, but he is a novelist without talent and never gets published. Their relations cool, and she finds her only solace in visiting her father. (Positive and dupe at Toho, Tokyo.)

*Herringbone Clouds (Iwashigumo)
pr: Toho; orig. story: Tsuto Wada; sc: Shinobu Hashimoto; color 'scope ph: Masao Tamai; music: Ichiro Saito; cast: Chikage Awashima, Isao Kimura, Ganjiro Nakamura, Michiyo Aratama, Yoko Tsukasa et al. A woman trying to be independent in a traditional farming family. She is widowed and has difficulty with her mother-in-law and her own family. Trying to find some escape, she writes stories about farm life for a newspaper, but she falls in love with the married reporter, who leaves her when transferred to a new post. (FC; negative at Toho, Tokyo.)

1959   *Whistling in Kotan/A Whistle in My Heart (Kotan no Kuchibue)*
pr: Toho; orig. story: Nobuo Ishimori; sc: Shinobu Hashimoto; color 'scope ph: Masao Tamai; music: Akira Ifukube; cast: Akira Kubo, Ken Kubo, Ryoko Koda, Masayuki Mori, Eiko Miyoshi et al. Very sentimental story about rural life and racial prejudice in Hokkaido. (PFA/TO; negative at Toho, Tokyo.)

1960   **When a Woman Ascends the Stairs (Onna ga Kaidan o Agaru Toki)*
pr: Toho; orig. sc: Ryuzo Kikushima; 'scope ph: Masao Tamai; music: Toshiro Mayuzumi; cast: Hideko Takamine, Masayuki Mori, Tatsuya Nakadai, Reiko Dan, Daisuke Kato et al. Naruse's element again: the Ginza bar world. A widow who runs a bar finds nothing but exploitation by men and her greedy family. Trying to remain faithful to her dead husband, she fails as her emotions and her desire to lead a normal married life overcome her. But she spurns the one man who really loves her: the younger, financially insecure manager of her bar. (FC, PFA/TO, JS)

Daughters, Wives and a Mother (Musume Tsuma Haha)
pr: Toho; orig. sc: Toshiro Ide and Zenzo Matsuyama; color 'scope ph: Jun Yasumoto; music: Ichiro Saito; cast: Setsuko Hara, Hideko Takamine, Masayuki Mori, Aiko Mimasu, Reiko Dan et al. A sweeping portrait of the worst of the middle class through one extended family. All the relatives prey upon one woman whose husband has died and left her a large life insurance policy. A shrewish grandmother feels unwanted, a daughter's husband carries on with bar girls, and a son is deserted by his wife. The widow is the only one who shows any possibility of finding happiness through remarriage to a younger man. Many themes repeated from his 1952 *Lightning*. (Positive and negative at Toho, Tokyo.)

Evening Stream (Yoru no Nagare)
pr: Toho; orig. sc: Toshiro Ide, Zenzo Matsuyama; codir: Yuzo Kawashima; color 'scope ph: Tadashi Iimura and Jun Yasumoto; music: Ichiro Saito; cast: Yoko Tsukasa, Isuzu Yamada, Yumi Shirakawa, Takashi Shimura, Tatsuya Mihashi et al. Melodrama about a daughter who falls in love with her mother's lover and escapes into the world of the traditional geisha. Naruse filmed all of the older generation scenes and Japanese restaurant scenes, while

Kawashima did the younger generation and the geisha house scenes. (Positive and negative at Toho, Tokyo.)

The Approach of Autumn (Aki Tachinu)

pr: Toho; orig. sc: Ryozo Kasahara; 'scope ph: Jun Yasumoto; music: Ichiro Saito; cast: Nobuko Otowa, Yosuke Natsugi, Daisuke Kato, Chisako Hara, Seizaburo Kawazu et al. Sketches of lower-middle class life in the big city, in the first film bearing Naruse's name as producer. A boy whose father dies is sent to live with relatives who run a greengrocer's shop in Ginza. His mother works as a live-in hotel maid, and he eventually becomes friendly with the daughter of a kept woman. Made for release as a double bill with Kurosawa's *The Bad Sleep Well*. (Positive and negative at Toho, Tokyo.)

1961 *As a Wife, As a Woman/The Other Woman* (*Tsuma toshite Onna toshite*)

pr: Toho; orig. sc: Toshiro Ide and Zenzo Matsuyama; color 'scope ph: Jun Yasumoto; music: Ichiro Saito; cast: Hideko Takamine, Masayuki Mori, Chikage Awashima, Tatsuya Nakadai, Yuriko Hoshi et al. Melodrama about a girl who becomes the mistress of a wealthy professor. He takes the two children she bears him into his own childless home and sets her up as a bar madame. His wife finds out about the relationship and tries to prevent the woman from taking her children back. Theme that goes back to his 1932 *Not Blood Relations*. (JS)

1962 *Woman's Status* (*Onna no Za*)

pr: Toho; orig. sc: Toshiro Ide and Zenzo Matsuyama; 'scope ph: Jun Yasumoto; music: Ichiro Saito; cast: Hideko Takamine, Yoko Tsukasa, Reiko Dan, Akira Takarada, Chishu Ryu et al. Apparently such a mediocre film, it is not even accorded a place in film reference books. (Positive and negative at Toho, Tokyo.)

A Wanderer's Notebook/Lonely Lane (*Horoki*)

pr: Takarazuka Eiga/Toho; orig. story: Fumiko Hayashi; sc: Toshiro Ide and Sumie Tanaka; 'scope ph: Jun Yasumoto; music: Yuji Koseki; cast: Hideko Takamine, Akira Takarada, Daisuke Kato, Keiju Kobayashi, Kinuyo Tanaka et al. The life of writer Hayashi, adapted from her first autobiographical novel. The daughter of a traveling salesman moves all over the country and works to support herself and her mother when the two are abandoned. She sends her weak-willed mother back to the hopeless man she loves, works as a café waitress in Tokyo, and lives with various men as she gradually develops her passion for writing. Her success ruins her relationship with a writer who cannot get published. (Positive and negative at Toho, Tokyo.)

1963 *A Woman's Story* (*Onna no Rekishi*)

pr: Toho; orig. sc: Ryozo Kasahara; 'scope ph: Jun Yasumoto; music: Ichiro Saito; cast: Hideko Takamine, Akira Takarada, Tatsuya Nakadai, Yuriko Hoshi, Tsutomu Yamazaki et al. Another negligible work, not listed in film references. (Positive and negative at Toho, Tokyo.)

1964 *Yearning* (*Midareru*)

pr: Toho; orig. sc: Zenzo Matsuyama; 'scope ph: Jun Yasumoto; music: Ichiro

Saito; cast: Hideko Takamine, Yuzo Kayama, Mitsuko Kusabue, Yumi Shira-kawa, Aiko Mimasu et al. A story line that looks like a poor melodrama becomes a skillful psychological portrayal in Naruse's hands. A childless widow manages the store left by her husband in a provincial town, supporting her in-laws, including a young brother-in-law. Competition from new supermarkets leads the family to decide to change the business, cutting the diligent daughter-in-law out entirely. She had already hoped to turn the business over to the young brother, but he is lazy, incompetent, and refuses to get married. Finally he reveals that he has been in love with her for years, but she rejects him and returns to her own family home in another part of the country. He follows after her and commits suicide. (FC; negative at Toho, Tokyo.)

1966   *The Stranger within a Woman/The Thin Line (Onna no Naka ni Iru Tanin)*
pr: Toho; orig. story: Edward Ataya (phonetic); sc: Toshiro Ide; 'scope ph: Yasumichi Fukazawa; music: Hikaru Hayashi; cast: Keiju Kobayashi, Michiyo Aratama, Tatsuya Mihashi, Mitsuko Kusabue, Daisuke Kato et al. Unusual material for Naruse —a murder case he turns into a dark psychological study. An ordinary middle-class man murders his best friend's promiscuous wife, with whom he has been having an affair. No one suspects him, but he cannot bear his guilt and confesses all to his wife, who begs him to remain silent for the sake of her and the children. Realizing that he feels compelled to give himself up, she gives him an overdose of sleeping pills. *KJ* #10. (FC; negative at Toho, Tokyo.)

Hit and Run/Moment of Terror (Hikinige)
pr: Toho; orig. sc: Zenzo Matsuyama; 'scope ph: Rokuro Nishigaki; music: Masaru Sato; cast: Hideko Takamine, Eitaro Ozawa, Yoko Tsukasa, Toshio Kurosawa, Daisuke Kato et al. Melodrama of revenge. A widow's only son is killed in a car accident, and she accepts financial compensation from the man who confesses responsibility. Later she finds the woman who actually did it and seeks revenge, but the woman commits suicide. The widow is accused of murdering her, but she goes insane. (JS)

1967   **Scattered Clouds/Two in the Shadow (Midaregumo)*
pr: Toho; orig. sc: Nobuo Yamada; color 'scope ph: Yuzuru Aizawa; music: Toru Takemitsu; cast: Yuzo Kayama, Yoko Tsukasa, Daisuke Kato, Mitsuko Mori, Mitsuko Kusabue et al. Unlikely plot with a sensitive treatment. The husband of a pregnant young housewife is killed in a traffic accident just as his future was looking bright. The wife has an abortion, looks for work, and finally goes back to her home town in Hokkaido to work for relatives as a maid in their Japanese inn. She steadfastly refuses to forgive the young man respon-sible for the accident, though he has committed no crime and voluntarily sends her money from his meager salary every month. His own marriage prospects and future have been ruined by the accident, and he finds himself transferred to his company's branch in the widow's home town. They continually meet by accident and gradually fall in love, but at her earlier insistence, he has applied for another transfer and leaves for Southeast Asia. *KJ* #4. (FC, JS)

2 THE POSTWAR HUMANISTS

The end of the Pacific War in August 1945 heralded the advent of a cinema of new catch phrases for Japan. The U.S. Occupation of the defeated adversary brought with it a severe control of the film industry hardly varying in degree of censorship from the wartime Information Ministry. "National policy" films were forcibly replaced by "democratic" films, but even with the official guidelines, problems of interpretation were rampant.

The oldest generation had the most difficulty. Kenji Mizoguchi, for example, determined to make period films despite Occupation abhorrence of them, in 1946 managed to make the late eighteenth-century woodblock print artist Utamaro into a "democrat" simply because he did not (and could not) belong to the official hereditary Kano school of painters. The artist's democratic and emancipatory attitude toward women appeared to Mizoguchi to have consisted in falling in love with a number of them and painting them in the nude. The director would proceed to employ Christian imagery in his 1948 *Women of the Night*, about the plight of Osaka streetwalkers, whose patter necessarily includes a liberal sprinkling of American slang. Paradox may have been unavoidable.

Yasujiro Ozu similarly took to filming such unlikely subjects as the founding of an orphanage in his 1947 *Record of a Tenement Gentleman* and, for him, such awkwardly sordid material as a woman whose economic circumstances forced her to engage in prostitution while her husband was away at the front in *A Hen in the Wind*. Mikio Naruse fared worst of the three, making commercially successful sex films like *Delinquent Girl* (1949) and *White Beast* (1950). It would take films like Akira Kurosawa's *Ikiru* (1952) and Keisuke Kinoshita's *A Japanese Tragedy* (1953) to point out that "democracy" meant neither soliciting and then neglecting the people's claim to a decent life nor license to engage equally in the wrongs committed by others. Two decades later Shohei Imamura would be able to parody the popular notion of "democracy" as group sex in his 1966 *Pornographers*, but in the late 1940s it was very serious, if confusing business. It was only as the Occupation was preparing for withdrawal by April 1952 that the older generation of directors began to recover by returning to their prewar subject matter—Mizoguchi to his downtrodden women and period atmosphere, Ozu to family life removed from socio-political concerns, and Naruse to family life as an imprisonment in economic concerns.

The younger generation had less difficulty with the transition. Tadashi Imai (1912–), for example, who had made many of the most militaristic films during the war, glided easily into the Occupation command film *An Enemy of the People* (*Minshu no Teki*) in 1946, and by 1949 he was happily glorifying coeducational values and the P.T.A. in *Blue Mountains* (*Aoi Sammyaku*). By 1950 he had fully accepted democratic kissing in *Until the Day We Meet Again* (*Mata Au Hi Made*). Turning all the way to confirmed Communism and the succor of the underdog, the quality of his filmmaking remained subordinate to his political message until recently, when his politics gave way to commercialism in such endeavors as his 1976 remake of Naruse's *Older Brother, Younger Sister*.

Actress Hideko Takamine, like many others, groups Imai with Akira Kurosawa and Keisuke Kinoshita as most representative of the hopes and the reality of the postwar Japanese in her 1976 autobiography *Watashi no tosei nikki*, but the latter two directors have consistently surpassed Imai in the essentials of film storytelling: coherent structure and realistic characterization. The primacy of film aesthetics for Kurosawa and Kinoshita has been shared by Kon Ichikawa and Masaki Kobayashi, but all have a thematic concern in common. All can be counted among the postwar humanists.

"Humanism" carries a variety of connotations in Japan, where it is used as an English loan word in preference to any equivalent native term. Its dictionary definition describes the basic importance placed on human beings and their liberation, but in concrete terms it is its most recent historical usage that prevails in Japan, rather than the Renaissance ideal of humanistic studies. The humanism espoused by a Tadashi Imai is the "socialist humanism" that derives from the proletarian movement to revive the humanity of those who have been alienated by the capitalist system. But the more popular second definition of humanism is the one a Kurosawa, an Ichikawa, a Kinoshita or a Kobayashi would use in describing himself; as most people who still use the word in Japan define it, it is synonymous with humanitarianism.

As noted in Joseph L. Anderson and Donald Richie's *The Japanese Film* (1960), part of what the U.S. Occupation sought to effect was the promotion of citizen participation in government, labor voice in industry, as well as individual freedom and the eradication of feudalistic practices.

In this atmosphere, the authors suggest, there may have been some inadvertent promotion of Communism, which encouraged the devastating labor disputes in the Toho production company. It was against such a background in 1946 that Kurosawa made his eulogy to the persecuted prewar Kyoto communists, *No Regrets for Our Youth*, and that Kinoshita sang the praises of war objectors who had been jailed for their views in *Morning for the Osone Family*. While Ichikawa's debut was submerged in the Occupation controls and the struggle to form the Shin Toho company as it split from the beleaguered Toho, and Kobayashi returned from military detention to resume assistant director status, a more generalized humanism came to the fore.

By the early 1950s, Japan was beginning to recover economically (with some thanks due, ironically, to the Korean War from 1950 to 1953) and psychologically from the Pacific War. Movies had become big entertainment, and Japanese humanism blossomed with Kurosawa's existential bureaucrat in *Ikiru*, Kinoshita's good-hearted stripper Lily Carmen (1951 and 1952), and Ichikawa's pathetic little man heroes Mr. Lucky (1952) and Mr. Pu (1953). The Japanese film was entering its second golden age, and with it came a new emphasis on the freedom of the individual and his encounter with the sometimes comic but often oppressive stodginess of the society at large.

Masaki Kobayashi, whose first social protest film on a "war criminal" who has been incarcerated for eight years while his responsible superior has gone free, was forced to come from behind. After military duty and detention he was a long-time assistant to his contemporary Kinoshita; and when his *Thick-Walled Room* was completed in 1953, it was suppressed for three years because of the stridency of its message. But Kobayashi would later have ample opportunity to make his social criticism films before his most poignant plea for individual worth in a feudal society, the 1962 *Harakiri*. Straddling two generations, the postwar humanists and the New Wave, Kobayashi would gain from both.

Although total political freedom is never possible in feature films because of the cost and mass media aspects of the enterprise, in the mid-1950s the Japanese film came closest to artistic freedom. The economic conditions favoring the strength of the director as *auteur* brought the year 1953, following U.S. departure, a remarkable number of masterpieces. Not only did Mizoguchi offer *Ugetsu*, Ozu *Tokyo Story* and the meek Naruse three of his best, *Wife, Husband and Wife* and *Older Brother, Younger Sister*, but Kinoshita presented *A Japanese Tragedy*, Ichikawa *Mr. Pu*, Kobayashi his sensational *Thick-Walled Room*, and Kurosawa was at work on his finest film, to be released the following year, *Seven Samurai*.

By the end of the 1950s, however, television began taking its toll on the older viewers, and a whole new generation of potential moviegoers had to be wooed. "Individualism" came to extend to sex, violence and irresponsibility, and not even superheroes like Kurosawa's Sanjuro (1961 and 1962) and Kobayashi's Hanshiro Tsugumo could keep alive humanism for its own sake. The generation that introduced Japanese cinema abroad would lose its audience for socially responsible individualism at home. In another decade Kurosawa would leave Japan to make a tired *Dersu Uzala* (1975), Ichikawa would be making the most successful films in Japan, the content of which he himself finds so uninspiring he does not want them shown abroad, Kinoshita would escape into producing films for television, and Kobayashi, perhaps the most optimistic of all, would make use of television, which he detests, to film his feature *Kaseki* (1975) largely in Europe. It was another moral upheaval that was in store at the end of the 1950s, and it would be yet a newer generation that would bring Japanese cinema out of the postwar era.

AKIRA KUROSAWA

●Sanshiro Sugata (Sugata Sanshiro), 1943, Susumu Fujita (Courtesy of Yoichi Matsue.)

●The Most Beautiful (Ichiban Utsukushiku), 1944, Yoko Yaguchi (second from right)

●*No Regrets for Our Youth (Waga Seishun ni Kui Nashi)*, 1946, Setsuko Hara and Susumu Fujita (Courtesy of Yoichi Matsue.)

●*Rashomon (Rashomon)*, 1950, Masayuki Mori and Toshiro Mifune

●*Drunken Angel (Yoidore Tenshi)*, 1948, Takashi Shimura and Chieko Nakakita (Courtesy of Yoichi Matsue.)

●*Ikiru (Ikiru)*, 1952, Takashi Shimura and Atsushi Watanabe (Courtesy of

Seven Samurai (Shichinin no Samurai), 1954. Toshiro Mifune and Isao(Ko) Kimura (Courtesy of Yoichi Matsue.)

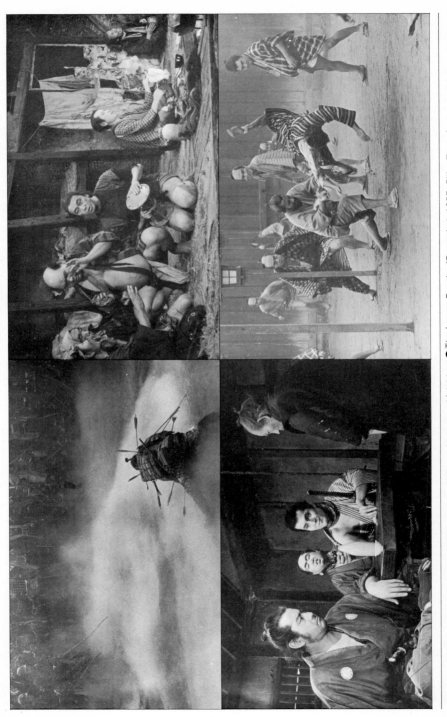

● Throne of Blood (Kumonosujo), 1957, Toshiro Mifune (Courtesy Yoichi Matsue.)

● The Lower Depths (Donzoko), 1957, Eijiro Tono (extreme right) and Koji Mitsui (second from right) (Courtesy of Yoichi Matsue.)

● Red Beard (Akahige), 1965, Toshiro Mifune (center) (Courtesy of Yoichi

●*The Blossoming Port (Hana Saku Minato)*, 1943, Ken Uehara (left) and Mitsuko Mito

●*Army (Rikugun)*, 1944, Kinuyo Tanaka

● A Japanese Tragedy (Nihon no Higeki), 1953, Shinichi Himori (left) and Yuko Mochizuki

● The Garden of Women (Onna no Sono), 1954, Mieko Takamine and Yoshiko Kuga

*You Were Like a Wild Chrysanthe-
mum (Nogiku no Gotoki Kimi Nariki),*
1955. Shinji Tanaka (left)
and Noriko Arita

●*Clouds at Twilight (Yuyake-gumo)*, 1956, Shinji Tanaka (left), Yuko Mochizuki and Yoshiko Kuga

●*A Candle in the Wind (Fuzen no Tomoshibi)*, 1957, Akiko Tamura (left), Hideko Takamine and Keiji Sata

●*The Ballad of the Narayama (Narayamabushi-ko),* 1958, Kinuyo Tanaka (left) and Teiji Takahashi

●*The River Fuefuki (Fuefukigawa),* 1960, Takahiro Tamura (left) and Hideko Takamine

● *Immortal Love (Eien no Hito)*, 1961, Hideko Takamine (left) and Tatsuya Nakadai

KON ICHIKAWA

● *A Billionaire (Okuman Choja),* 1954, Isao (Ko) Kimura (center)

● *The Heart (Kokoro),* 1955, Masayuki Mori and Tatsuya Mihashi

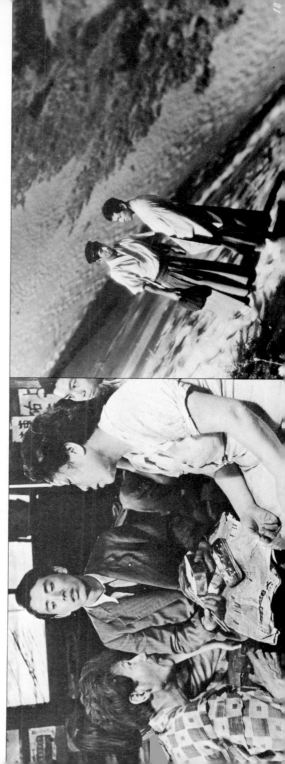

●Harp of Burma (Biruma no Tategoto), 1956, Shoji Yasui

● *Conflagration (Enjo)*, 1958, Raizo Ichikawa and Kayoko Honoo

● *Fires on the Plain (Nobi)*, 1959, Eiji Funakoshi and Mickey Curtis

● *The Key (Kagi)*, 1959, Machiko Kyo, Tatsuya Nakadai and Ganjiro Nakamura

●*Tokyo Olympiad (Tokyo Orimpikku)*, 1965

●*The Wanderers (Matatabi)*, 1973, Ichiro Ogura, Isao Bito and Kenichi Hagiwara

MASAKI KOBAYASHI

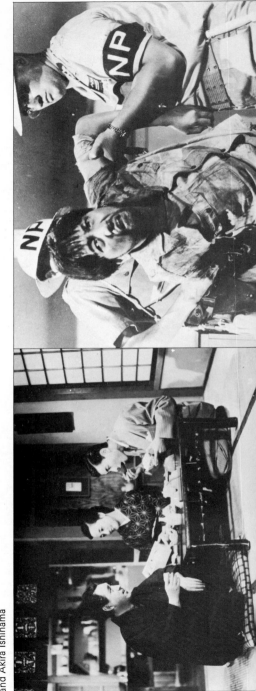

●*My Sons' Youth (Musuko no Seishun)*, 1952, Ryuji Kita, Kuniko Miyake
and Akira Ishihama

●*The Thick-Walled Room (Kabe Astuki Heya)*, 1953, Ko Mishima (center)

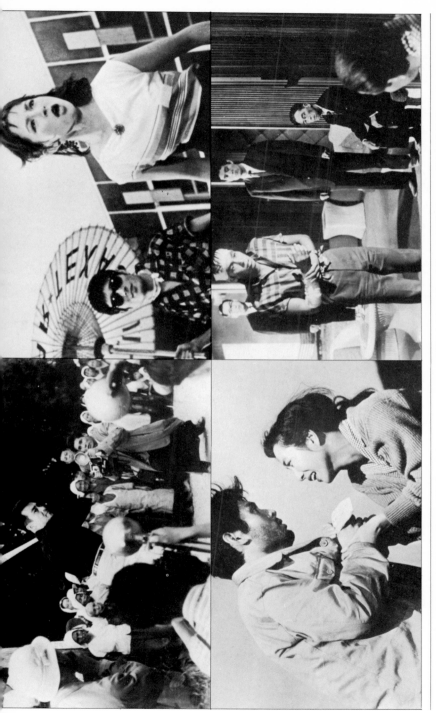

●*I'll Buy You (Anata Kaimasu)*, 1956, Minoru Oki (center)

●*The Human Condition (Ningen no Joken)*, 1959–61, Tatsuya Nakadai (left) and Michiyo Aratama

●*Black River (Kuroi Kawa)*, 1957, Tatsuya Nakadai (left) and Ineko Arima

●*The Entanglement (Karamiai)*, 1962, Minoru Chiaki (rear), Yusuke Kawazu, Tatsuya Nakadai, Seiji Miyaguchi and So Yamamura

●Harakiri (Seppuku), 1963. Tatsuya Nakadai (right) and Tetsuro Tamba

●Kwaidan (Kaidan), 1964. Tatsuya Nakadai

●Rebellion (Joiuchi), 1967. Toshiro Mifune (left) and Tatsuya Nakadai

●*Kaseki (Kaseki)*, 1975, Keiko Kishi (left) and Shin Saburi

AKIRA KUROSAWA

1910—

*In style we are completely different, but what
Kurosawa says is right.*

—Keisuke Kinoshita

If any living director can rightfully claim to represent the cinema of Japan throughout the world, that director can only be Akira Kurosawa. His *Rashomon* opened the eyes of the international public to the existence of a major film industry in Japan, and since that revelation it has always been his films that found the earliest and widest distribution as well as the widest praise. His domestic awards are amply supplemented with prizes from prestigious international film festivals such as Berlin and Moscow as well as Venice. His international acclaim culminated in Hollywood's Academy Award for *Dersu Uzala* as Best Foreign Film of 1976. He hastened to say he would like to have made it in Japan.[1]

There is more than a coincidental irony in the fact that the most famous Japanese director's Academy Award-winning film is a Soviet Mosfilm production, a Russian original story produced in the Russian language in the Soviet Union. Since it is probably safe to say that an ordinary Soviet production would never have come under consideration for the award, the question arises as to where a Japanese of Kurosawa's inter-national stature, concerns and demands can make films today.

The man is surrounded by an aura of greatness and a certain measure of secrecy. No one talks about his 1971 suicide attempt, and interviews can be obtained with him only with difficulty. While he is working on a script, he will see no one and divulge none of the contents. Among his personal friends he counts some of the most illustrious filmmakers in the world, such as John Ford, Satyajit Ray and Francis Ford Coppola. To some this atmosphere may appear intimidating, to others it may seem to be self-image inflation, but to most it should appear natural.

Kurosawa does in fact have friends and avid fans throughout the world, but he also has his share of detractors, especially in Japan of late. There are those who resent his condemnations of the Japanese film world, and there are those who feel his films no longer have a relevance to the life of the contemporary Japanese audience. Both these views have a certain validity, but Kurosawa's own attitudes remain justifiably unshakable. His production perfectionism and scale require financing and long-term scheduling that the faltering, safety-conscious Japanese major studios cannot risk; this tends to create mutual bitterness. On the other hand, Kurosawa's equal commitment to a humanistic ideal comes into direct conflict with the unspoken philosophy of the largely teenage contemporary audience—a self-centered, anti-sentimental conservative materialism. These people prefer to be terrified rather than inspired. For a Kurosawa who once described himself, when asked if he was a realist or a romantic, as a sentimentalist,[2] recognition of this prevailing mood must surely be a disappointment.

Yet a tenacious audience for Kurosawa always resurfaces in Japan. Revivals of *Seven Samurai* and *Ikiru* in the last few years have played to packed houses around the country, and dazzled viewers of a 1976 double-bill revival of *Yojimbo* and *Sanjuro* came away wondering why no one makes films that good any more. For a complete retrospective at the Tokyo National Museum of Modern Art Film Center in 1977 in celebration of Kurosawa's receipt of the cultural award rank Order of the Sacred Treasure in 1976, tickets were sold out more than two hours in advance for almost every screening. Obviously the critics who condemn his lack of militant leftism and the production companies who decry his excessive demands have missed the point that the faithfulness of his admirers underscores.

Like many masters of his generation, Kurosawa believes that film directors should keep quiet and let their works speak for them. His own extraordinary record reveals a consistently innovative, intellectual and entertaining approach. It was not without reason that his staff used to call him the "greatest editor in the world,"[3] but many other elements combine to give his films their particular strength. Above all, his stories, such as that of the aging bureaucrat transformed by impending death in *Ikiru* or the ragged men who save a whole village in exchange for nothing but room and board in *Seven Samurai*, treat life as a rich adventure in existential humanism transcending all national boundaries and inspiring even in times of the most intransigent apathy. Clothed in Kurosawa's superb dramatic pacing, vivid montage-with-camera-movement, and staging that constantly surprises, heroes of this nature satisfy the ineffable cravings of the hard-core moviegoer anywhere: they resemble us closely, with a Dostoyevskian realism that is "more real than real life," and yet the challenges they rise to make them superior human beings, imprinting them on our brains as models.

Wartime Beginnings

Kurosawa was born in Tokyo at the end of the Meiji Period to a family that had held samurai rank. His upbringing was strict, and it was at primary school that he developed a love of painting and film along with a skill at the traditional swordfighting art of *kendo*.[4] He attempted to become a painter for a time, but gave up because of chronic poverty, nevertheless the tonality and framing of his films reveal his artist's training. The realism revolution that Kurosawa brought about in filmed swordplay, with *Seven Samurai, Yojimbo* and *Sanjuro*, could probably not have been effected by someone without his experience with sword art.

Another great influence Kurosawa names from his days as an aspiring painter is that of Russian literature, especially Dostoyevsky. In the early 1930s, he became a member of the Japan Proletariat Artists' Group, largely in order to study the new art movements.[5] (White Russians brought many new art trends to relatively isolated Japan in the 1920s, and the influence of Soviet montage is evident in many Japanese films of the 1930s.) Kurosawa and his friends spent much of their time discussing nineteenth-century Russian literature, while his older brother, a former narrator for silent films, deepened his appreciation for movies. His interests of this era find expression in his later film adaptations of Gorky's *The Lower Depths* and Dostoyevsky's *The Idiot*, as well as in the treatment of *Scandal*, which has been called "a film in the Dostoyevsky manner."[6]

But Kurosawa's actual embarkation on a film career occurred almost by chance. In 1936, he faced the impossibility of support by his parents and answered a newspaper advertisement placed by P.C.L. (Photo Chemical Laboratories), which would later become the Toho studios. He was accepted from among hundreds of applicants and became an assistant director, but he had no particular love for the work until he joined the staff of director Kajiro Yamamoto, who consulted fully with his assistants instead of merely treating them as errand boys the way many did and still do.

In order to get ahead in Japan, assistant directors must spend all of their free time writing scenarios. It was no different for Kurosawa, who said that this may have been his period of richest imaginative power, although his work was "too technical."[7] His script on the life of architect Bruno Taut in Japan, *Daruma-dera no Doitsujin (A German at Dharma Temple)*, was one of the many he turned out as assistant director, and it is said to show one of his favorite dramaturgical devices of contrasting an extraordinary individual with the masses of ordinary people.[8] But it was not until 1943 that Kurosawa secured permission to direct his own work.

As soon as he saw the advance promotion for Tsuneo Tomita's novel, he knew *Sanshiro Sugata* was a film he could make. The day the book came out he read it and begged his producer to buy the film rights, and he shot the judo saga, he said, in a spirit of total enjoyment but with the objective of showing that Japanese films did not have to be made without technical virtuosity.[9] The result is a remarkable debut film that does what Kurosawa set out to do. Skillfully edited, it moves through five major combat scenes to the memorable climactic encounter between Sugata and his arch rival under the speeding clouds shadowing Ukyogahara plain. Supporting the excitement of the action are the themes of the hero's education and his awkward young love. Because he scrapped much of the novel's harping on patriotism and Japanese purity, critics in 1943 Japan found the film wanting in its portrayal of the spirit of judo.[10]

The education of the hero, a difficult progression toward spiritual enlightenment, would later become the theme of many of Kurosawa's films. He would take it up in the Sugata format as the personal struggle under tutelage of a wise older mentor in *Stray Dog, Sanjuro*, two of the relationships in *Seven Samurai*, extreme one-to-one form in *Red Beard* and finally in *Dersu Uzala. The Most Beautiful, No Regrets for Our Youth, Ikiru* and *Record of a Living Being* would present the hero in a solitary search for enlightenment without any single teacher. And conversely, the protagonist who rejects the option of setting out on this spiritual ascent ends by rushing headlong toward his doom, like the gangster of *Drunken Angel*, the greedy warlord in *Throne of Blood*, and the impetuous patriarch of another Shakespeare adaptation, the as yet unfilmed script "Ran" (Turmoil), based on *King Lear*. Kurosawa's existential humanism emerges in this education process because self-evaluation and searching for the right path almost invariably prove to entail movement toward active compassion. Kurosawa's own description of his goal in this approach is somewhat evasive, and yet at the same time more comprehensive. While calling himself a sentimentalist and insisting that a film must be both positive and constructive, he has denied attempting to make social films, and stresses that "what interests me is the drama, interior or exterior, of one man, and portraying this man through that drama."[11]

In *Sanshiro Sugata* Kurosawa employs this spiritual drama to create one of the most memorable images of the film. The unruly Sugata is being disciplined by his master, who tells him to remain submerged in the garden pond looking at the moon until he understands. Here Kurosawa introduces a catalytic image to the pond scene from the novel: meditating on his errors, Sugata turns to see a pure white lotus in full bloom a few feet away from him. Its unexpected beauty overwhelms his stubbornness, and he leaps from the pond having found humility. A parallel to this device appears nine years later in *Ikiru*, where the discouraged bureaucrat suddenly recognizes the toy rabbit as the symbol of bringing joy to children. After he is dead and the playground built in the slum, the toy rabbit reappears during his wake, just as Sugata's lotus recurs—less subtly—during his final battle as reminder of his enlightenment. Critics who seek to read a Zen interpretation into these humble objects' operation on the minds of the protagonists can amply justify their case, but in *Ikiru* the symbols are far more rationally integrated into the dramatic construction, perhaps too rationally for those who value a feeling of improvisation in film.

The personal struggle theme carries through *The Most Beautiful*, which underscores a far more strident support-the-war-effort message. But the heroine emerges as a real person despite the propaganda, because she is seeking her own identity through the socio-political situation in which she finds herself. Her rejection of the discouragement of influential people around her, her insistence on making her own contribution and meeting her own severe standards would be further developed in Kurosawa's most attractive postwar heroine, the determined idealist of *No Regrets for Our Youth.*

In *The Men Who Tread on the Tiger's Tail* Kurosawa attempted something completely different. From the serious period hero of *Sanshiro Sugata* and the serious contemporary heroine of *The Most Beautiful,* he turned to a serious classical Kabuki drama and added a comic hero, the humble porter played by Kenichi Enomoto. Such near sacrilege had never been dared before, and the film is so funny and unpropagandistic that it was not released. This foray into the comic form, which he completely overlayed on a classical suspense play, was an important step, revealing Kurosawa's innovative propensities from the earliest stages of his career. Later he would speak of *Yojimbo* and *Sanjuro* as his "first postwar comedies,"[12] although *The Men Who Tread on the Tiger's Tail* itself became a postwar film—released at last in 1952 when the U.S. Occupation ban on period films was lifted. It proved at that time to be quite competitively well made despite the wartime production limitations.

These three earliest films, all made during a time of low production standards and high propaganda demands, show that Kurosawa was more than, in the words of Kajiro Yamamoto, "ready . . . when his chance came."[13] His themes are already clear, his technique expert and his approach to genre experimental. There is in fact no major break between wartime and postwar in Kurosawa's concerns: he shows his drama of individuals and technical virtuosity from the outset. As a result, Kurosawa has not felt the need to repudiate his wartime works, as have some of the famous Communist directors such as Tadashi Imai and Satsuo Yamamoto, saying they had no choice but to make the most abject propaganda.[14] Other directors such as Yasujiro Ozu simply avoided making films at all after 1942, when material and ideological restraints became intolerably severe, but Kurosawa persisted in the search for his own cinematic expression.

Toward Humanism in the Postwar Individual

In discussing the impetus for his first postwar film, Kurosawa said: "I believed at that time that for Japan to recover it was important to place a high value on the self," and he added, "I still believe this."[15] Accordingly, he created a heroine in *No Regrets for Our Youth* who remains an uncompromising idealist despite social and political opposition as well as physical exhaustion. Like the heroine of *The Most Beautiful* before her and the hero of *Ikiru* after her, she places the highest demands on herself, setting an example that is often misunderstood by those around her and seen as eccentric or self-destructive.

The most moving sequence of the film, like that of *The Most Beautiful*, shows this character in highly tense visual terms, almost without dialogue. Just as the optical instruments factory girl works all night, thinking of the needs of the soldiers at the front, to make up for a lost lens, the delicate city woman Yukie (Setsuko Hara), followed by her mother-in-law to work in daylight for the first time, labors in the mud until the whole rice paddy is planted. Covered with dirt, she collapses in exhaustion on arriving home. Having seen the extended montage of their toil and the first joy on the women's faces at its completion, we experience total empathy with their frustration, sorrow and rage at the sight of their field the next day, trampled by persecuting villagers and bristling with placards accusing them of being spies and traitors. Without hesitation, Yukie begins removing the signs to start over, and her silent determination carries her mother-in-law, and finally her father-in-law, along in her fight against prejudice.

Silent determination in the face of bitter opposition would be the inspiring quality of the dying bureaucrat in *Ikiru* as well. Repeated images of Watanabe (Takashi Shimura), head bowed, standing immovable before embarrassed city officials and swaggering gangsters with his park project proposal, become the *leitmotif* of the second half of the film. We see him alone, staggering with the pain of his fatal cancer, and responding to the gangsters with a quiet gruesome smile that makes them turn away in terror at the realization that murder threats mean nothing to him. His baffled subordinates, like Yukie's in-laws and the factory girl's colleagues, are swept along without really comprehending this exemplary figure, recognizing his accomplishment only after his death.

Kurosawa has said that in *No Regrets for Our Youth* he was able to say something for the first time, and that the critical response at the time was unfavorable simply because the protagonist was female.[16] Yet from *Sanshiro Sugata*, through *The Most Beautiful, No Regrets for Our Youth*, and finally *Ikiru*, his ideas show a clear progression of emphasis on the individual finding self-definition, self-assertion, and finally a form of accomplishment that serves humanity. The choice of situations—Meiji Period martial arts competition, work for the war effort, persecution of Communists and bureaucratic stagnation—and of young and old, male and female protagonists from varying social backgrounds, reveals a dramatic focus that is bound neither by politics, age, nor sex, but by existential challenge to the individual.

Entertainment and the Kurosawa Family

Kurosawa's formation of a core group of staff and actors facilitated the development of his distinctive cinematic style. The young Toshiro Mifune first acted for him in *Drunken Angel*, a film of which Kurosawa said, "This is me at last."[17] The relatively fast pace of Kurosawa's films from this point on is constructed with the aid of Mifune's acting, which Kurosawa found to be lightning fast by comparison with most Japanese actors. His screen presence was in fact so strong that it changed the character balance of *Drunken Angel*, in which the alcoholic doctor played by Takashi Shimura was supposed to have been the hero. Mifune's agitated arrogance as the young gangster dying of tuberculosis assumed such dominance that his angry glare became a sensational new rebel movie star image.[18] But Kurosawa's subsequent casting of Mifune prevented him from stagnating in a gangster role mold. In *The Quiet Duel* he made Mifune a very strait-laced doctor, in *Stray Dog* a diligent rookie policeman, in *Scandal* a justice-seeking painter, in *Rashomon* a swaggering bandit, and in *Record of a Living Being* he had him play the aging industrialist grandfather when he was only 35 years old. In challenging his actors to break with their stage or screen type, Kurosawa has constantly challenged his own directorial powers.

Another addition to the Kurosawa family in *Drunken Angel* was composer Fumio Hayasaka, who brought sound-image counterpoint to the Japanese film for the first time with the "Cuckoo Waltz" as background for the gangster's most dismal moments walking in the black market district. Hayasaka's subsequent work with Kurosawa (much more so than his work with Mizoguchi) created some of the most memorable music in the Japanese cinema, which otherwise tends toward "Mickey Mousing" background music that deflates by overstressing what is already being shown on the screen. When Hayasaka died after composing the score for *Record of a Living Being*, a deeply grieved Kurosawa replaced him with Masaru Sato, who also outdid himself for Kurosawa, particularly in the comic score for some of the most gruesome sequences of *Yojimbo*.

With this production family, which included regular script collaborators and photographer Asakazu Nakai, Kurosawa proceeded to turn out his most popular entertainment movies. *Stray Dog, The Bad Sleep Well* and *High and Low* are thrillers with topical social themes of the type he initiated with *Drunken Angel*, and all show Mifune as a reflective, nearly obsessed protagonist who starts out seeking justice and ends up succumbing to humanism. Turning to the fresh entertainment potential of the period film, Kurosawa completely overturned the dull standard love versus duty conflicts to replace them with realistic struggles for food, survival and power. Clean-cut, pretty young men who pirouette and flick their swords a few times to destroy tens of adversaries at once are replaced by a filthy, scratching, heavy-drinking Mifune who tries to avoid violence but when forced to enters battle with his breath held. Ridiculous series of coincidences and ancestral relationships are replaced by a relentlessly logical plot development. Kurosawa's period films are so revolutionary in structure and characterization that some Japanese critics have found their origins in American Westerns.[19] Such analyses become ironic, however, in view of the fact that *Seven Samurai* and *Yojimbo* have both been remade in the west as Westerns: John Sturges' *The Magnificent Seven* and Sergio Leone's *A Fistful of Dollars*. Yet Kurosawa's orginals provide more than the shows of bravado of the remakes, for his are marked by what has been called an intellectual-ism,[20] or more specifically, a depth of characterization, a structural ex-perimentation, and an international selection of classic forms.

Classic Experiments

Not that there is any dearth of intellectuals among Japanese film direc-tors, but Kurosawa has been more courageous and insistent than others in putting through his method and materials. His first surprising stroke was the above-mentioned *Men Who Tread on the Tiger's Tail*, as far back as 1945, but Rashomon itself is an adaptation of two classic stories of early twentieth-century literature by Ryunosuke Akutagawa. Kurosawa, who firmly believes that every adaptation must be an interpretation,[21] added something that the nihilistic Akutagawa would have cringed at: a restoration of faith in humanity at the end in the woodcutter's adoption of the abandoned infant. Despite this fleeting touch of affirmation, how-ever, *Rashomon* remains a grimly cynical view of human beings' indul-gent evaluation of their own despicable behavior. The four different eyewitness-participant accounts of the same incident, showing the subjectivity of truth, constituted a revolutionary format and message for the film medium. Its refusal to select one truth from the many presented as the final, conclusive truth took Europe by surprise and ranked *Rasho-mon* as an overnight classic of world cinema, its echoes audible in the work of the avant-garde of the 1960s such as Alain Resnais' *Last Year at Marienbad*.

Nobody had wanted *Rashomon*. After two rejections, Kurosawa finally found a producer in Daiei, a company he had never worked with before. Film production companies everywhere look for the sure thing, which *Rashomon* did not appear to be, but Kurosawa in the 1950s was able to say he could always make what he wanted to because his films always made money.[22]

Following *Rashomon*, in 1951 Kurosawa attempted an adaptation of his favorite novelist, Dostoyevsky. Artistically *The Idiot* did not emerge as one of his best works, perhaps because of too much fidelity to the original, in which all of the main characters border on hysteria. But it contains some unforgettably beautiful scenes in the snows of Japan's northernmost island, Hokkaido, and it again shows the innovative determination of a Kurosawa who could find a company, Shochiku, willing to risk something as unheard of as a Russian classic set in Japan.

Throne of Blood, Kurosawa's 1957 *Macbeth* adaptation, was another project no other director would have dared to suggest. He was drawn to Shakespeare at this time by a desire to "film a well-constructed drama."[23] His Japanese Macbeth, a sixteenth-century warlord, again played by Mifune, is a greatly simplified character, lacking the self-doubt and eloquence of Shakespeare's original. But the visual effects, notably the eerie invasion of the castle by forest birds, the ghostly apparitions and movements borrowed from the Noh theater, the misty and forbidding locale, amply compensate for a shallowness in the characterization.

Today a film like *Throne of Blood*, with its elaborate, historically accurate castle built from scratch and its many months in production simply could not be made. Kurosawa's new script "Ran" (Turmoil), based on *King Lear* and set in the same era as *Throne of Blood*, requires the building of three castles and the use of hundreds of men and horses (the latter being far more expensive than people in Japan). With a tremendous budget the material might be assembled to produce "Ran," but it is doubtful whether the quality of cast required could be retained for the length of time Kurosawa puts into a film, since few can afford to relinquish their hectic bread-and-butter television commitments.

The opposite extreme of the lavish settings of *Throne of Blood* is the painfully confined single interior where almost all of the action takes place in *The Lower Depths*. Immediately following his Shakespeare interpretation, Kurosawa returned to Russian classics, this time Maxim Gorky's play. But again his goal was to make a film for a Japanese audience, and, believing the story would lose its realism if done as a period drama with wigs and other paraphernalia,[24] he adapted the setting and costumes to a kind of timeless poverty, and again dealt with the *Rashomon* problem of people's images of themselves. The squalor, desperation and intensity of interaction of the characters in the single interior—and even the ending a few steps outside is enclosed—are enhanced by the surprising device of refraining from all orchestral accompaniment. The only music is a nonsense song for which the tattered, grimy boarders play their own instruments as they dance. This bit alone required nearly a month of rehearsal for what becomes a grimly humorous sequence in Kurosawa's bleakest film.

A complex attitude lies behind Kurosawa's selection of material from the classics of world literature. Like most educated Japanese, he grew up with them and retains a deep personal attachment for them. But the fact remains that no other Japanese director has ever attempted to bring Shakespeare or Russian literature to a Japanese setting for a Japanese viewing public—and Kurosawa had always made films for the Japanese until *Dersu Uzala.* He has never catered to a foreign audience and has condemned those who do.[25] But he has also described his own predilection for the rational, well-wrought play in terms of internal cultural conflict: "Basically I began as a painter, so I have a great love of things Japanese—Noh drama, tea ceremony, haiku and *waka* [31–syllable poems]. But somehow that appears as a weakness, and I feel I mustn't fall into such a trap. Because of this, I cling all the more to the forceful occidental kind of drama."[26] This coexistence and dialectic between western and eastern arts finds its most obvious expression in Kurosawa's Shakespeare adaptations, where the visualization incorporates techniques and actual performances of Noh, while the overall structure of the drama retains the sharp clashes of western plot logic.

Kurosawa's Russian involvement began with his pre-film youth and extends through to the present. It fostered his internationalism well before he became internationally known—he was already filming *The Idiot* when *Rashomon* was winning at Venice, and when he was still an assistant director before the Pacific War he read and wanted to film the Arseniev story that finally became *Dersu Uzala.* Aside from his straightforward adaptations, however, a deeply ingrained nineteenth-century Russian literary cast can be seen in many of the characterizations in his original scripts. Those well versed in the subject find Russian literature prototypes for the alcoholic doctor in *Drunken Angel,* the lawyer in *Scandal,* the bureaucrat in *Ikiru,* the industrialist in *Record of a Living Being,* the relentless avenger of *The Bad Sleep Well,* and the haunted, wild-eyed criminals of *Stray Dog* and *High and Low.* All these characters share a somber, brooding quality and a need to take decisive moral action with many a personage from Dostoyevsky, Tolstoy and others. Though he has said he has never sought to make social films, the concern of these characters with a personal definition of social justice sets them apart from those who peopled the Japanese film before them, when villains tended to be purely evil and heroes were purely good, and a morality most often consisted of a sense of honor. Such complex characters and the dramatic structures that support them constitute a major aspect of Kurosawa's innovations. Many others lie in the technical area of filmmaking.

The Emperor's Way

Along with the development of his staff and cast "family" Kurosawa also formulated his own progressive and elaborate production style. He works with a large number of people, presiding with such incontrovertible authority that many used to call him "the emperor."[27] The group effort begins with the script, which Kurosawa has usually worked on with one or more of the team made up of Masato Ide, Hideo Oguni, Ryuzo Kikushima, Shinobu Hashimoto and Eijiro Hisaita. They always sequester themselves at a hotel or residence isolated from all distractions until the script is finished. Kurosawa described the process of writing *Seven Samurai,* for example, as a competition between himself and Hashimoto, "the technician," with Oguni, "the spirit . . . a great humanist," as the final arbiter.[28] Although he prefers not to write alone for the sake of deepening and broadening the concepts in the script, his early scripts and the recent *Dersu Uzala* are entirely Kurosawa's own.

Directing the actors forms another crucial element of Kurosawa's large productions. Not only does he require rehearsal to perfection, but he usually writes his scripts with a particular actor in mind for a role that will challenge his screen type. The flatness that results when Kurosawa breaks with his "family" tradition can be seen in the wooden performances of all but the two lead actors in *Dersu Uzala,* while the family interacts at its best in a bit like the song and dance sequence from *The Lower Depths.*

Art directors find Kurosawa no less exacting. Transporting black volcanic soil from Mt. Fuji to the Tokyo studio sets to assure matching effects, and having lacquer dishes order-made, as Kurosawa did for *Throne of Blood,* would make producers pale at the size of the art budget if attempted today. When it came to working with color for the first time in the 1970 *Dodeskaden,* Kurosawa again insisted on extraordinary effects, and even painted sets himself.

But perhaps one of the most impressive features of the Kurosawa film, carrying through *Dersu Uzala,* is the incorporation of weather effects. A seasonal awareness, a situating of stories in a natural environment, used to characterize the Japanese film in general, but what remains of this poetic tradition today is only tokenism, tribute to a bygone real-life lyricism. In Kurosawa's works nature has played a more forceful, often violent role. The oppressive heat in *Stray Dog* compounds the postwar atmosphere of crowded, frustrated discomfort. The bureaucrat's accomplishments in *Ikiru* are traced through his last few months from stifling, muggy summer to heavy fall downpours as he examines the muddy park construction site, and finally to the fluttering snowfall that accompanies his demise on the park swing. Thunderstorms and mist shroud the supernatural mystery as well as the worldly violence of *Throne of Blood,* and an overwhelmingly desolate foggy landscape expresses its supremacy over human passions at both the opening and close of the film. Such environmental effects are always integral to the story development in Kurosawa's work, but in *Dersu Uzala* nature itself assumes a dominance and directing capacity over the human responses.

From the panorama of the environment, the finely detailed sets, and the exhaustively rehearsed acting, Kurosawa's cameras pick out the most moving compositions. In some of his earlier films the combination of framing and blocking astounds the viewer with its single-camera intricacy. For example, when the bureaucrat in *Ikiru* listens to another patient's description of cancer symptoms in the hospital waiting room, he moves progressively away from the man and closer to the camera as the realization comes over him that he is suffering from that very disease. The camera moves almost imperceptibly, but by the end of this long take the background is blotted out as the bureaucrat stares out into space, hiding his look of horror from his interlocutor but showing it in closeup to the viewer. With the 1955 *Record of a Living Being,* Kurosawa was regularly using at least three cameras, finding that in this way the flow of acting could go on uninterrupted and he could select the best angles when editing. With the multicamera shooting of the battle scenes in *Seven Samurai* and the speeded-up action resulting from his daring use of telephoto lenses, Kurosawa became a notorious technical revolutionary. His shooting ratios were twenty feet exposed for every one used in the final film, and outcries arose against the waste of film stock. He countered with the argument that shooting time was actually reduced by this method, because due to the number of cameras actors lost their consciousness of a particular lens and action went faster and smoother, necessitating fewer retakes.[29] What does not seem so extraordinary by Hollywood standards remains anomaly to Japanese production companies, but the "emperor" has had his way with positive results.

It was only when Kurosawa switched to widescreen that the results lost something. With the exception of *Yojimbo,* in which photographer Kazuo Miyagawa found ways to pan successfully in the dark saké stall the hero uses as a base, Kurosawa's scope films take on a static, staged air, as if he had to strain to fill the broad space with interesting blocking of the actors—a case in point would be the scenes shot in the interior of the businessman's house in *High and Low.* With *Dersu Uzala,* however, Kurosawa conquered the problem of blurred edges in the pan shots by using 70 mm. film.

Editing puts the final film into Kurosawa's distinctive pace, which again sets him apart from Japanese tradition, for he cuts on motion of the subject and motion of the camera in a very western manner. At this stage also he selects from the mass of takes the split-second action details few other Japanese directors would have even bothered to film, as well as the longer dialogue shots coordinating actors' movement with almost imperceptible movement of the camera. And finally he discards what is too pretty, as he feels the camera should not call attention to itself, but subordinate itself to the action of the film.[30] The same director who made this statement, however, has always favored the very self-referential punctuation device of the wipe, in which one image pushes the preceding one off the screen with a clear line dividing the two. Such idosyncrasies can perhaps only be ascribed to artistic license.

Constant attention to fluid editing does not by any means imply that Kurosawa's pacing is always the same. The last sequence of *One Wonderful Sunday* is an excruciating twelve minutes of the boy conducting an imaginary orchestra in an empty amphitheater while his girlfriend appeals directly to the camera for the viewer to join in. Angles and focal lengths change, details of leaves scattering in the wind are intercut, but nothing makes the scene go any faster. For such reasons Kurosawa has later stressed that the script must be good to begin with because editing, though it is for him the most important phase of filmmaking, cannot salvage a bad script.[31]

A very different slow pace flows through *Red Beard, Dodeskaden* and *Dersu Uzala,* Kurosawa's most recent works. Perhaps in unwitting response to unfavorable criticism of the swift, sensationally virtuoso violence of *Yojimbo* and *Sanjuro* and the avenging ferocity of the police in *High and Low,* the 185-minute *Red Beard* has a studied slowness in keeping with its didacticism and anti-violence message. *Dodeskaden* has the languid flow of a series of interwoven anecdotes, no single one of which dominates the dramatic structure of the film. *Dersu Uzala,* on the other hand, has the slowness of a man overawed by nature, a protagonist growing old, and a filmmaker contemplating life after years of shooting in the inhospitable Siberian climate.

Seven Samurai

Kurosawa's longest and perhaps best film, a three-hour-and-27-minute period drama, illustrates some of the director's seldom-voiced principles of film structure at the same time as it overthrows fixed notions of the genre. The experience of viewing *Seven Samurai,* no matter how often repeated, never entails boredom or discomfort despite the film's unusual duration—even the music during the intermission is so pleasant one is reluctant to leave. American director Robert Wise said of Kurosawa that his primary quality was knowing how to tell a story,[32] a description that applies most aptly to the attention-riveting strength of this 1954 epic. Kurosawa himself has stressed the physical viewing experience in cinema by comparing it to the temporal art of music,[33] and as a maker of films that edify while entertaining, he dwells on audience psychology: "The spectator's receptiveness has limits. It cannot endure a number of undisguised truths brought to a culmination at the same time. They have to be pondered. So there have to be scenes for relaxation, scenes that are amusing although appearing to serve no purpose."[34] Following this precept, the best Kurosawa films unfold in a push-and-release rhythm, with vigorous action tempered by static dialogue, gripping suspense relieved by light romance or outright buffoonery. And at calculated intervals in the course of the unfolding come moments of Kurosawan truth.

Seven Samurai is essentially the story of the defense of a farming village threatened by marauding bandits. As such it is a war suspense film, concentrating on the assembly of the defense team, military training of the locals and fortification of the town, one offensive raid, two repulsions of enemy attacks and a final enclosed battle in which all the bandits are wiped out. Military strategy provides the structural backbone of the story, but what makes the film remarkable (and surpasses any remake) is the portrayal of the characters and the development of sociophilosophical themes.

Kambei (Takashi Shimura), the seasoned samurai tactician who first agrees to help the impoverished farmers who have nothing to offer but room and rice, personifies the undisguised truth of Kurosawan existential humanism. The farmers single him out for his selflessness and willingness to meet challenges when he saves a kidnaped child from the hands of a desperate thief. Posing as a monk to lure the kidnaper with food, he demonstrates not only an extraordinary courage, but a significant lack of attachment to his class image—he has his samurai topknot shaved off to appear as a bald-pated monk. In this way, through the early characterization of Kambei, Kurosawa suggests a theme of the breakdown of class distinctions, also a favorite concern of a director he greatly admires, Jean Renoir.

Kambei, with the grandiose horn accompaniment that enhances his image, becomes not only the hero of the common folk, but the mentor figure for two admirers who end by joining the task force he organizes. Behaving with proper samurai etiquette, the younger one, Katsushiro (Isao Kimura), seeks to assume the role of a traditional disciple, as Sanshiro Sugata had with his judo teacher. Like Sugata, Katsushiro provides an innocent young man character for Kurosawa to develop the theme of growing up, falling in love and assuming the awesome responsibilities of adulthood. Katsushiro also crosses class barriers by falling in love with a peasant girl, only to be rejected in the end in a touch reminiscent of Renoir but far less sentimental. He also undergoes the painful loss of a friend and idol, the master swordsman Kyuzo (Seiji Miyaguchi), and in the final battle he attains a traumatic manhood by killing for the first time.

The older admirer, the counterfeit samurai Kikuchiyo (Toshiro Mifune), embodying the rebellious qualities of many a postwar Kurosawa hero, finds himself attracted to Kambei as much out of curiosity as respect. Unlike the obedient Katsushiro, he does not articulate his submission to a superior, but watches, prods, criticizes, improvises and makes tragic mistakes while providing the major source of amusement in the film with his clowning—emphasized by his own personal bongo-drum, piccolo and bassoon theme music. Kurosawa uses this comic figure, however, to present an undisguised truth: that farmers are the sly and sniveling creatures they are largely because they have been abused and intimidated into it by the warrior class. Mifune's defensive tirade, his only serious speech in the film, reveals his own peasant origins and brings into the open the issue that the ending of the story underscores. When the bandits are destroyed, there is no longer any need for samurai, and the three survivors are ignored as the peasants resume their peaceful life work of planting. To people who have been exploited for centuries by warrior-landlords, these mercenaries are no more than a temporary necessary evil employed in order to combat their own kind. It has been suggested that this ending comprises Kurosawa's personal theory of contemporary Japan—that with the end of the Pacific War the necessary evil of a military establishment became unnecessary, and so Japan should remain pacifist.[35]

On a more universal level, the heroic efforts of the samurai, like those of the bureaucrat in *Ikiru*, remain unsung. Kurosawa's existentialists must accept the fact that there is no reward for their good deeds, and that human nature will not change because of their self-scarifice. Yet he has them decide that the little bit of good they can do, so that ordinary people can live in peace and with a modicum of comfort, is worth doing to the utmost, even to the point of death.

Such truths arise at intervals in the action, comedy, romance and ultimately Pyrrhic victory that provide the flow of *Seven Samurai*. One whole sequence, for example, the journey from the town to the remote mountain village after the samurai have been assembled, consists entirely of light diversion. Kikuchiyo, not as yet an official member of the group, tags along behind, appears out of nowhere with a whoop on the road ahead, and proudly shows his skill at catching fish with his bare hands as the samurai watch from their campsite at the top of the waterfall above him. The mountain scenery and Hayasaka's score in this sequence greatly enhance the lyrical, carefree mood. The result is a greater shock when they reach the village and find it deserted—the local population fears its saviors as much as it fears the bandits themselves. Demonstrating his usefulness by bringing out the farmers with the alarm bell, Kikuchiyo's familiarity with peasant psychology at last wins him a rank in the group of seven.

A similar pattern of push-and-release, tension to relaxation, sobriety to comedy, can be traced in each small segment of the film. The very opening shots, for example, give not only the verbal definition of the situation (the bandits will return to plunder after the harvest) and the visuals that clarify emotions of fear and desperation experienced by the peasants, but the alienating humor that keeps the story entertaining and unsentimental all the way through. The bandits appear in the distance first, and then ever closer, silhouetted against the sky on their galloping horses. Ominous percussion music accompanies the hoofbeats as they grow louder. They stop, discuss when to attack the village below them at the foot of the ridge again, and move thunderously out of the frame to the left. Suddenly the face of a terrified peasant pops up from the bushes the bandits were looking out over, and as he gulps for the camera it is impossible to stifle a laugh. The scene shifts abruptly to an overview of the village with the population assembled in the central clearing. The sound of wailing becomes audible as the camera cuts in closer to pick out members of the miserable crowd, obviously already informed of their impending doom. The tears and moaning prepare us for a scene of great pathos, but we are again surprised into laughter as the camera comes to rest in medium closeup on the posterior of a woman kneeling with her head to the ground and bouncing slightly with each statement she sobs out.

Such momentary ridicule, later developed more fully in the plot, prevents the portrayal of the farmers from deteriorating into a Soviet-style people's film glorifying the peasantry. It recalls, rather, the cynical Kurosawan realism of *Rashomon*. And yet the peasants play a revolutionary role in *Seven Samurai*, for there had never been a period film in Japan before in which peasants hired samurai.[36] In a neatly circular movement, it is the peasants who initiate the drama, and it is they, as Kambei declares, who emerge as victors in the end.

Seven Samurai is also unusual in that it is set in the chaotic era of civil wars, before the establishment of the centuries of relative peace called the Edo or Tokugawa Period (1600–1868), when most sword films take place. Kurosawa uses this period to create a novel action drama, while Mizoguchi uses it in *Ugetsu* to tell a story of the supernatural. Both directors in this way break with period film tradition.

Another firmly entrenched genre concept Kurosawa cast aside in *Seven Samurai* is the clean-cut gentility of the warrior. The masterless swordsmen who go to work for the farmers are all relatively unwashed and unkempt and poor—one has even been reduced to chopping wood for his dinner. Wealthy, aristocratic lineage comes up only as a matter of mockery in Kikuchiyo's stolen family register, and tactics take precedence over polite codes when it comes to waging war. The final battle scenes, with bamboo-spear-toting farmers and standing warriors attacking horsemen in a flurry of mud and hoofs, form a sharp contrast to the ritualistic dance-like encounters that preceded them in the standard period drama. In sum, Kurosawa hit upon a novel device that levels class structure in order to bring a new vision of historical realism and a new existential motivation to the Japanese costume picture.

Japan or the World

At the time of completion of *Seven Samurai*, Kurosawa was following an exceptionally rich pattern of his own. He moved freely from classic drama and literature adaptations like *The Lower Depths* and *Throne of Blood* to swashbuckling adventure stories like *The Hidden Fortress* and *Yojimbo*, and back again to the problems of the contemporary Japanese scene like *Record of a Living Being*, centered on the threat of atomic bomb contamination, and *High and Low*, a thriller exposing corruption in the government-industrial complex.

Gradually, however, the topicality for which Kurosawa was known in such postwar works as *Drunken Angel* and *Stray Dog* gave way to a greater universalism. *Ikiru*, though it presents much contemporary Japanese background atmosphere, marks the full force of his treatment of themes that have currency any time any place. The individual drama of this film also formulates a loud, clear message of existential humanism; a call for the extraordinary few to alleviate the plight of the unfortunate many.

But as Kurosawa himself became an ever more universal director in his themes as well as his personal reputation, the unfortunates at whom his heroes directed their humanism became less and less visible in contemporary Japan. By the time *Red Beard* was released in 1965, the postwar era of values like "humanism," "culture" and "democracy" was over. Those who still flock to see it today do so not because it says something about contemporary Japan, but because it is a kind of summary statement of Kurosawa's values and technical virtuosity. It has the requisite master-disciple relationship, the encounter of the young man with love and adult responsibility, the breathtaking Mifune fight scene (without swords), the helping of the poor and unfortunate and the thankless one-man opposition to accepted social injustice. Filmed in scope, it is a very frontal film, however, and as expertly as the visuals are handled, they lack the depth and movement of a masterpiece like *Seven Samurai*. The use of Beethoven's *Ninth Symphony* as the theme music adds to the overall impression that this film is a monument rather than a new statement.

Red Beard and the much later *Dodeskaden* were both made as independent productions, which accounts for some of their austerity of settings and visual format. (Kurosawa went independent at the request of the Toho studios, who thought there would be more money in it for them if they bought finished films from him instead of financing them at the outset.)[37] But it is the alienation of contemporary society from humanistic values that accounts for their feeling of didactic remoteness. A distance has come between Kurosawa and his audience, and by the time he comes to making films like *Dersu Uzala* in Russian, language itself seems to set up more barriers. The shantytown atmosphere of *Dodeskaden* is hard to find in contemporary wealthy Japan, and the man in unspoiled nature represented by Dersu is hard to find anywhere in the world. The devoted fans who revel in the Kurosawa message of humanism and challenge to the individual can find a good deal of what they want in these recent works, but the filmmaker himself faces a difficult choice.

For a world that demands a fixed idea of the Kurosawa film, the director can go anywhere in the world to produce his work. He has shown that he can present his universal messages in any language to any culture, and they will be well received. But for Kurosawa to continue growing, to see his films praised because they reach a new audience with new forms and new ideas, and not simply because they are "Kurosawa films," it may be necessary for him to resume filmmaking in Japan. The dilemma he faces is that of the established artist, the master. So many of his own works have become classics that the challenge of doing something new and different, which the fast-moving world of the feature film always requires, becomes a far more formidable task for him than for a director who is just beginning. But his consistent innovations in the past and his frequently reiterated commitment to an audience of his own countrymen indicate that he is more than willing to try. If Kurosawa can begin making films in Japan that speak to the underlying spiritual needs of an overeducated, overfed nation—and he is one of the very few who have the potential for spiritual and intellectual leadership—not only will his own work be revitalized, but its international currency will be, if anything, reinforced.

Notes

[1] Kurosawa's Academy Award press conference with Japanese newsmen, 1976.

[2] Yoshio Shirai, Hayao Shibata and Koichi Yamada, "L'Empereur" (The Emperor), *Cahiers du cinéma.* No. 182, 1966, p. 40.

[3] Donald Richie, *The Films of Akira Kurosawa* (Berkeley and Los Angeles: University of California Press, 1973), p. 193.

[4] *Ibid.,* p. 10.

[5] *Ibid.,* p. 11.

[6] *Ibid.,* p. 69.

[7] Akira Kurosawa and Masahiro Ogi, "Zen jisaku o kataru" (Kurosawa Talks about All His Films), reprinted from *Eiga Junkan* (Film Report) special 1956 New Year issue in *Sekai no eiga sakka 3: Kurosawa Akira* (Film Directors of the World 3: Akira Kurosawa) (Tokyo: Kinema Jumposha, 1973), p. 113.

[8] Tadao Sato, *Kurosawa Akira no sekai* (The World of Akira Kurosawa) (Tokyo: Sanichi Shobo, 1974), p. 19.

[9] Kurosawa and Ogi, *op. cit.,* p. 114.

[10] Sato, *op. cit.,* p. 39.

[11] Shirai et al., *op. cit.,* p. 37, p. 74.

[12] Kurosawa and Ogi, *op. cit.,* p. 133.

[13] Richie, *op. cit.,* p. 13.

[14] Sato, *op. cit.,* p. 65.

[15] Kurosawa and Ogi, *op. cit.,* p. 116.

[16] *Ibid.,* p. 116.

[17] *Ibid.,* p. 117.

[18] Sato, *op. cit.,* p. 121.

[19] Tadao Sato, *Chambara eiga shi* (History of Swordfight Movies) (Tokyo: Haga Shoten, 1972), p. 196 ff.

[20] Akira Iwasaki, "Kurosawa and His Work," *Japan Quarterly,* Vol. 12, No. 1, 1965, p. 62.

[21] Shirai et al., *op. cit.,* p. 37.

[22] Akira Kurosawa, Keisuke Kinoshita and Senkichi Taniguchi, "Rashomon to Nihon no eigakai" (*Rashomon* and the Japanese Film World), panel discussion, 1951, reprinted in *Gendai Nihon eiga ron taikei 1: Sengo eiga no shuppatsu* (Survey of Contemporary Japanese Film Theory 1, Beginnings of the Postwar Film) (Tokyo: Tojusha, 1971), p. 425.

[23] *Ibid.,* p. 427.

[24] Kurosawa and Ogi, *op. cit.,* p. 128.

[25] Kurosawa, Kinoshita and Taniguchi, *op. cit.,* p. 422.

[26] *Ibid.,* p. 427.

[27] Richie, *op. cit.,* p. 191.

[28] Kurosawa and Ogi, *op. cit.,* p. 124.

[29] *Ibid.,* p. 129.

[30] Shirai et al., *op. cit.,* p. 76.

[31] Richie, *op. cit.,* p. 185.

[32] Shirai et al., *op. cit.,* p. 75.

[33] *Ibid.,* p. 42.

[34] *Ibid.,* p. 76.

[35] Sato, *Chambara eiga shi, op. cit.,* p. 199.

[36] *Ibid.,* p. 197.

[37] Kurosawa and Ogi, *op. cit.,* p. 130.

AKIRA KUROSAWA: FILMOGRAPHY

1943 *Sanshiro Sugata (Sugata Sanshiro)*
pr: Toho; orig. story: Tsuneo Tomita; sc: Kurosawa; ph: Akira Mimura; music: Seiichi Suzuki; cast: Susumu Fujita, Denjiro Okochi, Takashi Shimura, Ryunosuke Tsukigata, Yukiko Todoroki et al. Martial arts film set in Meiji times in which the hero learns that judo is not just fighting but spiritual discipline. He defeats the villain and wins the girl in the end. Exciting combat scenes; superbly made film considering wartime conditions and the fact that it is his first. *Eiga Hyoron* #2. (FC, AB)

1944 *The Most Beautiful (Ichiban Utsukushiku)*
pr: Toho; orig. sc: Kurosawa; ph: Joji Ohara; music: Seiichi Suzuki; cast: Yoko Yaguchi, Takako Irie, Takashi Shimura, Ichiro Sugai, Asako Suzuki et al. Semi-documentary on girls working in a vital war industry, optical instruments. Centers on one girl who is determined to produce as much as the boy workers; her fanatical dedication leads her near to collapse, but she goes on. Blatant propaganda, but well edited and with almost convincing characterizations. (FC; negative at Toho, Tokyo.)

1945 *Sanshiro Sugata, Part II (Zoku Sugata Sanshiro)*
pr: Toho; orig. story: Tsuneo Tomita; sc: Kurosawa; ph: Hiroshi Suzuki; music: Seiichi Suzuki; cast: Susumu Fujita, Denjiro Okochi, Ryunosuke Tsukigata, Yukiko Todoroki et al. Sequel to the 1943 success, based on Tomita's epic novel. Nowhere near such acclaim as the first. (FC; negative at Toho, Tokyo.)

The Men Who Tread on the Tiger's Tail (Tora no O o Fumu Otokotachi)
pr: Toho; orig. story: Kabuki play *Kanjincho;* sc: Kurosawa; ph: Takeo Ito; music: Tadashi Hattori; cast: Kenichi Enomoto, Denjiro Okochi, Susumu Fujita, Masayuki Mori, Takashi Shimura et al. Medieval period drama about a legendary warrior hero escaping across a heavily guarded border with his loyal retainers disguised as monks. Kurosawa redesigned this serious, almost actionless play (the Kabuki itself is based on the Noh *Ataka*) as a vehicle for Enomoto, one of the most popular comedians of the day. He injects the commoner's viewpoint on these awesome nobles and provides much-needed humorous relief. But the authorities decided it did not promote the war enough —a valid judgment —and since feudal themes were banned by the succeeding U.S. Occupation, it was not released until 1952. A remarkable achievement considering there was almost no film stock in Japan at the time. (FC, AB)

1946 *Those Who Make Tomorrow (Asu o Tsukuru Hitobito)*
pr: Toho; codirectors: Kajiro Yamamoto and Hideo Sekigawa; orig. sc: Yusaku Yamagata and Kajiro Yamamoto; ph: Mitsuo Miura, Takeo Ito and Taichi Kankura; cast: Kenji Susukida, Chieko Takehisa, Chieko Nakakita, Mitsue Tachibana, Masayuki Mori et al. Kurosawa denies any responsibility for this film, which was a company command slapped together in one week. (No extant prints; negative at Toho, Tokyo.)

*No Regrets for Our Youth (*Waga Seishun ni Kui Nashi*)
pr: Toho; orig. sc: Eijiro Hisaita and Kurosawa; ph: Asakazu Nakai; music: Tadashi Hattori; cast: Setsuko Hara, Susumu Fujita, Denjiro Okochi, Eiko Miyoshi, Kokuten Kodo et al. A look back at the liberal thirties in liberal Kyoto and subsequent thought control and oppression during the war. Seen through the eyes of a young woman whose father and fiancé are both imprisoned for being leftists, her dedication grows as she is pressured to give up. Losing her activist husband, she goes to battle suspicion and resentment in his parents' farming village, where she gives up everything to become a farm woman. By far Kurosawa's most winning heroine; beautiful sequence of daughter and mother-in-law in the fields; some distracting bits of German expressionist technique. *KJ* #2. (FC; negative at Toho, Tokyo.)

1947 **One Wonderful Sunday (*Subarashiki Nichiyobi*)**
pr: Toho; orig. sc: Keinosuke Uekusa; ph: Asakazu Nakai; music: Tadashi Hattori; cast: Isao Numazaki, Chieko Nakakita, Ichiro Sugai, Midori Ariyama, Masao Shimizu et al. Contemporary story of a young couple in Tokyo who have no spending money but still try to enjoy a date. The girl spends most of the time trying to cheer up the boy, who becomes despondent because they cannot afford a model home they look at, cannot attend a concert because the cheap tickets are gone, and so on. The boy ends by conducting his own imaginary orchestra in an empty amphitheater while the girl pleads for all viewers to join in song. The girl's shock at the boy's desire to make love and the whole very long ending sequence look very dated now. *KJ* #6. (FC; negative at Toho, Tokyo.)

1948 ***Drunken Angel (*Yoidore Tenshi*)**
pr: Toho; orig. sc: Kurosawa and Keinosuke Uekusa; ph: Takeo Ito; music: Fumio Hayasaka; cast: Toshiro Mifune, Takashi Shimura, Michiyo Kogure, Chieko Nakakita et al. The slums of postwar Tokyo provide the setting for the conflict between an alcoholic doctor—the "drunken angel" of the title—and the arrogant, reckless gangster dying of TB whom he tries to save. Mifune's first great role in a "film in the Dostoyevsky manner." Firmly established Kurosawa as one of the great postwar directors. *KJ* #1. (FC, AB)

1949 **The Quiet Duel (*Shizuka Naru Ketto*)**
pr: Daiei; orig. play: Kazuo Kikuta; sc: Kurosawa and Senkichi Taniguchi; ph: Soichi Aisaka; music: Fumio Hayasaka; cast: Toshiro Mifune, Takashi Shimura, Miki Sanjo, Kenjiro Uemura, Chieko Nakakita et al. A young doctor who has contracted syphilis during the war from operating on an infected patient comes home and refuses to marry the woman he loves. Contrived, sentimental story with some redeeming moments. *KJ* #8. (FC, AB)

*Stray Dog (*Nora Inu*)
pr: Shin Toho; orig. sc: Ryuzo Kikushima and Kurosawa; ph: Asakazu Nakai; music: Fumio Hayasaka; cast: Toshiro Mifune, Takashi Shimura, Isao (Ko) Kimura, Keiko Awaji, Reisaburo Yamamoto et al. Detective story about a young policeman who has his pistol stolen and nearly goes crazy trying to get it back. As he comes to know more about the thief in his investigation, he begins to

realize how like himself the young unemployed repatriate is. Well-made thriller with effective postwar chaos and squalor as background, though the final chase is a little too long. *KJ* #3; Geijutsusai Grand Prize. (FC, TO, AB)

1950   *Scandal (Skyandaru)*
pr: Shochiku; orig. sc: Kurosawa and Ryuzo Kikushima; ph: Toshio Ubukata; music: Fumio Hayasaka; cast: Toshiro Mifune, Yoshiko Yamaguchi, Takashi Shimura, Yoko Katsuragi, Noriko Sengoku et al. Contemporary story that criticizes irresponsible, sensationalistic journalism. A young painter and a popular singer meet very politely by chance at a resort hotel, and scandal-mongering journalists blow it up into a secret romance. The two decide to fight the press in court, and an impoverished old lawyer takes it upon himself to help. They win their case when the old lawyer finally admits the editor bribed him to lose. Good characterization of the lawyer, but the girl is very weak; exciting fast cutting in the final courtroom suspense buildup. *KJ* #6. (FC, AB)

*Rashomon (Rashomon)
pr: Daiei; orig. stories: Ryunosuke Akutagawa; sc: Kurosawa and Shinobu Hashimoto; ph: Kazuo Miyagawa; music: Fumio Hayasaka; cast: Toshiro Mifune, Machiko Kyo, Takashi Shimura, Masayuki Mori, Minoru Chiaki et al. Timeless period drama that remains Kurosawa's most oft-cited film. Revolutionary storytelling method gives four contradictory eyewitness accounts of the same rape-murder incident, each revealing the witness's own high estimation of himself. No correct answer emerges, but a humanistic message closes the film. *KJ* #5; Venice Film Festival Grand Prix, 1951. (FC, MOMA, JA)

1951   *The Idiot (Hakuchi)*
pr: Shochiku; orig. story: Fyodor Dostoyevsky; sc: Kurosawa and Eijiro Hisaita; ph: Toshio Ubukata; music: Fumio Hayasaka; cast: Masayuki Mori, Toshiro Mifune, Setsuko Hara, Takashi Shimura, Yoshiko Kuga et al. The famous story of the too honest and good-hearted prince, the perverse beauty and the gloomy merchant's son set in the snows of Hokkaido instead of Petersburg. The beauty toys with the affections of both men, while the prince is also attracted to an upstanding general's daughter. Jealousy and resentment come to a head in the end when the merchant's son stabs the beauty and, in a departure from the original, both men go insane. Plot fidelity to the original, but the music and theatrical acting turn it into a tear-jerker. (FC, NY)

1952   **Ikiru (Ikiru)*
pr: Toho; orig. sc: Kurosawa, Shinobu Hashimoto and Hideo Oguni; ph: Asakazu Nakai; music: Fumio Hayasaka; cast: Takashi Shimura, Nobuo Kaneko; Kyoko Seki, Miki Odagiri, Yunosuke Ito et al. Kurosawa's clearest statement of existential humanism in a story of a bureaucrat who bypasses red tape in order to help others and give his own life meaning. A city hall section chief on the verge of retirement realizes he is dying of cancer and has only a few months to live. Finding no solace in his own son and daughter-in-law, in the debauchery he tries for the first time, or in the friendship of an energetic young woman, he turns to a slum park proposal gathering dust on his desk and fights all the other bureaucrats to see it built. After his death, his coworkers and re-

lations realize what he has accomplished during his wake. The wake becomes tedious after about 45 minutes, but seeing this man through others' eyes finally makes him a super-hero. *KJ* #1. (FC, AB)

1954   *Seven Samurai (Shichinin no Samurai)*
pr: Toho; orig. sc: Kurosawa, Shinobu Hashimoto and Hideo Oguni; ph: Asakazu Nakai; music: Fumio Hayasaka; cast: Takashi Shimura, Toshiro Mifune, Seiji Miyaguchi, Isao Kimura, Daisuke Kato et al. Unconventional period drama epic in both scope and length. Seven ragged samurai set out to protect a poor farming village from bandit raids in exchange for nothing but room and board. Sharp characterizations of the battle-worn astute leader who inspires all, the master swordsman, the hero-worshiping boy who becomes a man, and especially the counterfeit samurai of peasant origin who tags along and provides the humor. Breathtaking telephoto battle scenes in rain and mud, catchy musical motifs for the characters, and a Pyrrhic victory that underscores Kurosawa's existential humanism. *KJ* #3; Venice Film Festival San Marco Silver Lion. (FC, MOMA, TO, AB)

1955   *Record of a Living Being (Ikimono no Kiroku)*
pr: Toho; orig. sc: Kurosawa, Shinobu Hashimoto and Hideo Oguni; ph: Asakazu Nakai; music: Fumio Hayasaka; cast: Toshiro Mifune, Eiko Miyoshi, Yutaka Sada, Minoru Chiaki, Haruko Togo et al. Contemporary drama about one man's fear of the atomic bomb and his attempt to save himself and his family. An elderly and wealthy industrialist, he tries to persuade his family and mistresses to move with him to Brazil, but none of them wants to change his life. In their defiance, his factory burns down and they have him declared insane. A topical story that loses something over time, but one of Mifune's most astoundingly skillful performances in the role of the old man. *KJ* #4. (FC, AB)

1957   *Throne of Blood (Kumonosujo)*
pr: Toho; orig. play: Shakespeare's *Macbeth*; sc: Kurosawa, Shinobu Hashimoto, Ryuzo Kikushima, and Hideo Oguni; ph: Asakazu Nakai; music: Masaru Sato; cast: Toshiro Mifune, Isuzu Yamada, Minoru Chiaki, Takashi Shimura, Akira Kubo et al. A shallow, stupidly ambitious Macbeth as a Japanese medieval lord. Adaptations from the Noh make the three witches, who forecast his rise and fall into a white-haired apparition at a spinning wheel, and his lady into a sinister, soundlessly floating figure. Far more interesting than the characterization and story of this man who murders his friends and benefactors to rise to power, only to be shot down by his own men when the woods begin to move toward his castle, is the stylization of the cinematic technique. *KJ* #4. (FC, AB)

The Lower Depths (Donzoko)
pr: Toho; orig. play: Maxim Gorky; sc: Hideo Oguni and Kurosawa; ph: Ichio Yamazaki; music: Masaru Sato; cast: Toshiro Mifune, Isuzu Yamada, Ganjiro Nakamura, Kyoko Kagawa, Eijiro Tono et al. Another Russian original transported, very successfully, to late feudal Japan, and a masterpiece of staging in a single interior. A collection of derelicts and their miserly landlords find their lives changed by the inspiration of an itinerant priest, the only good-willed

character in the group. One commits suicide, while an arrogant thief finally tries to rid himself of the vicious landlady for the woman he really loves, her younger sister. But the girl rejects him and the landlady turns him over to the police for the inadvertent murder of her husband. All music is "real" —the derelicts' song and an irritating tinker's tapping. *KJ* #10. (FC, AB)

1958   *The Hidden Fortress (Kakushi Toride no San Akunin)*
pr: Toho; orig. sc: Shinobu Hashimoto, Ryuzo Kikushima, Hideo Oguni and Kurosawa; 'scope ph: Ichio Yamazaki; music: Masaru Sato; cast: Toshiro Mifune, Kamatari Fujiwara, Minoru Chiaki, Misa Uehara, Susumu Fujita et al. Pure entertainment period film set during the sixteenth century civil wars. A young princess is trying to travel across a war-torn area with her clan treasure and her loyal retainer, who tricks two peasants into helping them. Plenty of humor in the antics of the two low-life characters, and Kurosawa overturns period drama clichés by having the princess dress for rough travel, talk like a man, and criticize her retainer for sacrificing his sister in her place. Awe-inspiring pinnacles setting recalls many a Western. *KJ* #2; Berlin Film Festival Director's Prize; International Critics' Award, 1959. (FC, TO)

1960   **The Bad Sleep Well (Warui Yatsu Hodo Yoku Nemuru)*
pr: Kurosawa Prod./Toho; orig. sc: Shinobu Hashimoto, Hideo Oguni, Ryuzo Kikushima, Eijiro Hisaita and Kurosawa; 'scope ph: Yuzuru Aizawa; music: Masaru Sato; cast: Toshiro Mifune, Tatsuya Mihashi, Masayuki Mori, Takashi Shimura, Kyoko Kagawa et al. Thriller about a young man who hides his identity in order to expose the ruthless corruption in a construction company with government ties that caused his father's death. He ingratiates himself with the boss and gets engaged to his daughter, but in the end he relents and realizes he is really in love with the girl. Very tense drama with a timeless quality; marks the successful debut of Kurosawa's own production company. *KJ* #3. (FC, TO, AB)

1961   **Yojimbo (Yojimbo)*
pr: Kurosawa Prod./Toho; orig. sc: Ryuzo Kikushima and Kurosawa; 'scope ph: Kazuo Miyagawa; music: Masaru Sato; cast: Toshiro Mifune, Eijiro Tono, Tatsuya Nakadai, Isuzu Yamada, Daisuke Kato et al. Almost hard-boiled Western in samurai guise, and Kurosawa at his best. Two gangs are fighting for control of a feudal-period town when a super-swordsman masterless samurai arrives. Basing himself in a drinking stall to view the action, he forces a showdown in which the two sides wipe each other out by selling his services to both of them. Softhearted touches as the hero reunites a woman kept as collateral with her husband and baby and sends a farm boy back to his parents. Brutal humor largely centered on a coffinmaker and his wares and a variety of other caricatures. *KJ* #2; Venice Film Festival Best Actor (Mifune). (FC, AB)

1962   *Sanjuro (Tsubaki Sanjuro)*
pr: Kurosawa Prod./Toho; orig. story: *Hibi Heian* by Shugoro Yamamoto; sc: Ryuzo Kikushima, Hideo Oguni and Kurosawa; 'scope ph: Fukuzo Koizumi; music: Masaru Sato; cast: Toshiro Mifune, Yuzo Kayama, Tatsuya Nakadai, Keiju Kobayashi, Reiko Dan et al. The same hero as in the preceding film be-

comes mentor to a group of young, idealistic samurai trying to root out corruption in their clan administration. He opens their eyes to the fact that they are supporting the wrong man and are about to be betrayed, and goes on to preside over the gradual freeing of hostages and exposure of the real evil elements. The period film stereotypes all become comic next to the filthy but wily Sanjuro, but this film is not as funny, and more talky and didactic than the previous. *KJ* #5. (FC, TO, AB)

1963 *High and Low (Tengoku to Jigoku)*
pr: Kurosawa Prod./Toho; orig. story: *King's Ransom* by Ed McBain; sc: Ryuzo Kikushima, Hideo Oguni and Kurosawa; 'scope ph: Asakazu Nakai; music: Masaru Sato; cast: Toshiro Mifune, Tatsuya Nakadai, Kyoko Kagawa, Tsutomu Yamazaki, Tatsuya Mihashi et al. Humanistic thriller in which a self-made shoe magnate loses everything to save his chauffeur's son, kidnapped by mistake in place of his own child. A ruthless police investigator traces the criminal through his drug addiction, but the chase costs lives, and the motive is revealed as a poor boy's jealousy of the rich man. *KJ* #2. (FC, TO)

1965 *Red Beard (Akahige)*
pr: Kurosawa Prod./Toho; orig. story: Shugoro Yamamoto; sc: Ryuzo Kikushima, Masato Ide, Hideo Oguni and Kurosawa; 'scope ph: Asakazu Nakai and Takao Saito; music: Masaru Sato; cast: Toshiro Mifune, Yuzo Kayama, Tsutomu Yamazaki, Kyoko Kagawa, Miyuki Kuwano et al. Talky period film centering on a master-disciple relationship between a conceited young doctor who has studied Dutch medicine and a feisty old doctor who runs a public clinic. The young man gradually learns humility, patience and fortitude through the old man's example, defying a geisha house madame and her gangster associates to help the poor and exploited. Very long and rather static, but characterizations are excellent. *KJ* #1; Moscow Film Festival Soviet Filmmakers' Association Prize. (FC, AB)

1970 *Dodeskaden (Dodesukaden)*
pr: Yonki no Kai/Toho; orig. stories: Shugoro Yamamoto; sc: Kurosawa, Hideo Oguni and Shinobu Hashimoto; color ph: Takao Saito and Yasumichi Fukuzawa; music: Toru Takemitsu; cast: Yoshitaka Zushi, Kin Sugai, Hisashi Igawa, Kunie Tanaka, Noboru Mitani et al. Kurosawa's first and richly experimental color film, also marking the inception of the production company formed by him, Kon Ichikawa, Keisuke Kinoshita and Masaki Kobayashi. Not a plot movie, it is rather a collection of portraits of slum people, forming a hymn to the tenacity and imagination of the poor. The whole is tied together by the trolley-driving dream of a retarded boy, the title his imitation of the trolley sound. Moments of raucous humor as well as extreme pathos in thievery, begging, murder, adultery and death by food poisoning. *KJ* #3; Geijutsusai Prize for Excellence. (FC, JA)

1975 *Dersu Uzala (Dersu Uzala)*
pr: 41 Inc./Soviet Mosfilm; orig. story: Vladimir Arseniev; sc: Kurosawa; color 70 mm. ph: Asakazu Nakai, Yuri Gantman, Fyodor Dobronravov; music: Isac Schwalz; cast: Maxim Munzuk, Schemeikl Chokmorov, Yuri Salomin, Sve-

trana Danielchenka et al. Turn-of-the century Russian story about a solitary old woodsman in Siberia that allowed Kurosawa to develop his master-disciple theme with a spectacular natural setting. The leader of a geodesic survey team finds Dersu in the wilds, and he becomes a guide to the party, instructing them in nature's ways. Over a period of several years the surveyor reencounters Dersu and learns that he is going blind. He brings the old man to his home in the city, where the old man loses in his conflict with civilization. Breathtaking battles with the ferocity of nature. Moscow Film Festival First Prize; Academy Award 1976 Best Foreign Film; *KJ* #5.

KEISUKE KINOSHITA

1912—

*He can do anything; no one has as much
breadth as he does. He's a real
film genius, the only one in the
postwar era.*

—Masaki Kobayashi

Among the postwar masters of the Japanese cinema, Keisuke Kinoshita is the only one for whom the movies were his first love and true calling. Even today, when he has virtually retired into television production from the directing of feature films—aside from giving in to five years of pressure to make the 1976 *Love and Separation in Sri Lanka*—it is still the movies that fascinate him and for which he pours out ideas. With his own peculiar combination of modesty and pride, "I can't help it," he laughs, "ideas for films have always just popped into my head like scraps of paper into a wastebasket."[1]

The result is that this small and gentlemanly director has proved to be the most prolific giant of his generation, turning out some 42 films in 23 years. The temptation is to assume that such a prodigious output could only characterize someone who repeated himself continually. But Kinoshita has consistently surprised critics by refusing to be bound by genre, technique or dogma. He has excelled in both comedy and tragedy; the "home drama" of the contemporary family in isolation from social problems, and period films exposing social injustices; "all location" films and films shot completely in a one-house set, he has pursued a severe photographic realism with the long-take, long shot method, and he has gone equally far toward stylization with fast cutting, intricate wipes, tilted cameras, and even medieval scroll-painting and Kabuki stage techniques. Each film has had some major facet of experimentation for Kinoshita. But he claims that his determination to try everything has prevented him from becoming a master of any one thing: "Everything I've done has been somehow half-baked."[2] Others would disagree, for there are many who, like director Masaki Kobayashi, a Kinoshita pupil, attribute his breadth to genius. Kinoshita's modesty might even be motivated by guilt, for he repeatedly apologizes for having had such a wonderful time and doing exactly as he pleased throughout his film-making career.[3] It is the apology of the gifted natural talent who cannot understand why providence has singled him out for greater endowment than his fellows.

Despite his many innovations, however, there is a consistency to Kinoshita's work. It is the high value placed on innocence, purity and beauty that has caused him to be labeled "the eternal youth."[4] His own statement that "I have always believed since I was a child that beautiful things were true" has been extended to include the friendships of youth, maternal love, youth's dreams of the future, and young love.[5] His social and political criticism has accordingly been leveled at whatever and whoever deceives these pure and innocent notions. Kinoshita may consequently be accused of a certain naiveté, even a studied sentimentality, for many of the purest notions are inevitably betrayed with the course of simply living, and investing these moments with the weight of tragedy is of course going too far. But Kinoshita's persistent naiveté, his devotion to a sentimental ideal of purity and beauty, is precisely what lends his films their characteristic flavor. In his finest endeavors he succeeds in creating a nostalgia for these values that is next to excruciating. For the Japanese, who have revered simplicity, honesty, purity, devotion and especially straight-forwardness since the days of the samurai, the infallible attraction of the Kinoshita film has lain in seeing heroes who appear to be ordinary people like themselves, but are actually as pure, innocent and good as they would like to be. And yet there is no duplicity, no hypocrisy in Kinoshita's characterizations. The director who believes what is beautiful and pure is the truth sees all kinds of movies, and his most recent favorite at this writing is Sylvester Stallone's *Rocky*. It is part of what he sees as a long current of "beauty" in American films, and if Kinoshita has foregone other ideals in the course of his career, he has not given up on this one: "I admire beautiful, simple, pure relationships between individuals. These are what we need for world understanding and peace. We must have something to believe in."[6]

Movie Runaway

Kinoshita was born in December 1912 in Hamamatsu, Shizuoka Prefecture, about half-way between Tokyo and Kyoto, where his family had a grocery store. By the time he was eight years old, he was already a passionate movie fan, and was sure he wanted to become a film director. But he dutifully attended technical high school in Hamamatsu, and in his late teens unwillingly began study for entrance examinations to the college his parents wanted him to attend. But just at this time Hamamatsu became the location for the shooting of a period film, and the actors came to shop for local products at the Kinoshita store. Keisuke befriended actor Junosuke Bando, who helped him run away to Kyoto, where most period films are still made, and where he thought he would not be found, since runaways from Hamamatsu always headed for Tokyo.[7] But his grandfather came after him and took him back home the next day. The outcome of this display of rebellious devotion was felicitous, however, as Yasujiro Ozu's resistance to his family's opposition to a film career had been about a decade before: if the boy is so determined, they concluded, they ought to let him go into movies. "I'm the only director I know of who has always been this crazy about film,"[8] says Kinoshita, as if it were a congenital disease that turned out to be a blessing.

Resigning themselves to their son's desires, the family set about trying to help him, and at last his mother secured an introduction to Shochiku's Kamata studios, where Ozu, Naruse, and Yasujiro Shimazu were already creating their contributions to the first golden age of

Japanese cinema—with the *shomin-geki* genre. But the response to Kinoshita's appeal was that he would have no chance of entering as an assistant director without a university education, but there might be room for him as a photographer.[9] Although neither Shimazu, Ozu, nor Naruse had had a university education, Kinoshita believed what he was told and immediately applied to the Oriental Photography School, where he was told he could not be admitted without at least a half year's practical experience. Undaunted, he went to work in a photography shop in Tokyo's Hibiya district. He soon fought with the owner and moved to another shop in the Kanda district, and finally gained enough experience to enter the school. After graduating he was ready to apply to Shochiku, only to be told no camera assistants were needed, but he would be welcome in the film processing laboratory. Kinoshita's determination never flagged, however, and he took the job. "If it doesn't work out," he thought, "I can always go back to Hamamatsu and open a photography shop."[10] This was in 1933.

From the processing laboratory, which he hated, Kinoshita was at last summoned to the photography section to work under the chief cinematographer for Yasujiro Shimazu. He would spend three years as a camera assistant, during which he developed his personal ideas about composition and editing and made a bargain with his colleague Hiroshi Kusuda to take him along as his cinematographer should he succeed in becoming a director.[11] His seniors would scold him for watching the acting rehearsals instead of concentrating solely on the camera, Kinoshita recalled, but finally one of the several Shimazu assistants to become great directors in their own right, Kozaburo Yoshimura (1911–), told him he really ought to switch to the directors' section.[12] Shimazu himself asked Kinoshita's superior to send him over to become assistant director after he had been camera assistant for two years, but the chief refused, and Kinoshita spent another year at the camera before Shimazu came directly to him. He accepted, only to incur the wrath of both the chief cinematographer and all the assistant directors he was bypassing without taking the entrance examination for their section. Shimazu tried to make peace, but Kinoshita said he never felt so trapped in his life.[13] With his entry into the Shimazu group, chief assistant Shiro Toyoda (1906–77) was promoted to director and would go on to make many excellent films, while Yoshimura became next under Shimazu.

Kinoshita would spend another six years as assistant director, working like a slave and without respite for the tyrannical Shimazu. "Yoshimura and I got the worst of it," Kinoshita said, "but in retrospect I'm glad he was reluctant to let his assistants work for anyone else."[14] Although Kinoshita became chief assistant to Yoshimura when he was promoted in 1939, it is Shimazu that he names as his real mentor. "He relied heavily on his intuition," Kinoshita says, "and didn't like calculating everything in advance," which Kinoshita says is very much like his own method. "When the actors come onto the set in full costume and makeup for the first time, it changes the director's image. It grows in fits and starts during the shooting process. I learned this from Shimazu."[15] Out of this experience came Kinoshita's own intuitive, experimental approach as well as his autocratic attitude toward his own production staff, whom he did not like to lend.

But at Shochiku the real criterion for advancement was scriptwriting for Shiro Kido, and Kinoshita set about this too with a vengeance. "I knew everything I submitted would be rejected, so I'd write a melodrama, give it to him, and have a comedy ready by the time the melodrama came back, and then start on a tragedy."[16] It was a good experience, Kinoshita feels, in developing variety, for he turned out about two scripts a month before he was promoted, some three a year thereafter, as he was also writing for Yoshimura. Just when he was about to make a test film for his promotion, however, he was drafted, and on return was sent back to Yoshimura's staff. It was another year of writing scripts under the uncomfortable conditions of the Pacific War before the definitive promotion, deserved many times over, came at last in 1943.

Purity and Laughter

The first script Kinoshita wrote with Kido's blessing was rejected by the Information Ministry, but the second, *The Blossoming Port*, passed censorship, and he set out with a large budget and star cast to film on location in the southern Kyushu port town of Amakusa. Kinoshita was radiantly confident and had a wonderful time, with a·full 40 days spent on location and another 20 in the studio. He feels he owes much to Kido for giving him such a rousing start and all the way along for "bringing him up" as a director.[17] Indeed his debut 1943 *The Blossoming Port* shows occasional odd technical indulgences, such as a fantasy rear-screen projection sequence during a carriage ride into town, but overall has the look of an experienced director's work.

As with the first film Kinoshita's friend Akira Kurosawa made the same year, *The Blossoming Port* reveals much of what would come later. The idyllic seaport location would reappear in *Twenty-Four Eyes* (1954) and *Lovely Flute and Drum* (1967). The city-country contrast would be a theme of comedies like the Carmen set. Most striking, however, is the comedy form, with which Kinoshita would establish the highest reputation in the postwar era rivaled only by Kon Ichikawa, and then rush off in other directions and return to it only periodically. It has been held that in Japan "comedy of character is rare and satire is almost unheard of," and that "both would be even more rare were it not for the work of Keisuke Kinoshita. . . ."[18] *The Blossoming Port* is built around a confrontation between two stereotypes, city slickers and country bumpkins. A great deal of the hilarity derives from the breaking of these set images, however. The two crooks quickly reveal their lack of slickness by bungling their arrival in town: both come posing as the same person. After they straighten things out between themselves, the one who takes a painter's role (Ken Uehara superbly cast against his romantic type) then proceeds to destroy his stereotype further by falling in love with a local girl. She in turn proves to be not quite the gullible simpleton the crooks have taken all the townspeople for, and confronts him with the fact that she knows what they are up to. Unlike Kurosawa's 1943 *Sanshiro Sugata,* which presages the introspective, self-perfecting, existential hero, the Kinoshita debut is a drama made from close personal relationships in search of purity. When the purity emerges and the social conditions allow it to flourish, we have comedy—the crooks relent in shame and end by taking nothing.

Kinoshita would pursue comedy of the sort he began with *The Blossoming Port* into the postwar era, with no change in the values he upholds. Just as he satirized city slickers, country bumpkins, and blind reverence for University of Tokyo graduates (as one of the crooks also pretends to be) in his first film, he went on to satirize the nouveau riche and the impoverished aristocracy in *A Toast to the Young Miss* (1949), the feudalistic patriarch and the independent postwar individualist family he tries to control in *Broken Drum* (1949), city and country again in *Carmen Comes Home* (1951), and all manner of postwar stereotypes in *Carmen's Pure Love* (1952). The avaricious, lazy and untalented playboy artist, his wealthy playgirl fiancée, her militarist-politician mother, and Carmen the stripper's conviction that she is an artist, all come under the fire of Kinoshita's gags and witty dialogue. Much later he would revive his satire in the tyrannical suburban grandmother and the pseudo-tough hoodlums of *A Candle in the Wind* (1957), and the bored bourgeoisie confronted with a sweet-potato vendor who turns out to have been the grandmother's first love in *Spring Dreams* (1960). The Kinoshita flavor of optimistic sentimentality infuses all these comedies: class differences and country-city barriers can be broken down, and this is usually brought about by love as a matter of individual choice. This is best seen in *A Toast to the Young Miss,* but is a strong theme also in *Broken Drum* and *Spring Dreams,* where daughters defy parents' commands and pick their own husbands. Kinoshita's comedy, in sum, affirms the movie myths of love conquering all and the good, honest, and pure succeeding in the end.

The Carmen character, however (Hideko Takamine cast against her serious, intelligent type), introduces greater complexity and consequently greater realism into the comic portrayals. Not only is she a country girl with a citified veneer of outrageous manners (smoking cigarettes, for example) but she retains such pure good-heartedness and innocence that she verges on stupidity (there is talk in *Carmen Comes Home* of her having been kicked in the head as a child by a cow). Kinoshita takes a kind of "blessed are the simple-minded" attitude toward her, but he does not let her win in the end. Carmen shows yet another virtue, one that becomes the key to Kinoshita's tragedies: she continues in her self-sacrifice, both for her "art" and for her love, even when she knows she is not loved in return.

Reverse Angle

The thinness of the line between comedy and tragedy cannot be over-stressed in Kinoshita's case. One of the reasons he was able to move back and forth so freely between the two is that his protagonists in both retain the same traits—innocence, devotion, and self-sacrifice. Just as his villainous protagonists in *The Blossoming Port* are redeemed by discovering their own capacity for self-sacrifice, his tragic heroes—who are almost all heroines—accept this virtue as given. Again in the tragic realm, little difference between a wartime style and a postwar refinement of the same ethical stance can be found in Kinoshita's work.

Army (1944) has been maligned as a fascist film,[19] as well all films made under wartime Information Ministry regulations may be. In actuality, however, it is a film about a family focusing on the relationship of devotion between mother and son. The father, honest and unbending, is one of those male characters Kinoshita has been criticized for making "more shame-conscious than necessary for men"[20]—ashamed of anything impure or less than straightforward, which is why he makes a poor businessman. But at the time Kinoshita was subjected to virulent criticism for his ending to the film, in which his own philosophy completely undermines the war effort. Scenarist Ikeda had written only one sentence, "The mother sees the son off at the station," and told Kinoshita he expected the director, being who he was, would improvise as he saw fit in any case.[21] Kinoshita has the mother (one of the late Kinuyo Tanaka's great mid-career roles) refuse at first to see off her son, called up for duty at the front, because she knows she will cry. Alone in the shop she feels a sudden dizziness come over her. In closeup she begins to recover, mumbling to herself the code of the military man. The camera moves in closer on her distracted, almost crazed face and her mumble begins to fade, replaced by the sound of bugles. She revives, the camera pans around the empty house, and finally picks her out in long shot running down the street. A fast montage of the crowd of well-wishers rushing to the station increases the tension. The mother, stumbling through the mobs of flag-waving, shouting townspeople, catches sight of her son in uniform, marching with the others. Orchestral music rises as the camera shows the crowd running; the mother cries; the troops march; the film ends with a low angle medium closeup on her tear-stained face, praying as the crowd jostles her from all sides.

Needless to say, the emotion that surges up in this ending is hardly one that promotes a war effort. The very length of the scene, the close concentration on the mother's almost delirious sorrow at her son's departure —rather than on his enthusiasm or readiness to die—turns the whole into exactly what it was labeled by the Information Ministry, an "anti-war film." His next project on the Kamikaze troops was rejected because the Ministry now felt that such a director could never portray the correct spirit of the suicide corps. The next was also rejected, this time because it had nothing to do with national policy. Kinoshita was ready to quit film, recognizing his inadequacies: "I can't lie to myself in my dramas. I couldn't direct something that was like shaking hands and saying 'come die.' "[22] Like Kurosawa, Kinoshita could not keep himself from pursuing authentic emotions and realistic characterizations despite national policy; both were criticized and ended—Kinoshita a year earlier—by waiting out the end of the war.

Immediately after the war, Kinoshita took up the very same theme he had introduced in *Army*. In *Morning for the Osone Family* (1946) a widow whose personal beliefs and child-rearing method have been very liberal has to stand by as two of her sons die in military service and the third is imprisoned for his anti-war publications. The film also introduces Kinoshita's only real, incorrigible villain, the militarist uncle who encourages the youngest son's enlistment in the Kamikaze corps. As in *Army*, the central focus is really on the women, the mother and daughter, their recognition of what is right and their inability to make themselves heard. The daughter's pleas for justice are treated as insolence by her uncle, and the mother simply gives in to the man's insistence on running his dead brother's family. Kinoshita shows the mother as weak, never openly renouncing her beliefs but allowing them to be denigrated and her authority trampled upon. In the face of a brother-in-law whose viciousness is supported by the society at large, her own ethical purity has no power.

Kinoshita's women, the central figures in all of his tragedies, always know that war, political oppression, class distinctions and individual selfishness are evils. Their values always side with freedom of expression, love of family and, at the same time, romantic love, and overall honesty and straightforwardness. What they do in situations where their values are threatened is endure, sometimes in silence and suffering, sometimes protesting, but in extremity they choose death rather than forfeit the purity of their emotion and commitment. Such is the case of the persecuted girl who has been sent to the prison-like boarding school to keep her away from the boy she loves in *The Garden of Women* (1954), as well as the self-sacrificing mother abandoned and scorned by her children in *A Japanese Tragedy* (1953). In *The Ballad of the Narayama* (1958) the aging heroine, in a horrifying self-sacrifice so that others in the family can eat, destroys her front teeth and hastens her own death. In Kinoshita's great chronicle tragedies *The River Fuefuki* (1960) and *Twenty-four Eyes* (1954, his most popular film in Japan), the war-hating heroines endure the loss of husbands and children, unable to restrain them from participating. The schoolteacher of *Twenty-four Eyes* opposes the persecution of leftists and the fascism that leads to war by resigning from her job. In what is perhaps Kinoshita's most heart-rendingly simple, sentimental film (and one of his own favorites), the 1955 *You Were Like a Wild Chrysanthemum*, the young country girl mutely gives up the younger boy she loves and who loves her because his mother has greater social ambitions for him. Subjected to an early arranged marriage, she dies in pregnancy, clutching his letters but never having uttered his name. In *The Bitter Spirit* (1961), a woman forced to marry into a powerful local family endures far from mutely, but endures nonetheless, until she can help her children escape from the feudalistic surroundings that ruined her own life.

This consistent strain of morally pure if not always courageous women who sacrifice, endure, and sometimes even bring about change (*The Garden of Women, The Bitter Spirit*) act as the conscience and the vindicators of the female movie-going audience. Whether they emerge as politically weak or, in very rare cases like the aforementioned, as strong, whether they suffer at the hands of the family system or represent its most loving and comforting aspects, their moral imperative is always purity of feeling. They partake of a dominant flavor in the films of the Shochiku company that began as early as the development of the Kamata studios' style by Shiro Kido in the 1920s. Kamata went into the making of films for a female audience—the so-called woman's film (*josei eiga*)— because "women have much stronger feelings than men" and because "art is founded on feeling; movies are art, so women would necessarily view movies as important."[23] But even more important than the emotional basis of dramatic films for Kido was the moral basis: "The old morality oppressed women and in so doing gave rise to many dramatic situations . . . they had nothing to rely on but maternal love. Kamata movies tried to cultivate obedience and gratitude on the part of the children toward mothers for their many sacrifices. We made women our allies and praised their virtues."[24] Kinoshita, avowedly raised by Kido, continued this tradition at Shochiku's postwar Ofuna studios, and became in the 1950s the major creator of women's films labeled as "Ofuna flavor"— warm, sentimental, subscribing to myths of basic human goodness, romantic love and maternal righteousness. The director's work is by no means limited to this viewpoint on life, but his most popular films— comedies and tragedies alike—have displayed these traits.

Beyond Genre

Kinoshita's method, from the very beginning of his career, prevented him from falling into a single genre trap. Already as an assistant director he experimented with melodrama, tragedy, comedy, light romance, as much variety as possible in order to make an impression on Kido. When he became a director he continued alternating genres as the ideas overcame him, always testing out new methods as he treated new material. His philosophy of beauty and purity, with the sentimentality it engenders, and some of his staff members, are perhaps the only constants in the staggering multitude of subjects and techniques in his work. In this respect, he is very much like his friend Kurosawa, whose philosophy of existential humanism and individualism pervades an entire career. But in the prolific Kinoshita's case, there are almost twice as many films in which to find this marriage of constant philosophy and varying form. He has been compared, because of his musical methods, including song as diversion or commentary on the action, with René Clair, whom he met in France in 1951.[25] But Kinoshita himself denies any single influence from abroad: "Yes, I loved Clair very much when I was young, but Duvivier . . . I always wanted to be a director like Julien Duvivier—he did everything. And Renoir . . . I would say my own style really changed after I saw Jean Renoir's *The River* [made in India in 1951] . . . and Billy Wilder, and Carol Reed . . . but you see, I like too many different things, so I could never stop naming directors whose work has impressed me."[26]

Kinoshita, unlike Kurosawa and Kon Ichikawa, has always preferred to write his own original scripts. However, he has worked with a number of scriptwriters, including Tadao Ikeda (*Army*) and Kogo Noda (*The Good Fairy*, 1957), who also wrote for Yasujiro Ozu and Mikio Naruse; Eijiro Hisaita (*Morning for the Osone Family, Apostasy*, 1948, and *The Yotsuya Ghost Story*, 1949), who also wrote for Kurosawa; his own sister Yoshiko Kusuda (*Clouds at Twilight*, 1956); and some who were or would become directors in their own right: Akira Kurosawa (*The Portrait*, 1948), Kaneto Shindo (*A Toast to the Young Miss*), Masaki Kobayashi (*Broken Drum*), and Zenzo Matsuyama (*Distant Clouds*, 1955). After 1956, however, with only one exception, all of his scripts are his own, including the literary adaptations. Earlier he was encouraged to stimulate his own style by using other people's ideas, but now he insists his own ideas are the best and the quickest. "Unless you are working with a great scenarist, like Hisaita, for example, who took my idea for *Morning for the Osone Family* and did exactly as I wanted him to, they are all very jealous of every word they've written. Trying to make corrections is too time-consuming and troublesome. My mind is always ahead of theirs by several steps anyway."[27] Perhaps as a result of doing all his own scripts, however, his later works show a certain uniform sentimentality. Nevertheless, the breadth of material is immediately evident in everything from adaptations of serious modern novels like *Apostasy,* based on Toson's *Hakai* (*The Broken Commandment*), to the boisterous Carmen comedies, to reflections on oppression of the peasants in the feudal era like *The River Fuefuki.*

In his treatment of actors, Kinoshita presents the opposite of the mute severity of a Mikio Naruse. Hideko Takamine, who stars in some eleven Kinoshita films, including masterpieces such as the Carmen comedies, *The Garden of Women, Twenty-four Eyes, The River Fuefuki* and *The Bitter Spirit,* aside from admiring the many different types of women Kinoshita can portray with great depth, finds him easy to work with because he is so straightforward about likes and dislikes, praise and blame.[28] She quotes him as repeating, "The two types of people I can't stand are the stupid and the slow," and (whenever he took a shot he liked), "see what a good director I am?!"[29] In Takamine's estimation, Kinoshita would seem to share with Kon Ichikawa the conviction that actors have to be treated with great tenderness or they cannot perform well, while demanding almost as much of his staff as he did of himself. A measure of the enthusiasm of the players who have worked with Kinoshita—and he has worked with many top stars and introduced many a new face ("Nothing can equal their freshness, and besides, the experienced actors lead them.")[30]—is the fact that Takamine thinks she appeared in more Kinoshita films than she actually has. Credit must be given to what she describes as his "maternal" attitude—he was also intermediary for her marriage to his assistant, Zenzo Matsuyama.

A familiar approach carries over into Kinoshita's cinematography, which has always been executed by his brother-in-law and former colleague in the Shochiku photography section, Hiroshi Kusuda. Again this is a way for Kinoshita to retain total control over his films. "When I first started out Kido opposed the idea of having a director and a cinematographer who were both unknowns working together, but I got my way. I knew I had to have someone who would do exactly as I wanted, and Kusuda and I had agreed on this."[31] As in the case of scriptwriters, Kinoshita finds cinematographers with their own way of doing things more of a hindrance than help. He designs every camera setup himself.

With his inspirational method of shooting, this is of course a necessity. "Only the director can know how one shot is going to follow another," he maintains, "and besides, I had to start out as a cinematographer, so I know what to do."[32] His confidence has aided him in attacking as wide a variety of photographic situations as dramatic situations. The 1946 *Morning for the Osone Family* was all shot with a one-house interior set (except for the ending the U.S. Occupation forced him to shoot at a prison, and which he feels subverts the aesthetic intention of the film); the 1948 *Woman* was all shot on the steep hillsides, farms and winding streets of the seaside resort town of Atami. The 1951 *Carmen Comes Home*, most of it, too, shot on location, was the first all-color feature-length film in Japan; fortunately, Kinoshita shot it simultaneously in black-and-white, which doubled the work, because the early Fuji film process did not prove lasting. In 1955, to give an antique flavor to the recalled story, he used masks throughout *You Were Like a Wild Chrysanthemum*. In the 1958 *Ballad of the Narayama*, he used color, widescreen, spotlighting, dimming and curtains for scene changes, and set that drop or slide out of the frame to simulate the feeling of the Kabuki stage. For the 1960 *River Fuefuki*, he drew on his training in the processing laboratory to achieve medieval battle picture-scroll effects: eerie green, lavender, and sepia cloud patterns, and cartouches with the names of the famous battle scenes intrude constantly to remind us of the aesthetic recording of this ghastly sixteenth-century reality.

Music has, like cinematography, been a family affair for Kinoshita. When his brother Chuji, who had studied composition, had no work at the end of the war, he invited him to come work with him. Since 1946 all of Kinoshita's film music has been done by his brother, who even plays the role of the pianist brother in *Broken Drum*. In comedies and lighter musical films like their first one together, *The Girl I Loved* (1946), the Kinoshita brothers team excells, but Chuji's experimental approach has served other films less well—the flamenco guitar theme in *The Bitter Spirit*, for example, sounds disturbingly inappropriate to western ears, but perhaps startled the Japanese no more than Fumio Hayasaka's use of Ravel's "Bolero" did in Kurosawa's 1950 *Rashomon*.

When it comes to editing, Kinoshita feels he has done enough. "Except for Kurosawa, the Japanese follow a shooting order that is exactly the same as the finished film. If you want a closeup in between two medium shots, you stop and shoot that closeup." He leaves the editing to the staff editor because, he says, "After doing my own writing, directing of actors and camera setups, I'd rather have a little time left to eat, drink, and talk about movies with my friends."[33] At the rate Kinoshita made films, however, usually producing two for every one the company requested, one wonders where he found any free time at all.

A Japanese Tragedy

Although Kinoshita's production rate was extraordinarily fast, like most directors he retains deepest affection for the works on which he spent the most time and had the largest budget. For Kinoshita, predictably, there is no single favorite, but several that tend to be his most technically experimental and his most tragic: *The River Fuefuki, You Were Like a Wild Chrysanthemum, The Ballad of the Narayama, The Scent of Incense* (1964), and *A Japanese Tragedy*.[34] The story behind the making of *A Japanese Tragedy* fully reveals the depth of Kinoshita's feeling for it.

In exchange for Akira Kurosawa's script for *The Portrait* in 1948, Kinoshita had promosed to write a script for a Kurosawa assistant who was to be promoted.[35] He felt an obligation to do a good job, and gathered a great deal of information for the film, gradually becoming so interested in it he was loathe to give it away. But when he turned it over to Toho, they decided it was too difficult for that particular director, and in fact would not be a good commercial risk.[36] A delighted Kinoshita immediately had Shochiku buy it back and he set about filming it in 1953, using newsreel footage in a way that had never been done before to produce one of his most moving films.

A Japanese Tragedy has been called "a *haha-mono* or 'mother film,' but one of the very finest."[37] In essence this means it succeeds in doing what Shiro Kido said the Kamata film was designed to do in the late twenties and early 1930s: show that the self-sacrificing mother deserves gratitude and obedience. Indeed the widowed mother who has to work as a maid in a resort inn to support her two contemptuous children strongly recalls the middle-aged geisha of Mikio Naruse's 1933 *Apart from You*. In Kinoshita's modern version of the unappreciated mother story, however, there is no one to convince the children to love their mother but the mother herself, and her attempts at demanding her due end in miserable failure. What Kinoshita shows, by combining parts of the broad contemporary scene with newsreel footage and newspaper headlines, and flashbacks from the past of the mother and her two nearly adult children, is that social conditions are responsible for the tragedy. The very same year Yasujiro Ozu said he was making a film about the breakdown of the Japanese family system in *Tokyo Story*, but actually made a film about the acceptance of permanent separation and lowered expectations, Kinoshita's film showed not just lack of love for their elders on the part of children, but shame, scorn, exploitation and abuse. And he points to identifiable causes for both the children's callousness and the mother's suffering: all is part of the aftermath of that great deceit, the Pacific War.

Haruko (Yuko Mochizuki), who lost her husband in the war, has worked at every manner of degrading occupation in order to raise her two children. She is uneducated and trusting, and as a result loses even her one possession, her land, to her unscrupulous brother-in-law (Shinichi Himori), who promises to care for the children but actually lets his wife mistreat them and teach them their mother is "off having a good time in her flashy clothes" when she works to support them in another town. By the time they are young adults, they have learned to think that money will solve all of their problems. Haruko works in Atami to send her daughter Utako (Yoko Katsuragi) to sewing and English conversation schools and her son Seiichi (Masami Taura) to medical school in Tokyo. But the two children use their education as excuses to keep demanding more money from their mother and live in freedom away from her. Utako is raped while a young girl and hates men. She takes revenge on her married English teacher (Ken Uehara) who falls in love with her, and ruins his family life. Seiichi announces to his mother that he intends to become the adopted son of a wealthy physician who lost his own child in the war, and when the distraught Haruko rushes to Tokyo to see him about Utako, all he talks of is changing the family records. Completely rejected by her children, Haruko throws herself in front of an oncoming train on the way back. Only her two friends back in Atami, a street musician (Keiji Sata) and the inn's cook (Teiji Takahashi) remain to speak of her as a good person.

While its morality is quite traditional, the form of *A Japanese Tragedy* is one of the most modern of its time. A series of about 21 very fast-cut scenes showing the progress of the mood of the postwar reconstruction age precedes the title and credit sequences. These show montages of newspaper headlines on war crimes trials, newsreel footage of the courtroom scenes, the pardoned Emperor greeting the cameras, and jump through intertitles to the present-day political dissatisfaction and social unrest—demonstrations, strikes, assassination attempts, suicides, poverty and gangster takeovers. Before he focuses on his protagonists, Kinoshita uses an intertitle to warn, heavy kettle drums, bells, and cymbals on the soundtrack, that this story is an allegory about a problem that is so close to us that it could spread throughout Japanese soil.

Through such devices, the realism of the story is extremely calculated. Deep focus, long-take photography in the opening sequences at the Atami inn stresses the bustling, vulgar actuality of the scene, and song is smoothly incorporated in the character of the street musician. The flashbacks show determinism of the personalities of the vicious, cold children. Cutting from the boy and girl facing each other across a table of food, the first flashback shows them as small children in the identical composition. We then see the ruins, the mother getting black-market rice for them, and talk of hunger and disease. The most telling part of this flashback sequence is in the sister's classroom, however, where the teacher writes the subject for an essay on the blackboard: "New Japan." A pupil asks why they were taught the war was good before, but now it is a "mistake." She accuses the teacher of deceiving them, but the teacher responds, "No, I was deceived along with everyone else." From a closeup of the sister's face, newsreel footage of riots, trains derailing, police and military troops and exploding bombs follow. In subsequent flashbacks, more reasons for the children's mercenary, selfish attitudes appear: a street politician lectures on the meaning of democracy while the two small children watch in the crowd. What emerges is that if someone else does wrong, freedom allows me to do the same. The camera cuts to a Japanese girl and a U.S. serviceman kissing, the children observing, and then their mother laughing with a man under the light of a street lamp.

Kinoshita's message explodes all over the screen through his montage and manipulation of time. He even worked out with Kusuda how to get the contemporary dramatic footage to match the old newsreels, and was extremely proud of the results.[38] The war was a case of insincerity, deceit, and the distortion of the meaning of democracy in the postwar era is just as impure, resulting in children who destroy their own parents out of avarice and contempt. Kinoshita drives home all that Ozu left out of *Tokyo Story* except as a joking conversational reference—extreme parental self-sacrifice and severe neglect on the part of children in return. The deterministic form of the film construction, couched in surprising experimental feats, underscores Kinoshita's immutable philosophy of purity, maternal love and beauty, which are corrupted by outside, impersonal, unfeeling political and social forces.

Ofuna Flavor

There is a noticeable change in the sting of Kinoshita's message after *A Japanese Tragedy*, and the following year's *Garden of Women*. By the time he reached the subsequent *Twenty-four Eyes* the protest became submerged in sentimentality. The schoolteacher of the small Inland Sea community resigns when books she believes are good for teaching purposes are condemned as "Red" literature, and she does not return to her job until after the war's end. But the greater emphasis of the story is on its "three-handkerchiefs"[39] aspects of the film, the widowed teacher's personal sorrows and courage. It would be this sentimental quality that director Nagisa Oshima would point to as the finest example of "Ofuna flavor" when he and others sought to overthrow Shochiku's calcified forms in the late 1950s and early 1960s.[40] It was a glorification of purity and innocence that became, for the eager and sophisticated young of the New Wave generation, inapplicable to their own lives. The destructive violence and sexuality, the potential insincerity of ordinary people that they insisted were part of daily life were what Kinoshita would have labeled as unbeautiful, and therefore not part of what he feels society and film should be.

Kinoshita had found long before Oshima that social protest in film had no effect. He was disappointed in Japan in the war and nearly quit film when he had just begun, but he came back again. After his sojourn in France in 1951 he returned with a new critical eye to Japan and made his finest satires and deepest social tragedies. But, he says, "the Japanese people did not take me seriously, and I decided it was useless to try to say anything meaningful to them."[41] *The Garden of Women* shows a school headmistress whose cruelty results from her own hidden tragedy in youth, but Kinoshita's message is that people like her should nevertheless be deposed, just as children like Haruko's in *A Japanese Tragedy* are in the wrong no matter how understandable their behavior may be. But starting with *Twenty-four Eyes* the evil in society becomes more a-nonymous, less possible to pinpoint and attack, and Kinoshita's protagonists become simultaneously weaker. The "eternal youth" has never changed his ideas, as his admiration of *Rocky* shows, but his presentation of the pure, the meek, the honest, the young has become even more indulgent. A film like his 1963 *Sing, Young People!* refuses to deal with the possibilities he confronted so openly in *A Japanese Tragedy* and somewhat less rationally as late as 1956 in *The Rose on His Arm*. His sympathies remain with the young, the loving family, and all who retain the purity and innocence of youth. "Today the word 'young' [the English loan word *yangu*], as far as I can see in the media, is synonymous with 'idiot.' I think it's outrageous what mindless trash the young people allow to be foisted upon them today,"[42] he says, reconfirming his respect for youth and wishing they would protest.

Nevertheless, Kinoshita remains almost totally ensconced in television production, where he cannot make movies with the wonderful scenic long shots that marked his style and have been perpetuated by younger directors like Yoji Yamada at Shochiku. "But," he says, "I still have too many ideas for movies, and if I had to work in theatrical films I'd only be able to make one a year at the most under today's bad financial conditions. To make features now requires too much compromise with the financiers who demand a sure thing—and of course I'm no good at compromise."[43] Many today decry the loss of Keisuke Kinoshita to the tiny screen in the little box, but he believes his audience remains at home, and in his seven years of television production, his dramatic series have been among the most popular in the country. "Of course I would rather make features," he admits, "but in television I can do whatever I want and a lot of it."[44]

Notes

1 Author's interview with Keisuke Kinoshita, May 1977.
2 *Ibid.*
3 *Ibid.*
4 Tsuneo Hazumi, "Hyoden: Kinoshita Keisuke" (Critical Biography: Keisuke Kinoshita), *Kinema Jumpo* (Tokyo), No. 115, 1955, p. 33.
5 Toru Ogawa, *Gendai nihon eiga sakka ron* (Theories on Contemporary Japanese Film-makers) (Tokyo: Sanichi Shobo, 1965) p. 73.
6 Kinoshita interview, *cit.*
7 Keisuke Kinoshita, "Jisaku o kataru" (Keisuke Kinoshita Talks about His Films), *Kinema Jumpo*, No. 115, 1955, p. 35.
8 Kinoshita interview, *cit.*
9 Kinoshita, *op. cit.*, p. 35.
10 Kinoshita interview, *cit.*
11 *Ibid.*
12 Kinoshita, *op. cit.*, p. 35.
13 *Ibid.*, p. 36.
14 *Ibid.*, p. 36.
15 Kinoshita interview, *cit.*
16 *Ibid.*
17 *Ibid.*
18 Joseph L. Anderson and Donald Richie, *The Japanese Film: Art and Industry* (New York: Grove Press, 1960), p. 372.
19 Tadao Sato, *Nihon eiga shiso shi* (History of the Intellectual Currents in Japanese Film) (Tokyo: Sanichi Shobo, 1970), p. 253.
20 Ogawa, *op. cit.*, p. 75.
21 Kinoshita, *op. cit.*, p. 38.
22 *Ibid.*, p. 38.
23 Shiro Kido, *Nihon eiga den: Eiga seisakusha no kiroku* (The Story of the Japanese Film: A Movie Producer's Record) (Tokyo: Bungei Shunjusha, 1956), pp. 52–54.
24 *Ibid.*
25 Anderson and Richie, *op. cit.*, p. 373.
26 Kinoshita interview, *cit.*
27 *Ibid.*
28 Hideko Takamine, *Watashi no tosei nikki* (My Professional Diary) (Tokyo: Asahi Shimbun-sha, 1976), vol. 2, pp. 187–88.
29 *Ibid.*, pp. 192–93.
30 Kinoshita interview, *cit.*
31 *Ibid.*
32 *Ibid.*
33 *Ibid.*
34 *Ibid.*
35 *Ibid.*
36 Kinoshita, *op. cit.*, p. 46.
37 Anderson and Richie, *op. cit.*, p. 188.
38 Kinoshita, *op. cit.*, p. 46.
39 Edwin O. Reischauer, introduction to *Twenty-four Eyes* in P. B. S. television series, *The Japanese Film*, 1975.
40 Nagisa Oshima, *Sengo eiga: Hakai to sozo* (Postwar Film: Destruction and Creation) (Tokyo: Sanichi Shobo, 1963), p. 18.

[41] Kinoshita interview, *cit.*
[42] *Ibid.*
[43] *Ibid.*
[44] *Ibid.*

KEISUKE KINOSHITA: FILMOGRAPHY

1943 **The Blossoming Port (Hana Saku Minato)*
pr: Shochiku (Ofuna); orig. story: Kazuo Kikuta; sc: Yoshiro Tsuji; ph: Hiroshi Kusuda; music: Jo Abe; cast: Eitaro Ozawa, Ken Uehara, Mitsuko Mito, Chishu Ryu, Eijiro Tono et al. From his debut work, Kinoshita shows his taste for comedy of character, idyllic locations, romance and faith in human good-heartedness. Two adventurous crooks attempt to defraud the entire population of a sleepy southern port town by posing as long-lost heirs to a defunct shipyard they intend to "revive." Collecting money from all the townspeople, they intend to abscond with it, but one of them falls in love with a local girl, and finally both are won over by the sincerity of the people and the outbreak of the war. Eiga Hyoron #4. (FC; dupe positive at Shochiku, Tokyo.)

The Living Magoroku (Ikite Iru Magoroku)
pr: Shochiku (Ofuna); orig. sc: Kinoshita; ph: Hiroshi Kusuda; music: Hikaru Saotome; cast: Ken Uehara, Yasumi Hara, Reikichi Kawamura, Mitsuko Yoshikawa, Fumiko Okamura et al. Confused story aimed at promoting food production for the war effort, but with underlying themes of attacking superstition and encouraging young love. A family of rural gentry is finally persuaded to give up their fields to grow crops for the troops when the local military advisor convinces them that their son will not die if the ground is broken. It turns out that the ailing son suffers not from tuberculosis, but mere nervous exhaustion. Interwoven is an irrelevant story about establishing the identity of a prized sword. (FC; negative at Shochiku, Tokyo.)

1944 *Jubilation Street (Kanko no Machi)*
pr: Shochiku (Ofuna); orig. sc: Kaoru Morimoto; ph: Hiroshi Kusuda; cast: Ken Uehara, Eijiro Tono, Mitsuko Mito, Choko Iida et al. Made to promote the drive to evacuate the cities, this story focuses on one particular family waiting for the father to come home, their fears about leaving until he does, and their relations with the other people and businesses on their street. (FC; dupe positive at Shochiku, Tokyo.)

*Army (Rikugun)
pr: Shochiku (Ofuna); orig. story: Ashihei Hino; sc: Tadao Ikeda; ph: Yoshio Taketomi; cast: Kinuyo Tanaka, Chishu Ryu, Ken Mitsuda, Haruko Sugimura, Ken Uehara et al. Amazingly honest film that should have been war propaganda. Three generations of a family with a career military tradition are traced from feudal times down to the current Pacific War. Attention focuses on the son of the second generation, who has been unable to live up to the family tradition because of poor health and also proves a failure as a merchant because of his military frankness. His own son is also a weakling, and he fears that this boy too will prove a military failure. But the son grows strong in his adolescence, and the film closes with his tearful mother following the parade as he goes off to the front. One-scene, one-take technique with much camera movement. Criticized on release —and justly so —for being anti-war. (FC; dupe positive at Shochiku, Tokyo.)

1946 *Morning for the Osone Family (Osone-ke no Asa)*
pr: Shochiku (Ofuna); orig. sc: Eijiro Hisaita; ph: Hiroshi Kusuda; music: Takaaki Asai; cast: Haruko Sugimura, Eitaro Ozawa, Mitsuko Miura, Eijiro Tono, Shin Tokudaiji et al. A bitter look back at responsibility for the war, a new inter-pretation of democracy as popular justice instead of license, and encourage-ment for women to assert themselves. A widow with three sons and an out-spoken daughter relies on her militarist brother-in-law to manage the family during the war. The oldest son is jailed for his pacifist thoughts, and the uncle breaks his niece's engagement as a result. The two younger sons are drafted and both die, and by the end of the war the widow realizes that her brother-in-law's counsel has all been self-aggrandizement. She throws him out and joy-fully receives her newly released pacifist son as morning dawns for the liberal family. *KJ* #1. (FC; dupe positive at Shochiku, Tokyo.)

The Girl I Loved (Waga Koi Seshi Otome)
pr: Shochiku (Ofuna); orig. sc: Kinoshita; ph: Hiroshi Kusuda; music: Chuji Kinoshita; cast: Yasumi Hara, Kuniko Igawa, Chieko Higashiyama, Yoshindo Yamaji, Junji Soneda et al. Pastoral idyll about a farm boy who loves the orphan girl he grew up with, only to see her marry a handicapped school teacher from the village. Kinoshita's first work with his brother's music, inter-weaving songs in René Clair style and creating the best of his escapist senti-mentality. *KJ* #5. (FC; dupe positive at Shochiku, Tokyo.)

1947 *Marriage (Kekkon)*
pr: Shochiku (Ofuna); orig. idea: Kinoshita; sc: Kaneto Shindo; ph: Hiroshi Kusuda; music: Chuji Kinoshita; cast: Ken Uehara, Kinuyo Tanaka, Eijiro Tono, Chieko Higashiyama, Kuniko Igawa et al. Promotion of postwar female emanci-pation ideals as a young woman opposes her family and marries the man of her own choice. (Non-circulating print; dupe positive at Shochiku, Tokyo.)

Phoenix (Fushicho)
pr: Shochiku (Ofuna); orig. story: Yoshiro Kawazu; sc: Kinoshita; asst. dir: Masaki Kobayashi; ph: Hiroshi Kusuda; music: Chuji Kinoshita; cast: Kinuyo Tanaka, Toyoko Takahashi, Keiji Sata, Isamu Kosugi et al. Melodrama set in wartime and including one of the shocking new kiss scenes. Two young people are finally able to marry, but the war intervenes almost immediately and the husband never returns from it. The wife, however, lives on like an ever-reviving phoenix through her destructive experiences. (FC; dupe positive at Shochiku, Tokyo.)

1948 *Woman (Onna)*
pr: Shochiku (Ofuna); orig. sc: Kinoshita; asst. dir: Masaki Kobayashi; ph: Hiroshi Kusuda; music: Chuji Kinoshita; cast: Mitsuko Mito, Eitaro Ozawa et al. Melodramatic semi-thriller about a long-suffering woman and the worthless man she loves, but with an unusual emancipation twist. A Tokyo dance-hall girl goes to a hotspring resort to meet her former lover. He begs her to run away with him, finally admitting that he was involved in a robbery. He convinces her her career is worthless anyway and invokes their old love for each other. She makes an effort to stay with him, but realizes she will be im-

plicated in his spontaneous criminal acts. She escapes amid a crowd during a fire in a resort town and returns to her job in Tokyo. Typical Kinoshita beautiful seaside locations, but too many forced action scenes. (FC; dupe positive at Shochiku, Tokyo.)

The Portrait (*Shozo*)
pr: Shochiku (Ofuna); orig. sc: Akira Kurosawa; asst. dir: Masaki Kobayashi; ph: Hiroshi Kusuda; music: Chuji Kinoshita; cast: Kuniko Igawa, Kuniko Miyake, Mitsuko Miura, Ichiro Sugai, Chieko Higashiyama et al. With the idea of challenging his own patterns, Kinoshita asked his forceful friend Kurosawa to do this script, but the result is cinematically reserved in Kinoshita's usual style. A woman who is a mistress poses for a portrait in which she is rendered as a pure and honest person. Her own self-image is changed by this experience and she runs away from her unsavory patron to change her life. (FC; dupe positive at Shochiku, Tokyo.)

Apostasy (*Hakai*)
pr: Shochiku (Kyoto); orig. novel: Toson Shimazaki; sc: Eijiro Hisaita; asst. dir: Masaki Kobayashi; ph: Hiroshi Kusuda; music: Chuji Kinoshita; cast: Ryo Ikebe, Yoko Katsuragi, Osamu Takizawa, Jukichi Uno, Yoshi Kato et al. Social protest film showing Kinoshita's sentimental humanism. A young schoolteacher, member of Japan's pariah class, hides his identity until the pariah intellectual leader he admires is killed. Rumors spread about his heritage and school authorities try to have him removed, but he confesses before his sobbing pupils, and the message of freedom and equality is heavily underscored with tears. Interesting to compare with Kon Ichikawa's 1961 version of the same story. *KJ* #6. (FC; negative at Shochiku, Tokyo.)

1949   *A Toast to the Young Miss/Here's to the Girls* (*Ojosan Kampai*)
pr: Shochiku (Ofuna); orig. sc: Kaneto Shindo; asst. dir: Masaki Kobayashi; ph: Hiroshi Kusuda; music: Chuji Kinoshita; cast: Shuji Sano, Setsuko Hara, Sugisaku Aoyama, Keiji Sata, Sachiko Murase et al. Sentimental egalitarianism in a love story that crosses class barriers. A lower-class entrepreneur on his way up is proposed a match with a lovely girl of an aristocratic family. He soon learns her household is bankrupt and hoping he will bail them out, and he feels he has none of the refined culture this girl enjoys. But in the end the girl herself realizes she is really in love with this boorish but charmingly frank and devoted young man, and she runs off to stop him from leaving town in despair. KJ #6. (FC; dupe positive at Shochiku, Tokyo.)

The Yotsuya Ghost Story, Parts I and II (*Yotsuya Kaidan, I-II*)
pr: Shochiku (Kyoto); orig. Kabuki play: Namboku Tsuruya; sc: Eijiro Hisaita; asst. dir: Masaki Kobayashi; ph: Hiroshi Kusuda; music: Chuji Kinoshita; cast: Kinuyo Tanaka, Ken Uehara, Haruko Sugimura, Choko Iida et al. New interpretation of the famous story of revenge by the spirit of a scorned wife. Leftist playwright Hisaita's script concentrates on the human relations elements and foregoes much of the grotesquerie. (FC; dupe positive at Shochiku, Tokyo.)

Broken Drum (Yabure-daiko)
pr: Shochiku (Kyoto); orig. sc: Kinoshita and Masaki Kobayashi; asst. dir: Masaki Kobayashi; ph: Hiroshi Kusuda; music: Chuji Kinoshita; cast: Tsuma-saburo Bando, Sachiko Murase, Masayuki Mori, Jukichi Uno, Chuji Kinoshita et al. Rollicking satire on the nouveau riche. A blustering father tries to run his family, composed of very modern strong individuals, along feudal authoritarian lines. Teased by all, he fails and relents. *KJ* #4. (FC; dupe positive at Shochiku, Tokyo.)

1950 *Engagement Ring (Konyaku Yubiwa)*
pr: Shochiku (Ofuna); orig. sc: Kinoshita; ph: Hiroshi Kusuda; music: Chuji Kinoshita; cast: Jukichi Uno, Kinuyo Tanaka, Toshiro Mifune, Mitsuko Yoshikawa, Nobuko Otowa et al. Beautiful seaside locations in a maudlin love story about a wife who nearly deserts her sick husband for the young doctor who is treating him. (FC; dupe positive at Shochiku, Tokyo.)

1951 *The Good Fairy (Zemma)*
pr: Shochiku (Ofuna); orig. story: Kunio Kishida; sc: Kogo Noda and Kinoshita; ph: Hiroshi Kusuda; music: Chuji Kinoshita; cast: Masayuki Mori, Chikage Awashima, Rentaro Mikuni, Yoko Katsuragi, Chishu Ryu et al. Protest against scandal-mongering in the press centering around a young reporter sent to cover a divorce case in which his sympathy for those involved makes him fudge the assignment. Impressive snow country settings; Mikuni's debut film. (FC; dupe positive at Shochiku, Tokyo.)

Carmen Comes Home (Karumen Kokyo ni Kaeru)
pr: Shochiku (Ofuna); orig. sc: Kinoshita; asst. dir: Masaki Kobayashi; ph: Hiroshi Kusuda; music: Chuji Kinoshita and Toshiro Mayuzumi; cast: Hideko Takamine, Shuji Sano, Chishu Ryu, Kuniko Igawa, Takeshi Sakamoto et al. Musical satire on postwar manners involving Tokyo stripper Lily Carmen and her colleague Akemi meeting the baffled folks back home in the country. They find themselves shunned, ridiculed and lonely until they put on a benefit performance for the local elementary school and leave town as heroines. Takamine as a remarkable comedienne. *KJ* #4. (FC; dupe positive at Shochiku, Tokyo.)

A Record of Youth (Shonenki)
pr: Shochiku (Ofuna); orig. story: Isoko Hatano; sc: Sumie Tanaka and Kinoshita; ph: Hiroshi Kusuda; music: Chuji Kinoshita; cast: Akiko Tamura, Akira Ishihama, Chishu Ryu, Rentaro Mikuni, Toshiko Kobayashi et al. Another critical look at wartime thought control, couched in a story of a boy growing up in the country. His father, formerly a university English professor, spends all his time reading and doesn't help his mother with the work at all. The boy finally comes to understand when his father is accused of being anti-war and tells him if he must die he wishes to spend every possible minute left reading his liberal books. (FC; dupe positive at Shochiku, Tokyo.)

Fireworks over the Sea (Umi no Hanabi)
pr: Shochiku (Ofuna); orig. sc: Kinoshita; ph: Hiroshi Kusuda; music: Chuji Kinoshita; cast: Michiyo Kogure, Yoko Katsuragi, Chishu Ryu, Keiji Sata,

Rentaro Mikuni et al. Undistinguished melodrama with a huge cast set in a port town in northern Kyushu. Hastily executed so that Kinoshita could leave for France. (FC; negative at Shochiku, Tokyo.)

1952   ***Carmen's Pure Love** (Karumen Junjosu)*
pr: Shochiku (Ofuna); orig. sc: Kinoshita; asst. dir: Masaki Kobayashi; ph: Hiroshi Kusuda; music: Chuji Kinoshita and Toshiro Mayuzumi; cast: Hideko Takamine, Masao Wakahara, Chikage Awashima, Toshiko Kobayashi, Eiko Miyoshi et al. Stripper Carmen again devoted to her art and a playboy artist she meets by accident. Postwar confusion of ideals of patriotism, liberation, and equality interestingly expressed through tilted camera angles and camera movement. Parodies on all the extreme types, especially the superpatriot played by Miyoshi. Originally shot in color as well as BW, but the process was unsuccessful. *KJ* #5. (FC; negative at Shochiku, Tokyo.)

1953   ***A Japanese Tragedy** (Nihon no Higeki)*
pr: Shochiku (Ofuna); orig. sc: Kinoshita; asst. dir: Masaki Kobayashi; ph: Hiroshi Kusuda; music: Chuji Kinoshita; cast: Yuko Mochizuki, Yoko Katsuragi, Masami Taura, Keiji Sata, Ken Uehara et al. Sentimental criticism of postwar ruthless individualism. At the close of the war, a widowed mother makes every possible sacrifice to bring up her ungrateful son and daughter. They gradually reject her in their search for the material comforts she cannot provide by working as a maid at an inn, and she commits suicide in despair. Newsreel footage intercut throughout integrates the individual mother's tragedy into the larger historical context. *KJ* #6. (FC; negative at Shochiku, Tokyo.)

1954   ***The Garden of Women** (Onna no Sono)*
pr: Shochiku (Ofuna); orig. story: Tomoji Abe; sc: Kinoshita; ph: Hiroshi Kusuda; music: Chuji Kinoshita; cast: Mieko Takamine, Hideko Takamine, Keiko Kishi, Yoshiko Kuga, Takahiro Tamura et al. Protest against vestiges of feudalism in the teaching profession, reminiscent of Leontine Sagan's 1931 *Mädchen in Uniform.* A proud and severe headmistress in a private girls' school shows leniency to a rich girl despite her leftist ideas and extreme cruelty toward a poor girl sent to school to keep her from getting married. Rebellion breaks out when the poor girl commits suicide. *KJ* #2. (FC, PFA/SH)

***Twenty-four Eyes** (Nijushi no Hitomi)*
pr: Shochiku (Ofuna); orig. story: Sakae Tsuboi; sc: Kinoshita; ph: Hiroshi Kusuda; music: Chuji Kinoshita; cast: Hideko Takamine, Yumeji Tsukioka, Toshiko Kobayashi, Kuniko Igawa, Chishu Ryu et al. Chronicle of a teacher and her pupils in a small Inland Sea village beginning in 1928 and carrying through twenty years of their joys and sorrows. Criticism of wartime thought control and the tragedies wrought in the lives of the island people, presented in a very touching and sincere reserved camera style with emphasis on the beauty of the setting. *KJ* #1. (FC, PFA/SH, AB)

1955   *Distant Clouds (Toi Kumo)*
pr: Shochiku (Ofuna); orig. sc: Kinoshita and Zenzo Matsuyama; ph: Hiroshi Kusuda; music: Chuji Kinoshita; cast: Hideko Takamine, Keiji Sata, Takahiro

Tamura, Kuniko Igawa, Akira Ishihama et al. Melodramatic love story exploiting the setting of the old castle town of Takayama. After many years a man returns home before being sent away to a new job, and he falls in love with a local young widow. She too is attracted to him, but gossip, sabotage, and anxiety on the part of relatives conspire to keep the woman with her dead husband's family. (FC, PFA/SH)

You Were Like a Wild Chrysanthemum (Nogiku no Gotoki Kimi Nariki)
pr: Shochiku (Ofuna); orig. story: Sachio Ito; sc: Kinoshita; ph: Hiroshi Kusuda; music: Chuji Kinoshita; cast: Noriko Arita, Shinji Tanaka, Chishu Ryu, Takahiro Tamura, Haruko Sugimura et al. Story of unrequited love resulting from a mother's ambitions for her son. An old man returns to his home town in the mountains after 60 years and recalls his youth in flashbacks, remembering the cousin he loved but was not allowed to marry because he was to go away to school. While his own worldly success went as planned, she was forced into marriage and died from early childbirth. *KJ* #3. (FC, PFA/SH)

1956 *Clouds at Twilight (Yuyake-gumo)*
pr: Shochiku (Ofuna); orig. sc: Yoshiko Kusuda; ph: Hiroshi Kusuda; music: Chuji Kinoshita; cast: Shinji Tanaka, Yuko Mochizuki, Takahiro Tamura, Yoshiko Kuga, Eijiro Tono et al. Delicate treatment of the transition from childhood illusions to the reality of adulthood. A boy whose family runs a fish shop fantasizes with his close friend about what they see through a telescope, his window to a world where he escapes from his ties to the shop. His ambitious older sister marries for money and deserts her family, his friend moves away, and when his father dies he reluctantly but dutifully takes over the family business. (FC, PFA/SH)

The Rose on His Arm (Taiyo to Bara)
pr: Shochiku (Ofuna); orig. sc: Kinoshita; ph: Hiroshi Kusuda; music: Chuji Kinoshita; cast: Akira Ishihama, Katsuo Nakamura, Sadako Sawamura, Yoshiko Kuga, Noriko Arita et al. Kinoshita's response to the *taiyo-zoku* ("sun cult") films about rebellious youth. A lower-class boy despises his hardworking mother and gets involved with petty gangsters at first, then a rich boy who makes a plaything out of him. He ends by breaking his mother's heart. *KJ* #9. (FC, PFA/SH)

1957 *Times of Joy and Sorrow/The Lighthouse (Yorokobi mo Kanashimi mo Ikutoshitsuki)*
pr: Shochiku (Ofuna); orig. sc: Kinoshita; color ph: Hiroshi Kusuda; music: Chuji Kinoshita; cast: Hideko Takamine, Keiji Sata, Katsuo Nakamura, Masako Arisawa, Yoko Katsuragi et al. Chronicle of two generations of a family that operates lighthouses, covering the period from 1935 up to the present. Their vicissitudes during the war and after, treated with gushing sentimentality. *KJ* #3; Geijutsusai Grand Prize. (FC; negative at Shochiku, Tokyo.)

A Candle in the Wind/Danger Stalks Near (Fuzen no Tomoshibi)
pr: Shochiku (Ofuna); orig. sc: Kinoshita; ph: Hiroshi Kusuda; music: Chuji

Kinoshita; cast: Hideko Takamine, Keiji Sata, Akiko Tamura, Shinji Nambara, Toshiko Kobayashi et al. Comedy of family relations recalling Kinoshita's 1949 *Broken Drum*. Everyone in this suburban household is after everyone else's money, but when they win a valuable camera in a contest, the schemes come to a head, only to be further complicated by a group of young thieves who have their eye on the house. (FC, PFA/SH)

1958 ***The Ballad of the Narayama (Narayamabushi-ko)**
pr: Shochiku (Ofuna); orig. story: Shichiro Fukazawa; sc: Kinoshita; color 'scope ph: Hiroshi Kusuda; music: Tameharu Endo; cast: Kinuyo Tanaka, Teiji Takahashi, Yuko Mochizuki, Seiji Miyaguchi, Yunosuke Ito et al. Allegory about parent-child relationships, skillfully employing Kabuki stage techniques. In the remote mountains certain poor villages traditionally abandon the aged on a mountaintop in order to ensure that the younger people can eat. The heroine, near 70, forces her unwilling and loving son to follow the horrible tradition. *KJ #1*. (FC, SH)

The Eternal Rainbow (Kono Ten no Niji)
pr: Shochiku (Ofuna); orig. sc: Kinoshita; color 'scope ph: Hiroshi Kusuda; music: Chuji Kinoshita; cast: Teiji Takahashi, Yoshiko Kuga, Takahiro Tamura, Kinuyo Tanaka, Chishu Ryu et al. Documentary-like treatment of life in a north Kyushu steel town, touching on many people's joys and tribulations and emphasizing collective life. (FC, PFA/SH)

1959 **Snow Flurry (Kazabana)**
pr: Shochiku (Ofuna); orig. sc: Kinoshita; color 'scope ph: Hiroshi Kusuda; music: Chuji Kinoshita; cast: Keiko Kishi, Ineko Arima, Yoshiko Kuga, Yusuke Kawazu, Chishu Ryu et al. Typically resplendent, nostalgic location for a rural story. Various residents of a farming village suffer under the onus of feudalistic tradition and gradually extricate themselves. (FC, PFA/SH)

The Bird of Springs Past (Sekishuncho)
pr: Shochiku (Ofuna); orig. sc: Kinoshita; color 'scope ph: Hiroshi Kusuda; music: Chuji Kinoshita; cast: Keiji Sata, Ineko Arima, Masahiko Tsugawa, Akira Ishihama, Toyozo Yamamoto et al. Set against the mountain scenery of Aizu, sentimental story of the friendship of five young men and how it is affected over the years by war, illness, postwar progress and the like. Poor construction and pacing. (FC, PFA/SH)

Thus Another Day (Kyo mo Mata Kakute Ari Nan)
pr: Shochiku (Ofuna); orig. sc: Kinoshita; color 'scope ph: Hiroshi Kusuda; music: Chuji Kinoshita; cast: Teiji Takahashi, Yoshiko Kuga, Kankuro Naka-mura, Kanzaburo Nakamura, Takahiro Tamura et al. Melodrama set in the Karuizawa mountains involving a white-collar worker's family, a retired career military man and threatening gangsters. (FC, PFA/SH)

1960 ***Spring Dreams (Haru no Yume)**
pr: Shochiku (Ofuna); orig. sc: Kinoshita; color 'scope ph: Hiroshi Kusuda; music: Chuji Kinoshita; cast: Mariko Okada, Yoshiko Kuga, Eitaro Ozawa, Shuji Sano, Chishu Ryu et al. Upper-class family comedy with fresh, biting

repartee. The family's life is thrown into confusion by a sweet-potato vendor who has a stroke in their house. (FC, PFA/SH)

*The River Fuefuki (Fuefukigawa)
pr: Shochiku (Ofuna); orig. story: Shichiro Fukazawa; sc: Kinoshita; color 'scope ph: Hiroshi Kusuda; music: Chuji Kinoshita; cast: Hideko Takamine, Takahiro Tamura, Somegoro Ichikawa, Shima Iwashita, Mannosuke Nakamura et al. Period drama chronicle about five generations of a poor farming family during the war-torn sixteenth century. Their doom is finally brought about by the young people's ambitions to become warriors. Experimental techniques incorporating medieval battle scroll-painting effects. *KJ* #4. (FC, SH)

1961 ***The Bitter Spirit/Immortal Love (Eien no Hito)**
pr: Shochiku (Ofuna); orig. sc: Kinoshita; 'scope ph: Hiroshi Kusuda; music: Chuji Kinoshita; cast: Hideko Takamine, Tatsuya Nakadai, Keiji Sata, Nobuko Otowa, Akira Ishihama et al. Another chronicle film with an overpowering setting: Mount Aso. A rural woman loves a man from the same town, but he goes off to war and she is raped and forced to marry the son of the village headman. She never recovers from her resentment of her husband, and helps her children escape from him. Greatly flawed by inappropriate flamenco guitar score. *KJ* #3. (FC, PFA/SH)

1962 **This Year's Love (Kotoshi no Koi)**
pr: Shochiku (Ofuna); orig. sc: Kinoshita; 'scope ph: Hiroshi Kusuda; music: Chuji Kinoshita; cast: Mariko Okada, Teruo Yoshida, Masakazu Tamura, Chieko Higashiyama, Chieko Naniwa et al. As the title implies, this is a sentimental love story made for New Year's release. (FC, PFA/SH)

The Seasons We Walked Together (Futari de Aruita Iku Shunju)
pr: Shochiku (Ofuna); orig. poetry: Doko Kawano; sc: Kinoshita; 'scope ph: Hiroshi Kusuda; music: Chuji Kinoshita; cast: Hideko Takamine, Keiji Sata, Toyozo Yamamoto, Yoshiko Kuga, Chieko Baisho et al. Family drama about a man repatriated after the Pacific War and unable to find work. He becomes a road construction worker, and he and his wife labor many years to see their son through college. Landscape settings again play a major role. (FC; negative at Shochiku, Tokyo.)

1963 **Sing, Young People! (Utae Wakodo-tachi)**
pr: Shochiku (Ofuna); orig. sc: Taichi Yamada; color 'scope ph: Hiroshi Kusuda; music: Chuji Kinoshita; cast: Tsutomu Matsukawa, Yusuke Kawazu, Shinichiro Mikami, Kei Yamamoto, Shima Iwashita et al. Comedy about university life and one student who becomes a television star. Plot lacks realism, but dialogue, especially between parents and children, is often amusing. (FC, PFA/SH)

Legend of a Duel to the Death/A Legend, or Was It? (Shito no Densetsu)
pr: Shochiku (Ofuna); orig. sc: Kinoshita; color and BW 'scope ph: Hiroshi Kusuda; music: Chuji Kinoshita; cast: Shima Iwashita, Mariko Kaga, Kinuyo Tanaka, Go Kato, Bunta Sugawara et al. Hokkaido setting for a melodrama

Kinoshita originally intended to make right after the war. A country girl is about to be married to the son of the village headman when it is revealed that he was involved in war crimes. A duel with pistols consummates the unlikelihood. (FC, PFA/SH)

1964 **The Scent of Incense (Koge)*
pr: Shochiku (Ofuna); orig. novel: Sawako Ariyoshi; sc: Kinoshita; 'scope ph: Hiroshi Kusuda; music: Chuji Kinoshita; cast: Mariko Okada, Nobuko Otowa, Kinuyo Tanaka, Haruko Sugimura, Go Kato et al. Very long story of the bitter relations between a mother and daughter in the geisha world. The mother is conceited and wanton, but much as the daughter resents her, she obeys. *KJ* #3. (FC, SH)

1967 *Lovely Flute and Drum (Natsukashiki Fue ya Taiko)*
pr: Kinoshita Prod./Takarazuka Eiga/Toho; orig. sc: Kinoshita; color 'scope ph: Hiroshi Kusuda; music: Chuji Kinoshita; cast: Yosuke Natsuki, Mayumi Ozora, Kumeko Urabe, Kazuya Kosaka, Kamatari Fujiwara et al. Attempt to recapture the nostalgia of Kinoshita's 1954 *Twenty-four Eyes* with a similar Inland Sea setting and focus on children who live in poverty but still have happy experiences. *KJ* #9. (FC, SH)

1976 *Love and Separation in Sri Lanka (Sri Lanka no Ai to Wakare)*
pr: Toho Eiga/Haiyuza Eiga Hoso; orig. sc: Kinoshita; color 'scope ph: Asakazu Nakai; music: Chuji Kinoshita; cast: Kinya Kitaoji, Komaki Kurihara, Hideko Takamine, Keiju Kobayashi, Keiko Tsushima et al. Love story about two Japanese who meet in Colombo and console each other's loneliness. Melodramatic and sentimental.

KON ICHIKAWA

1915—

*Because he makes films only for the sake
of making films, Kon Ichikawa's
work has a kind of innocence and very pure
pleasure. In the technical realm he has
been the most influential in pointing out
directions for the avant-garde of my generation.*

—Masahiro Shinoda

Kon Ichikawa, a cigarette clamped between his teeth, his head cocked to one side, then to the other, and gesticulating for emphasis, loves to talk. He not only talks, with a broad western Japanese accent, but has written with equal enthusiasm about himself and his work, and his view of what movies are.

In his writing as well as his conversation, certain terms emerge with such frequency that they must be taken as guiding principles. "Contemporaneity" and "self-exploration" retain for him special significance that in turn applies to "aesthetic consciousness" and "self-expression." In the course of his 30-odd years as a director, the content, tone and look of his films have necessarily varied in keeping with these principles, of which "contemporaneity" remains the most basic. "Movies move," says Ichikawa, "with an overwhelming concreteness, unlike music and literature, which can create an atmosphere that transcends time."[1] The feature film is, in Ichikawa's mind, inextricably tied to the present, in everything from the living people and landscapes it records to its editing style.

Ichikawa insists that since film is a temporal art of such vivid concreteness, the thought that goes into its making must also be contemporary. He strives to be a man of his times, which undoubtedly accounts in large measure for his persistent energy. His approach to his times entails interpreting the works of his literary contemporaries for the screen. Regarding his start as a director he said, "My own life experience was not very rich, [so I decided to] absorb other people's ideas in my own way, and see what sort of answers emerged from putting them on film."[2] He has tackled a surprising diversity of material, from serious novels by Junichiro Tanizaki *(The Key)* and Yukio Mishima *(Conflagration)*, to Taizo Yokoyama's famous comic strip, *Mr. Pu.* Not content to select subject matter from the present to reflect his sought-after contemporaneity, he has gone back to the past to reinterpret not only turn-of-the-century novels by Soseki Natsume *(The Heart* and *I Am a Cat)* and Toson Shimazaki *(The Outcast),* but also pre-World War II films by Teinosuke Kinugasa *(An Actor's Revenge)* and Yutaka Abe *(The Woman Who Touched Legs).* In the mid-1960s he began to delve still further into contemporaneity by making documentaries, such as the deeply moving 1965 *Tokyo Olympiad,* one of the first sports documentaries to favor people's feelings over the simple recording of events.

Emerging in the immediate postwar generation of directors, along with Akira Kurosawa and Keisuke Kinoshita, Ichikawa began as a maker of melodramas. These were succeeded by the ironic comedies that won him a reputation as spokesman for the postwar frustrations felt by the little man. When he then went on to do literary adaptations that included war films as well as stories about young renegades and lascivious old men, it was the critics who became frustrated. Ichikawa's constant search for

new challenges through his subject matter has made him impossible to
label. He himself has said, "I don't have any unifying theme—I just make
any picture I like or any that the company tells me to do."[3] He has therefore suffered accusations of immorality, absence of world view, and other
notions, usually including that expressed by director Nagisa Oshima:
"He's just an illustrator."[4]

Yet Ichikawa's evasion of labels does not diminish the clarity of his
idea of what good filmmaking is. His ironic characterizations, breathtaking compositions—he is unquestionably one of the best manipulators
of widescreen in the world—and abrupt editing style have assured his
own aesthetic consciousness a permanent rank in contemporary film history. If his irony and aestheticism do not sit well with social-problem-
oriented Japanese critics, they are warmly received abroad. Since
Ichikawa won the San Giorgio Prize at the 1956 Venice Film Festival for
Harp of Burma, his foreign devotees wait with eager anticipation for
each new film.

Illustration as Approach

Born in what is now part of the city of Ise in Mie Prefecture, Ichikawa
grew up as a rather sickly child and spent most of his free time drawing.
Asked what he wanted to be when he became an adult, he would invariably answer, "a painter." As a boy he also became an avid movie
fan, going to see all the great prewar samurai movies. He soon became enthusiastic about foreign films as well, notably Charlie Chaplin's, and began to ponder how he could combine a painter's career with this twentieth-century moving art. His revelation came through Walt Disney.
"Seeing *Mickey Mouse* and *Silly Symphony*, I realized that pictures and
film were deeply, organically related. All right, I decided, I'm going to try
making animated films too."[5] Disney was the catalyst that opened Ichikawa's eyes to his own possibilities in film, and he long continued to
name Disney and Chaplin as his ideals. This was not so much for their
direct influence on his work (although the father in *I Am Two* is moved
to buy a television set when he hears that his little son likes cartoons, and
the same film contains a kind of *hommage à* Disney animated banana
sequence), but for their method of production: "self-capitalized, self-
written, self-directed and self-distributed. I think this is the fondest dream
of the film artist."[6]

In the 1930s Ichikawa finished technical school in Osaka, and, hearing
that J.O., a rental film studio in Kyoto, had its own animation department,
he went to work there straight away. When J.O. later became a full-
fledged production company, Ichikawa would experience the kind of
work responsibility that was his ideal. The animation department was

dissolved, and he alone remained to think up the stories, write the scenarios, supervise the painting and photography and edit each animated film.

Later, Ichikawa was shifted to the position of assistant director in the new feature-film-making staff. He worked under four different directors, all of whom he admired as strong individualists. Among them was Yutaka Abe, who had received his film training in Hollywood as a member of Sessue Hayakawa's retinue (Abe played Hayakawa's valet in Cecil B. DeMille's 1915 *The Cheat*). Paying the highest possible tribute to his mentor, Ichikawa remade Abe's 1926 comedy, *The Woman Who Touched Legs*, in 1952. But always true to himself, he did it in his own way, giving it a coherent plot and animating parts of it.

By the time the Pacific War began, J.O. had merged with P.C.L., a company that made advertising films, to form the Toho feature film company, and Ichikawa was transferred to Tokyo. There, during the war, he worked on his first feature. *A Girl at Dojo Temple* was originally planned as an animated film, but since this would have required too much work at a time when there was a shortage of labor because of the war, he made it with puppets instead. It is noteworthy that he at first wanted to adapt Ryunosuke Akutagawa's *Rashomon, In a Grove* (later these formed the basis for Kurosawa's famous international success in 1950), or *The Nose*, but he was told that these were material for a great director and not a beginner like himself, so he went to the Kabuki story *Musume Dojoji*.[7] But the war ended before the film could be released, and the U.S. Occupation authorities confiscated it because the scenario had not been submitted for prior censorship review. To this day Ichikawa does not know what happened to his debut creation; all that remains of it are his planning sketches.

Ichikawa takes the epithet "illustrator" as anything but an insult. It was with the intention to illustrate that he began his filmmaking career, and he still calls himself an illustrator. Since an illustrator is necessarily concerned with composition, one can safely say that a good measure of his films' breathtaking "Ichikawa look" is due to his illustrator's eye. But perhaps more than anything else, this attitude expresses the humility with which he approaches his subject matter and the reliance upon others—especially his wife, Natto Wada—to which he readily admits.

Natto and Literature

Asked why so many of his films are literary adaptations, Ichikawa first responds, "Pure coincidence," but on further reflection he decides it was "because I started working with my wife."[8] Script collaboration with Natto Wada, who had a special flair for literary adaptations, goes back to before they were married and the first film Ichikawa calls his own, *A Flower Blooms,* released in 1948. It was Wada who suggested Ichikawa try adapting Yaeko Nogami's novel for the screen. By 1949 Wada had joined the staff as coscenarist on *Human Patterns,* and she would remain Ichikawa's closest collaborator through the 1965 *Tokyo Olympiad.*

Ichikawa has described their system of scriptwriting as something like living with the material.[9] They would both read the novel (almost invariably a company assignment), discuss it, and develop the script over a period of months in the course of their daily activities. The basic tone of the film would be decided first—melodrama, comedy, thriller—then the dramatic high point determined, and the number and personality of the characters decided. From that point they worked on the settings and dialogue, and Wada would do the final writeup.

The director looks back on those days with obvious nostalgia. "Women . . . well, my wife is very meticulous," he sighs, "so she always did a complete and beautifully detailed scenario," from which he could proceed directly to mapping out the continuity, compositions and camera setups. "The way movies are made nowadays there isn't time to do that, and here I am still reworking the dialogue and even worrying about the casting after shooting has already begun [on *The Devil's Bouncing Ball Song*]."[10]

After *Tokyo Olympiad,* with such fine scenarios as *Harp of Burma, Conflagration, The Key Fires on the Plain* and *Bonchi* to her credit, Wada retired from scriptwriting. Ichikawa explains that his wife feels that humanity is gone from the contemporary cinema. "She doesn't like the new film grammar, the method of presentation of the material; she says there's no heart in it any more, that people no longer take human love seriously."[11] And indeed if one compares a Wada scenario like *Harp of Burma* or *I Am Two* to any Ichikawa has directed since 1965, it becomes apparent that while humor and feeling for the human condition remain, some of the warmth of affirmation and optimism is gone.

Recently, Ichikawa has worked frequently with scenarist Shuntaro Tanikawa, whom he names as his favorite collaborator. "But," confided one of his producers, "when we really want Ichikawa to do something, the only way to get him to change his mind is through his wife."[12]

"Christie" and Humanity

If Natto Wada's collaboration has been a great asset in Ichikawa's serious literary adaptations and his early melodramas, his own personal taste runs in the vein of thrillers and biting satire. Since the immediate postwar era when translated foreign mysteries became extremely popular in Japan, Ichikawa has read everything he can get his hands on. His idol is Agatha Christie, whose view of human nature fascinates him. "I can't understand why she was never given a Nobel Prize," he says.[13] He has such great admiration for her that since 1957 he has used the penname "Christie" for his own scenarios, of which *The Pit* and *The Devil's Bouncing Ball Song* have actually been thrillers. "Unfortunately," he laments, "when I'm working on a thriller myself, I can't stand reading those written by others, so one of my favorite pastimes has to be suspended."[14] As testimony to Ichikawa's abilities in the genre, his adaptation of mystery writer Seishi Yokomizo's *The Inugami Family* was the biggest Japanese movie hit of 1976, grossing nearly six million dollars.

What may be the key phrase in Ichikawa's description of his passion for mysteries is "view of human nature." He himself is able to deal with all kinds of material because he seeks to interpret different views of human nature, and in so doing find and express his own. The result is a very clinical examination of human motives that leads him away from sentimentality and toward irony. He would like to be more optimistic. "I look around for some kind of humanism," he has said, "but I never seem to find it."[15] It is from his objectivity that both his comedy and tragedy emerge, for at times the attempt to deal with the human condition is comically pathetic, as in *A Billionaire*, and at times it is tragically ironic, as in *Fires on the Plain* or *Conflagration*.

Ichikawa used to divide his works into "dark" and "light" moods. He no longer does so, recognizing that his ironic view of human beings places both tones within the same film. In *I Am a Cat*, for example, the cat who observes the comic foibles of the humans around him ends his frustration by committing suicide in despair. Yet the moment his corpse is found floating in a barrel of water is one of the funniest in the whole film. Ichikawa admits he has tendencies toward black comedy— although at the time he vigorously denied that *The Key* was a black comedy—and says he would like to be able to make a real one, "but in Japan it's impossible. In any case, I'm a very light person, so I'm irresistibly drawn to dark things."[16]

Production and Perfection

Ichikawa, who admires Kurosawa very much, always describes him as a perfectionist and admits that he himself has many of the same tendencies. Time and money, the most difficult-to-come-by requisites in filmmaking, are the causes of chagrin for both directors. Ichikawa's arguments with the production company over his first war film, *Bungawan Solo*, as far back as 1951, caused him to virtually disown the film. Unable to meet the shooting schedule, he lost editing control to the producers and even saw footage shot by someone else put into the final product.

The most famous imbroglio occurred over Ichikawa's beautifully humanistic *Tokyo Olympiad*, which marks a near revolution in sports documentaries. The finished two-hour-and-45—minute film, on which Wada also worked, eschews the mechanical recording of each event to close in on the emotional reactions of both participants and audience, and the story within the big event of the lonely runner from the brand-new African country of Chad brings out the full meaning of the Olympics on an individual scale. The company, having expected television-style records of scores and fast finishes and no more, expressed outrage by claiming one could not tell if the film was about the Olympics or about people. The foreign versions of the film were pared down to half the full length, Ichikawa left the Daiei company for good, and the film went on to claim the biggest box office to that date in Japan.[17] In short, Ichikawa insists on being allowed to make his own kind of film. No matter what the original impetus for a particular work, Ichikawa says, "I'm happy if I can express myself through it."[18]

Observing Ichikawa on the set one gets some idea of what his perfectionism consists of. He is everywhere, altering lighting, checking camera angles, joking with the staff and jumping in to coach the actors between shots. The atmosphere is busy, but not hectic, as his authority keeps everything running smoothly and cheerfully.

Ichikawa used to draw up "continuity"—in Japan this means shot-by-shot measurement and design of each cut in advance so as not to waste any film stock—but now there is no time for this. He relies heavily on the staff to turn out a fast, quality production. He has not only preferred scenarists, but favorite cameramen, composers, art directors and lighting experts. However, he is always ready to move with the times, as his beloved contemporaneity requires changes in personnel to achieve changes in style. This is especially true for his casting, which he says constitutes 60 percent of the finished film (in 1960 he ascribed 70 percent to this aspect), "because the actors have to convey the intentions of the director, who does not appear before the cameras."[19]

However, despite the high percentage Ichikawa assigns to the importance of casting, he is tempted to give equal weight to editing. Once the film is shot, Ichikawa spends an equal amount of energy dubbing in the sound and supervising every cut, again to the chagrin of impatient producers. Here too is a source of the "Ichikawa look"—those abrupt cuts and startling sound effects.

Ichikawa has devoted years of study to the directors of the past, including Mizoguchi, Ozu, Kurosawa, Kinoshita and recently Pasolini. "I learned a tremendous amount from them," he admits, "and then I started all over on my own.''[20] As meticulous as the planning may be, each film is a new experiment for him, and he maintains that only God knows what the result will be. "A director says at the outset, 'I want to convey this particular idea or bring out that particular feeling' of a work, but he never knows what he will do until he has done it. Then he can look at his film and say, 'Oh, so that's what I meant.' "[21] It is because of this youthful energy, curiosity, and spirit of adventure that an Ichikawa in his sixties is still one of the most modern and active directors in Japan.

Irony in Self-Expression

Like Keisuke Kinoshita, Ichikawa has made a transition from comedy to tragedy in the course of his career. But unlike Kinoshita, Ichikawa did not progress from humor into sentimentality, which is perhaps one of the reasons he has not been favored by Japanese critics. Just as he has said he looks for humanism but cannot find it, he feels that the same objectivity that rejects sentimentality gives rise to comedy.[22]

In the first half of the 1950s, Ichikawa's most successful films, including *Mr. Pu, Mr. Lucky, The Blue Revolution* and *A Billionaire,* were all comedies. The basis of the humor in these works is comedy of manners, as in the great Kinoshita comedies, but their pure Ichikawa flavor resides in their ironic view. The hero of *A Billionaire* provides a typical example of the failure of goodness as a principle for dealing with reality. A new employee of the income tax office, he is sent out to investigate a case of chronic tax evasion. The family in question lives in a hovel with 18 children and a demented boarder upstairs who has not paid any rent in over a year and, when she is not working on a road construction crew, spends all of her spare time manufacturing an atomic bomb. The family, whose business failed years before, looks with envy at the tax official's lunchbox, extravagant by their standards. This same lowly government employee goes on to arouse widespread indignation by confessing to taking a bribe—of ¥10,000 (about $30)—over which he tries to commit suicide, and in the process inadvertently exposes a huge tax fraud by a politician. In a touch that remains highly contemporary, the politician's refrain on the witness stand is "I have no recollection. . . " Ichikawa's ironic message is that the tax laws, designed for justice, oppress the poor while the rich go on abusing them, and the normal working of society sees the honest man as a mere troublemaker. When society is held up to objective scrutiny, ethical standards are a mere illusion.

The leap from comic pathos to ironic tragedy is not so great as it might seem, as Ichikawa's analytical approach to human behavior bridges the two. In 1955, he began making films with obsessive tragic heroes whose anguish is that of the soul. Even when material suffering is involved, as in *Fires on the Plain,* where the Japanese soldiers are starving, diseased and ill-clothed, the spiritual issues are greater: the senselessness of war, the failure of religion to preserve human decency or even to console, and the most horrifying negation of the humanity of one's fellow man—cannibalism. Consistently throughout, from the 1955 *The Heart* to the 1973 *The Wanderers,* Ichikawa rejects the sentimentality of the happy or warmly tearful ending. His tragic heroes, like his comic heroes before, remain condemned as outcasts, rebels, obsessed or inconsolable. But this harsh perspective on life finds some mitigation in moments of humor and an exquisite audio-visual presentation throughout.

The Heart marks the beginning of Ichikawa's grim psychological studies. Based on Soseki Natsume's early twentieth-century novel *Kokoro,* it presents a middle-aged hero, "Sensei" ("teacher"), who is so obsessed by guilt that he ends by destroying himself. The young student who adopts this man as his mentor begins to wonder why he isolates himself from society and treats his wife with such coldness. The answer comes in a letter written to the student prior to Sensei's suicide. For his entire adult life he has felt responsible for the death of his closest school friend, who committed suicide when Sensei won the hand of the woman his friend had confided he himself wished to marry. Sensei has never been able to tell his wife the truth, with the result that he has closed himself off from her over the years as the living symbol of his guilt. The final denial of solace through human communication comes at the end, when the student, who has rushed back to Tokyo from his dying father's bedside at the news of Sensei's death, is turned away by the bereaved wife.

Even this bitterly pessimistic story, shot in beautiful monochrome shadowy interiors and stark landscapes, has humorous punctuation. After a long and serious discussion in a bar, Sensei leaves the student alone to continue drinking, but the boy finds the bottle empty. Later in a park, the two sit down on a bench and unwittingly frighten off a pair of newlyweds. No viewer can suppress an ironic smile as the student's mother tries to put his university diploma on display and it keeps falling down, or as a yawning postal messenger delivers a telegram bringing desperate news.

Ironic reversal prevails even in a film with a message of benevolence like *Harp of Burma,* made the year after *The Heart* and Ichikawa's first prize-winning work. The story of the Japanese soldier who foregoes repatriation to remain in Burma at the end of the Pacific War in order to bury the dead can move the susceptible to tears. His vain efforts to persuade a hysterically fanatical group of his countrymen to surrender rather than die following the armistice, and his subsequent horror and pity facing the innumerable Japanese corpses strewn around the countryside never fail to inspire. When he plays familiar melodies on his Burmese harp, and British and Japanese soldiers raise their voices together to the tune of "Home Sweet Home," *Harp of Burma* really seems to show "men's capacity to live with one another" for which it won the Venice San Giorgio Prize. But often overlooked is the fact that this army private turned Buddhist monk has survived to become a doer of good deeds because he was rescued and nursed back to health after the massacre of the Japanese holdouts by a real Buddhist monk, whose robes he then stole with the simple intention of disguising himself to traverse the Burmese countryside unharmed. All of his exemplary moral conduct thereafter is made possible by this most ungrateful, but very human, act of base thievery.

Like *Harp of Burma, Fires on the Plain* shows the Japanese at war in Asia in an adaptation from a novel. But while Shohei Ooka's novel is narrated by a man who is repatriated and recovering, with a new Christian view of life and suffering, Ichikawa's hero is condemned, walking with his hands raised into Filipino peasants' rifle fire. Nor is this hero a moral paragon, outraged as he may be by his comrades' cannibalism. Not only does he kill the Japanese purveyor of "monkey meat," but he murders a defenseless Filipina woman in cold blood simply because she screams in terror at the sight of him.

The spiritual wasteland of *Fires on the Plain* too abounds in humor that is so ironic as to be macabre. Audiences laugh uproariously when a dying man no longer able to move points to his arm and says to the shocked hero, "You can eat this part," and when the unwary hero allows a wily old gangrenous soldier to rob him of his only valuable possession, a single hand grenade. In Ichikawa's bleakest film, this humor relieves only momentarily; its aftereffect compounds the gloom.

Ichikawa reaches his peak of macabre humor with *The Key,* his free adaptation of Junichiro Tanizaki's novel. The core group of unsavory characters offers not one with any redeeming qualities. An elderly Kyoto gentleman of some means knows that his physical stamina is deserting him, but is determined to maintain a sexual relationship that satisfies his beautiful younger wife. He discovers that he requires not only drugs, but jealousy and prohibition to keep himself aroused, and he draws his daughter's future husband, who hopes for financing for his own hospital in exchange, into a relationship with his wife. Everyone in this little circle, including the falsely modest wife, knows what everyone else is up to. The whole game culminates in the old man's death from overstimulation, to no one's surprise but the maid's. When the plain daughter then realizes she will have to share her husband with her mother, she tries to poison her, only to be outdone by the maid, who poisons all three of them. In this final twist—a surprising addition to the novel—laughter closes the film. The maid confesses she has killed all those horrible people, but the police think she is simply delirious with grief and send her home. Although Ichikawa has insisted that this film is not a black comedy, he does allow that of all the authors he has adapted, he feels his own aesthetic consciousness is closest to Tanizaki's, and that this proximity has something to do with perverseness.[23]

Obsessive, isolated protagonists continue to parade through Ichikawa's works, from the pariah schoolteacher who is "passing" in *The Outcast* to the three country boys devoted to the gangster code in *The Wanderers*, and even to the philosophical cat who relinquishes life in despair in *I Am a Cat*. But of all the twisted, frustrated, paranoid heroes in his films, his own favorite remains the stutterer acolyte of *Conflagration*.[24]

Conflagration

Ichikawa's favorite film was not one he wanted to make. He rejected the proposal several times, fearing that a film based on Yukio Mishima's bestselling *Kinkakuji (The Temple of the Golden Pavilion)*, because it was such a highly abstract and conceptual novel, would turn out to be nothing more than a digest.[25] Finally, he allowed himself to be persuaded, recognizing the necessity of putting his own interpretation on the work. He expended four months from initiation to completion of the scenario and location hunting.

With his scriptwriters Natto Wada and Keiji Hasebe, Ichikawa assessed the various possible interpretations of Mishima's novel and met also with the author himself. The conclusion, despite Wada's wish to fashion the film into a melodrama, was to make the complicated, perverse and finally perverted acolyte Mizoguchi into an absolutist whose own standard of purity finds nothing in the real world that measures up to it. As the primary source of Mizoguchi's disillusionment, they decided to focus on the relationship between his parents.[26] In the film, Mizoguchi (played by Raizo Ichikawa) therefore emerges as a much more sympathetic character than in the novel, and his mother takes on qualities of dim-witted villainy.

Ichikawa tells the story in flashbacks, beginning from Mizoguchi's interrogation by police after he has burned the pavilion (called "Shu-kaku" in the film because of opposition to the use of the real name by Kyoto monks).[27] The central time frame of the film begins with Mizoguchi's arrival at the temple and builds up to his act of arson, after which the opening time frame resumes, and the film ends with investigators getting out of a car to examine his straw-mat-covered corpse on the ground where he jumped from the train that was taking him to Tokyo for incarceration. But within the central time frame there are also flashbacks to a third time and place: the lonely coast of northwestern Japan where Mizoguchi spent his childhood. By interchanging these time frames, Ichikawa picks out the incidents and images from Mizoguchi's life that shape his obsessions and build his motivations toward destruction of his symbol of pure beauty, Shukaku.

The opposition between Mizoguchi's contempt for his mother and his worship of the purity of Shukaku emerges through these contrasting time frames with an acuteness that dialogue or narration could never convey. His mother (Tanie Kitabayashi) arrives to visit him in Kyoto, but he refuses to see her, running off to scrub the floors of Shukaku instead. She comes after him as air raid sirens begin to sound, but he refuses to let her into the pavilion, his stuttering face in closeup showing utter terror. As she drags him away from the pavilion, the scene dissolves to his dead father covering the boy's eyes as a kimono slips along the floor into the next room, followed by a shot of his mother with another man. When his father then says to him on the cliffs by the windy sea that Kyoto's Shukaku makes him forget the sordidness of the world, the relationship between the pavilion and the boy's parents has already asserted itself with visual force.

Characterization in Ichikawa's films rarely foregoes humor, and the vain pettiness of the head of the Kyoto temple (Ganjiro Nakamura) provides a fine vehicle. He first appears dressed in a white kimono in his quarters, putting on makeup in front of a mirror. Later he puts on a little show for Mizoguchi, who happens to be cleaning the garden when a beggar comes to the temple. At first the abbot ignores him, but when he catches sight of Mizoguchi, he magnanimously presents the beggar with a coin. This hypocritical monk, who later turns out to be having an affair with a geisha, becomes another object of Mizoguchi's contempt despite his good intentions toward the boy. Without these little characterizing visual details, Mizoguchi's attitude would elicit little sympathy.

In Mishima's novel, the incident of the tourist's induced miscarriage reveals the depth of Mizoguchi's self-contempt and resulting capacity for evil more than anything else. In Ichikawa's film this event is an accident brought about by the stutterer's desire to protect the purity of Shukaku, and behind it lies the contemporary "pain of the age."[28] Ichikawa feels the novel expressed. From a flashback to Mizoguchi's first view of the exquisite pavilion we proceed to a closeup of his desperate face as he runs into it to escape his importunate mother. Significantly, this is followed by a long shot of G.I.s getting off a train, which creates a visual association between Mizoguchi's inner turmoil and the U.S. presence in Japan resulting from the war defeat. People in the temple then

converse with a new smattering of English words about how the finances
are improving. A dissolve shows a quiet lily pond, and then the imposing
Shukaku, which now appears threatened by those improving finances.
Immediately juxtaposed to the magnificent image of purity is a squabble
taking place in the garden between a G.I. and a Japanese woman who is
refusing to have an abortion. She runs up to the door of Shukaku and
tries to get in. The horrified Mizoguchi pushes her away and she falls,
clutching her abdomen in pain. The G.I. then jubilantly rewards Mizoguchi for his inadvertent service in getting rid of the baby by giving him a
carton of cigarettes. In Ichikawa's interpretation, Mizoguchi's destructive
view of the world gradually builds in this way as he encounters corruption at every turn. His final act of setting fire to Shukaku is to prevent it
from being further sullied by such unclean human beings as his mother,
these irreverent tourists, and the greedy and lascivious head of the
temple. The pain of the age is that postwar reconstruction brings yet
more corruption, and purity is nowhere to be found.

The tragic destruction of the symbol of purity brings with it the moment of highest audio-visual excitement in the film. Kazuo Miyagawa's
photography, with its characteristic fluid movement, varied angles and
subtle light and shade, attains one of its triumphs in the roaring flames of
Shukaku with the desperate, choking Mizoguchi silhouetted against the
holocaust. Ichikawa triumphs as well with the sound, as the crackling
blaze dissolves into Kashiwagi (Tatsuya Nakadai), Mizoguchi's club-
footed sinister friend, softly and gleefully playing his flute. Through
this sequence of sound and images alone, the symbolic destruction of
absolute purity and the victory of corruption is complete; not a word
of unnecessary dialogue intrudes.

Art above All

Since *Conflagration*, Ichikawa has embarked on a staggering variety
of cinematic endeavors, yet his ironic view and superb craftsmanship
remain consistent. With a literary adaptation like Soseki's *I Am a Cat* he
recaptured the pleasure of working with great classics;[29] with *Toppo
Gigio and the Missile War* and part of *I Am Two* he revived his love for
animation; with *Tokyo Olympiad* and *Youth* (1968) he demonstrated
a remarkable talent in documentaries; and with *The Wanderers* he
interpreted *Easy Rider* as a Japanese period drama. He insists that it is
only by dealing with such diverse subject matter that he can find
himself and what he wishes to express.

The critics may grumble about his inconsistent world view in his
excessive variety, but Ichikawa's irony prevails. The self-possessed
child's-eye-view of *I Am Two* is as convincingly presented as the self-

recognition attained through illness by the arrogant adolescent of *Her Brother*, or the defeat met by the three innocent young men of *The Wanderers*. Ichikawa sees that a search for human understanding at times presents insurmountable difficulties; sometimes there is room for optimism (as perhaps at age two), but more often the question, as in *Tokyo Olympiad*, remains "What have they won?" and the ironic truth is that even a gold medal provides no answer to the problems of living.

The producers may grumble about Ichikawa's work pace and expenses, but his artistry prevails. His insistence on a first-rate staff and cast and adequate time to dub and edit his films has never led him astray, as the phenomenal success of *Tokyo Olympiad* proved. Even a film as off-beat as his remake of *An Actor's Revenge*, a trite story serving as a vehicle for theatrical acting and audio-visual virtuosity, is coming into its own more than ten years after it was made. The fact remains that the grumblers keep coming back for more from this perfectionist, and there are many who reluctantly call him a genius.

If there are any legitimate complaints, they come from the man himself. In making fatuous thrillers like the all-time success *The Inugami Family*, he admits he is compromising. "All of us who want to make films now have to compromise. I look for the contemporary in my films, and contemporary Japan demands movies like *The Inugami Family*."[30] But Ichikawa is humble enough to go on making films with no moral viewpoint in the hope that somewhere along the way he will be able to express something of himself in the work—in the sharp-edged montage structure, the unsettling compositions, the intricate lighting and stylized colors, the disturbing sound effects.

Notes

1 Author's interview with Kon Ichikawa, January 1977.
2 Kon Ichikawa and Natto Wada, *Seijocho 271 Banchi* (Tokyo: Shirakaba Shobo, 1961), p. 89.
3 Donald Richie, "The Several Sides of Kon Ichikawa," *Sight and Sound*, Spring 1966, p. 85.
4 Author's conversation with Nagisa Oshima, May 1974.
5 Ichikawa and Wada, *op. cit.*, p. 81.
6 *Ibid*, p. 128.
7 *Ibid*, p. 86.
8 Ichikawa interview, *cit*.
9 Richie, *op. cit.*, p. 86.
10 Ichikawa interview, *cit*.
11 *Ibid*.
12 Author's conversation with Kiichi Ichikawa, November 1976.
13 Ichikawa interview, *cit*.
14 *Ibid*.
15 Richie, *op. cit.*, p. 86.
16 Ichikawa interview, *cit*.
17 *Sekai no eiga sakka 31: Nihon eiga shi* (Film Directors of the World 31 : The History of the Japanese Film) (Tokyo: Kinema Jumposha, 1976), p. 204.
18 Ichikawa interview, *cit*.
19 *Ibid*.
20 *Ibid*.
21 Ichikawa and Wada, *op. cit.*, p. 54.
22 Ichikawa interview, *cit*.
23 *Ibid*.
24 *Ibid*.
25 Ichikawa and Wada, *op. cit.*, p. 45.
26 *Ibid*, p. 47.
27 *Ibid*, p. 50.
28 Ichikawa interview, *cit*.
29 *Ibid*.
30 *Ibid*.

KON ICHIKAWA: FILMOGRAPHY

1946 *A Girl at Dojo Temple (Musume Dojoji)*

pr: J.O./Toho; sc: Ichikawa and Keiji Hasebe; dolls: Puppe Kawasaki; music: Tadashi Hattori. Variation on the traditional Kabuki story of the monk Anchin and his tragic love for Kiyohime. Ichikawa makes Anchin a bronze bell-maker and has Kiyohime sacrifice herself for the sake of completion of the new temple bell, from which no one but Anchin can draw a sound. When he rings it, her ghost emerges from it to dance. Confiscated by U.S. Occupation authorities, all trace of this film has been lost.

1947 *1001 Nights with Toho (Toho Senichiya)*

pr: Shin Toho; planning: Fuku Nakamura; ph: Akira Mimura; cast: Hisako Yamane, Susumu Fujita, Yataro Kurokawa, Hideko Takamine et al. Hodgepodge film marking the debut of the Shin Toho company. Ichikawa was responsible for only some of the footage. (No extant prints; negative at Toho, Tokyo.)

1948 *A Flower Blooms (Hana Hiraku)*

pr: Shin Toho; orig. story: Yaeko Nogami; sc: Toshio Yasumi; ph: Joji Ohara; cast: Hideko Takamine, Ken Uehara, Hideko Mimura et al. Melodrama about a girl from a wealthy family who gets involved with a leader of the student movement, but finds her new ideals destroyed when he gets one of her friends pregnant. (No extant prints; negative at Toho, Tokyo.)

365 Nights (Sambyaku-rokujugo Ya)

pr: Shin Toho; orig. story: Masajiro Kojima; sc: Kennosuke Tateoka; ph: Akira Mimura; music: Tadashi Hattori; cast: Ken Uehara, Hisako Yamane, Yuji Hori, Chizuko Nogami, Hideko Takamine et al. Melodrama about a Tokyo girl and an Osaka girl who are both in love with the same boy. Conceived as a two-part, two-location film, the Osaka girl loses out in the end, with action marked by an American-style shoot-out. (FC)

1949 *Human Patterns (Ningen Moyo)*

pr: Shin Toho; orig. story: Fumio Niwa; sc: Yoshikazu Yamashita and Natto Wada; ph: Joji Ohara; cast: Ken Uehara, Yoshiko Yamaguchi, Chiaki Tsukioka, Goro Aoyama et al. Sad and complex love relationships centering on a good-hearted young man. His old school friend, now a company president, is pressuring an unhappy girl who prefers the poor young man. His own fiancée, however, leaves him for the company president. Wada's first scriptwriting for Ichikawa. (No extant prints or negative.)

Passion without End (Hateshinaki Jonetsu)

pr: Shin Toho/Shinseiki; orig. sc: Natto Wada; ph: Joji Ohara; music: Ryoichi Hattori; cast: Yuji Hori, Chiaki Tsukioka, Tatsuo Saito, Yoshiko Yamaguchi, Yunosuke Ito et al. Melodrama about a modern composer who marries a woman who turns out to be someone else's wife. (FC)

1950 *Sanshiro of Ginza (Ginza Sanshiro)*

pr: Shin Toho; orig. story: Nobuo Aoyagi; sc: Naoyuki Hatta; ph: Jun Yasumoto; music: Nobuo Iida; cast: Susumu Fujita, Takashi Shimura, Hisako Yamane, Akiko Kazami, Choko Iida et al. Action melodrama about a young doctor who runs a clinic in Ginza. He hides the fact that he is a sixth rank judo expert because of an agreement with a local gangster, whom he injured when he was a student. But when the woman he loves is threatened by violence, Sanshiro breaks his promise and wreaks havoc among the gangsters. (FC)

Heat and Mud (Netsudeichi)
pr: Shin Toho; orig. story: Soju Kimura; sc: Ichikawa and Ryoichi Sakaya; ph: Minoru Yokoyama; cast: Susumu Fujita, Harue Tone, Yuji Hori, Eijiro Tono, Eitaro Shindo et al. Action film about a man who has stolen a million yen, taken a bar girl with him and escaped to Hokkaido. He is pursued by a former doctor and a spectacular fight takes place in which the girl escapes to her lover. (Print edited for television FC.)

Pursuit at Dawn (Akatsuki no Tsuiseki)
pr: Tanaka Prod./Shin Toho; orig. story: Jun Nakagawa; sc: Kaneto Shindo; ph: Minoru Yokoyama; cast: Ryo Ikebe, Jun Tazaki, Michitaro Mizushima, Yoko Sugi, Chizuko Nogami et al. Documentary-style treatment of the new "people's police force" set in the back alleys of Tokyo's Shimbashi district. Sequences shot from inside the police box looking out show the beginnings of Ichikawa's inventive camera style, but much of the film looks like police promotion. (No extant prints or negative.)

1951   *Nightshade Flower (Ieraishan)*
pr: Shoei Prod./Shin Toho; orig. sc: Kenro Matsuura and Ichikawa; ph: Minoru Yokoyama; cast: Ken Uehara, Asami Kuji, Harue Tone, Chiaki Tsukioka et al. Melodrama with reminiscences of the war, one of the many films about the black market and repatriates made around this time. A former army doctor finds the girl he fell in love with at the front. He is ill, but when he finds that she is trying to sell her body to pay for his treatment, he goes into hiding. He is finally killed trying to help one of his wartime subordinates. (No extant prints or negative.)

The Lover (Koibito)
pr: Shin Toho; orig. story: Haruo Umeda; sc: Natto Wada and Ichikawa; ph: Minoru Yokoyama; cast: Ryo Ikebe, Asami Kuji, Koreya Senda, Sachiko Murase, Tanie Kitabayashi et al. A study of human affections with a melodramatic flavor. The day before her wedding, a girl goes out one last time with an old male friend. In the course of the day she discovers that her feelings toward him are more than just friendly, but she comes home smiling that night. (No extant prints or negative.)

The Man without a Nationality (Mukokuseki Mono)
pr: Toyoko Eiga/Toei; orig. story: Jun Takami; sc: Toshio Yasumi; ph: Minoru Yokoyama; cast: Ken Uehara, Ichiro Sugai, Chikako Miyagi, Yunosuke Ito et al. Something of an anti-war film with two unsavory lead characters. One, a strategist during the war, has killed a subordinate and stolen his money. He

goes on to make the dead man's wife his mistress and tries to make her sister participate in his schemes. The other man, a witness to the evil doings of the first, was a spy during the war and has had his citizenship revoked. (No extant prints or negative.)

Stolen Love (*Nusumareta Koi*)
pr: Aoyagi Prod./Shin Toho; orig. story: Jiro Kagami; sc: Natto Wada and Ichikawa; ph: Minoru Yokoyama; music: Akira Ifukube; cast: Asami Kuji, Masayuki Mori, Koroku Kawakita, Takashi Shimura, Michiko Kato et al. Light romance about an unemployed dancer who goes to a banker who has always liked her to find out how he feels about marriage. He replies that love is after all a game, and she decides to prove it. Picking an impoverished painter she pretends is her fiancé, she asks the banker to make him famous. The painter's talent is duly recognized, and the banker finally proposes, only to see the girl go off with the painter. (FC)

Bungawan Solo (*Bungawan Solo*)
pr: Shin Toho; orig. story: Shozo Kanagai; sc: Natto Wada and Ichikawa; ph: Minoru Yokoyama; cast: Ryo Ikebe, Hisaya Morishige, Yunosuke Ito, Asami Kuji et al. Love tragedy set in wartime Java. Three deserters from the Japanese army hide at the home of some Javanese villagers, and one of the men falls in love with the daughter. On the day the war ends, the lovers are killed by military police. Unable to finish shooting on schedule, Ichikawa lost final cut on the film and left Shin Toho in the ensuing arguments. (No extant prints or negative.)

Wedding March (*Kekkon Koshinkyoku*)
pr: Toho; orig. sc: Toshiro Ide, Natto Wada and Ichikawa; ph: Tadashi Iimura; cast: Ken Uehara, Hisako Yamane, Yoko Sugi, Hajime Izu, Fubuki Koshiji et al. Light romance about a young man who wants to become a writer. He reads novels so much of the time he loses his job. His girl friend goes to plead with his boss in his behalf and finds herself hired instead. The boss's wife becomes suspicious, but in the end all is righted and the young couple marry. (No extant prints; negative at Toho, Tokyo.)

1952 ### Mr. Lucky (*Rakkii-san*)
pr: Toho; orig. story: Keita Genji; sc: Katsuhito Inomata; ph: Tadashi Iimura; cast: Yukiko Shimazaki, Keiju Kobayashi, Hiroshi Koizumi, Yoko Sugi, Tatsuo Saito et al. A "salaryman film" made before Toho became known for this genre. An office worker enjoys the affections of two girls, one who works in the same section, and the other the daughter of a very wealthy family. The office girl introduces the rich girl to another boy who likes her, and she is sacrificed to a marriage of convenience. Mr. Lucky, true to his name, gets a promotion and transfer to another city, but no girl. (No extant prints; negative at Toho, Tokyo.)

Young People (*Wakai Hito*)
pr: Toho; orig. story: Yojiro Ishizaka; sc: Naoya Uchimura, Natto Wada and Ichikawa; ph: Kazuo Yamada; cast: Ryo Ikebe, Yukiko Shimazaki, Asami Kuji,

Hiroshi Nihonyanagi et al. Set at a mission school in Hokkaido, the story of a student who gets involved in the love affair between two teachers. Not as successful as Shiro Toyoda's 1937 version of the same story. (No extant prints; negative at Toho, Tokyo.)

The Woman Who Touched Legs (*Ashi ni Sawatta Onna*)
pr: Toho; orig. story: Bumatsu Sawada; sc: Natto Wada and Ichikawa; ph: Jun Yasumoto; cast: Fubuki Koshiji, Ryo Ikebe, So Yamamura, Mariko Okada, Yunosuke Ito et al. Remake of Yutaka Abe's 1926 comedy with more plot. A lady pickpocket returns to her home in the country to seek revenge for the death of her father, who committed suicide when accused of being a wartime spy. Pursued by a young local policeman, she ends up falling in love with him. (No extant prints; negative at Toho, Tokyo.)

This Way, That Way (*Ano Te Kono Te*)
pr: Daiei; orig. story: Nobuo Kyoto; sc: Natto Wada and Ichikawa; ph: Senki-chiro Takeda; cast: Yoshiko Kuga, Masayuki Mori, Mitsuko Mito, Yuji Hori et al. Comedy about a man whose wife demands more respect for her talents. Further complications arise from the arrival of her insufferable niece. Based on a radio serial. (No extant prints; negative at Daiei, Tokyo.)

1953 ### *Mr. Pu (Puu-san)*
pr: Toho; orig. story: Taizo Yokoyama; sc: Natto Wada, Ichikawa and Jumei Eirai; ph: Asakazu Nakai; cast: Yunosuke Ito, Fubuki Koshiji, Isao Kimura, Kaoru Yachigusa, Yoko Sugi et al. The comedy for which Ichikawa is best known as a postwar satirist. A teacher at a continuation school who is not getting ahead in the world goes to the Ginza and is hit by a car. A student he asks to help him demands money, and the girl he loves snubs him. The vulgar politician responsible for the accident publishes his memoirs from jail and becomes popular. The teacher realizes that he is simply too good-hearted and will never get anywhere. (No circulating prints; negative at Toho, Tokyo.)

The Blue Revolution (*Aoiro Kakumei*)
pr: Toho; orig. story: Tatsuzo Ishikawa; sc: Katsuhito Inomata; ph: Masao Tamai; cast: Koreya Senda, Asami Kuji, Rentaro Mikuni, Daisuke Kato, Michiyo Ko-gure et al. A story similar to *Mr. Pu*, but put on the level of the bourgeois intelligentsia. The central character, a historian, runs into trouble all around him, but eventually others solve his problems for him. (No extant prints; negative at Toho, Tokyo.)

The Youth of Heiji Zenigata (*Seishun Zenigata Heiji*)
pr: Toho; orig. story: Kodo Nomura; sc: Natto Wada and Ichikawa; ph: Seiichi Endo; cast: Tomoemon Otani, Yunosuke Ito, Yoko Sugi, Hajime Izu et al. Period comedy about a famous Edo personality who as a young man comes into some counterfeit money. (No extant prints; negative at Toho, Tokyo.)

The Lover (*Aijin*)
pr: Toho; orig. story: Kaoru Morimoto; sc: Natto Wada and Toshiro Ide; ph: Masao Tamai; cast: Ichiro Sugai, Fubuki Koshiji, Mariko Okada, Ineko, Arima,

Rentaro Mikuni et al. Light romance about a widowed director of melodramas who decides to remarry with a dancer. Humor and confusion as their two families are united. (No extant prints; negative at Toho, Tokyo.)

1954 *All of Myself (Watashi no Subete o)*
pr: Toho; orig. story: Kazuo Kikuta; sc: Haruo Umeda, Tatsuo Asano and Ichikawa; ph: Mitsuo Miura; cast: Kinuko Ito, Ryo Ikebe, Ineko Arima, Ken Uehara, Sumiko Hidaka, Hiroshi Nihonyanagi et al. Melodrama about an office worker in love with the president's daughter, and a painter in love with an unfortunate beauty who enters the Miss Universe contest (Kinuko Ito was actually third runner-up in this pageant). (No extant prints; negative at Toho, Tokyo.)

*A Billionaire (Okuman Choja)
pr: Seinen Haiyu Club/Shin Toho; orig. sc: Ichikawa, Kobo Abe, Taizo Yokoyama, Keiji Hasebe and Natto Wada; ph: Takeo Ito; music: Ikuma Dan; cast: Isao Kimura, Yoshiko Kuga, Isuzu Yamada, Yunosuke Ito, Eiji Okada, Sachiko Hidari et al. Various contemporary stereotypes converge on a helpless new income tax office employee, who gets in trouble with all of them because he is too honest. Very fast-moving sketches of a corrupt politician, a jaded geisha, an impoverished family with 18 children and a boarder who works as a day-laborer and manufactures atomic bombs at night. (FC; negative at Toho, Tokyo.)

Twelve Chapters on Women (Josei ni Kansuru Junisho)
pr: Toho; orig. essays: Sei Ito; sc: Natto Wada; ph: Mitsuo Miura; cast: Keiko Tsushima, Hiroshi Koizumi, Ineko Arima, Asami Kuji, Ken Uehara et al. Story of how a couple who have been engaged for nine years finally get around to getting married. (No extant prints; negative at Toho, Tokyo.)

1955 *Ghost Story of Youth (Seishun Kaidan)*
pr: Nikkatsu; orig. story: Bunroku Shishi; sc: Natto Wada; ph: Shigeyoshi Mine; cast: Mie Kitahara, So Yamamura, Tatsuya Mihashi, Yukiko Todoroki, Hisako Yamane, Michiko Saga et al. Literary adaptation made to compete with the other big production companies' versions of the same author's works. Not the best of Ichikawa. (No extant prints; negative at Nikkatsu, Tokyo.)

*The Heart (Kokoro)
pr: Nikkatsu; orig. story: Soseki Natsume; sc: Katsuhito Inomata and Keiji Hasebe; ph: Takeo Ito; cast: Masayuki Mori, Michiyo Aratama, Tatsuya Mihashi, Shoji Yasui, Akiko Tamura et al. The first of Ichikawa's dark psychological dramas centering on guilt. A student who develops a friendship with a man he calls "teacher" notices that the man's relations with his wife are strained. The boy goes home to the country to see his dying father, only to hear that his mentor has committed suicide. A letter from the older man reveals that he has never been able to overcome his feeling of guilt over having stolen his wife from his best friend in his student days, with the result that the friend committed suicide. (No circulating prints; negative at Nikkatsu, Tokyo.)

1956   *Harp of Burma (Biruma no Tategoto)*
pr: Nikkatsu; orig. story: Michio Takeyama; sc: Natto Wada; ph: Minoru Yokoyama; music: Akira Ifukube; cast: Shoji Yasui, Rentaro Mikuni, Tanie Kitabayashi, Taketoshi Naito, Jun Hamamura et al. An obsessive main character who
comes to a humanistic end. A young Japanese soldier in Burma during the war
is sent to convince a group of holdouts in the mountains that the war is over.
He fails to move the fanatics, all of whom are killed. Surviving by stealing a
Buddhist monk's robes, he begins to act out the monk's role as he tries to get
back to his regiment for repatriation. But the mountains of war dead move
him to begin burying corpses, and he remains in Burma as his fellows leave
for home. Venice Film Festival San Giorgio Prize; *KJ* #5. (FC, JA)

Punishment Room (Shokei no Heya)
pr: Daiei; orig. story: Shintaro Ishihara; sc: Natto Wada and Keiji Hasebe; ph:
Yoshihisa Nakagawa; cast: Hiroshi Kawaguchi, Ayako Wakao, Takashi
Kodaka, Masayoshi Umewaka, Seiji Miyaguchi et al. Sex and violence youth
genre film of the type called *taiyo-zoku* ("sun cult"), made popular by novelist
Ishihara. Overwrought moralistic critical reaction caused trouble for Ichikawa,
who insisted he sought only contemporaneity. A rebellious delinquent student
puts sleeping powder in a girl's beer and rapes her. She falls in love with him,
but he rejects her. Her irate family and other outraged students then punish the
boy themselves. (No circulating prints; negative at Daiei, Tokyo.)

Nihombashi (Nihombashi)
pr: Daiei (Kyoto studios); orig. story: Kyoka Izumi; sc: Natto Wada; ph: Kimio
Watanabe; cast: Chikage Awashima, Fujiko Yamamoto, Eijiro Yanagi, Ayako
Wakao, Ryuji Shinagawa et al. An old favorite melodrama from the Shimpa
stage about the proud head of a geisha house and a famous beauty whose rivalry brings tragedy. (No extant prints; negative at Daiei, Tokyo.)

1957   *The Crowded Streetcar (Manin Densha)*
pr: Daiei (Tokyo); orig. sc: Natto Wada and Ichikawa; ph: Hiroshi Murai;
cast: Hiroshi Kawaguchi, Michiko Ono, Chishu Ryu, Haruko Sugimura et al.
Satire on contemporary ills in which overcrowded Japan appears on the verge
of bursting at the seams. A new university graduate cannot find a job, and in
the course of his desperate search he drives his father crazy and gets gray hair
himself. He ends up as a messenger boy for a primary school. (No extant
prints; negative at Daiei, Tokyo.)

The Men of Tohoku (Tohoku no Zummutachi)
pr: Toho; orig. story: Shichiro Fukazawa; sc: "Christie" (Ichikawa); 'scope ph:
Kazuo Yamada; cast: Hiroshi Akutagawa, Chieko Naniwa, Hajime Izu, Eiko
Miyoshi, Minoru Chiaki et al. Bizarre tale of the misery of second and third sons
in northern Japan, who were not allowed to marry or own property. Focuses
on one particular man whose miseries are compounded by bad breath, so that
no one can bear to come near him. He dreams of a land of women beyond the
northern mountains, and in the end sets out in that direction. (No circulating
prints; negative at Toho, Tokyo.)

The Pit (Ana)
pr: Daiei (Tokyo); orig. sc: "Christie" (Ichikawa); ph: Setsuo Kobayashi; cast: Machiko Kyo, So Yamamura, Eiji Funakoshi, Tanie Kitabayashi, Kenji Sugawara et al. Comedy, romance and social commentary mixed into a thriller. A woman reporter loses her job for writing a story on police corruption using a real model. A friend persuades her to go into hiding and sell the idea of a contest to find her to the weekly news magazines. But when she goes to a bank to borrow money, the banker and his subordinate plan to accuse her of embezzling. Some of the ideas were a little too far fetched. (No extant prints; negative at Daiei, Tokyo.)

1958 **Conflagration (Enjo)*
pr: Daiei (Kyoto); orig. story: Yukio Mishima; sc: Natto Wada and Keiji Hasebe; 'scope ph: Kazuo Miyagawa; music: Toshiro Mayuzumi; cast: Raizo Ichikawa, Tatsuya Nakadai, Ganjiro Nakamura, Tanie Kitabayashi, Yoko Uraji, Michiyo Aratama, Tamao Nakamura et al. Chilling story of the stutterer acolyte obsessed with beauty made famous by Mishima's fictionalized account of an actual event, *Kinkakuji (The Temple of the Golden Pavilion)*. The young man who resents his mother's promiscuity and his father's weakness finds worse corruption surrounding him at his temple and his school, where a crippled friend enjoys seducing women. Flashbacks build up to the acolyte's final inability to find any solace and his desperate arson of the golden pavilion. Ichikawa and photographer Miyagawa prove a superb combination, strengthened by Mayuzumi's avant-garde music. *KJ* #4. (FC, MOMA, NY)

1959 *Goodby, Hello (Sayonara, Konnichiwa)*
pr: Daiei (Tokyo); orig sc: "Christie" (Ichikawa) and Kazuo Funabashi; color 'scope ph: Setsuo Kobayashi; cast: Machiko Kyo, Ayako Wakao, Hitomi Nozoe, Kenji Sugawara, Hiroshi Kawaguchi et al. Light romance full of mixups. For family reasons a girl decides not to get married, and sends a friend to tell her fiancé. The friend falls in love at first sight with him, while the girl who has given him up is suddenly plied with the attentions of the boy her own younger sister likes. (No extant prints; negative at Daiei, Tokyo.)

*The Key/Odd Obsession (Kagi)
pr: Daiei (Tokyo); orig. story: Junichiro Tanizaki; sc: Keiji Hasebe, Natto Wada and Ichikawa; color 'scope ph: Kazuo Miyagawa; music: Yasushi Akutagawa; cast: Machiko Kyo, Junko Kano, Tatsuya Nakadai, Ganjiro Nakamura, Tanie Kitabayashi et al. Disturbing story of the marital relations between a middle-aged beauty and her elderly husband, who keeps himself going sexually with injections, jealousy and taking photographs of his nude, sleeping wife. Their daughter's ambitious but impoverished fiancé is drawn into the relationship, and the daughter burns with jealousy. Ichikawa's ending to this twisted affair is a surprise quite different from the novel. *KJ* #9. (FC, MOMA, JA)

*Fires on the Plain (Nobi)
pr: Daiei (Tokyo); orig. story: Shohei Ooka; sc: Natto Wada; 'scope ph: Setsuo Kobayashi; music: Yasushi Akutagawa; cast: Eiji Funakoshi, Mickey Curtis, Osamu Takizawa, Hikaru Hoshi, Jun Hamamura et al. Bleak picture of the close

of the Pacific War in the Philippines, but marked by Ichikawa's ironic humor. Retreating Japanese soldiers fight starvation and embittered Filipinos, who build signal fires on the plains. The hero finds himself murdering for a bit of salt, becoming feverish with starvation, and finally realizing the "monkey meat" some of his comrades are eating is really human flesh. Ichikawa's interpretation of the novel removes the Christian possibility of salvation, and all escape is closed off. *KJ* #2. (FC, JA)

A Woman's Testament, Part Two: Women Who Sell Things at High Prices (Jokyo II: Mono o Takaku Uritsukeru Onna)
pr: Daiei (Tokyo); orig. story: Shofu Muramatsu; sc: Toshio Yasumi; color 'scope ph: Hiroshi Murai; cast: Fujiko Yamamoto, Eiji Funakoshi et al. Second part of an omnibus, the other parts of which were directed by Kozaburo Yoshimura and Yasuzo Masumura. Comic love story in which a writer wins a beautiful real estate saleswoman who has been trying to trick him. (MOMA; negative at Daiei, Tokyo.)

1960   ** Bonchi (Bonchi)*
pr: Daiei (Kyoto); orig. story: Toyoko Yamazaki; sc: Natto Wada and Ichikawa; color 'scope ph: Kazuo Miyagawa; music: Yasushi Akutagawa; cast: Raizo Ichikawa, Ayako Wakao, Tamao Nakamura, Isuzu Yamada, Fubuki Koshiji, Ganjiro Nakamura, Machiko Kyo et al. Horrifying but terribly funny picture of a traditional matriarchy in Osaka. "Bonchi" is an affectionate term used for a son in the area, but not for a son who is a full-fledged adult. This son is so dominated by his mother and grandmother that his wife is turned out of their traditional merchant household. He turns to a life of dissipation, which pleases his women at home as long as he doesn't have any sons. Browbeaten by women on all sides, Bonchi survives the war and begins to realize what a failure he is. (FC; negative at Daiei, Tokyo.)

* Her Brother (Ototo)
pr: Daiei (Tokyo); orig. story: Aya Koda; sc: Yoko Mizuki; color 'scope ph: Kazuo Miyagawa; music: Yasushi Akutagawa; cast: Keiko Kishi, Hiroshi Kawaguchi, Masayuki Mori, Kinuyo Tanaka, Kyoko Kishida et al. Ichikawa's most nearly sentimental film, about familial affection. A devoted sister postpones getting married partly because her crippled mother cannot manage the household, partly because her rebellious brother needs constant bailing out of trouble. Their writer father is too busy to pay attention to them and pursues a laissez-faire policy until his son contracts TB. On his deathbed, the boy realizes he has been a burden to everyone, and that love has been there all along. *KJ* #1; Geijutsusai First Prize. (FC, MOMA; negative at Daiei, Tokyo.)

1961   *Ten Dark Women (Kuroi Junin no Onna)*
pr: Daiei (Tokyo); orig. sc: Natto Wada; 'scope ph: Setsuo Kobayashi; music: Yasushi Akutagawa; cast: Eiji Funakoshi, Fujiko Yamamoto, Keiko Kishi, Mariko Miyagi, Tamao Nakamura, Kyoko Kishida et al. A mock thriller about a television producer surrounded by jealous women, each of whom wants him all to herself. When he hears the jealousy is driving them to thoughts of murdering him, he appeals to his usually totally neglected wife. She devises a staged mur-

der that throws the others off the track for a while, but she ends by dumping her hopelessly run-around husband on his number one mistress. Purposely stagey acting and arty camera and lighting work. *KJ* #10. (FC; negative at Daiei, Tokyo.)

1962 **The Outcast/The Broken Commandment (Hakai)*
pr: Daiei (Kyoto studios); orig. story: Toson Shimazaki; sc: Natto Wada; 'scope ph: Kazuo Miyagawa; music: Yasushi Akutagawa; cast: Raizo Ichikawa, Shiho Fujimura, Hiroyuki Nagata, Rentaro Mikuni, Kyoko Kishida et al. Dark psychological drama of a young man's inner struggle with the secret that he is a member of Japan's pariah class. "Passing" to the point of becoming a school teacher, his admiration for an outspoken author who is also an outcast brings exposure, but he follows his father's commandment and denies his heritage, only to see his mentor murdered. *KJ* #4. (FC; negative at Daiei, Tokyo.)

*I Am Two/Being Two Isn't Easy (Watashi wa Nisai)
pr: Daiei (Tokyo); orig. story: Toshio Matsuda; sc: Natto Wada; color 'scope ph: Setsuo Kobayashi; music: Yasushi Akutagawa; animation: Ryuichi Yokoyama; cast: Eiji Funakoshi, Fujiko Yamamoto, Kumeko Urabe, Kyoko Kishida et al. A very funny and touching film narrated from the viewpoint of a baby, who observes the fault-finding, worrying, loving world of adults. Much is not to his liking, but he proceeds full of hope and energy. *KJ* #1. (FC, JA)

1963 **An Actor's Revenge (Yukinojo Henge)*
pr: Daiei (Kyoto); orig. story: Otokichi Mikami; sc: Daisuke Ito, Teinosuke Kinugasa and Natto Wada; color 'scope ph: Setsuo Kobayashi; cast: Kazuo Hasegawa, Fujiko Yamamoto, Ayako Wakao, Ganjiro Nakamura, Raizo Ichikawa et al. An old favorite story done as a breathtaking avant-garde experiment, made to celebrate actor Hasegawa's 300th film appearance. Ichikawa had him play the same double role —Kabuki actor of female roles and small-time gangster —that he had played in Kinugasa's 1935 version of the same story. The actor, aided by the mysterious gangster, succeeds in avenging his parents, but not without having both a beautiful rich girl and a female thief-assassin fall in love with him. The silly story allowed Ichikawa full play for his visual fancy, and there are color and composition surprises throughout the film. (NY)

Alone on the Pacific (Taiheiyo Hitoribotchi)
pr: Ishihara Prod./Nikkatsu; orig. story: Kenichi Horie; sc: Natto Wada; color 'scope ph: Yoshiyuki Yamazaki; music: Yasushi Akutagawa and Toru Takemitsu; cast: Yujiro Ishihara, Kinuyo Tanaka, Masayuki Mori, Ruriko Asaoka et al. Psychological study based on Horie's actual experience. A young man sets out alone in a small sailboat, and in the course of long hours of calm followed by furious gales, he comes to understand a great deal about his family relationships. *KJ* #4; Geijutsusai First Prize. (FC; negative at Ishihara Promotion, Tokyo.)

1964 *The Money Dance/Money Talks (Zeni no Odori)*
pr: Daiei (Tokyo); orig. sc: "Christie" (Ichikawa); color 'scope ph: Kazuo Miyagawa; cast: Shintaro Katsu, Chiemi Eri, Jun Hamamura, Roy James, Shiro

Otsuji et al. Comedy about a man who cannot tolerate evil, but finds out that the people he works for are a gang of murderers. More Katsu than Ichikawa. (No circulating prints; negative at Daiei, Tokyo.)

1965   **Tokyo Olympiad (Tokyo Orimpikku)*
pr: 13th Olympic Organizing Committee/Toho; sc: Natto Wada, Yoshio Shirasaka, Shuntaro Tanikawa and Ichikawa; color 'scope ph: Shigeo Hayashida, Tadashi Tanaka, Kinichi Nakamura, Kazuo Miyagawa and Shigeichi Nagano. Revolutionary sports documentary that concentrates on the human, rather than the athletic, aspect of the games. Beautifully edited cutaways to audience closeups show the variety of response to the competitive efforts in the stadium, and the runner from the new African country of Chad, who has most of his story told in his isolation from the other participants. The agony of the cross-country race provides a moving, exhausting ending to a 2-hour-45-minute film that is never boring. *KJ #2.* (TO, AB)

1967   *Toppo Gigio and the Missile War (Toppo Jijo no Botan Senso)*
pr: Perego/Ichikawa Kon Prod.; orig. sc: Ichikawa, Rokusuke Nagai, Alberto Ongaro, Frederico Caldora; ph: Shigeichi Nagano; puppeteer: Maria Perego. Disastrous Italian coproduction with the Italian mouse puppet, Toppo Gigio, as hero. (No circulating prints.)

1968   *Youth (Seishun)*
pr: Asahi Shimbunsha/Asahi Television News/Toho; sc: Ichikawa. Documentary on the 50th Japan High School Allstar Baseball Game. Concentrating on one boy, a pitcher from a rural school, Ichikawa begins with winter practice and follows the joys and sorrows of preparation for the big game. (No circulating prints.)

1969   *Kyoto (Kyoto)*
pr: Olivetti Co.; sc: Ichikawa. Beautiful half-hour color documentary on Japan's ancient capital, capturing all of its dark serenity. (MOMA, Olivetti Co.)

1970   *Japan and the Japanese (Nihon to Nihonjin)*
pr: Expo '70 Organizing Committee; sc: Ichikawa. Short documentary full of Ichikawa's clinical view of life and his ironic humor, as when a breathtaking panorama of the Japan Alps tilts down to a colossal traffic jam. (No circulating prints.)

1972   *To Love Again/Pourquoi (Ai Futatabi)*
pr: Toho; orig. sc: Shuntaro Tanikawa; color 'scope ph: Kiyoshi Hasegawa; cast: Ruriko Asaoka, Renaut Verley, Tetsuo Ishidate, Seiji Miyaguchi et al. A self-consciously arty and superficial love story. A Japanese girl who fell in love with a French boy while studying in France sees him again in Tokyo. She feels that their relationship is impossible because of cultural differences, but he doesn't understand why. (TO)

1973   *The Wanderers (Matatabi)*
pr: Ichikawa Kon Prod./ATG; orig. sc: Shuntaro Tanikawa; color ph: Setsuo Kobayashi; cast: Ichiro Ogura, Isao Bito, Kenichi Hagiwara, Reiko Inoue et al. Ichikawa's parody of gangster films and his own version of *Easy Rider*. Three

farm boys in nineteenth-century Japan leave home to find a better life as petty gangsters. In their penniless attempt to observe the code of obligation to hosts and local bosses, they are victimized by all and each other. One of them dies of gangrene from a foot wound, another is forced to kill his father and sell his girlfriend. The remaining two fight over a point of order in the code, and one of them trips and falls over a cliff to his death. A very funny film, but most of the humor is pathos. *KJ* #4. (TO)

1975 **I Am a Cat (Wagahai wa Neko de Aru)*
pr: Geiensha/Toho; orig. story: Soseki Natsume; sc: Toshio Yasumi; color ph: Kozo Okazaki; cast: Tatsuya Nakadai, Mariko Okada, Juzo Itami, Nobuto Okamoto, Yoko Shimada et al. Adaptation of a very essay-like novel that succeeds on its caricature and clinical view of human beings. A cat who lives in the home of a poor schoolteacher around the end of the nineteenth century observes and comments on the poses and presumptuousness he sees around him. Discouraged by the death of his sweetheart next door and his inability to communicate with the humans, he commits suicide. The pompous students, confused teacher, and obnoxious nouveaux riches are delightful stereotypes. (No circulating prints; negative at Toho, Tokyo.)

1976 *Between Women and Wives (Tsuma to Onna no Aida)*
pr: Geiensha/Toho; codirector: Shiro Toyoda; orig. story: Harumi Seotuchi; sc: Toshio Yasumi; color ph: Kozo Okazaki and Kiyoshi Hasegawa; music: Masaru Sato; cast: Yoshiko Mita, Mayumi Ozora, Wakako Sakai, Akiko Nishina, Meiko Kaji, Takahiro Tamura, Yusuke Okada et al. Story of the loves, disappointments and work of four sisters from a traditional Kyoto paper shop. Character study takes precedence over action. (TO)

The Inugami Family (Inugami-ke no Ichizoku)
pr: Kadokawa Haruki Jimusho/Geiensha/Toho; orig. story: Seishi Yokomizo; sc: Norio Nagata, Shinya Hidaka and Ichikawa; color ph: Kiyoshi Hasegawa; music: Yuji Ono; cast: Koji Ishizaka, Mieko Takamine, Yoko Shimada, Rentaro Mikuni, Shuji Otaki, Ryoko Sakaguchi et al. A bafflingly complicated thriller that reveals the dastardly internecine rivalries in a wealthy industrialist's family. The horrifying series of murders that occur over the succession to the old man's wealth is unraveled by an early twentieth-century Japanese version of the scruffy investigator Colombo. A light work that is more fun than fear, and the biggest box office success in Japanese film history. *KJ* #5.

1977 *The Devil's Bouncing Ball Song (Akuma no Temari-uta)*
pr: Toho; orig. story: Seishi Yokomizo; sc: "Christie" (Ichikawa); color ph: Kiyoshi Hasegawa; cast: Koji Ishizaka, Keiko Kishi, Tomisaburo Wakayama et al. Hasty sequel to the previous Yokomizo detective story adaptation.

Island of Horrors (Gokumonto)
pr: Toho; orig. story: Seishi Yokomizo; sc: "Christie" (Shinya Hidaka and Ichikawa); color ph: Kiyoshi Hasegawa; music: Shinichi Tanabe; cast: Koji Ishizaka, Reiko Ohara, Mitsuko Kusabue, Yoko Tsukasa, Shin Saburi et al. Intrepid detective Kindaichi (Ishizaka) tracks down a triple murderer using haiku poem clues.

1978   ***Queen Bee*** (***Joobachi***)
pr: Toho; orig. story: Seishi Yokomizo; sc: "Christie" (Shinya Hidaka, Chiho Katsura and Ichikawa); color ph: Kiyoshi Hasegawa; music: Shinichi Tanabe; cast: Ishizaka Koji, Chie Nakai, Tatsuya Nakadai, Keiko Kishi, Yoko Tsukasa, Norihei Miki et al. Hopefully the last of the Yokomizo adaptations.

MASAKI KOBAYASHI

1916—

*As a contemporary and friend I feel very
close to Masaki Kobayashi, but I am
convinced that the seriousness of his pursuit
of aesthetics in film is something quite
unique.*

—Kon Ichikawa

Of the four outstanding directors emerging in the immediate postwar era, Masaki Kobayashi bears the deepest scars of the Pacific War. The personal experience and philosophical problems of the greatest trauma of twentieth-century Japan have become for him the raw materials of his art. It was the war that not only caused him to become a filmmaker, but considerably delayed his actual start at making his own films. It also instilled in him the determination to make his epic trilogy *The Human Condition* (1959–61) the most intense evaluation of wartime responsibility, and suffused all of his work with a deep concern for social justice, whether set in the present, as in *The Thick-Walled Room* (1953), about the war-crimes trials, or the past, as in his Cannes prize-winner on feudal morality, *Harakiri* (1962).

A tall, soft-spoken man who always wears a hat, Kobayashi is completely straightforward about his likes and dislikes. He adores his mentor, Keisuke Kinoshita; Canada, where he has been accorded the full recognition he deserves in the west; and ancient art. He hates rushing through his work—shooting no more than three takes a day, as he did on *Kwaidan* (1964), would be his ideal—and he hates television—when his television series *Kaseki* was shown in 1974, he refused to watch it; he had shot the eight one-hour programs only as footage from which to edit the feature 213–minute film.[1]

Because of his meticulous perfectionism, his insistence on doing material he wants to do, and his late start, Kobayashi has produced surprisingly few films compared with the output of his contemporaries. He will not admit to having any favorites among his own works, insisting "They're all like my children to me"—but he does admit to having a single direction in his career: "I always wanted to be a maker of films that comment on society."[2] Even his most recent *Kaseki,* the highly introspective story of a successful businessman who learns in late middle-age while traveling in Europe that he has cancer, comments on society in the broad sense that Japan today is so much a member of the community of developed nations that the locale and the problem of the film necessarily become universal. Kobayashi has said, "The relationship of an individual's consciousness to his setting is my main theme."[3] The same is true of Kobayashi's next project, *Tun-huang,* which takes place in ancient China's Sung dynasty and which he hopes to film in China using actors from all over the world.[4]

But aside from the social commentary thread in Kobayashi's work, there is also a consistent aesthetic strain. Kobayashi as an art-lover and art historian is manifested in the way he illuminates his films, as seen in the graphic composition of *The Thick-Walled Room,* the emphatic use of Japanese architecture and family crest designs in *Harakiri,* and the critical tour of the Musée Rodin and a romanesque church in *Kaseki.* In the purely cinematic realm of sound-image-motion coordination, his work explores much that future art historians will study.

Far from Beauty Past

Kobayashi was born in Hokkaido where he attended public schools until entering Waseda University in Tokyo in 1933. He enrolled in the philosophy department of the literature faculty, but actually studied Oriental art until he graduated finally in 1941. Under Professor Yaichi Aizu who was, he maintains, a great influence on him, Kobayashi pursued the art of early Japan, China, Southeast Asia, as well as that extending all the way through India to Greece. "I would have gone on, he says, "but the Pacific War had begun. In art history I knew it would require many more years of painstaking research for me to make a contribution, and the war made the future too uncertain. But with film, I thought there might be a chance of leaving something behind."[5] He entered Shochiku's Ofuna studios in May of that year and, sure enough, worked there a scant eight months before being drafted in January 1942.

By April he was in Manchuria at Harbin. His opposition to the cruelty of the Imperial Japanese Army system could only be expressed by refusing to rise above the rank of private, which he remained for the duration of his military service.[6] This passive resistance immediately recalls the actions of the pacifist hero of his epic *The Human Condition*, about whom he has indeed said, "I am Kaji in the film."[7] Not only were his experiences in Manchuria very much like those of the hero Kaji, but when he had the sets built in Hokkaido, he made the environment look as much as possible like what he himself had seen.[8] In 1944 he was transferred to the defense of Miyakojima in the Ryukyu Islands, where he saw the end of the war. But he was kept in a detention camp in Okinawa for a full year thereafter, and it was not until November 1946 that he returned to Shochiku. "This too was a very strange experience," he says, avoiding a precise verbal description, "someday I want to make a film about it, too."[9] One suspects he still has much to say about the American Occupation that he could not say in *The Thick-Walled Room* or *Black River* (1957). While Kurosawa, Ichikawa, and Kinoshita, whose staff he was to join, had all been making films during the preceding five years, Kobayashi had been off fighting a war he has called "the culmination of human evil,"[10] and had to begin again from scratch.

The Kinoshita School

By 1947 Kobayashi was seriously carrying out the work of assistant director on Kinoshita's staff at Ofuna. He would fulfill the customary six-year stint as assistant, and even coscript Kinoshita's 1948 comedy *Broken Drum*. Also among the major Kinoshita films on which he assisted are *Woman* (1948), *A Toast to the Young Miss* (1949), the Carmen comedies (1951–52), and *A Japanese Tragedy* (1953). Kobayashi recalls that this era, just before he himself was promoted, was the time of his mentor's "most severe, most rigorous" work, which he greatly admires.[11] From Kobayashi's first entry into Shochiku in 1941 to the completion of his debut film, *My Sons' Youth*, in November 1952, it had been over eleven years. To celebrate his promotion, Kinoshita himself wrote the script for Kobayashi's next film, the 1953 *Sincerity*. The novice director, though only four years younger than Kinoshita, was very careful to listen to his senior's advice on what sort of films Shochiku (i.e., the company president, Shiro Kido) would like.[12]

Kobayashi is very proud of the fact that he was the first graduate of the "Kinoshita School," an actual organization within the Shochiku company. Other noted directors who followed him are Zenzo Matsuyama, Yoshiro Kawazu (1926–), and Yoshishige Yoshida (1933–) ; the latter would become, along with Nagisa Oshima, one of the most vociferous and most French-influenced of Japan's New Wave. The Kinoshita School was thus a very prestigious organization, with Yasujiro Ozu as "P.T.A. chairman," and actress Kinuyo Tanaka (Kobayashi's cousin) as "vice chairman." (Kobayashi, who spent every day for several months at the dying Tanaka's hospital bedside in 1976–77, also remains grateful to her for her advice and strictness with him when he decided on a film career: "You must prove yourself on your own," was her admonition.")[13] Kobayashi's early work, with the great contrast between his Kinoshita-style endeavors and intimations of the later direction he would carve out for himself, shows him as a director who, because of his late start, straddles two very different generations in his style.

The critical response to Kobayashi's first films was astonishment at the youthful freshness and lyricism in the work of someone who had undergone such a long apprenticeship.[14] This lyricism is of course the Kinoshita legacy. In his debut film *My Sons' Youth*, not only does the sentimentality of Chuji Kinoshita's score dominate the content of the film, but the story itself is a pure "home drama" of a middle-class household, entirely removed from pressing socio-political concerns. Keisuke Kinoshita's story of unattainable, pure love in the subsequent *Sincerity* is very much like the script his sister would write for him in the 1956 *Clouds at Twilight*. But Kobayashi almost tripped himself irretrievably with his 1953 *Thick-Walled Room*, and it was only by returning to the Kinoshita fold with the 1954 *Three Loves* and Yoshiko Kusuda's very first script, *Somewhere under the Broad Sky*, again with Chuji Kinoshita's music, that he reinstated himself in Shiro Kido's favor. He secured his position by following these with two scripts by the second Kinoshita School graduate, Zenzo Matsuyama, who incorporated the standard Kinoshita elements of pure love and pure friendship, and country-city tensions—some of the essentials of sentimentality in the Kinoshita of the 1954 *Twenty-four Eyes.* Kobayashi's instinct of self-preservation within the Shochiku system was correct. In Kinoshita he had an excellent teacher and powerful patron. While none of the early films he made under direct Kinoshita tutelage are bad films, they are more his mentor's late style than his own, and very different from what Kobayashi already knew he wanted to do as a director.

Judgment for Today

A progression straight from *The Thick-Walled Room* (1953) to *I'll Buy You* (1956) was what Kobayashi had in mind, but the first film was too outspoken for the society of the day. Today it appears harmless enough; if anything, it seems more flattering to the American military than to the Japanese. But it is based on the actual diaries of low-ranking war crimes prisoners, and indicates very clearly through flashbacks that they were only following orders about which they had no choice in the inhumanly cruel Imperial Army system. Further sympathy for the scapegoats is en-sured by showing the effects of their years of incarceration on their loved ones—a pure country girl becomes a prostitute catering to American GIs. The subject was volatile enough to cause Shiro Kido to shelve it for three long years because of what he repeatedly contended was an act of his own conscience because "films should be art, not polemics," all the while affirming Kobayashi's talent as a director.[15] Current reference sources and Kobayashi himself, however, maintain that it was U.S. Occupation pressure that forced Kido's decision.[16]

The political repercussions of the 1953 shelving of *The Thick-Walled Room* sent Kobayashi back into lyrical *shomin-geki* dramas of lower middle-class life again, but the artistic exploration of the film presages the method of the coming generation of the New Wave. He had stepped outside of the system to find a scenarist who was a complete amateur to film, seven years before Masahiro Shinoda would do the same. When Kobayashi approached Kobo Abe and asked him to do a script for him, the novelist was still a believer in the justice of the Communist system, and this belief enters the finished film. By the time Abe began working with Hiroshi Teshigahara (1927–), the director with whom he became an internationally renowned team, his political philosophy was under-going the doubt and redirection toward surrealism that produced *Pitfall* (*Otoshiana,* 1962) and *Woman in the Dunes* (*Suna no Onna,* 1964). Kobayashi and Abe also instituted what was to become later New Wave

practice by forming their own production company and securing Shochiku's promise of distribution. Shochiku did not uphold its side of the
agreement, however, and Kobayashi's supportive fellow-directors saw
to it that *The Thick-Walled Room* won the Peace Culture Prize when it
was at last released in 1956.[17]

By the time he was allowed to do what he wanted to again, Kobayashi narrowed his sights to a particular profession, and went back to
Shochiku scriptwriter Zenzo Matsuyama. The message of *I'll Buy You* was
just as scathing as the indictment three years before, however. Following
in the footsteps of the "severe, rigorous" Kinoshita of the 1953 *Japanese
Tragedy,* Kobayashi portrays a young baseball star who scorns all close
relationships (girlfriend, manager, other family members) to go where
the money is. His icy character is fully delineated before any interaction
with other people occurs: we see him crush a spider with the end of his
baseball bat for no apparent reason. But it is not the star who is the only
numb figure in the baseball world. His manager, the protagonist scout
armed with bribe money, and all the other scouts accept corruption as a
way of life. The full horror of the moral irresponsibility of the whole society of Japan's most popular sport since well before the Pacific War is
expressed in one scout's political philosophy: "A horse needs reins, a
dog a master, a country a prime minister." Compared to Akira Kurosawa's
exposé of corruption a few years later in *The Bad Sleep Well* (1960),
Kobayashi's portrayal is far more pessimistic: no one can even attempt
to buck the system, and the coolest, most unfeeling opportunists are the
winners all around.

After completing another exposé, this time of the sordid corruption
around U.S. military bases in Japan, the 1957 *Black River,* Kobayashi set
about working on a long-cherished project. *The Human Condition* was
to be a long, hard look back at the Pacific War and its immorality. But as
was also the case with Kurosawa's 1950 *Rashomon,* the film that would
establish Kobayashi's international reputation was a film nobody would
let him make. He had read Jumpei Gomikawa's six-volume novel (quite
a task in itself) when it first appeared and had immediately bought the
rights for the Ninjin independent production company. It later became a
best seller, but the other major studios and even Shochiku still refused to
let him make the film, until he threatened to quit.[18] The six parts of the
novel, compressed into three feature films, each over three hours long,
took Kobayashi four years to make. He was already into production on
"Part II" after the domestic success of "Part I" when news came that he
had won the San Giorgio Prize at Venice. The story is an excruciating one,
sentimentalized in moments by the participation of Kobayashi's long-
time allies, scriptwriter-director Zenzo Matsuyama and composer Chuji
Kinoshita. But the saga of the pacifist Kaji (played to perfection by

Kobayashi's discovery Tatsuya Nakadai), forced into the Imperial Army and tortured into being cruel not only toward the enslaved Chinese but toward his inferiors in the Japanese system, forced to lead his troops into certain death, and finally trapped as a war criminal by the Soviets, is so full of the truth of war's reversal of all human values that over-emotionalizing the horror is certainly understandable. In fact, in all of Kobayashi's attacks on what subverts humanism in contemporary—or any—society is the loss of emotion. It is this emotional rigidity, the negation of common feeling with one's fellow man, that threatens life itself.

The same humanistic appeal for the retention of emotion lies behind the portrayal of viciousness in his 1962 *Inheritance*. But here, as in *I'll Buy You*, the universal motivation is selfish greed. In showing the contemporary bourgeoisie and those who believe they have something to gain from these people, Kobayashi never allows character change or any kind of enlightenment as Kurosawa does in everything from the 1952 *Ikiru* bureaucrat to the 1963 shoe magnate of *High and Low*. For Kobayashi, the good, like Kaji, never win, but their failure can inspire. The bad, like the whole array of unfeeling characters (with the exception of the helpless innocents: the baseball star's girlfriend and the millionaire's illegitimate but violent son, who only become hardened by their experience in *I'll Buy You* and *The Inheritance*), never change, but Kobayashi makes them so unattractive that we can feel no sympathy for them. He denies that he is pessimistic, but admits "it is very easy to become so after examining the history of humanity. You have to try hard to be optimistic."[19]

Kobayashi says there is absolutely no difference for him in the feeling of making period or contemporary films.[20] The history of humanity, in other words, reveals oppression and lack of human feeling in every age, so that Kobayashi understands "the past as the present."[21] The feudal loyalty and concomitant inhumanity demanded of the samurai families in both *Harakiri* and *Rebellion* (1967) are the same as the demands made by the Imperial Army in *The Thick-Walled Room* and The *Human Condition*. In the postwar era, the dehumanizing values of the Pacific War and the age of the warrior are replaced by the equally dehumanizing pursuit of money in *I'll Buy You*, *Black River*, *The Inheritance* and even, until the hero's enlightenment, in the 1975 *Kaseki*. When the lonely businessman Itsuki (Shin Saburi in the best performance of his career) is given a reprieve from death, however, his final agony consists in facing a return to finances and unsatisfying social forms. The undeniable (much as Kobayashi does deny it) pessimism of this view of human society has been tempered only by an acute sensitivity to dramatic action pacing and an ever-increasig auditory-visual aestheticism.

Select Offspring

The care Kobayashi devotes to each film is expressed in his attitude toward his works as his children, an affection evident in every phase of the
filmmaking process. With the exception of his early Shochiku days, he
did not even accept material other than that of his own choice. The
independent production and experimental script method begun in *The
Thick-Walled Room* indicated the direction he would follow. However,
in having the novelist Abe write for him, he did not demand a professional
script. "He wrote something novelistic, and I went over it and made it
into a real scenario."[22] Kobayashi has done this ever since. Even when
his name does not appear among the scriptwriters he works with, which
have also included such illustrious names as Shinobu Hashimoto (*Harakiri* and *Rebellion*), who also worked with Kurosawa, and Yoko Mizuki
(*Kwaidan*, 1964), who worked with Mikio Naruse, Kobayashi goes over
every script until it is exactly what he wants.[23]

For Kobayashi casting is an important element of a style that is
simultaneously critical of the unhealthy vestiges of the past and something that looks to the future. In this context he was very pleased to
discover Tatsuya Nakadai, an actor with strong classical stage training
combined with the youth capable of representing the contemporary
Japanese.[24] For any director the actor becomes vehicle for his social,
psychological and aesthetic statement; as Kurosawa developed a family
of actors, and Oshima would after him, Kobayashi came to rely on
Nakadai as his personal representative on the other side of the camera.[25]

When he began making period films with *Harakiri* in 1962, Kobayashi
began a new exploration of formal beauty. He had already been using
widescreen since *The Human Condition*, but after the somewhat televi-
sion-like contemporary sets of *The Inheritance* he decided upon a reduction and stress of the compositional elements of Harakiri. "I wanted a
mixture of symbolism and realism, so I imposed the harsh contrasts of
white sand and black kimonos, and the domination by the Japanese
family crest motif."[26] When he saw that this was successful at the Cannes
Film Festival, he wanted to go a step further with the formal beauty of
Kwaidan.

As with *Harakiri*, the music was done first; and now, working with
avant-garde composer Toru Takemitsu, who had been discovered for the
screen by the New Wave director Shinoda, the tone was a new and eerie
freshness to combine with the visuals of the four ghost stories. Kobayashi speaks with great enthusiasm of Takemitsu's ingenious use of the
most Japanese of sounds made into concrete music electronically, a
different effect for each story: wood being split, very hard stones, found
only on the island of Shikoku, being struck, the small non-verbal vocal

accompaniments to music in the Noh drama, and a highly specialized shamisen style used only for the theater. It took a half-year of dubbing to perfect the sound-image combination, the part of filmmaking Kobayashi says is most important to him and which he says he had a wonderful time doing.[27]

In the visuals for *Kwaidan* as well, what Kobayashi did indicates his devoted aesthetic concern. For his first color film he wanted complete tonal control, so he looked until he found an unused airplane hanger, built all the sets inside it, and painted everything himself. He then proceeded to film at his own pace: one or two, at most three final takes a day. He was rewarded for his loving care with a second place in the domestic polls and a Special Jury Prize at Cannes. His exploration of traditional Japanese aesthetics is best combined with his philosophical themes, however, in his 1962 black-and-white film *Harakiri*, which has been called his "single finest film."[28]

Harakiri

Even at the end of the sixteenth century's civil strife, when the warrior became an anachronism, the samurai's code required that he guard his honor at all costs. If he found himself in compromising circumstances, such as poverty so dire as to threaten his life, honor demanded that he commit ritual suicide rather than lie, steal, or become a mercenary in order to survive. Samurai who lost their masters in battle or assassinations often had to face this situation as *ronin*, warriors without a lord to serve. The theme of *Harakiri*, which means ritual suicide, is the inhumanity of this requirement for those who dutifully adhered to it, and the hypocrisy of those who enforced its practice. Kobayashi's aim is to show that "honor and bravery are a false front," as the hero says.

The somewhat wordy story is organized by flashbacks strung together through the narration of two main characters. The narration is all very calm and composed, in contrast to the build-up of action, suspense, and anguish in the flashback sequences. The climax these prepare for is a "violent tragic attack of individual human dignity directed at empty institutional pride,"[29] the same heartless glory that drove 47 to their deaths in the famous *Chushingura* story of the loyal retainers, and thousands more to the same end in the Pacific War.

A bedraggled masterless samurai of the Geshu clan, Hanshiro Tsugumo (Tatsuya Nakadai), comes to the Edo residence of Lord Ii requesting permission to commit ritual suicide in some corner of the lord's mansion. He is received with some hesitation by Kageyu Saito (Rentaro Mikuni), a high-ranking samurai of the Ii household, who remarks that a *ronin* of the same clan had come there earlier for the very same purpose.

He asks whether Tsugumo would like to hear what happened to him.

Here the flashbacks begin, showing the arrival of the young man, Motome Chijiwa (Akira Ishihama). The samurai of the Ii house deliberate on what to do about him, since the reason for his request is obviously poverty. One of them, Hikokuro Omodaka (Tetsuro Tamba), insists that he should not be given money and sent away, much less should he be given employment because this would only bring more impoverished *ronin* to their door. He says that for the sake of the reputation of the Ii, the man should be forced to carry out his stated plan of suicide. But they decide to play with him first, and he is told he will be granted an interview with the heir of the house. He waits, enthusing about his good fortune, hoping he will be given employment. But he is then informed the interview is impossible, and he must immediately change from the formal clothing they have given him into the white robes for suicide which are now thrust at him. The Ii have decided not only to make an example of him for other desperate *ronin*, but to torture him psychologically and physically in the process.

Chijiwa attempts to escape but is forced back. Omodaka even refuses to grant him one or two days postponement, telling him he must follow the code and keep his word. In the course of the preparations they have also discovered that Chijiwa's sword has nothing but a bamboo blade— his poverty has obviously forced him to sell the metal blade. In spite of this they are determined to make him go through with the suicide, and Omodaka tells him that in acting as his second he will observe the code properly and wait to behead him until he is completely dead. The bamboo blade is of course too blunt to cut his flesh, and Chijiwa in desperation finally falls on it and bites off his tongue in order to die.

After hearing this story of the Ii's brutality and Chijiwa's courage, Tsugumo calmly promises that he will not do anything as cowardly as biting off his tongue to die. He refuses the white ritual robes they offer him and proceeds to the white platform set up in the courtyard.

Tsugumo requests Omodaka as a second, but he has taken a leave of absence from his clan duties. Saito sends a messenger to bring him, and while they wait, Tsugumo offers to pass the time by telling them his life story.

"Motome Chijiwa was a man of some acquaintance to me," he begins, and the second series of flashbacks soon reveals that he was actually Tsugumo's adopted child and son-in-law. Chijiwa's father too had been a victim of suicide for honor, and he had put his son in Tsugumo's care. He grew up to become a teacher and married Tsugumo's daughter, Mino (Shima Iwashita). The young couple had a very difficult time financially, with first Mino and then their baby falling ill. Chijiwa tried every possible means of making money, selling off all of their possessions and seeking work as a laborer, which he was refused because of his status as a samurai. Hearing that some of the great clan households in Edo employed *ronin* who came to them asking to be allowed to commit suicide, he decided to go and try it in spite of the risk. He was returned a few days later as a corpse by three members of the Ii clan.

While Tsugumo tells the story, various messengers arrive to report that all three men he requested as seconds—the same three, including Omodaka, who had brought back Chijiwa's body—are "ill." Tsugumo tells a story which explains why they are ill. He has searched out each one of them and engaged him in combat to take his topknot, the symbol of his rank as a samurai and of his adult manhood.

Tsugumo insists on his right to choose a second according to the code, but Saito orders him killed. He kills several of the men who attack him and wounds many others. Finally he commits *harakiri* as he said he would, but they finish him with pistol shots, completely contravening the samurai code.

The closing scene shows Saito telling his subordinates that "nothing unusual happened today," and the men who were killed "all died of illness." The clan records are to show only that a man named Hanshiro Tsugumo of the Geshu clan was granted permission to commit ritual suicide on the grounds on the Ii mansion.

Harakiri is a film that abounds in symbols, some of them visual and some verbal. All pertain to the historical image of the samurai and are used in ironic fashion. The first visual symbol appears immediately after the opening titles: a closeup of a face mask and great battle helmet, complete with the hornlike prongs that indicate high military rank. The camera then moves back to show the full suit of armor above which the mask and helmet sit, with mist rising around it. The effect, enhanced by Toru Takemitsu's score, is eerie and grotesque. There is no narration over this, but the audience later learns that this armor represents the ancestors of the Ii house. The household members address it directly in their consultations over what to do about these *ronin* applying for permission to commit suicide, and generally they treat it with utmost reverence and respect, apologizing to it for the dishonor and disturbance incurred by granting the requests. The irony of this sham is fully brought out in the final scene of the attack on Tsugumo. In the heat of the combat, he knocks over the armor and holds it up to help defend himself. Kobayashi's point here is that the Ii samurai are actually cowards, and that this symbol of military might and dignity is a completely empty one. The initial awe inspired by the camera treatment, mist effects, and music in the beginning is totally overturned in the end.

The second visual symbol, which follows the armor in the opening sequence, is the daily record book of the clan. It forms the opening and closing circle of the film and represents the lies of recorded history. In the beginning the open book is shown in closeup and a narrator reads the entry for the day in 1630 when "there were no incidents of note except. . . ." There is then a cut to a man approaching the gate of an imposing mansion, and the audience soon learns that this is Tsugumo. Tsugumo will go on to expose all the hypocrisy, cowardice, and cruelty covered up by this record book, but the final sequence of the film will be the same passage from the same book, noting only that his suicide took place. Kobayashi's message is that the lies of recorded history prevail through the unjust power structure, despite the courage and uprightness of a few men like Tsugumo, a *ronin* without political backing. The whole story of his accusation and challenge to them will be ignored to protect the honor of the clan.

A third symbol is the samurai sword. Kobayashi uses it not only to show the cruelty of the Ii, but to contrast the attitudes of father and son-in-law. For the samurai the sword represented his identity and social role. He was required by law to wear it, and along with his shaved front hair and topknot, it immediately informed anyone he came in contact with of his rank in the top of the four social classes of the Edo period. However, for Chijiwa, poverty is more real than the symbolism of his sword, and he sells the blade to keep his family alive. When Tsugumo learns of this he is shocked; such a drastic solution would never have occurred to him, he says, no matter how poor he became. But through his son-in-law's action Tsugumo learns the lesson of the meaninglessness of such symbols.

The Ii, on the other hand, exercise the utmost of cruel mockery of the sword symbol by making Chijiwa commit suicide with his bamboo blade. Because he has violated the reverence due his own sword, Chijiwa is actually dying a shameful "dog's death," not the honorable death of a samurai at all. His painful struggle to perform the ritual according to the code is therefore also meaningless, and what the Ii do by forcing him to go through with it amounts to outright murder of the most sadistic kind. Kobayashi's point is what Chijiwa actually believes, that the rank and respect automatically due a samurai through the symbol of his sword are worthless when he has nothing to eat and cannot pay a doctor to examine his sick child.

In the course of Tsugumo's revenge for the murder of his son-in-law, a fourth symbol comes into play, the topknot. He takes the three men's topknots by fighting them honorably, and all but Omodaka prove to be cowards in the process. Divesting them of their topknots is the equivalent of taking their swords; according to the samurai code, it would be better for them to die than be subjected to such shame. But they simply take a leave of absence from their clan duties, committing suicide only when

Tsugumo makes their shame public by requesting them as seconds. Tsugumo's revenge is thus extremely subtle. He could have killed all of them, but instead his attack is on the symbols they claim to live by, the same kind of symbols they invoked to murder Chijiwa.

A fifth symbol is the rhetoric of the samurai code. The phrase that recurs throughout the film and that Masahiro Shinoda would also twist in his 1969 *Double Suicide* is "A samurai does not have two words," meaning he never lies, but the Ii use it against Chijiwa to prevent him from postponing his suicide by even one or two days. If they really believed in this phrase, which implies the trustworthiness of the samurai, they should have let him go on the assumption he would come back. But the Ii's sadistic intention is abuse of the code, and the irony lies in the fact that they demand strict adherence to it, while they themselves have no compunctions about lying and far worse—even murder.

Harakiri avoids the sentimentality of some of his earlier films, such as *The Human Condition,* through a new emphasis on visual-auditory aesthetics with the cold formality of compositions and Takemitsu's electronic score. But none of Kobayashi's social protests is diminished in the film's construction—its Mizoguchi-like circularity bitterly denies any hope for human progress, and the character of Tsugumo, with whom we have become so involved, effects no change in the unjust system. His valiant, superhuman fight, as breathtaking as the action is, remains a futile sacrifice of his own life.

Forward and Back

Kobayashi does not have real slumps, since he makes so few films (only 19 to date), but it was too long between the successes of *Harakiri* and *Rebellion* to the back-door entry of *Kaseki* into feature competition from the tawdriness of television. In the 1968 *Youth of Japan,* Kobayashi attempted to return in a contemporary drama to his theme of the inhumanity of the Pacific War, and in his 1971 *Inn of Evil* the only positive note is an odd Kinoshita-type faith in the power of pure love to inspire hardened criminals to do good deeds. Perhaps Kobayashi recognized what was so hard for Kurosawa to cope with, and what sent Kinoshita into television, where the older audience can still be reached, and what makes Ichikawa continue to make features with an attitude of guilty compromise: postwar humanism is dead. After *Inn of Evil* Kobayashi developed as many as ten new film projects, including a fourth part to *The Human Condition* on the Tokyo war crimes trials and a script on the Vietnam War. "But," he sighs, "all of them were rejected. . . . and all of them were social criticism films."[30]

In fact *Kaseki* came about because of the failure of the same postwar humanists to agree on what should be done with their organization Yonki no Kai. They all lost time, money and energy trying to write a script together; then, realizing they were each too stubborn as individuals, they helped Kurosawa make *Dodeskaden* (1970) instead. But they still had great financial losses to recoup, and the consensus was to do a television series. Kobayashi agreed only on the condition that he be allowed to make a feature from it. "Actually, this was ideal," he maintains, "because no feature film company would have accepted a project on a late middle-aged widower with cancer."[31] What Kurosawa did in 1952 in *Ikiru* could only be done for television today. His achievement, though he denies it constitutes a shift in direction for him, is the *Ikiru* message turned inside-out: the worst fate may be living, after having discovered an escape from the boredom of devotion to a family and a business image in a purely personal relationship and the evaluation of the past. Humanism emerges in *Kaseki* in an entirely new light for Kobayashi, as the study of human emotion. The contemporary problem of living cannot be solved by the old humanism's view of personal satisfaction to be achieved by doing good deeds. The consistent Kobayashi touch, as in all of his finest works, like *Harakiri, Rebellion, The Human Condition, The Thick-Walled Room*, leaves the individual condemned. But now the force that crushes him is no longer the external evils of society, but his own power of introspection.

For a man who appears so vigorous, Kobayashi seems to be preparing for the end in much the same way his protagonist Itsuki reflected on death. For ten years he has cherished the project of a film adaptation of Yasushi Inoue's novel *Tun-huang*, situated in the ancient city of Buddhist cave temples in China.[32] "I have to do this film," he insists, "I can't die until I do."[33] But at the same time he has tens of other projects he will do if the conditions are right for his meticulous approach—the danger of his stopping on completion of *Tun-huang* is probably very, very slight.

Notes

[1] Author's interview with Masaki Kobayashi, May 1977.

[2] *Ibid.*

[3] Joan Mellen, *Voices from the Japanese Cinema* (New York: Liveright, 1975), p. 139.

[4] Kobayashi interview, *cit.*

[5] *Ibid.*

[6] Claude R. Blouin, "Kobayashi, l'homme et l'oeuvre" (Kobayashi, the Man and His Work), *Cinéma Québec* (Montreal), vol. 3, No. 5, 1974, p. 40.

[7] Mellen, *op. cit.*, p. 147.

[8] Kobayashi interview, *cit.*

[9] *Ibid.*

[10] Mellen, *op. cit.*, p. 145.

[11] Kobayashi interview, *cit.*

[12] *Ibid.*

[13] *Ibid.*

[14] *Nihon eiga kantoku zenshu* (Dictionary of Japanese Film Directors) (Tokyo: Kinema Jumposha, 1976), p. 174.

[15] Shiro Kido, *Nihon eiga den: Eiga seisakusha no kiroku* (The Story of Japanese Film: A Movie Producer's Record) (Tokyo: Bungei Shunjusha, 1956), p. 225.

[16] Kobayashi interview, *cit.*

[17] Akira Iwasaki, *Nihon eiga sakka ron* (Theories on Japanese Film Directors) (Tokyo: Chuo Koronsha, 1958), p. 112.

[18] Kobayashi interview, *cit.*

[19] Mellen, *op. cit.*, p. 147.

[20] Kobayashi interview, *cit.*

[21] *Ibid.*

[22] *Ibid.*

[23] *Ibid.*

[24] *Ibid.*

[25] *Ibid.*

[26] Mellen, *op. cit.*, p. 141.

[27] Kobayashi interview, *cit.*

[28] Donald Richie, *Japanese Cinema* (New York: Doubleday Anchor, 1971), p. 137.

[29] Tadao Sato, *Nihon eiga shiso shi* (History of the Intellectual Currents in Japanese Film) (Tokyo: Sanichi Shobo, 1970), p. 99.

[30] Kobayashi interview, *cit.*

[31] *Ibid.*

[32] Translated by Jean Moy for Kodansha International, in press.

[33] Kobayashi interview, *cit.*

MASAKI KOBAYASHI: FILMOGRAPHY

1952 *My Sons' Youth* (*Musuko no Seishun*)
pr: Shochiku (Ofuna); orig. story: Fusao Hayashi; sc: Sadao Nakamura; ph: Kurataro Takamura; music: Chuji Kinoshita; cast: Akira Ishihama, Chishu Ryu, Kuniko Miyake, Yoko Kozono et al. Very short, light, episodic first film showing strong Kinoshita home drama influence. Indulgent study of the middle-class life of a father and his two adolescent sons, the trivial joys and sorrows of first dates and sibling rivalry, with atmosphere created by the sentimental music. (PFA/SH; negative at Shochiku, Tokyo.)

1953 *Sincerity* (*Magokoro*)
pr: Shochiku (Ofuna); orig. sc: Keisuke Kinoshita; ph: Toshiyasu Morita; cast: Akira Ishihama, Kinuyo Tanaka et al. Sentimental love story that is more Kinoshita's than Kobayashi's. A boy studying for university entrance examinations falls in love for the first time with a beautiful young invalid he can admire only through the window of her sickroom. (No circulating prints; negative at Shochiku, Tokyo.)

*The Thick-Walled Room (*Kabe Atsuki Heya*)
pr: Shinei Prod./Shochiku; orig. ideas: diaries of B- and C-class war-crimes prisoners; sc: Kobo Abe; ph: Hiroshi Kusuda; music: Chuji Kinoshita; cast: Ko Mishima, Torahiko Hamada, Keiko Kishi, Toshiko Kobayashi, Eitaro Ozawa et al. Kobayashi's very strong first protest against political and social injustice. In this well-edited film, flashbacks show that those imprisoned for as long as eight years were often forced into criminal acts by wartime superiors who went free. Fear of U.S. reaction prevented the release of the film until 1956, but the portrayal of the U.S. military is not particularly unfavorable. The emphasis is rather on the overall effects of war, including footage of the Korean war, Japanese torturing an American POW in the Pacific War, and a Japanese woman who becomes a prostitute through her contact with U.S. Occupation forces. (FC; negative at Shochiku, Tokyo.)

1954 *Three Loves* (*Mittsu no Ai*)
pr: Shochiku (Ofuna); orig. sc: Kobayashi; ph: Seiji Inoue; cast: Isuzu Yamada, Ko Mishima, Yunosuke Ito et al. Three-part film full of sentimental humanism. A scholar and his wife worry about their son who loves only birds and butterflies; a young couple are too poor to get married; a man becomes a priest when his wife leaves him. (No circulating prints; negative at Shochiku, Tokyo.)

Somewhere under the Broad Sky (*Kono Hiroi Sora no Dokoka ni*)
pr: Shochiku (Ofuna); orig. sc: Yoshiko Kusuda; ph: Toshiyasu Morita; music: Chuji Kinoshita; cast: Keiji Sata, Yoshiko Kuga, Hideko Takamine, Akira Ishihama, Kumeko Urabe et al. Sentimental uplift for the underdog in a lower middle-class family drama. A handicapped girl in a small shop district of the growing industrial town of Kawasaki hopes to marry while receiving only unacceptable offers, individuals worry about loneliness without a big family, and a shop boy sees his own positive energy as related to the lovely smoke-belching chimneys of the surrounding factories. A strong Kinoshita flavor,

with the script by the director's sister and music by his brother. (PFA/SH; negative at Shochiku, Tokyo.)

1955   *Beautiful Days* (*Uruwashiki Saigetsu*)
pr: Shochiku (Ofuna); orig. sc: Zenzo Matsuyama; ph: Toshiyasu Morita; cast: Yoshiko Kuga, Isao Kimura et al. Indulgent story of friendship tinged with sorrow. A young girl whose brother was killed in the war lives with her grandmother, and the two run a florist shop. The events center around the love and friendship between the girl and three classmates of her dead older brother. (PFA/SH; negative at Shochiku, Tokyo.)

1956   *The Spring* (*Izumi*)
pr: Shochiku (Ofuna); orig. story: Kunio Kishida; sc: Zenzo Matsuyama; ph: Toshiyasu Morita; cast: Ineko Arima, Keiji Sata et al. Love story with sensitive treatment of the role of self-respect, set against a background of the conflict of city versus country. (Non-circulating print and negative at Shochiku, Tokyo.)

*I'll Buy You (*Anata Kaimasu*)
pr: Shochiku (Ofuna); orig. story: Minoru Ono; sc: Zenzo Matsuyama; ph: Yuharu Atsuta; music: Chuji Kinoshita; cast: Keiji Sata, Keiko Kishi, Minoru Oki, Yunosuke Ito, Mitsuko Mito et al. Social protestor Kobayashi's chilling exposé of corruption in the world of professional baseball. A ruthless scout sets out to recruit a top high-school star at any cost, with extensive interior monologue as he plans his attack. He seeks out all relatives and acquaintances when the boy himself turns down the bribe, wrecks the boy's relationship with his girlfriend, and perpetrates family quarrels that are finally resolved when the boy is bought. In the process, the boy's avaricious guardian dies. *KJ* #9. (FC, PFA/SH; negative at Shochiku, Tokyo.)

1957   **Black River* (*Kuroi Kawa*)
pr: Shochiku (Ofuna); orig. story: Takeo Tomishima; sc: Zenzo Matsuyama; ph: Yuharu Atsuta; cast: Fumio Watanabe, Ineko Arima, Tatsuya Nakadai et al. Exposé of corruption around U.S. military bases in Japan, casting blame on the Japanese social system for allowing prostitutes, gamblers and gangsters to prey on soldiers. Touches of melodrama in first starring role for Nakadai. (Non-circulating print and negative at Shochiku, Tokyo.)

1959   **The Human Condition, Part I: No Greater Love* (*Ningen no Joken I-II*)
pr: Kabukiza/Ninjin Club/Shochiku; orig. novel: Jumpei Gomikawa; sc: Zenzo Matsuyama and Kobayashi; 'scope ph: Yoshio Miyajima; music: Chuji Kinoshita; cast: Tatsuya Nakadai, Michiyo Aratama, Chikage Awashima, Ineko Arima, Keiji Sata et al. Pacifism and social criticism with genuine feeling set in wartime Manchuria. A young Japanese pacifist is drafted and sent to experience the miserable conditions of a mine in Japanese-controlled Manchuria. He tries to improve the lot of the native slave laborers, but is accused of conspiracy, is tortured and sent in to active duty. First adaptation of the epic six-volume novel. *KJ* #5; Venice Film Festival San Giorgio Prize. (FC, AB)

*The Human Condition, Part II: Road to Eternity (*Ningen no Joken III-IV*)
pr: Ningen Prod./Shochiku; orig. novel: Jumpei Gomikawa; sc: Zenzo

Matsuyama and Kobayashi; 'scope ph: Yoshio Miyajima; music: Chuji Kinoshita; cast: Tatsuya Nakadai, Michiyo Aratama, Keiji Sata, Kei Sato, Yusuke
Kawazu et al. The hero sees the brutal treatment of Japanese army recruits
and tries to make discipline more human when he is promoted, but he only
precipitates the hatred of other officers. In a decisive battle he is one of the
three survivors in his detachment. *KJ* #10. (FC, AB)

1961   *The Human Condition, Part III: A Soldier's Prayer (Ningen no Joken V-VI)*
pr: Shochiku/Ninjin Club; orig. novel: Jumpei Gomikawa; sc: Zenzo Mat-
suyama, Koichi Inagaki and Kobayashi; 'scope ph: Yoshio Miyajima; music:
Chuji Kinoshita; cast: Tatsuya Nakadai, Michiyo Aratama, Tamao Nakamura,
Yusuke Kawazu et al. The Japanese surrender and the hero is caught by
Soviet troops on his way home. He is imprisoned under miserable conditions
with many other Japanese who would never return home, escapes into the
Siberian snow and dies dreaming of rejoining his wife. *KJ* #4. (FC, AB)

1962   *The Entanglement/The Inheritance (Karamiai)*
pr: Bungei Prod./Ninjin Club/Shochiku; orig. novel: Norio Nanjo; sc:
Koichi Inagaki; 'scope ph: Ko Kawamata; cast: So Yamamura, Keiko Kishi,
Tatsuya Nakadai, Minoru Chiaki, Seiji Miyaguchi et al. The horrors of wealth
in the Japanese family system. A dying patriarch announces his desire to
leave much of his riches to his three illegitimate children, whose whereabouts
are unknown. A vicious search begins with imposters, blackmail, and even
murder coming into play. All the imposters are outwitted by a young secretary
who convinces the man he has made her pregnant even at death's door. The
man dies with everything willed to the baby, and the secretary has a "miscarriage," keeping all the money for herself. (SH)

    Harakiri (Seppuku)
pr: Shochiku (Kyoto); orig. novel: Yasuhiko Takiguchi; sc: Shinobu Hashimoto; 'scope ph: Yoshio Miyajima; music: Toru Takemitsu; cast: Tatsuya
Nakadai, Akira Ishihama, Shima Iwashita, Tetsuro Tamba, Rentaro Mikuni
et al. Kobayashi's first period film, an indictment of the emptiness of the samurai code in the face of poverty and established power. At the end of the feudal
era when many professional warriors are unemployed, a young man requests
permission to commit ritual suicide on the grounds of a wealthy household,
hoping to be given money or work instead. He is ruthlessly forced through the
suicide, and his father-in-law comes to avenge his death. The flashback
monologue builds to a breathtaking climax in which the father slays most
of the swordsmen who set upon him to cover the household's shame. *KJ*
#3; Cannes Film Festival Special Jury Prize, 1963. (FC, AB)

1964   *Kwaidan (Kaidan)*
pr: Ninjin Club/Toho; orig. stories: Yakumo Koizumi (Lafcadio Hearn); sc:
Yoko Mizuki; color 'scope ph: Yoshio Miyajima; music: Toru Takemitsu;
cast: Rentaro Mikuni, Michiyo Aratama, Tatsuya Nakadai, Keiko Kishi, Katsuo
Nakamura, Kanemon Nakamura, et al. Kobayashi's first color film; four bril-
liantly photographed ghost stories without any particular message. Perhaps
his most commercially successful film based on Lafcadio Hearn's interpretation of the traditional stories "Black Hair," "The Snow Princess," "Earless

Hoichi'' and ''In a Cup of Tea.'' *KJ* #2; Cannes Film Festival Special Jury Prize, 1965. (FC, TO, TW)

1967   **Rebellion/Samurai Rebellion (Joiuchi)*
pr: Mifune Prod/Toho; orig. story: Yasuhiko Takiguchi; sc: Shinobu Hashimoto; color 'scope ph: Kazuo Yamada; music: Toru Takemitsu; cast: Toshiro Mifune, Go Kato, Tatsuya Nakadai, Michiko Otsuka, Yoko Tsukasa et al. Another attack on the feudal code and its abuse of individuals. A vassal's son is ordered to marry his lord's concubine, who has been replaced while giving birth to his child. The young man accepts the cast-off woman, and the couple have been happily married for two years when the lord suddenly demands the woman's return, since her child has become his heir. The vassal family rebels at this outrage in a spectacular swordfight ending. *KJ* #1; Venice Film Festival Critics' Association Prize, 1967. (FC, TO)

1968   *The Youth of Japan/Hymn to a Tired Man (Nihon no Seishun)*
pr: Tokyo Eiga/Toho; orig. story: Shusaku Endo; sc: Sakae Hirosawa; color 'scope ph: Kozo Okazaki; music: Toru Takemitsu; cast: Makoto Fujita, Michiyo Aratama, Toshio Kurosawa, Wakako Sakai, Kei Sato et al. Anti-war social drama that also shows the dullness of contemporary life. Character contrast between a father whose youth was spent in wartime and his postwar son. The father's youth is recalled when he meets his army superior and his first love in the government patent office where he now works. Rather strident in showing the man's attempted desertion in wartime, the brutality of the punishment, and his resulting deafness. *KJ* #7. (FC, JS)

1971   *Inn of Evil (Inochi Bo ni Furo)*
pr: Haiyuza Eiga Hoso/Toho; orig. story: Shugoro Yamamoto; sc: Tomoe Ryu (Yasuko Miyazaki); color 'scope ph: Kozo Okazaki; music: Toru Takemitsu; cast: Kanemon Nakamura, Komaki Kurihara, Tatsuya Nakadai, Kei Yamamoto, Wakako Sakai et al. Period film about a gang of thieves who are won over by young love. A young member of a gang of smugglers finds out that his girl-friend has been sold into prostitution. Desperate for money, he enlists the help of his fellows. During a dangerous job, three of them are killed but one escapes with the money to redeem the girl. The police close in on their restaurant hideout in the end. *KJ* #5. (JS)

1975   **Kaseki (Kaseki)*
pr: Haiyuza Eiga Hoso/Yonki no Kai/Fuji Television; orig. story: Yasushi Inoue; sc: Shun Inagaki; color ph: Kozo Okazaki; music: Toru Takemitsu; cast: Shin Saburi, Hisashi Igawa, Keiko Kishi, Kei Yamamoto, Komaki Kurihara et al. New direction in a subtle human drama originally made for TV as a 13-part series. An elderly executive learns while on a European business trip that he is dying of cancer. He steels himself gradually while recalling his dead wife and pursuing a fascination with a Japanese woman married to a wealthy Frenchman. On his return to Japan, his family finds out about his condition, which he has kept secret, and doctors persuade him to have an operation. The operation succeeds, and he is left baffled about what to do about his reprieve. *KJ* #4. (NY)

③ THE NEW WAVE AND AFTER

Toward the end of the golden age of the 1950s the commercial viability of the Japanese film industry was coming into question, and an upheaval nearly equivalent to the French New Wave was in store. The situation was worst in the Shochiku Company because the female audience for the "Ofuna flavor" films was beginning to stay home and watch television. Although Masaki Kobayashi was also distributed by Shochiku, he was producing his trilogy *The Human Condition* independently, and the unequivocal critical success of his few, very meticulously made films of social commentary was not the bread-and-butter for the company that the Ofuna studio directors provided.

In his 1963 collection of articles *Sengo eiga: Hakai to sozo* (Postwar film: Destruction and Creation), Nagisa Oshima, a young Shochiku assistant director and film critic, labeled Keisuke Kinoshita's 1954 *Twenty-four Eyes* as the apogee of Ofuna flavor, but decried the fact that films exactly like it were still being made. Equally famous, more sentimental love melodramas were produced by other Ofuna directors at an even faster rate than Kinoshita's two or three a year. Commercial high points for the genre were the two-part 1953–54 *What Is Your Name?* (*Kimi no Na wa*) by Hideo Oba (1910–) and the trilogy plus overview 1962–64 *Tree of Promises* (*Aizen Katsura*) by Noboru Nakamura (1913–). By the time Yoshitaro Nomura (1919–) was remaking Kozaburo Yoshimura's 1938 *Warm Current* (*Danryu*) for the second time in 1966, "Ofuna flavor" had become a thoroughly pejorative term, and Kinoshita himself was on the verge of entering television.

Oshima stressed that the morality and the form of the Ofuna film had no relevance to the real life and thought of the new film audience to whom an appeal had to be made. This new audience was "the postwar generation, that bears no scars from the war, that has grown up amid the destruction of feudal Japanese morality, that believes in nothing but a world with itself as center, and that is because of this pure and active in effecting its personal goals." The company, having little financial choice, decided to gamble on letting the young upstarts show if they could pull in an audience. Oshima attacked the New Left, Masahiro Shinoda parodied it, and Yoshishige Yoshida offered the sex and mindless violence of university student life in *No Good* (*Rokudenashi*). It was 1960, and the height of the "Ofuna Nouvelle Vague." In another two years it would be over, but it would have done its job.

Attention focused on the younger directors everywhere, in a burst of vitality unknown since the days the movies themselves were young. Kihachi Okamoto (1924–) brought the young into the Toho company's theaters to see his superfast action gangsters and wartime mercenaries, most notably in the two-part *Free-Agent Hoodlums* (*Dokuritsu Gurentai*, 1959–60). Susumu Hani (1928–) introduced a new kind of dramatic reconstruction using non-professional actors and handheld cameras in his eye-opening 1960 *Bad Boys* (*Furyo Shonen*) about reformatory inmates. Shohei Imamura, who had left Shochiku to join the newly reestablished Nikkatsu company in 1954, appealed to the young with the confusion and earthiness of his early black comedies and social commentary, fully establishing himself with the 1961 *Pigs and Battleships*. But the new content of sex and violence would soon calcify into genre for the majors: Nikkatsu would lay claim to soft-core pornography and Toei would entrench itself in gangster films. The young men who had made and benefited most from the New Wave phenomenon would all go on to form their own independent production companies.

Oshima loudly formed his own company as early as 1961, but did not actually start producing until around the time both Shinoda and Imamura had followed suit in 1965–66. These three matured very quickly in their approach to filmmaking, and all came to center on the common problem of being Japanese today. Leaving behind the universal humanism of the earlier decade, they sought to make a different kind of film that was only for the Japanese. Oshima took a politico-sociological approach, Shinoda a historical and Imamura a cultural anthropological one, but all dealt with the problem with a new self-consciousness. Their cinematic form, like that of the French New Wave, was also influenced by a desire to overthrow the narrative and technical conventions established by the studio system.

With small but significant production and distribution assistance from such groups as the Art Theater Guild (ATG), which owned six theaters, some of the finest works of the 1960s were made. Oshima's *Death by Hanging* (1968) and Shinoda's *Double Suicide* (1969), for example, were ATG releases, while, Oshima says in discussing prospects for Japanese cinema of the 1980s (*Eiga Hyoron*, September 1973), Imamura's 1968 *Profound Desire of the Gods* marked the end of the majors' willingness to distribute this "different kind of film." Directors with great potential who remained within the studio system saw their talents submerged in formula films. Such is the case for Okamoto (except when he did his 1966 *Human Bullet [Nikudan]* and 1975 *Tokkan* [Tokkan] for ATG) and Shochiku's Yoji Yamada (1931—), whose chances for varied expression have been destroyed since the company found it could exploit his Tora-san "Lovable Tramp" (*Otoko wa Tsurai-yo*) format 20 times over since 1969.

In the 1970s both independent productions like ATG and the majors themselves are stumbling toward financial ruin. In 1973 Oshima, always at the forefront, dissolved his production company and announced that production conditions were back to zero—if the project was good, since the majors were losing money on their formulas, they might finance anything. But there has been little of such risk-taking on the part of the majors despite the failure of remake after remake. Television on the one hand and foreign films on the other conspire to keep the young away from the theaters specializing in Japanese films. Oshima himself has perhaps found a solution in making Japanese films that are released in Japan as foreign movies—his 1976 *Realm of the Senses* was shown in a foreign film house, with French subtitles and so badly whited out by the censors it seemed even more alien.

The young directors of the 1960s are no longer young, as Masaki Kobayashi has pointed out in an interview by Joan Mellen in *Voices from the Japanese Cinema* (1975). They have not yet been replaced by a new generation for the 1970s because the majors have failed to develop new talents—in the vicious circle of bad financial returns, they have failed to promote assistant directors at the same time as they have kept the established directors doing dull formula films. Although Shohei Imamura has founded a film school that provides training unavailable within the industry itself, it may be too late to save the major film studios. The concern of the moneymen who have usurped artistic control of the Japanese film is the sure, cheap thing. Untried talent is too uncertain for them, and big name directors like Kurosawa and Kobayashi are too expensive. All they can offer the mostly teenage audience is remakes with new stars' faces plugged in, which is why people like Keisuke Kinoshita complain that the word "young" today is virtually synonymous with "idiot." The rationale of the industry is merely to stay alive, regardless of how poor a product it may be turning out. The Japanese film, which in 1971 in *Japanese Cinema* Donald Richie called the last cinema in the world to retain its individual flavor—an individuality greatly enhanced by the 1960s directors' exploration of the Japanese consciousness—, stands at the brink of losing that individuality. Unless a second New Wave phenomenon, an overturn of existing structures and practices, takes place very soon, others will follow the direction Kurosawa, Oshima, and Kobayashi are beginning to set: as artists they will place filmmaking itself above the importance of Japan, and they will go elsewhere to create.

SHOHEI IMAMURA

● *Stolen Desire (Nusumareta Yokujo)*, 1958, Minako Kazuki

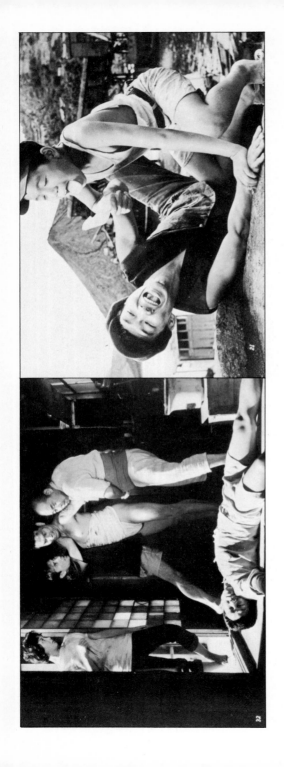

●*Endless Desire (Hateshi Naki Yokubo)*, 1958, Misako Watanabe, Ko Nishimura, Takeshi Kato, Taiji Tonoyama, and Shoichi Ozawa (clockwise from left)   ●*My Second Brother (Nianchan)*, 1959, Shoichi Ozawa

● *The Insect Woman (Nippon Konchuki)*, 1963, Sachiko Hidari

● *Pigs and Battleships (Buta to Gunkan)*, 1961, Hiroyuki Nagato

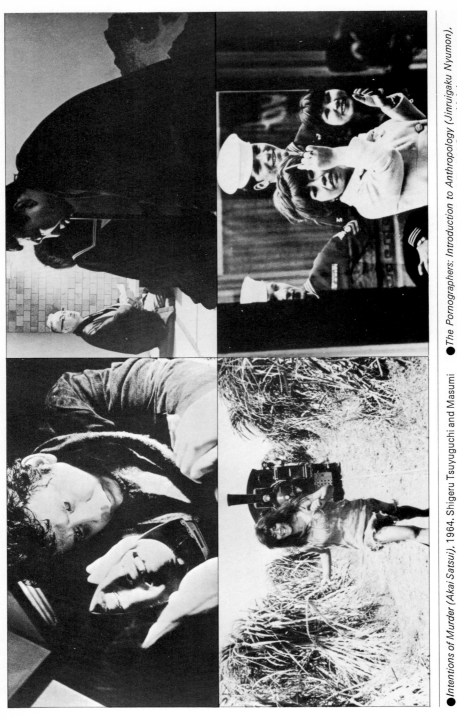

●Intentions of Murder (Akai Satsui), 1964. Shigeru Tsuyuguchi and Masumi Harukawa

●The Profound Desire of the Gods (Kamigami no Fukaki Yokubo), 1968,

●The Pornographers: Introduction to Anthropology (Jinruigaku Nyumon), 1966, Ganjiro Nakamura (left rear) and Shoichi Ozawa (right)

●History of Postwar Japan as Told by a Bar Hostess (Nippon Sengo Shi:

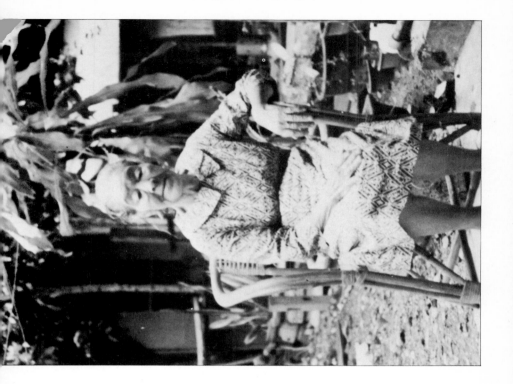

NAGISA OSHIMA

● *A Town of Love and Hope (Ai to Kibo no Machi)*, 1959, Fumio Watanabe (left) and Kakuko Chino

Cruel Story of Youth (Seishun Zankoku Monogatari), 1960, Yusuke Kawazu and Miyuki Kuwano

● *The Sun's Burial (Taiyo no Hakaba)*, 1960. Masahiko Tsugawa and Isao Sasaki   ● *Death by Hanging (Koshikei)*, 1968, Yun-do Yun

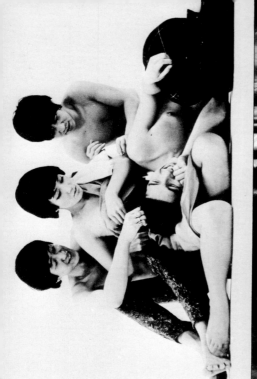

● *Three Resurrected Drunkards (Kaette Kita Yopparai),* 1968

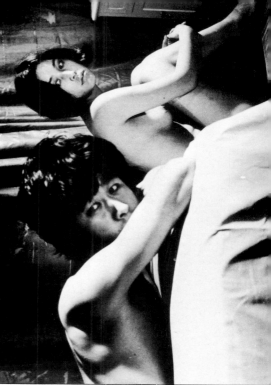

● *Diary of a Shinjuku Thief (Shinjuku Dorobo Nikki),* 1969, Tadanori Yokoo and Rie Yokoyama

● Boy (Shonen), 1969, Fumio Watanabe (right), Akiko Koyama (left) and
Tetsuo Abe (center)

● The Man Who Left His Will on Film (Tokyo Senso Sengo Hiwa), 1970,
Kazuo Goto

● *The Ceremony (Gishiki)*, 1971, Kei Sato (center)

● *The Realm of the Senses (Ai no Koriida)*, 1976, Tatsuya Fuji, Eiko Matsuda and Akiko Koyama

MASAHIRO SHINODA

● *Tears on the Lion's Mane (Namida o Shishi no Tategami ni)*, 1962, Kyoko Kishida and Takashi Fujiki

● *Pale Flower (Kawaita Hana)*, 1963, Takashi Fujiki

● *Assassination (Ansatsu)*, 1964, Tetsuro Tamba

● With Beauty and Sorrow (Utsukushisa to Kanashimi to), 1965, Kaoru Yachigusa (left) and Mariko Kaga

● Clouds at Sunset (Akanegumo), 1967, Shima Iwashita (left) and Kei Sato

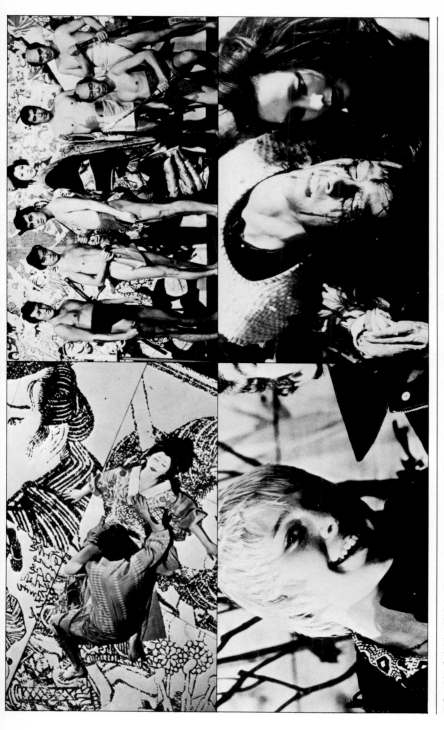

● *Double Suicide (Shinju Ten no Amijima)*, 1969, Shima Iwashita and Kichiemon Nakamura

● *Sapporo Winter Olympic Games (Sapporo Orimpikku)*, 1972, Janet Lynn (skater)

● *The Scandalous Adventures of Buraikan (Buraikan)*, 1970, Shima Iwashita (center)

● *Himiko (Himiko)*, 1974, Masao Kusakari and Rie Yokoyama

●*Under the Cherry Blossoms (Sakura no Mori no Mankai no Shita)*, 1975.
Shima Iwashita and Tomisaburo Wakayama

SHOHEI IMAMURA

1926—

*Nobody understands what is real and what
is fantasy. Imamura's crime for the Japanese
critics and pundits is that he mixes the
two indistinguishably.*

—Shuji Terayama

from an interview with Joan Mellen, *Voices from the Japanese Cinema*, 1975

By the time I left Shohei Imamura's office in the Yokohama Broadcast Film Institute (Yokohama Hoso Eiga Semmon Gakuin), the hurried urbanites on the street looked like actors in costume and the skyscrapers like big-budget movie sets. We had been talking about the shrines dedicated to the fox god Inari, which Imamura assured me adorned the top of every modern office building around Yokohama station. "You may think all that is real," said the slightly graying, no longer plump director of the Institute, gesturing toward the dreary cityscape outside, "but to me it's all illusion. The reality is those little shrines, the superstition and the irrationality that pervade the Japanese consciousness under the veneer of the business suits and advanced technology."[1]

His statement reinforces the themes and structures of his films, which pursue the sometimes humorous, sometimes awesome undercurrents of human motivations and reject traditional dramatic narrative. But more important for Imamura, his statement and his films reflect the reality of Japanese life. He elaborated with an example: "The man whose construction company built this school is a friend of mine. We are both busy but manage to get together occasionally. But he always has to check his calendar to make sure our appointment doesn't fall on a "great good fortune" (*tai-an*) day, because those are all booked solid with ground-breaking ceremonies."[2] Imamura marvels at the fact that ordinary pocket memos in Japan record these lucky days, and that no contemporary Japanese would dare build a house, much less a multistory building, without performing the Shinto religious dedication ceremony on a carefully selected lucky day. "The Japanese are not religious," he hastens to add, "these rituals, those fox shrines, are simply part of everyday life—much as I imagine Christianity is part of everyday occidental life. You don't feel right unless you observe these things."[3]

Like the other representatives of his generation, Nagisa Oshima and Masahiro Shinoda, Imamura searches for the essence of Japaneseness through his works. Like them, he too began his filmmaking career in the Shochiku company's Ofuna Studios and reacted against their craftsmen's orthodoxy and gentility epitomized by Yasujiro Ozu. But Imamura set off in a very different direction from his peers. He searches for essential Japaneseness not through direct politico-social or historical commentary, as he feels the Japanese "did not change as a result of the Pacific War—they haven't changed in thousands of years!"[4] He searches much more literally, doing a cultural anthropologist's footwork, covering Japan from the snowbound north where the extended family remains under the supervision of the patriarch, and then the oldest son (*The Insect Woman, Intentions of Murder*), to the southern islands around Okinawa, where sisters are sacred and shamanesses reveal the secrets of heaven (*The Profound Desire of the Gods*). Though Imamura himself is a Tokyoite and university graduate, he cannot resist the lure of the uneducated lower classes and the more primitive outlying regions. "Even when I was supposed to make a film situated in the center of modern Tokyo (*Nishi Ginza Station*), somehow I ended up on a deserted island."[5]

Imamura's discoveries have exposed the underside of Japan, the antithesis of the Zen-tinged aestheticism and quiet resignation of Ozu. He has said, "I want to make messy, really human, Japanese, unsettling films."[6] Accordingly, his works are peopled with greedy, lustful, deceitful, vicious, vulgar, humorous and often very touching characters. His ribald black humor and indomitable bovine heroines have repelled European audiences, who seem to cherish a Noh-play, tea-ceremony and Kenji Mizoguchi image of Japan, but have won him a loyal following among critics and the young in Japan. Always on the verge of documentary, even in his dramatic films, Imamura seeks to sound the depths of his characters and their cultural formation, bringing out the fine lines between illusion and reality, fiction and what he calls "nature."

Into and Against Ofuna

Imamura's first love was not movies, nor was he ever part of the primitive, earthy, resilient vitality of the lower and outer reaches of Japanese society portrayed in his films. Born and raised in Tokyo, he was the son of a physician and attended all the elite primary and secondary schools that should have set him on a course toward the University of Tokyo and a comfortable, sedate business or government career.

But two factors led him on a divergent path. One was an active interest in modern theater, instilled in him by his older brother when he was still in middle school, and the other can only be called an innate aversion for the presumptuousness of the upper class. In prewar thought-controlled Japan, Imamura said, he came to view the police as a power to be feared, while his classmates looked upon them as servants at their disposal.[7] From an early age then, his attitudes coincided with those of ordinary people rather than those of the privileged class into which he was born.

Imamura has jokingly referred to Nagisa Oshima as a samurai, while he considers himself to be a country farmer, but, in fact, when he finished high school his intention was to enter the agriculture faculty of the national university in Hokkaido.[8] He failed the examination, however, and rather than face the draft, entered a technical school in Tokyo. The day after the close of the Pacific War he quit this institution and began to prepare to enter Waseda University's literature faculty in occidental history.

During his six immediate postwar years at Waseda Imamura would begin a life of dire economic straits that would continue until well after he became a successful director. He was almost too busy to attend lectures as his schedule was filled not only with the resumption of his theatrical activities but also numerous part-time jobs. He wrote plays and appeared on stage with many of the core group of actors he would later work with in his films: Shoichi Ozawa, Kazuo Kitamura, Takeshi Kato and others.[9]

His Waseda friends all entered the modern theater world, but Imamura, after a brief Stint with a company that leased garbage boats in Tokyo Bay (one of which he turned into a "sociological field research boat," giving guided tours to school groups), joined Shochiku as an assistant director in 1951. Though he had never been particularly interested in movies, he said he chose film production over contemporary theater because it seemed "more professional."[10] But he was by no means to abandon theater in his film career.

Like Oshima and Shinoda, Imamura became assistant director at Shochiku's Ofuna Studios, and like Oshima, he reacted with revulsion to the Ofuna tradition. His response was perhaps more visceral than Oshima's political, international rebellion, however, because he found himself at the outset assisting Yasujiro Ozu on *Early Summer* (1951). Claiming no influence whatsoever from Ozu, Imamura went on to assist him on the 1952 *Flavor of Green Tea over Rice* and his masterpiece *Tokyo Story* (1953). "I wouldn't just say I wasn't influenced by Ozu," Imamura asserts, "I would say I didn't want to be influenced by him. The fact that his directing of actors, for example, was cast into too rigid a mold was repugnant to me."[11] But he worked for him in silence until he left Shochiku. He also worked with other directors, such as Masaki Kobayashi and Yuzo Kawashima (1918–63), but his closest friend and mentor became Yoshitaro Nomura, best known for his most recent films, such as *The Castle of Sand* (*Suna no Utsuwa*, 1974). "I remember talking over my departure from Shochiku in the bath with Nomura. There were 50 assistants ahead of me in line at Shochiku, and I was marrying the administrator who took care of all of us—she was the most visible woman in my life. Nomura urged me to go to Nikkatsu right away."[12]

Imamura did not dislike the comfortable, tepid atmosphere of Shochiku, but he felt it would in the long run be harmful to his artistic growth. "For the first three years assistant directors talk a lot of theory and aesthetics and feel resentful toward the older established directors who confine their pronouncements to things like 'nice shot.' But then the younger ones too grow up and stop talking."[13] The activity around the reestablishment of Nikkatsu, which had stopped production in 1941, was quite exciting. Directing talent was being recruited from Shochiku, administrators from Daiei, and still others from Shin Toho. Imamura went to Nikkatsu with high hopes, much energy and Ozu's blessings.

Nikkatsu Regionalism, Comedy and Theater

The new company proved to be challenging at least to Imamura's patience. He had hoped to work with Kon Ichikawa, who was rumored to be moving to Nikkatsu as well,[14] but this never transpired, and Imamura's first two assisting jobs were with movie stars becoming directors. So Yamamura's social drama *Black Tide* (*Kuroi Ushio*, 1954) was followed by Kinuyo Tanaka's poetic romance, *Moonrise* (*Tsuki wa Noborinu*, 1954). By this time, Imamura had had enough of stars trying to direct films, and begged for relief.[15] As a result, much to his chagrin, he was teamed up with Yuzo Kawashima, who had also come to Nikkatsu from Shochiku. Imamura disliked the idea of working with someone he already knew—later he would part ways with his photographer, Shinsaku Himeda, so that both of them could find stimulation from working with new people—but his association with Kawashima proved a fruitful one. The older director's off-beat, individualistic comedies are said to have been a strong influence on the rough, humorous quality of Imamura's films, which stand in marked opposition to the urban sophistication of Shochiku's Ofuna flavor.[16] Kawashima would be so important in Imamura's life that he even wrote a critical biography of him, *Sayonara dake ga jinsei-da* (*Life Is Only Goodby*, Tokyo: Nobel Shobo, 1969). The last film on which they worked together, and Imamura's last job as an assistant director, *Sun Legend of the Shogunate's Last Days* (*Bakumatsu Taiyo Den*, 1958) is considered one of Kawashima's very best.

When Imamura at last came to direct a film of his own, the material suggested to him by his producer was particularly well suited to his tastes. The story of the internal stresses in a troupe of traveling actors who perform Kabuki highlights, alternated with a strip chorus line, presents the full-blown boisterousness of Imamura's off-color humor. The women in the audiences shriek and sigh over the simpering poses of the Kabuki actors, while the men hoot and ogle at the strip show.

Off-stage, the older men in the troupe seek out women from among their local fans, a love triangle nearly destroys the cohesiveness of the family-run company, and a farm girl leaves home to become a stripper in the chorus line. Imamura's only complaint, similar to Oshima's about his debut film, was that the company changed the title—the straightforward "Tent Theater" would become the pandering *Stolen Desire*.[17]

Because Imamura expresses such vehement antagonism to Ozu's style, one cannot help but compare the story of *Stolen Desire* with

Ozu's 1934 *Story of Floating Weeds* and the color and sound remake he would produce the year after Imamura's film, *Floating Weeds*. It is as if Imamura set out to put in everything Ozu leaves out of his story of a traveling Kabuki troupe and its relationships with the population of a provincial town. Imamura's emotional confrontations are impulsive, open, verbal, and often physically violent, while Ozu's are all meticulously subtle. The locals, in a relationship Imamura would return to time and again, are far from resigning themselves to exploitation by the city people passing through. They enjoy a robust relationship of mutual commerical and sexual exploitation with them. Where Ozu treats life in its indirectness, refinement, and acceptance of things as they are, Imamura seizes on bold forthrightness, earthiness and a positive, primal life energy. Even with a troupe split up by romance and plagued by debts, the troupe's enthusiasm revives, and they leave town amid a roar of cheers, which covers two of the actors' last attempt to steal a goose.

If influences are to be sought for Imamura's developing style, they may be found in entirely unexpected quarters. While his stated antipathy for Ozu's methods is only reconfirmed by seeing his work, a not-so-odd affinity emerges with the style of another less senior director, Akira Kurosawa. Like the touch of the master editor of the postwar era, Imamura's cutting is fast, and his camera movement follows close into the often breakneck, rough and tumble action of his films. Like Kurosawa, he varies angles constantly, though he tends to favor an objectifying overhead Kurosawa avoids, and his fluid framing makes expressive use of depth of field. But perhaps more Kurosawan than any other aspect of Imamura's style is his use of music, especially in his early films like *Stolen Desire*. The judicious, unsentimental, most often comic use of western instruments recalls Fumio Hayasaka's score for Kurosawa's masterpiece, the 1954 *Seven Samurai*. These echoes are all the more understandable in view of the fact that Toshiro Mayuzumi, the avant-garde composer who has worked with Imamura since his first film, was a disciple of Hayasaka. While both Ozu and Mizoguchi employed Mayuzumi to modernize their later films—the former in his 1959 *Ohayo* and 1961 *The End of Summer* and the latter in his 1954 *The Woman of the Rumor* and 1956 *Street of Shame*—their traditional stories and film styles would have been better served by Mayuzumi's Hayasaka-like abilities than his twanging electronic tendencies. It has only been with Imamura that Mayuzumi has progressed smoothly from Hayasaka comic instrumentation to appropriately eerie avant-gardism, in keeping with the director's own stylistic development.

Stolen Desire, aside from treating a theatrical milieu with which Imamura had some personal experience and showing his action-comedy abilities, reveals two tendencies that would grow in his subsequent

292   *Shohei Imamura*

works. His predilection for regional flavor and dialect begins with the cheap entertainment districts of Osaka's rough Kawachi area in *Stolen Desire* and immediately, intuitively, sets out for a provincial farming village. *Nishi Ginza Station*, his next command film, begins in central Tokyo as ordered, but moves to a tropic island. His third film, *Endless Desire*, begins at a provincial train station, and while the characters split up and return to Osaka to gather capital for the pursuit of their nefarious excavations, their activities center in the sleepy town of Himeji, where they excercise their instinctive greed, jealousy, laziness and lust in colorful and vulgar Osaka dialect. By the following year, 1959, with *My Second Brother*, the whole film, except Nianchan's foray to Tokyo to look for work, is shot in the grim, squalid location and thick dialect of a southern Kyushu coal-mining town. However, this film, a company assignment based on the diary of a little girl, shows much less of Imamura's other strong tendency, that of revealing the intuitive cunning and determined self-interest of Japanese women.

Women Will Out

When confronted with the idea that his film heroines represent an "eccentric image of the modern Japanese woman,"[18] Imamura has an immediate retort. "My heroines are true to life—just look around you at Japanese women. They *are* strong, and they outlive men. Self-sacrificing women like the heroines of Naruse's *Floating Clouds* [1955] and Mizoguchi's *Life of Oharu* [1952] don't really exist."[19] The creative eccentricity that can be ascribed to Imamura lies in the realm of cinematic genre, for he rejects both the slow pace and the long-suffering image of the "woman's film." His women not only hold their own, they increase it, and they fight dirty with no pangs of conscience.

These authentic Japanese women inhabit Imamura's films from the outset. In *Stolen Desire* the younger sister, who has made up her mind that she wants the young idealist director working with the troupe, pesters him, seduces him, and forces him to choose between her and her older sister-in-law. In the end he is out of the troupe and stuck with her, since the married woman preferred to stay with her husband. She mocks at his depression and yanks him along by the hand to get to where she wants to go. In *Endless Desire* the central female character dupes all her male accomplices through seduction, playing off jealousies, and finally even murder, while a young local girl wreaks havoc among suitors by stating flatly that she will go where the most money is in marriage.

These early hard caricatures give way in the 1961 *Pigs and Battleships* to a warmer, less rational, but equally forceful girl in Haruko (Jitsuko Yoshimura), who is determined to escape from what appears to be her sordid fate as a prostitute near the U.S. naval base at Yokosuka. In her character Imamura embarks on his devoted research of the relationship between two problems: "the lower part of the human body and the lower part of the social structure, on which the reality of daily Japanese life obstinately supports itself."[20] Haruko tries to persuade her boyfriend to give up working for the gangsters who, along with the prostitutes, have assembled to welcome and prey upon the American visitors. Her older sister makes her living off the foreigners, but Haruko resists. When her feckless boyfriend (Hiroyuki Nagato plays the naively ambitious boy role in all these early films) tells her to do the same, in her anger she gets drunk and is raped. But she does not submit to violence without retaliation: she steals the three drunk Americans' money. Her boyfriend dies, tricked by his employers and caught in a gang war, and through her tears Haruko screams insults after his departing corpse. Left with no alternative in Yokosuka but to join her sister in prostitution, Haruko suddenly bolts, in all her makeup and bouffant, high-heeled finery, to go work in the factory town of Kawasaki. This vitality and instinct for self-preservation in the face of tragic adversity would be the mark of all Imamura's later heroines.

During the two-year interval between *Pigs and Battleships* and his next film, Imamura was not resting. He struggled with his production company, which refused to let him make *Intentions of Murder* once they had read the finished script and realized it was not a thriller.[21] He wrote scenarios for other directors, including that for his friend and colleague Kirio Urayama's first film, *The Street with the Cupola* (*Kyupora no Aru Machi*, 1962). He directed a play called *Paraji* at the request of his friend actor Shoichi Ozawa, and he traveled to Amami Oshima Island on a "scenario hunting" expedition with his new coscenarist, Keiji Hasebe. He lived in abject poverty, but at last he persuaded Nikkatsu to let him make *The Insect Woman*, which would present the fully developed Imamura heroine, a woman whose responses to life's challenges resemble the instinctive grubbing and flight of an insect.

"I wanted to work away from the pattern of suffering and pathos of the usual 'woman's film' life story," Imamura explains, "so I used freeze frames and humor to make the spectator laugh at her and therefore stand in a critical position."[22] Indeed the tragicomedy in the life of Tome (Sachiko Hidari) distances the viewer, yet as the flow of her life takes her from deceived country innocence to labor union activities to a possibly incestuous relationship with the man who is her legal father, to maid's work, prostitution, a new mystical religion and call-girl management in Tokyo, the internal logic of her character justifies her vicissitudes and never fails to fascinate. Her path to materialism, deceit and self-pity is set by what she experiences as a young woman in the country. As she writes in the bad poem that begins her diary, "I work for my country and household, but now I write my diary all alone." Both her country and her family take advantage of her trust—Japan loses the war and her family sends her into maid/mistress service to cover their debts. Not surprising, then, that Tome decides to live for herself, and with no compunctions about abusing others to get what she wants.

When he was at last given permission to make *Intentions of Murder* the following year, Imamura again pursued the antithesis of the standard female film image in Sadako, who slowly and dumbly takes to deceit to resist the abuses of the northern Japanese family system in which women have power only through their sons. "Masumi Harukawa (who had played the unsavory, slovenly mistress of an American soldier in *The Insect Woman*)," crowed Imamura, "was perfect. She was everything Ofuna would never allow an actress to be."[23] The image of the heroine he sought for *Intentions of Murder* fits all of the women of his mature works: "Medium height and weight, light coloring, smooth skin. The face of a woman who loves men. Maternal. A lukewarm feeling. Good genitals. Juicy."[24] Neither conventional beauty nor a model's slenderness is part of the ideal.

Sadako is overwhelmingly ordinary. Barely competent as a housewife—when seeing her husband off on a business trip she brings an undershirt instead of the dress shirt he asked for—she spends a great deal of her time watching television, much to her stingy husband's annoyance. Her reaction to being raped is that she must commit suicide, but before she can face taking her life she devours a huge meal.

Her suicide is also prevented by the desire to see her beloved six-year-old son one last time. This deformed child represents another of Imamura's recurrent themes, already broached in *The Insect Woman* and further developed in *The Profound Desire of the Gods*. Although Sadako herself does not know it, she is the granddaughter of her husband's family patriarch's mistress. She and her husband are thus of the same blood, and their child the product of an inadvertent incestuous union, very much part of Japanese culture in Imamura's view.

Raised as a maid in her husband's household, Sadako's main concern is to attain the security of having her son entered in the family register as her husband's child rather than as his grandparents', a procedure which has not taken place because of her lowly status and her husband's powerlessness as a second son. It is the threat to her potential security that makes her decide to murder the rapist who falls in love with her, gets her pregnant and begs her to run away with him. Her slow, stolid intuition emerges victorious at the end. Their escape train to Tokyo is caught in snowdrifts, and her lover dies of a heart attack when Sadako cannot bring herself to let him drink the poisoned tea she has prepared. She simply denies that she is the woman in the photographs taken by her husband's jealous mistress, who is hit by a car and killed while snapping Sadako collapsing from the pain of a miscarriage. Sadako goes to family court to have her son's registration changed, and pretending she "didn't know it would cause such trouble," attains a legal wife and mother's rights. The last scene shows her tending her own silkworms, dreamily enticing one along her skin with a mulberry leaf just as she did as a lascivious adolescent. Sadako has had her cake and eaten it too, and the dangers of the whole affair have stimulated her to act toward the ensuring of her security.

Imamura's 1966 film based on Akiyuki Nosaka's prize-winning novel *The Pornographers*, his first with his own independent production company, bears the title *Introduction to Anthropology*, and it duly encapsulates many of the threads that the filmmaker finds to be immutable in Japanese civilization. Again set in the sleazier parts of Osaka and played in rich dialect, the story follows an 8 mm. pornographic filmmaker's search for meaning in life. The widow whom Subuyan (Shoichi Ozawa, for whom Imamura wrote the script) loves refuses to marry him out of what appears to be blind loyalty because her husband asked her on his deathbed to keep his name. But superstition plays a strong role in her loyalty: every time she does something bad, the carp born when her husband died splashes in its tank, and one day an itinerant priest tells her that her husband's soul cannot rest because of her. She has a slight heart attack at the news, but while the carp splashes she seeks comfort in sex with Subuyan.

He in turn, much as he loves the widow, is drawn to her teenage daughter, who allows him to buy kisses from her. The incest theme comes into the open when the widow, who has also allowed her 19-year-old son to fondle her in bed, realizes she will soon die and asks Subuyan to marry her daughter and take over the running of the beauty shop with her. Incest appears even in a movie within the movie sequence when the pornographers are filming a rape scene. The uncooperative actress turns out to be the middle-aged "rapist's" own retarded daughter, genuinely frightened because she doesn't recognize the man she usually makes love with.

Subuyan is rejected by his mistress' daughter, however, and having concluded that life is only beautiful as long as it remains erotic, he sets about building himself a model in the image of the dead widow to cure his impotence. Explaining why he has come to hate real women, he gives the cold-hearted daughter as an example: "They blame other people for everything, but they're actually greedy, lying lechers." In this statement Subuyan shows the reverse of what Imamura, who admitted to recognizing his own lecherous tendencies in the course of making this film,[25] appreciates in the Japanese woman. She is motivated equally strongly and without any internal feelings of contradiction by a deep concern for the legal forms of lineage that protect her rights and self-esteem through property and children, by a proto-religious superstition that a super-human order controls at least part of her life, and by her untrammeled appetites. The interplay of these motivations makes her humorous, awesome and attractive to Imamura, and his goal has been "to portray the unsounded depths of woman by peering at her in unguarded moments like a voyeur."[26]

Toward Documentary

In *The Pornographers* Imamura sought this profound reality by using hidden camera techniques, making the spectator feel as much a voyeur as the pornographer hero or the director himself. But already much earlier he had begun to reject traditional dramatic film methods in order to achieve a greater realism. For *The Insect Woman* he used a real-life model, a 40-year-old former prostitute, and the shooting was all done on location with sync-sound using wireless microphones. Imamura wanted to "do away with the accepted convenience of sets and post-synchronized sound" (in most Japanese films any location sound is still post-synchronized) as well as try something different from the dramatic narrative perfection of a "well-made scenario" like *Intentions of Murder*.[27] The urge for such authenticity, says Imamura, came not from the influence of the French New Wave, but again was a reaction against his Ofuna and Ozu training.[28]

The film that epitomizes his search for real-life drama is the 1967 *A Man Vanishes*, but at the same time it points out the necessary fiction imposed by the filmic medium. From police missing persons files, Imamura selected the man who seemed the most ordinary and met Yoshie, the strong-willed fiancée who was looking for him. Unable to find an amateur who could spare the time, he selected Shigeru Tsuyu-guchi, who had played the rapist in *Intentions of Murder*, to be the interviewer-investigator who accompanies her. Hidden, hand-held cameras and wireless microphones following the actual search reveal a startling transformation: within the first twelve minutes of the film Yoshie has lost all sincere interest in finding her fiancé, though a medium tells her that her older sister knows the answer, and by the middle of the film she is declaring her love for the dumbfounded actor. The ending is a purposely inconclusive freeze frame when Imamura himself steps in to destroy the "set" where the two sisters are confronting each other, neither ready to give an inch. In defending the "manipulation" and "invasion of privacy" of which he was accused, Imamura refuses to take all responsibility, saying that Yoshie used him as much as he used her plight to make a film. "Now I think maybe the title should have been 'When a Woman Becomes an Actress' . . . anyway I like the fact that everyone showed his worst in the film—Yoshie became an actress, and Tsuyuguchi became an amateur."[29] Imamura had had a feeling that fiction would emerge from fact, and it did so in the form of Yoshie's love scene, the spontaneous result of her consciousness of becoming a film personality.

The same sort of unexpected emotional twist would occur during the filming of the 1970 *History of Postwar Japan As Told by a Bar Hostess* when Imamura himself was the off-screen interviewer. Again Imamura sought documentary authenticity in the spontaneous reactions of a lower-class Japanese woman, "Madame Omboro", to newsreel footage of the major postwar events coinciding with developments in her own life. They do not touch her, however. "No one cried over such a stupid thing," she says about the emperor's radio address ending the Pacific War; "There they go again," she says about student riots; "I only believe what I've seen with my own eyes," she says about Vietnam War massacre photos. Meaning in her world comes through the new Soka Gakkai religion and getting all she can out of the Americans she sees as too gentlemanly to have committed the atrocities portrayed. Married to an American young enough to be her son, she announces her intentions: "No matter what happens, I'm going to stick to him until I get U.S. citizenship. When everything is mine, I'll leave him flat." Her own observations and those of the people involved in her postwar life gradually reveal Madame Omboro to be another of Imamura's strong-willed, deceitful and self-deceiving, highly sensual women. As in *A Man Vanishes*, the characterization emerges without a dramatic framework from the spontaneous actions of the woman herself. Imamura's documentary technique produces the record of individual personalities as much as the record of historic events.

The Profound Desire of the Gods

Imamura's 1968 film, also known as *Kuragejima: Tales from a Southern Island,* arose from the impulse to document the confrontation between a waning primitive culture and the goals and mores of modern civilization, and it remains his most visually striking film. Filmed in color and 'scope entirely in the southern Ryukyu Islands, this 2-hour-55-minute film has been called "an at times uneasy but always fascinating combination of documentary, epic, melodrama, and philosophical dissertation."[30] Playing once more with illusion and reality, Imamura goes back to the myths of the founding of human society in the Ryukyus—one of the likely sources of the Japanese people—and shows how the primitive beliefs survive, even beneath the veneer of modernization.

The original source for the film was in fact the 1962 play *Paraji,* which presented superstition as part of the satisfaction of a need to feel at home in modern, compartmentalized, industrialized society. The installation of shrines in mammoth apartment complexes around Osaka at that time[31] corresponds to the appeasement of that ineffable discomfort a builder would feel if he did not carry out the Shinto ground-breaking ceremony on a lucky day. Modern civilization may hide these inalienable beliefs, but the blindness of the Tokyo engineer to the dancing figure of Toriko, the shamaness on the train tracks at the end of *The Profound Desire of the Gods,* is merely a temporary lapse. The reality of Japanese myth, superstition and closeness to nature will always find expression eventually, for this is the feeling of being at home.

The society of the Ryukyus offers much that coincides with Imamura's own tastes. Unlike the northern patriarchal system seen as oppressing women in *The Insect Woman* and *Intentions of Murder,* the southern tradition venerates women who, in ages past and in the primitive vestigial "Kuragejima" society Imamura portrays, perform the role of spritual leaders of the community as shamanesses (*noro*) through direct, trance-induced communication with the gods. The sibling incest theme, celebrated in the film's opening song about the founding of Ryukyu society ("brother and sister become man and wife; together they begin an island") and one of the dramatic motifs of the action, is expressed in terms of worship of the mystical power of sisters. "When the men go out fishing, for example," says Imamura, "they take a lock of their sister's hair as a talisman to ward off evil. And the dead, like Toriko and Uma at the end of the film, remain with the living, expressing their opinions when asked at the grave site. It takes maybe three or four years before the spirit withdraws so far into the realm of the gods that you can't converse with it any more. We live with the dead."[32] The red sail of Uma's boat is still seen occasionally by fishermen at sea, and Toriko dances on despite Coca-cola, jet planes and steam locomotives.

In the film, the myths are interwoven with the actuality of modern civilization's encroachment on the island. Nekichi (Rentaro Mikuni), like Terauchi in Oshima's 1971 *The Ceremony,* is the son of his own grandfather, and is in love with his own sister, Uma (Yasuko Matsui), the local shamaness. He has been a soldier and has learned to use dynamite and guns. His employment of these devices incurs the wrath of the community, who fear the vengeance of the gods, for they believe that all must be returned to nature. Twenty years earlier in Nekichi's field a huge phallic stone stood up. The reason for the anger the gods so expressed was deemed to be Nekichi himself who had just returned from the war and had a strange relationship with his sister. His punishment was to dig a hole into which the boulder could fall. This he has been doing for 20 years. His sister is imprisoned at the spring and his son ostracized. Though incest is part of the myth and the reality of Kuragejima life, it is nevertheless taboo, and placation of the gods, return to harmony with nature is in order. This nature constantly makes itself felt through cut-away closeups of snakes, ants, owls, a pig falling into the clutches of a shark at sea, and thunderous cicada song on the soundtrack.

Into this scene comes the Tokyo engineer (Kazuo Kitamura) to survey how irrigation of sugar cane fields can be effected. He is duly received as a god from over the sea—Imamura points out the similarity in the Japanese women's welcome of the American ships at the end of *Pigs and Battleships*[33]—to be placated and incorporated. With Nekichi's son Kametaro (Choichiro Kawarazaki) as his guide, he learns the local people will work for nothing, but the sacred spring may not be used. The engineer is given a local girl, Kametaro's crazy sister Toriko (Hideko Okiyama), whom he finally accepts. Gradually he forgets time and responsibility, participating in the island life and festivals, but he is recalled to Tokyo.

Nekichi succeeds at last in felling the stone, though Ryugen (Yoshi Kato), the old man who ordered Nekichi and Uma's punishment and separation, commands him to stop when the end is in sight. Ryugen dies making love to Uma, and Nekichi, vindicated, decides to go to a new island with his sister and begin a new life, like the gods of old. Angry islanders, including Kametaro, believing Nekichi murdered Ryugen, pursue them wearing ferocious masks. In a horrifying but beautiful chase, the uncomprehending Nekichi is beaten and dragged from his boat as the sharks wait. Uma, who has betrayed her status as shamaness, is tied to the mast and set adrift. The avengers mask themselves again and pick up their paddles in the stillness of sunset.

Five years later all in the family are dead, except Kametaro, who realizes his dream of escape and goes to Tokyo. Rumor has it that Toriko, who replaced Uma as shamaness, has become a rock and still waits for the return of the engineer. Kametaro returns from Tokyo, a "scattered place where you are not yourself," and drives the new steam engine. The engineer and his family come to the island, where the old man who sings the song of the myth of the founding now accepts ten yen coins for his tunes. Kametaro slams on the brakes to keep from hitting Toriko, dancing happily on the train tracks, but no one else can see her.

"Primitive culture is very weak in the face of modern civilization,"[34] says Imamura, and his film, with the apparent triumph of industrial society over the dreamy way of life of the natives of Kuragejima, shows the inferiority the primitive experiences in confronting technology. Kametaro, the transitional character who leaves the island, personifies this inferiority complex. On the other hand, escape is also the dream of Nekichi and Uma, who are subjected to the sanctions of the primitive culture itself. "There is good and bad on both sides," says Imamura, "but," and as in Shinoda's views, echoes of Waseda University studies in classic Japanese theater are audible here, "I happen to be more interested in the Japan that flourished before the artistic decadence fostered by political isolation in the feudal period."[35] The energy, in other words, lies in the primitive forms, and so it is that Imamura seeks out the places and people least molded into a rigid modernity—the southern islanders and the female escapees from the frozen north. His deepest character studies are the lower-class provincial women who embody the intuition, superstition and surviving primitivism of original Japaneseness. In figures like Haruko, Tome, Sadako, the widow and her sullen daughter in *The Pornographers*, Uma and Toriko, Madame Omboro, and even Yoshie and her sister in *A Man Vanishes*, Imamura does not preach; he celebrates, peers through chinks in walls, and laughs indulgently. He can sympathize also with those who would escape from the overwhelming lusty grasp of these marvelous primitives—epitomized by the man who vanished and finally even Subuyan the pornographer—but from his own point of view the attraction outweighs the fear. The engineer returns with his family, but he does return; Kametaro, while working for the technological society that is changing the island, returns because he cannot bear its culmination, the atomization of Tokyo. The need for a feeling of cultural-emotional unity must be fulfilled, and Imamura is confident that the unifying bonds always reemerge—shrines on top of office buildings, perhaps? "No, I am not a pessimist," he smiles, "and the Japanese are very stubborn."[36]

The Legacy of Japan

Since the completion of *History of Postwar Japan As Told by a Bar Hostess* in 1970, Imamura has shifted his areas of activity but not his major concerns. Not only has he founded the Yokohama Broadcast Film Institute (1975), he has carried his anthropological research yet farther afield, to Southeast Asia. Beginning in 1971 he traveled to Malaysia and Thailand searching for Japanese soldiers who did not come home after the Pacific War. His goal is to find out why, and the answers he gets from these men in his television documentaries reflect strong criticisms of Japanese society. Notable is the verdict of an expatriate doctor: "Avarice has led the Japanese astray." Another colorful character, Private Fujita, who does come home for a visit accompanied by Imamura's camera and microphones, encounters unhappy squabbles with his relatives. "The Japanese have had their heads turned by money and become utter fools," he laments. Still others, the women who were sent abroad as prostitutes before and during the war, become the subject of a documentary now released as a feature, *Karayuki-san*. The 74-year-old woman who helps Imamura search for those who shared her experience in Southeast Asia is perhaps the most moving of all in her modest dismissal of all the suffering she underwent: "It was such a long time ago," she says.

In 1977, dividing his time between lecturing and administration at his very successful school and his own filmmaking activities, Imamura is returning to features. The subject matter is of course documentary, from police records of a murder case written up as a book by Kyuzo Saki, *Fukushu suru wa ware ni ari* (Revenge Is for Us). And again Imamura seeks to overthrow established dramatic forms in treating his material. "What fascinates me is the fact that the murder takes place completely by chance, and it occurs at the end. The problem for me is involving the spectator in these marvelous characters up until that surprising moment."[37] Building on a theme of attitudes toward death, the finished work promises to be yet another anthropological study in Imamura's continuing probe into the nature of the Japanese.

Notes

1 Author's interview with Shohei Imamura, April 1977.
2 *Ibid.*
3 *Ibid.*
4 *Ibid.*
5 Rikiya Tayama, *Nihon no eiga sakkatachi: Sosaku no himitsu* (Japanese Filmmakers: Secrets of Creation) (Tokyo: Daviddosha, 1975), p. 15.
6 Quoted in Heiichi Sugiyama, "Imamura Shohei ron" (On Shohei Imamura), *Sekai no eiga sakka 8: Imamura Shohei* (Film Directors of the World 8: Shohei Imamura) (Tokyo: Kinema Jumposha, 1975), p. 30.
7 Tayama, *op. cit.*, p. 8.
8 *Ibid.*, p. 9.
9 *Ibid.*, p. 10.
10 *Ibid.*, p. 11.
11 *Ibid.*, p. 12.
12 Interview, *cit.*
13 *Ibid.*
14 *Ibid.*
15 Tayama, *op. cit.*, p. 13.
16 Sugiyama, *op. cit.*, p. 25.
17 "Imamura Shohei zen jisaku o kataru" (Shohei Imamura Talks about All His Films), *Sekai no eiga sakka 8, op. cit.*, p. 64.
18 Joan Mellen, *The Waves at Genji's Door: Japan through Its Cinema* (New York: Pantheon, 1976), p. 301.
19 Imamura interview, *cit.*
20 Quoted in Koichi Yamada, "Les Cochons et les dieux: Imamura Shohei" (Pigs and Gods: Shohei Imamura), *Cahiers du cinéma*, No. 166, Mai-Juin 1965, p. 31.
21 "Imamura Shohei zen jisaku o kataru," *op. cit.*, p. 66.
22 Imamura interview, *cit.*
23 "Imamura Shohei zen jisaku o kataru," *op. cit.*, p. 73.
24 *Imamura Shohei no eiga* (The Films of Shohei Imamura) (Tokyo: Haga Shoten, 1971), p. 101.
25 "Imamura Shohei zen jisaku o kataru," *op. cit.*, p. 75.
26 *Imamura Shohei no eiga, op. cit.*, p. 97.
27 "Imamura Shohei zen jisaku o kataru," *op. cit.*, pp. 68–69.
28 Imamura interview, *cit.*
29 "Imamura Shohei zen jisaku o kataru," *op. cit.*, p. 82.
30 Donald Richie, *Japanese Cinema* (New York: Doubleday Anchor, 1971), p. 166.
31 *Imamura Shohei no eiga, op. cit.*, p. 159.
32 Imamura interview, *cit.*
33 "Imamura Shohei zen jisaku o kataru," *op. cit.*, p. 72.
34 Imamura interview, *cit.*
35 *Ibid.*
36 *Ibid.*
37 *Ibid.*

SHOHEI IMAMURA: FILMOGRAPHY

1958 *Stolen Desire (Nusumareta Yokujo)*

pr: Nikkatsu; orig. story: Toko Kon; sc: Toshiro Suzuki; 'scope ph: Kurataro Takamura; music: Toshiro Mayuzumi; cast: Osamu Takizawa, Hiroyuki Nagato, Yoko Minamida, Michie Kita, Shinichi Yanagisawa et al. Ribald comedy about the confused, complex life of a family troupe of traveling actors from the sleazy, rough Kawachi area of Osaka. The young director, who quit university for love of the theater, is secretly in love with the son's wife, but is pursued by the unmarried younger daughter. In the course of their successful, then violent appearance in a small village, these relationships come into the open. In their noisy departure from the village the daughter-in-law has decided she cannot leave her husband, who goes so far as to offer to quit the troupe, and the director is stuck with the younger sister. The original title was 'Tent Theater,'' but the company changed it, much to Imamura's embarrassment. (FC; negative at Nikkatsu, Tokyo.)

Nishi Ginza Station (Nishi Ginza Eki-mae)

pr: Nikkatsu; orig. idea and sc: Imamura; 'scope ph: Hisanobu Fujioka; music: Toshiro Mayuzumi; cast: Frank Nagai, Shinichi Yanagisawa, Ko Nishimura, Shoichi Ozawa, Kyoko Hori et al. Completely nonsensical comedy Imamura was forced to make to promote singer Frank Nagai. He pleaded tone deafness, but was told he could make whatever he wanted as long as the title song came at the beginning, middle and end. The story centers on a man who periodically lapses into reliving his happy wartime love affair with a native girl on a tropic island. The company said Imamura tricked them. (FC; negative at Nikkatsu, Tokyo.)

Endless Desire (Hateshi Naki Yokubo)

pr: Nikkatsu; orig. story: Shinji Fujiwara; sc: Toshiro Suzuki and Imamura; 'scope ph: Shinsaku Himeda; music: Toshiro Mayuzumi; cast: Hiroyuki Nagato, Sanae Nakahara, Ko Nishimura, Taiji Tonoyama, Misako Watanabe et al. Rough black comedy showing the first of Imamura's ruthlessly determined women. A motley collection of five people meet at a railroad station to find and dig up a cache of morphine buried in an airraid shelter during the war. The widow of the man who buried it, an owner of a Chinese restaurant, a gangster, a pharmacist, and a junior high school teacher form the group who find a butcher shop built on the site of the airraid shelter. They set about renting a building from which to dig a tunnel and collecting funds to finance the work. The interpersonal relationships become hilariously confused as the hired son of the building owner falls in love with the butcher shop owner's daughter but is seduced by the widow, who ends up by poisoning the men who remain at the end, including her lover the pharmacist, and escaping with the morphine. But she falls off a bridge under construction, and the next morning the river is full of dead fish floating belly up in the autumn sun. (FC; negative at Nikkatsu, Tokyo.)

1959   *My Second Brother (Nianchan)*
pr: Nikkatsu; orig. story: Sueko Yasumoto; sc: Ichiro Ikeda and Imamura;
'scope ph: Shinsaku Himeda; music: Toshiro Mayuzumi; cast: Hiroyuki
Nagato, Kayo Matsuo, Takeshi Okimura, Akiko Maeda, Tanie Kitabayashi et
al. This company assignment, based on the diary of a ten-year-old girl of
Korean descent, is an atypically pure and simple story for Imamura, who
said the factual basis made it difficult to portray any villains. But his preferences
come through in the harsh location and the remarkable vitality of the poor,
socially outcast characters. In the midst of the post-Korean War coal-mining
recession in Kyushu, the death of a father leaves four siblings to fend for
themselves. Strikes, protracted layoffs and poverty finally split the family up,
but the ambitious little Nianchan runs away to Tokyo to look for a job. He is
apprehended and sent back to Kyushu, but keeps his determination to succeed.
Along with poverty and ethnicity, problems of education and social work are
sensitively presented, and to Imamura's embarrassment the film was awarded
the Education Minister's Prize. *KJ* #3. (FC; negative at Nikkatsu, Tokyo.)

1961   **Pigs and Battleships (Buta to Gunkan)*
pr: Nikkatsu; orig. sc: Hisashi Yamauchi; 'scope ph: Shinsaku Himeda; music:
Toshiro Mayuzumi; cast: Hiroyuki Nagato, Jitsuko Yoshimura, Yoko Minamida, Shiro Osaka, Sanae Nakahara et al. Tragi-comic study of the lowest
stratum of the Japanese social scale encountering the U.S. military presence
at the Yokosuka naval base. Haruko is the typical lower-class Imamura
heroine who finds her innocence impossible to protect but survives on her
own determination. She tries to keep the boy she loves from getting involved
with gangsters who are dealing in black-market pigs, but he is sucked into the
structure of pseudoloyalty, dying in the end in a bizarre shoot-out and pig
stampede. Haruko looks only to escape from the atmosphere of prostitutes and
mobsters, but she does not manage to do so until she has been gang-raped by
American soldiers. Superb low-life energy, humor and semi-documentary
seediness. *KJ* #7. (FC; negative at Nikkatsu, Tokyo.)

1963   **The Insect Woman (Nippon Konchuki)*
pr: Nikkatsu; orig. sc: Keiji Hasebe and Imamura; 'scope ph: Shinsaku Himeda;
music: Toshiro Mayuzumi; cast: Sachiko Hidari, Kazuo Kitamura, Jitsuko
Yoshimura, Seizaburo Kawazu, Hiroyuki Nagato et al. Through the story of
one woman who grubs like an insect to survive and succeed on her own,
Imamura shows rural life in wartime and city life during postwar reconstruction.
Tome is actually the illegitimate daughter of a woman who leads a very unset-
tled life, and she herself, after the death of her village boyfriend in the war and
desertion by her lover at the paper mill where she becomes involved in union
activities, goes on to bear an illegitimate daughter for whom she is determined
to provide at all costs. She goes to Tokyo and works as a maid, but ends up a
prostitute. Gradually learning the way of controlling such operations, she
rebels against the cruel madame and sets up her own call-girl ring. As she
grows older, however, her girls in turn oppose her, and her own daughter steals
her lover and persuades him to set her up in business. But the daughter simply

walks off with the older man's money and goes to live with her country lover, where Tome comes to be impressed by her daughter's practicality and ability to find her own happiness. Three generations of illegitimate women prove to succeed, unfazed by war, conventional morality, poverty or weak exploitative men. *KJ* #1. (FC; negative at Nikkatsu, Tokyo.)

1964   **Intentions of Murder (Akai Satsui)*

pr: Nikkatsu; orig. story: Shinji Fujiwara; sc: Keiji Hasebe and Imamura; 'scope ph: Shinsaku Himeda; music: Toshiro Mayuzumi; cast: Masumi Harukawa, Shigeru Tsuyuguchi, Ko Nishimura, Yoshi Kato, Yuko Kusunoki et al. Another inarticulate, plain country girl who survives by pure instinct. The story, based on a single real person and set in the harsh climate and rigid family system of northern Japan, forms Imamura's tightest dramatic script. Sadako is home alone when she is suddenly attacked by an intruder. Flashbacks retell her past as a girl brought from Tokyo to Sendai when her grandmother dies, growing up tending silkworms and becoming a maid in the household where she now has a son and tends the ailing head of the house. The rapist returns again and again, swearing he is in love with her and begging her to run away with him to Tokyo. She becomes pregnant by him and finally, impulsively, decides to run off with him, but their train is caught in snowdrifts. Attempting to walk over a high pass to the next town, the man is seized with a heart attack, and Sadako runs away, leaving him to die in the snow. Her victory is complete when she steadfastly denies she was the woman accompanying that man, although a jealous longtime mistress of her husband has taken photographs to prove it, and she and her son are finally officially entered in the family register. *KJ* #4. (FC; negative at Nikkatsu, Tokyo.)

1966   **The Pornographers: Introduction to Anthropology (Jinruigaku Nyumon)*

pr: Imamura Prod./Nikkatsu; orig. story: Akiyuki Nosaka *(Erogoto-shi)*; sc: Imamura and Koji Numata; 'scope ph: Shinsaku Himeda; music: Toshiro Mayuzumi; cast: Shoichi Ozawa, Sumiko Sakamoto, Keiko Sagawa, Masaomi Kondo, Ichiro Sugai et al. Back to an Osaka location for a humorous but pathetic view of the men who make the blue movies. The marginal main character is having a love affair of convenience with his dying landlady, who tries to pass her daughter on to him. He becomes progressively more obsessed and simultaneously disgusted with the lechery of his customers and, always skirting run-ins with the police, finally escapes into a world of perfect women —a mannequin he fabricates in the image of the lost woman he loves. Imamura originally suggested this film project as a joke, and ended up being told to make it himself. He does not prefer it among his works, but it is one of the most appreciated. *KJ* #2. (FC; negative at Nikkatsu, Tokyo.)

1967   **A Man Vanishes (Ningen Johatsu)*

pr: Imamura Prod./Nihon Eiga Shinsha/ATG; planning: Imamura; ph: Kenji Ishiguro; music: Toshiro Mayuzumi; cast: Yoshie Hayakawa, Shigeru Tsuyu-guchi, Sayo Hayakawa, Imamura et al. Planned by selecting one woman who filed a missing persons police report and helping in her search for her lover, the final development of this film shows the impossibility of drawing a line between fact and fiction. The acidic Yoshie quickly loses interest in finding the man she suspects her sister has murdered, and proceeds to fall in love with the actor-interviewer who accompanies her on her search. When piecing together the bits of evidence finally necessitates a confrontation between the sisters, Imamura himself steps into the standoff and has the room fall apart to show that it is a studio set. Full of spontaneity in sync-sound recording and hidden camera work, and a startling treatment of a real social problem. *KJ* #2. (FC; negative at ATG, Tokyo.)

1968 *The Profound Desire of the Gods/Kuragejima: Tales from a Southern Island (Kamigami no Fukaki Yokubo)*
pr: Imamura Prod/Nikkatsu; orig. sc: Imamura and Keiji Hasebe; color 'scope ph: Masao Tochizawa; music: Toshiro Mayuzumi; cast: Rentaro Mikuni, Choichiro Kawarazaki, Kazuo Kitamura, Hideko Okiyama, Yasuko Matsui et al. Practical civilization and primitive myth collide in the industrial development of the Ryukyu Islands, and the outcome is a stalement in perpetuity. An engineer from Tokyo leaves his wife and family behind to come as the advance researcher for his construction company to the virtually untouched island of Kuragejima. In encountering the local customs, religion and interpersonal relationships, he grows more disoriented daily. A woman who appears to be the local shaman priestess is loved by her own brother but nevertheless makes constant sexual advances to the baffled engineer. He observes the brother digging a sacred pit, puzzles over the powerful local superstitions and non-money economy, and is finally presented with an apparently demented girl who makes him forget Tokyo altogether. Finally the brother and sister lovers, as in old Okinawan myth, escape together by sea, but the villagers set out to punish them, and the demented girl is set up as the new priestess. The engineer goes back to Tokyo and returns later with his family to find a railway and Coca-cola a new part of the island culture, but an apparition of the demented girl dances on the train tracks. *KJ* #1. (FC; negative at Nikkatsu, Tokyo.)

1970 *History of Postwar Japan as Told by a Bar Hostess (Nippon Sengo Shi: Madamu Omboro no Seikatsu)*
pr: Nihon Eiga Shinsha/Toho; planning: Imamura; ph: Masao Tochizawa; music: Harumi Ibe; interviewing: Imamura; cast: Emiko Akaza, Etsuko Akaza, Akemi Akaza, Chieko Akaza et al. Inspired by Imamura's persistent fascination with the American military port town of Yokosuka, and the production company's request to do a documentary report on Japan in the quarter century since the Pacific War. Selecting a middle-aged woman who had operated a bar for U.S. military men and was now married to an American, he had her reconstruct her own life while commenting on newsreel footage of major political and social events he showed her on the abandoned barroom wall. In the course of the interviews, "Madame Omboro's" outcaste social status, the impossibility of having a normal marriage, her determined practicality and earthy sense of humor emerge. Omboro has nothing but scorn for the great events of her time, however, and her daughter's primary interest is revealed as the desire to live up to the phenomenal strength of her own

mother and see to her own and her daughter's financial security. Finding himself the object of Omboro's growing affection, Imamura was relieved when her husband whisked her away to the U.S. His search for the view of the most ordinary of people again led him into a story with no ending. (Positive and negative at Toho, Tokyo.)

1975   *Karayuki-san, the Making of a Prostitute* (*Karayuki-san*)
pr: Imamura Prod./Shibata Organization; planning: Imamura; ph: Masao Tochizawa. Part of a series of documentary films made for television in which Imamura traces Japanese who were sent to Southeast Asia and for various reasons decided not to return. "Karayuki-san" were young women sold into prostitution and sent out for use largely by the Japanese military before the Pacific War. Many were from outcaste backgrounds, or simply so poor that their families sold them under duress. Imamura traces women who often spent their lives in bondage, providing for families at home who were too ashamed of them to take them back. Many as a result have remained in the countries where they were stationed, preferring the life of expatriates, though many still live in poverty. A very moving portrayal of undefeated, surviving women. (Non-circulating print at Shibata Organization, Tokyo.)

NAGISA OSHIMA

1932—

I'm a country farmer; Nagisa Oshima is a samurai.

—Shohei Imamura

from Rikiya Tayama, *Nihon no eiga sakka-tachi: Sosaku no himitsu,* 1975

Originator of the New Wave movement that began in 1959, Nagisa Oshima has commanded more attention, both at home and abroad, than any of his contemporaries. In Japan his work has been treated as the supreme expression of the psychology of a whole age,[1] while in the west he has been called variously controversial and difficult,[2] innovative and inaccessible,[3] and "the least inscrutable of all Japanese directors."[4] Despite the wide divergence of opinions about his intelligibility, most critics seem to agree that Oshima is quite revolutionary. Clearly, he is controversial, as the recent furor over his hard-core pornographic film, *Realm of the Senses* (1976), demonstrates, but he does not like to be labeled a maker of revolutionary or politically, activist films. Oshima feels that a filmmaker works in and records movements, but he does not make them because he cannot keep himself out of his product. "I believe all of my films are films made within a movement, even those from before the inception of Sozosha [his own production company]. But all of them bear my personal mark, and this is what movies are."[5]

It is almost as if Oshima's own remarks are a response not only to the critics' pressure to make him a revolutionary, but to the direction taken by one of the first filmmakers to influence his work, Jean-Luc Godard. Oshima's sympathy with the French New Wave from his first exposure to their work was in fact militant, and his admiration for Godard's style can be seen manifested in particular in his late 1960s films, such as *Three Resurrected Drunkards* (1968) and *Diary of a Shinjuku Thief* (1969). Like the forgers of the French New Wave, Oshima has theorized extensively on what film should be, and has produced two volumes on the subject, his 1963 *Sengo eiga: Hakai to sozo* (Postwar Film: Destruction and Creation) and the 1975 *Taikenteki sengo eizo ron* (A Theory of the Postwar Image Based on Personal Experience). Even the difference in the titles reveals the evolution of Oshima's cinematic thought from political art to personal statement. He moves, as his films have moved, with the climate of the times. The Oshima with a lion's mane of the last days of social criticism—*The Ceremony* (1971) and *Summer Sister* (1972)—has somehow become a short-haired television personality who wears lavender business suits (or did the last time I saw him). Yet, in spite of change, Oshima still agonizes over the role of film and the filmmaker in society. He speaks with a charming un-Japanese sarcasm about himself and other film directors ("Except for Jean-Marie Straub, I wouldn't trust any of the new German filmmakers—they have no class."),[6] but the barrage of theory and criticism always comes back to the crucial issue of the meaning of the act of filmmaking. This problem is so deep for Oshima that he has made at least one film devoted solely to it, his 1970 *Man Who Left His Will on Film*. He has also described his entire experience as a filmmaker in terms of constant evaluation, condemnation, and vindication only if his films survive as documents—even without his name attached to them.[7]

It is this documentary impulse that has caused Oshima's work to be called journalistic[8] by some and unartistic[9] by others. Oshima's primary concern has always been freedom of expression, which necessarily brings politics and social issues into his films. The abuse of power and the oppression of individuals and whole segments of the population have been his themes from the earliest criticism of the Communist youth movement, *Night and Fog in Japan* (1960) to his bitterly satirical indictment of the Japanese attitude toward Koreans, *Death by Hanging* (1968). Even *Realm of the Senses*, in which Oshima pursues the idea of personal fulfillment much more deeply than ever before, is an indirect lashing out at Japanese film censorship in that he went outside Japan in order to have the freedom to make a truly erotic film. The topicality of some of his films, such as *Three Resurrected Drunkards*, the title song taken from a popular novelty hit of the same year, requires a familiarity with some of the most fleeting aspects of popular culture as well as with more lingering social issues. Nevertheless,this journalistic quality is part of what Oshima values as his personal expression. Three of the films he cherishes most, *Night and Fog in Japan*, *A Treatise on Japanese Bawdy Song* (1967) and *Death by Hanging*, deal with extremely volatile subjects: intraparty ethics of Japanese Communists and injustice toward Koreans. When he says he likes these best among his own films because "only I could make them,"[10] Oshima does not mean that he is the only filmmaker with the courage to approach such issues, but that he is the only one with enough inside knowledge to do so.

In the course of his nearly twenty years as a film director, however, Oshima has attained considerable artistry in a willy-nilly fashion. The impulse to record and comment on society remains with him, but a turning inward appeared about the time of his 1969 *Boy*. The psychological exploration of escape fantasy continues through the frustrations of *The Ceremony* (1971) and culminates in the ignorance of the state and the acting out of fantasy in *Realm of the Senses*. The depth of these recent characterizations, abetted by a richer technical control, looks suspiciously like art.

No Regrets

If a left-leaning humanism was the mark of the filmmaking generation of the immediate postwar era, Oshima led a new cinematic movement in the 1960s with portraits of his disillusionment with the organized left. As a young man Oshima had never considered becoming a film director, and in fact avoided having anything to do with the film industry throughout his university career. While his acquaintances in Kyoto, where most period films were made, earned pocket money as extras, Oshima cleaned bathrooms for the sanitation department rather than associate himself with the glamor and wealth of the movie world.[11] Still, he indicates that certain films stood out as ideological signposts in his youth.

Oshima was born on March 31, 1932 in Kyoto, but moved to Okayama Prefecture where his father, a samurai descendant, worked as chief of a government fishery experiment station. When Nagisa was six years old, his father, whom he describes as an accomplished amateur painter and poet,[12] died, and his mother moved back to Kyoto with him and his sister. His childhood was lonely: his health was poor, and his mother went to work to support the family within a few years of her husband's death. His father had left a large library, half of which consisted of books and periodicals on Communist and Socialist thought; during the war Oshima devoured these forbidden fruits in solitude.[13]

He tired of reading and loneliness, however, and in middle school, like the hero of his 1971 *Ceremony*, he became absorbed in the group activity of baseball. He did not excel in this sport, and soon developed an interest in postwar literature to the extent that he began writing poetry and novels. "I'm not at all proud of them," he says, "and in any case I again tired of this solitary activity."[14] By his second year in high school, he was already splitting his time between student activism and dramatics.

His admission to Kyoto University seemed to him a natural progression—it did not occur to him that he might fail the entrance examination to this prestigious national university.[15] He cites a film he had seen at the age of 14 as being influential in his choice of school: Kurosawa's 1946 *No Regrets for Our Youth*. The model for the heroine's father, "Professor Yagihara," was the famous Kyoto University law professor, Yukitoki Takikawa (1891–1962). As Oshima now sees it, the film is a superficial idealization of the 1933 Takikawa Affair, when the professor was dismissed from his post for publishing a liberal tract.[16] Nevertheless, Oshima claims it was this attempt at free speech in the face of fascist militarism that inspired him to enter the law faculty of Kyoto University.[17] It was the same Professor Takikawa who later in 1953 refused Oshima and the student group he led the right to hold meetings on the Kyoto University campus.

It has been suggested that while the logic of Oshima's films may be comprehensible, their sentiment may not be readily understandable to viewers who have not shared in the experiences of student activism.[18] Indeed, his disillusionment with the monolithic power of the Japanese Communist Party and his frustration over the inability of smaller groups to effect change appear openly as recurrent themes in his films, beginning with the 1960 *Night and Fog in Japan* and going on to the

1966 *Violence at Noon* and the 1970 *Man Who Left His Will on Film*. His very personal despair lies rooted in his experiences as vice president of Kyoto University's student association, and later as president of the Kyoto Prefecture Student Alliance. In 1951, when the emperor visited Kyoto University, Oshima and his colleagues, having been denied their request for open questions and answers, carried a huge placard imploring the emperor not to allow himself to be deified again because so many students who were their seniors had been killed in the war in the name of his divinity.[19] The result of the "Emperor Incident" was the dissolution of the student association.

In 1953, however, the association was revived by popular demand, and Oshima became regional leader. When the university refused to allow them to meet on the campus, pressure mounted for an open confrontation. A mass demonstration ensued. The police joined the confrontation, over 70 people were injured, and punishment was meted out to six students. Efforts to have the punishment rescinded were frustrated by the onset of winter vacation, and Professor Takikawa published a statement blaming the occurrence of the 1953 "Kyoto University Incident" excesses on the failure to deal more harshly with the 1951 "Emperor Incident."[20]

In effect, the student movement was crushed, and a despondent Oshima went on for his senior job interviews as the new year began. That spring, with deep awareness of his responsibilities, he watched Kinoshita's *The Garden of Women*. Not only was the setting recognizably modeled on Kyoto Women's University, where he had many friends, but direct references were made in the film to "last year's Kyoto University Incident," which the heroine says symbolizes the fact that boys, unlike girls, go to school for more than graduation and marriage.[21] This film about academic freedom for women left Oshima feeling that his failure to resist Communist demands for confrontation had brought about the violent incident, and worse yet, the result had been the complete suppression of academic freedom. In retrospect, Oshima names the Communist Party as a major source of his frustrations, because its cell leadership system made it impossible "to have things go as I wanted."[22]

He emerged from the winter battle branded as a "Red Student" which hampered his search for a job. 1954 was a bad year. Previously, among his fellow-students, there had been extensive debate about the ethics of entering industries related to the Korean War, but with the termination of hostilities, employment in Japan was plummeting. Thinking that the Osaka office of the prestigious *Asahi Shimbun* newspaper might still take a "Red Student" despite the nationwide Red Purge of the late forties and early fifties, Oshima's first try was for journalism. But he was rejected by the *Asahi*, and even by the textile and paper companies he subsequently tried. Even his closest advisor at Kyoto University steered him away from a possible research position because he was "too showy for such a career;" thus, he was left with only his friends in dramatics to turn to.[23] One of them happened to be going up to Tokyo to take the Shochiku Ofuna Studios entrance examination, and Oshima went along to distract himself from his melancholy and "to degenerate."[24] He found two thousand applicants assembled to compete for five openings for assistant directors.

Ofuna Nouvelle Vague

Oshima placed first in the examination. During a break in the examination, one of the Shochiku assistant directors administering the test had revealed to him the meaning of a code word in the questions that baffled everyone. An angry Oshima went ahead and wrote the exam he knew they wanted instead of exposing the trick, and he greeted the year 1954 with shame; in his desperation for a job he had temporarily abandoned his beliefs.[25] When he entered Shochiku in April, he knew nothing about making movies—not even that they were shot one take at a time.[26]

As an assistant director Oshima did not consider himself attached to the staff of any one particular director. He worked first with Yoshitaro Nomura, once or twice with Masaki Kobayashi and, out of preference for Hideo Oba's (1910–) liberal attitude, on every film Oba made during the five-year duration of his assistantship. He says, "I never became a 'great assistant director' who runs hard at the director's bidding . . . . If I thought the work was boring, I'd quit and go home."[27] He stressed self-assertion as his own criterion for a good assistant director, and worked as little as possible for others, assisting on only 15 films in 5 years. He expended his energies instead on scriptwriting, completing 11 scenarios before his 1959 promotion and publishing them in the assistant directors' magazine. Like his French counterparts, he also engaged in vehement film criticism for a number of publications beginning in 1956. His preference for the spontaneity he found in the new films from France and Poland was thus as public as his aversion for the Ofuna system and the glossy, well-made stories of American and American-influenced films, which he labeled as "the enemy."[28] Advocating freedom of expression and freshness at the cost of commercial veneer, his art politics placed him loudly and clearly in a camp allied with the incipient French New Wave, and his theoretical stance later garnered critical support when he made his directing debut.

To Oshima it remains a complete mystery why he was singled out for promotion when Ofuna formula films were at their nadir. It was clear that Shochiku was in the throes of a financial crisis, and Shiro Kido was about to take matters into his own hands to produce a film by a new director.

His system was to launch a new talent with the new director's own original scenario, and this time his specified goal was a film with "a social
quality."[29] Oshima's script "The Boy Who Sold His Pigeon" was duly
selected, but the company did not like the title. By the time the printed
shooting script reached his hands, Oshima was chagrined to find it had
become "A Town of Love and Hope." Whenever he sees this title at the
top of his filmography, the resentment he feels he will probably never
overcome brings tears to his eyes.[30]

The 1959 *A Town of Love and Hope* has the look, but not the feel, of an
Ofuna film. Keisuke Kinoshita's staff, notably cinematographer Hiroshi
Kusuda, lent their services with sincerity to help the novice Oshima.
Yuko Mochizuki, who had played the abandoned mother in Kinoshita's
1953 *A Japanese Tragedy*, again appeared in the role of a tearful lower-
class mother. But the morality of the story turned Ofuna on its ear.

The high school student who sells his homing pigeon to a rich girl,
knowing it will return to him, has the furtiveness of someone conscious of
his wrongdoing, but aware that his family's poverty gives him no choice.
Giving up a higher education, he takes and passes the entrance examination for the company owned by the rich girl's father, but her self-righteous
brother refuses to give him a job after finding out about the pigeon incident. Ofuna humanism would have required the boy to show contrition
and apologize, and the wealthy brother to show magnanimity and hire
him. Instead the boy shows anger and, in a burst of impotent rage, destroys the pigeon's cage. Even his pathetic mother will not condemn her
son—she had encouraged him to sell the pigeon. The disillusioned rich
girl convinces her brother to shoot the hapless pigeon, symbol of her
attempt at a relationship with the poor boy, with his rifle, and with the
rifle report and the falling bird the film ends.

Shiro Kido saw the "social" film he had put himself behind, thinking in
terms of Shochiku's traditional support for the little man, and promptly
expressed his anger: "This seems to be saying that rich and poor can never
join hands . . . . this is a 'tendency film'!"[31] Oshima had let his beliefs find expression in his very first film, only to see it labeled with a
term describing the early 1930s films, showing contrast between economic classes. Company retaliation was immediate. *A Town of Love and
Hope* was released only in small, out of the way theaters, and for half a
year Oshima was given no further work.

But as in the French New Wave, the relationship between the critical
world and the new directors proved crucial. Oshima had been criticizing
the critics' indifference to the formula film plight of young directors for a
number of years in print, and now they rallied to his cause. The critical
response to his first film, made when he was 27 years old, was so favor-
able that the company could not ignore it and had to give him another

chance. In 1960, as he released *Cruel Story of Youth*, Shochiku was banking on him and the other young directors Yoshishige Yoshida and Masahiro Shinoda, and the "Ofuna Nouvelle Vague" was in full swing.

But Oshima immediately objected to the label the journalists had borrowed from France and that Shochiku publicity had taken up with enthusiasm. He maintained that there were too few "new directors" to constitute a "wave," and moreover that they were all working within the restrictions of the company system, which hampered the emergence of a true avant-garde. He further lamented that it had only been a coincidence that both he and Yoshida had taken delinquent students as the protagonists of their films, and that their purpose in using sex and violence —to overthrow the standard morality of the Ofuna formula—had been misinterpreted. He stressed, as he called for the destruction of a "nouvelle vague" meaning nothing more than exploitation of youth, sex, and violence, that there was a need for continuing revolt if the avant-garde was to survive.[32]

Indeed, the actions of the young delinquents in *Cruel Story of Youth* were sensational at the time. But as in *A Town of Love and Hope*, there is a chillingly hopeless rage behind their attitude. Against a background of anti-U.S.-Japan Security Treaty demonstrations, the boy and girl talk about sex. They proceed to a dirty waterfront where timber floats in the glaring sun. He chases her, slaps her, and throws her in the water. "I can't swim!" she screams, but when she continues to refuse to "behave," the boy steps on her fingers clinging to a log. He threatens to satisfy her sexual curiosity, drags her out of the water, and begins to kiss her roughly. The camera moves up to the sun, then down to her clothes strewn over the logs. The two go on to more dangerous games with sex and violence, flaunting their ruthlessness in the face of disillusioned adults. "We have no dreams, so we can't see them destroyed," the boy insists, and, when reprimanded by the police, he maintains that the only wrongdoing lies in getting caught. The girl, after an abortion and abandonment, jumps from a speeding car, and the boy is beaten to death by a gang of hoodlums. With this film, employing a hand-held camera reminiscent of Jean-Luc Godard's *Breathless* (*A Bout de Souffle*, 1958) but fully in keeping with the angry, defiant and jagged mood of the story, Oshima became the "darling of the age."[33]

In the same year, he rushed on to make *The Sun's Burial* about the vicious path to survival in Osaka's biggest slum. Again rape, murder and gang warfare are a way of life, and the heroine, who has learned to despise all sentimentality, even tries to strangle her own father when he cheats her. In contrast to the Ofuna flavor, Oshima shows that only the strong and unfeeling can survive, that the weak and the good are utterly expendable. It was a very successful film.

In Oshima's next film, the sun, an image of hope for Japan, has disappeared altogether, and it was a fluke that he was allowed to make such a dark, vindictive statement. Taking up leadership of an avant-garde movement, he persuaded the company that the traditional audience had to be ignored, and an appeal had to be made to a new audience to come into the theaters.[34] Shochiku was desperate enough to listen, but foolish enough to believe that because it was about a wedding, it could be exploited as a melodrama.[35] *Night and Fog in Japan* is about the failure of the left to put a stop to the U.S.-Japan Security Treaty in the bloody 1960 demonstrations. Like the Alain Resnais short film *Night and Fog* (*Nuit et Brouillard,* 1955), from which it takes its name, it is a narration, a memory and an argument. One long discourse from beginning to end, it indicts the selfishness and innocence of the student left as well as the inhuman rigidity of the Japan Communist Party in a reconstruction of the events and attitudes leading up to the 1960 debacle. The party dogma is represented by the wealthy young leader who picks out the prettiest girl and condemns the students for not joining with the workers, but autobiographical figures also appear in the "ghost" activist from the past who comes to the wedding to accuse the cell group of cowardly inhumanity, and in a concerned young newspaper reporter who brings up the real issue of people being wounded in the struggle. The verdict is the failure of the left as the music rises over the strident declamations of the wealthy leader, and the camera picks out the sad and angry faces in the wedding assemblage. The film closes with fog in the still forest.

Oshima had worked with journalistic speed to produce three films on highly volatile issues in one year, and Shochiku had not been able to keep up with him. *Night and Fog in Japan* was dubbed a commercial failure, and it was pulled from circulation three days after release, probably as a result of political pressure stemming from the assassination of Japan Socialist Party leader Inejiro Asanuma.[36] In bitterness, Oshima left Shochiku, but his action had been foreseeable, perhaps inevitable, if he was to practice the revolutionary avant-gardism he preached. The instigator of the Ofuna Nouvelle Vague left Ofuna the same year the movement had begun.

Crime and Revolution

The revolt against the formula film culminated in Oshima's complete rejection of the studio system and his formation of his own production company, Sozosha (Creation Company), with his wife, actress Akiko Koyama, and other colleagues. He had tried to change the system from within (even at his own wedding he had made a speech denouncing Shochiku),[37] but instead he had been forced out. It would be several years before his predictions about the definitive loss of the mass audience would come true, and by 1966 the age of independent production would dawn in earnest. After the hectic pace of his production at Shochiku— one film every two months—he entered a period of varied activities: work with novelist Kenzaburo Oe (*The Catch*, 1961), a period film about an eighteenth-century revolutionary (*Shiro Tokisada from Amakusa*, 1962), and two years of travel around war-scarred Korea and Vietnam, making television documentaries as he went. In 1965, he returned to his earlier themes with a new vitality and scope in *Pleasures of the Flesh*, but it was not until much later that he came to assess the meaning of the themes he discovered looking back over his own work.

Entering Shochiku as a complete novice to film, Oshima had had no idea what kind of films he might want to make. After laboring for about a year as an assistant director and realizing that in this work he had acquired a real profession, he began to feel confident that he too might some day make ordinary, commercially successful films.[38] But he had no ink-ling of what sort of material he wanted to treat or how.

He began to understand only after he had already made a number of films of his own. He saw that he was extremely drawn to what society calls criminal behavior.[39] He observed, moreover, that the criminality portrayed in his films escalated. First his characters committed crimes because they had no choice, as in *A Town of Love and Hope*, and then either because they enjoyed it (*Cruel Story of Youth, Diary of a Shinjuku Thief*) or because they had no awareness that it was a crime (*Death by Hanging, Boy*). Indeed, in every Oshima film at least one murder, rape, theft or blackmail incident can be found, and often the whole of the film is constructed around the chronic repetition of such a crime. Worse yet, Oshima realized that as the crime in his films escalated, he had more frightening nightmares about himself committing crimes. He would in-variably commit rape and mass murder, be caught, and then escape to live an ordinary life for some time, only to be caught in his peaceful dis-guise.[40]

The punishment for his crimes would consist of the official destruction of his identity and permanent isolation in a deep black hole. As he faced a future of inactivity, he would suddenly regret not only the loss of his loved ones but the fact that he could no longer make films. He would awaken from these recurrent dreams with the lingering conviction that he was in fact guilty of some crime, that his actual daily life was only the calm period of grace before his detection and capture. He gradually came to the conclusion that his guilt feelings were related to the impurity that had entered his attitude toward revolution—he was, after all, a filmmaker and not a revolutionary, and it was the possibility of making films that was taken away from him as punishment in his dreams.

Although he was never a member of the Communist Party, Oshima has been a left sympathizer from his high school activist days through the student unrest of the late 1960s and early 1970s, as films like *Night and Fog in Japan, Diary of a Shinjuku Thief* and *The Man Who Left His Will on Film* openly show. He has always felt something in common with the oppressed, notably the 600,000 Japanese of Korean descent, the poor and women. "You might not think so to see me sitting here smiling and laughing," he says, "but that dark, oppressed side of me is always there."[41] The need for social revolution weighs upon him to such an extent that he has stated he looks forward to the defeat of Japan in its imperialism toward other Asian countries as the only means by which to effect social change.[42] Yet he is painfully aware that making films can do nothing to bring on this change or defeat.

While he still expresses admiration for the determination of filmmakers like Godard concerning their avid commitment to a revolutionary purpose in the filmic medium, Oshima is adamant in his belief that such a goal is doomed to frustration; hence the criminality complex apparent in his own films. He recognized at an early stage that he was not physically strong enough to be a revolutionary, and his early defeat in the "Kyoto University Incident" marked him for life. He turned to a much-needed job and later to the unshakable responsibilities of a family. A true revolutionary, Oshima feels, risks death at every turn because he is seen as a threat by the established order. Writing at 39, he concluded that no one had seen him as such a threat in his work as a filmmaker, because he was still alive. The great contemporary revolutionaries, such as Che Guevara, Malcolm X and Martin Luther King, had all been assassinated before reaching age 40, he observed, but he was more than likely to go on living.[43] The craving for revolution remains with him, but its expression is in the criminality—the rejection of the law of the state—of his protagonists.

Recently, Oshima has become more wistful, more philosophical in his interpretation of the political role of film, placing still higher value on individuality in art and life. While he now says "All movies are political,"[44] he sees no contradiction between such a view and his earlier claims that no film can be a political weapon. "Films have many meanings, among which is the political, but some people insist that the political meaning is the only valid one, and I have always opposed this view."[45] He maintains that filmmaking is for him a means of self-exploration, a personalism that cannot be exercised within a studio system any more than it can subordinate itself to a political goal. His interest is not only in political and social movements, which continue to appear as background, like the snatches of grim soldiers of imperial Japan in *Realm of the Senses,* but in how the individual responds and moves within these broader trends, and how they move within him. This relationship between the individual and society is best expressed, he has found, in the irrationality of crime and sex—forces that drive the individual without his own comprehension.[46]

With *Realm of the Senses*, his first new statement in four years, Oshima has reached an equilibrium in the tensions among crime, revolution and personalism. Sada and her lover Kichizo are not criminals for Oshima because they act spontaneously and lack the necessary complexes,[47] but in their pursuit of sexual fulfillment they are complete dropouts from society and politics. Oshima himself had earlier remarked upon the attraction of such a solution but concluded that he could not drop out any more than he could be a revolutionary. Nevertheless, while Oshima insists that the dropout's response is a positive one, the imperial troops representing the rise of fascism gnaw at everyone's consciousness.

Dead Flag Fantasies

Oshima is almost impossible to pin down stylistically, except in terms of recurrent favorite symbols. His first film, like his most recent, is a modestly straightforward story. In between, however, his technical experimentation has pushed far into territories very new to the Japanese cinema, but closely allied to the novelty of his content.

At the time of his second film, *Cruel Story of Youth*, Oshima was already employing the techniques of the French New Wave and cinema verité movements to suit his own ends. Hand-held cameras and jump-cuts introduce a new irrationality to stories of rebels who are far from sympathetic heroes. The amoral, violent young people of *Cruel Story of Youth* and *The Sun's Burial* have no traffic with traditional morality; they commit crimes with bland detachment, and Oshima often shows the grotesque results in alienating long shot. He forces us to evaluate the conditions giving rise to such impotent rebellion because we cannot identify with these frighteningly cold protagonists; the emotionally drained quality of action and cinematic presentation instead "invites a more intellectual response."[48]

With *Night and Fog in Japan* Oshima embarked on the interweaving of past and present to tell the story of the failure of the organized left. Much more a dialogue drama than a montage argument, the theatrical presentation takes on symbolic meaning with the spotlighting of characters and events against a pitch black background, all to be swallowed in fog at the end. The camera darts and circles in coordination with the extreme lighting effects, and the whole film is constructed of only 43 shots, in contrast to later films such as the 1966 *Violence at Noon*, an action allegory composed of some 1,500 shots.[49] As justification for such pendulum swings of technique, Oshima upholds the director's personal

feeling: "A film has to be enjoyable to make. If it fails, it means the director's feeling was not in it. I'm very self-indulgent, and I like to do extreme
things—the more enthusiastic I am, the more extreme my technique becomes."[50]

In the late 1960s when he was making *Death by Hanging, Three Resurrected Drunkards, Diary of a Shinjuku Thief* and *The Man Who Left
His Will on Film*, his narrative structures became so shattered and centrifugal that an audience expecting a story film would be instantly repelled by them. The bitter humor that overlies the destroyed narratives
is likewise unbearably black: the state tries to hang a man and succeeds
only in giving him amnesia, but he cannot be killed unless he recognizes
his crime, so reenactment is selected as the means of jogging his memory.
A Korean army deserter steals a Japanese boy's school uniform, but the
boy and his friends may have been Korean to begin with when the story
begins all over again, halfway through, with the same sequence of shots.
A boy who finds his only sexual stimulation in stealing books is turned in
by a girl sales clerk who proves not to be a store employee at all; the
bookstore owner aids the two in an unconsummated love affair; actors
assume their daily-life identities to talk about sex, then don costumes to
rape the "sales clerk." A high-school student agonizes over a friend's
apparent suicide, takes over the friend's girl and begins to see that the
"revolutionary" film the friend had been making was all about him; in
the end it is he who jumps from a building with the camera in his hand. A
terrible despair pervades these films, and our laughter catches in our
throats.

Rather than a Godardian alienation, it is a personal anguish that infuses
the deadpan acting in Oshima's films as well. This is especially remarkable in the lack of expression in the criminal children of *A Town of Love
and Hope* and the 1969 *Boy*. Neither will cry and neither will admit to
any wrongdoing. Their blankness is a cover for their pain, as Oshima's
own early development of an emotionless mask was to hide his sorrow
and loneliness.[51] But Oshima feels embarrassed by the obviousness in
the victimization of these children, and he regrets his own tendency toward sentimentality. He prefers a more complex structure that hides his
feelings at the same time as it reveals them.[52]

Much of the complexity derives from the interaction of individual motivations with a social reality, and a tension is created between social
symbols and personal fantasies. In discussing the structure of his 1969
Diary of a Shinjuku Thief, Oshima ascribed a major role to the power of
imagination: " . . . something that starts with imagination can change
reality. But this reality soon becomes something static and then another
imagining would change this, so there is continual reciprocity between
reality and fiction . . . ."[53] *A Treatise on Japanese Bawdy Song,*

Three Resurrected Drunkards and *Death by Hanging* all deal with a collective fantasy regarding Koreans and the escape fantasies of individual protagonists. *Boy* and *The Ceremony* show individual fantasies of escape from oppression: the child forced to participate in his parents' extortion racket dreams of salvation by monsters from the deep, and the young man caught in his family's cold web returns to a childhood fantasy baseball game in which everyone seems to love him and he feels in control of his destiny. The fantasy pervading the *Diary of a Shinjuku Thief*, however, is the very positive impulse to "steal the country" like the historical revolutionary Shosetsu Yui, a character in the play within the film. In this sense the fact that the hero's theft of Shosetsu Yui's identity at the end coincides with actual student demonstrations outside is highly significant. When we come to *Realm of the Senses*, there is no longer any fantasy, only exercise of desire.

That the most positive fantasy in the criminal films is that of wresting power from the state relates to Oshima's own activist background and the "anti-state" symbolism of his films. He has himself remarked on the gradual replacement of a rather hopeful image of the sun in his early films *Cruel Story of Youth* and *The Sun's Burial* by the negative outlook of night and fog. His disillusionment with leftist politics in Japan and his observation of the increasing oppression of individual freedom by the state came to be represented by the black-and-white image of the Japanese flag (actually a red sun centered on a white ground) from 1967 on. Compared with the vitality of the sun image, he has said, the flag represents something dead: the Japanese nation since 1960.[54] This black flag dominates the setting of the prison interrogation in *Death by Hanging*, where degradation and murder are carried out in the name of state justice, and it reappears as the object of ironic enthusiasm in all of Oshima's films since. Its reappearance, in color as well, becomes the criminal's refrain voiced in the script of *Death by Hanging*: "As long as the state makes the absolute evil of murder legal through the waging of wars and the exercise of capital punishment, we are all innocent." The flag becomes the symbol of injustice, and along with the songs that are sung in its presence, it shows the imprisonment of the popular consciousness in a false identity.

From the beginning, Oshima brought together a closely knit group of accomplices to his work. From his first film he has worked with actor Fumio Watanabe, who has played everything from the bourgeois older brother in *A Town of Love and Hope* to the tyrannical lazy father in *Boy* and the repatriated POW uncle in *The Ceremony*. Other regulars in Oshima's cast include Kei Sato, Mutsuhiro Toura and Akiko Koyama. He always works on his own scripts, but when he left Shochiku to form Sozosha, he took scenarists Toshiro Ishido and Tsutomu Tamura with him;

they have continued to collaborate. At the outset he wanted to work with cinematographer Ko Kawamata, who stayed with Shochiku; Oshima would develop the close camera relationship he wanted with Akira Takada. His later films are likewise marked by the avant-garde music of Hikaru Hayashi and Toru Takemitsu.

One of the first things Oshima learned was how to make films on a small budget, for this was one of the criteria of the Ofuna Nouvelle Vague. He prides himself on the ability to do this, but admits it does have an effect on the look of the film. Low budgets account for the straightforward stories of films like *Boy* and *Realm of the Senses*, and his 1965 *Diary of Yunbogi* is a documentary feat of narration and still photographs. Using an analogy from his beloved baseball, he says, "When you can only afford a mediocre pitcher, you don't let him throw too many curves."[55] With budget restrictions, theme becomes more important than virtuoso technique. But Oshima's main concern, no matter what the budget, is the making of his own personal statements in his films. One reason he feels he ends up with low budgets is because he cannot do what others want. "If someone brings me a script and asks how a particular scene should be handled, I can't imagine what to say. I can only do what I have created and loved from the beginning."[56]

The Ceremony

Along with *Death by Hanging, A Treatise on Japanese Bawdy Song* and *Night and Fog in Japan, The Ceremony* ranks as one of Oshima's own favorite films—the ones he feels only he could have made. At the same time, however, it is a film that he finds "sentimental"[57] in revealing an excess of his personal feelings. It is the complexity of its commentary on the whole 25-year span of Japanese postwar history that redeems the sentimentality for him—but obviously sentimentality means something different to Oshima than it does to others. His sentimentality is the amount of himself that he recognizes in the main character of the film, Masuo. But the problem Masuo faces is one faced by every Japanese who grew up in the postwar era, and to a great extent by the same generation throughout the world: how to find values to live by. Masuo's passivity is a kind of stopgap solution, and the one most of us accept to keep on living. Oshima has said of him, ". . . he keeps thinking of himself as a weak person, but he will probably become very powerful in the system."[58]

The story is that of a family, the Sakuradas, who come together and deal with one another only at the ceremonial occasions of weddings and funerals. The 25-year period of postwar history of the family and Japan is told in flashback by Masuo (Kenzo Kawarazaki), whom we see in the beginning with his cousin Ritsuko (Atsuko Kaku) on the way to their cousin Terumichi's desolate island. Ritsuko calls Masuo "relative person," and he begins to recall his first encounter with her and the rest of the Sakurada clan.

In 1947 Masuo and his mother are repatriated from Manchuria, which had been a Japanese colony since the 1930s. After arriving at the Sakurada provincial estate, they quickly learn their places in the family. Masuo is seated facing his grandfather, Kazuomi (Kei Sato), and his mother disappears from his life. He is cared for by his aunt Setsuko (Akiko Koyama), who was also in Manchuria as wife of a Chinese collaborator and for whom Masuo develops a deep fascination. Masuo also meets his tomboy cousin Ritsuko, Setsuko's daughter; Tadashi (Kiyoshi Tsuchiya), a cousin whose father is still being held in China as a war criminal; and the enigmatic cousin Terumichi (Atsuo Nakamura), who later proves to be Kazuomi's illegitimate son by a woman who was supposed to marry Masuo's father. In their first encounters it is Terumichi who immediately takes command, but Masuo asserts his own inalienable identity in his private ritual of putting his ear to the ground to listen for the voice of his dead brother, who was buried alive by their mother during the flight from Manchuria. The first ceremony is the death anniversary of Masuo's father, who committed suicide when the emperor renounced his divinity but kept his position as figurehead leader of the Japanese nation in 1946.

Farther along on their journey Masuo reminds Ritsuko of the first baseball game they all played together as children, with Setsuko as umpire. She does not remember, but Masuo recalls his mother's death in 1952, when he swore to give up baseball in penance for continuing to pitch a losing tournament instead of rushing to her side in her last moments. In this flashback he remembers Setsuko giving him his father's will, only to have it snatched from his hands by Kazuomi. Setsuko objects, reminding Kazuomi that because he raped her as a girl she was unable to marry the man she loved and for whom she was intended, Masuo's father. Kazuomi's response is to order her to submit to his sexual advances. An agonized Masuo watches Terumichi calmly step in and ask Kazuomi to relinquish his place. Masuo meanwhile becomes aware of his physical attraction for Ritsuko, who finds him burning his bat and glove, but she teases him into kissing her on the forehead as a relative should.

At the rail of the boat heading south, Masuo observes to Ritsuko that they were all born of Japan's regret at turning back from Manchuria. The third flashback ceremony shows the raucous wedding of the family's Communist Party member uncle Isamu (Hosei Komatsu) in 1956. At the ceremony, Tadashi confronts his repatriated war criminal father,

Susumu (Fumio Watanabe) who refuses to speak to him. Later, Masuo and Terumichi talk to him about how to deal with his frustrations, and Terumichi shows him how to wield the family sword, suggesting he kill Setsuko, who has said she wants to die. Masuo goes to talk to Setsuko and offers to die with her, but she turns him away, and he comes back to find Terumichi and Ritsuko have become lovers. The next morning Setsuko is found impaled on a tree with the samurai sword, and Kazuomi lables her death a suicide.

Masuo tends the seasick Ritsuko in the cabin of the boat and laments his loss of her. "You just want to be doomed," she responds, and when he asks her to marry him up on deck, she becomes violently seasick. Masuo recalls the fourth ceremony, his own mock wedding in 1961. The bride selected by Kazuomi does not appear due to an attack of "appendicitis," but Tadashi appears in his policeman's uniform and begins to read a right-wing manifesto in the midst of the pantomime marriage to "a pure Japanese girl untainted by foreign influences." He is dragged off and reported killed in a traffic accident a few minutes later. In the mixture of wedding and wake, Masuo makes love to a pillow and then to Kazuomi, whom Terumichi holds down to play the role of the "pure Japanese girl." Masuo then takes Tadashi's corpse out of its coffin and jumps in, dragging Ritsuko, whom he claims he always wanted to marry, after him. But she holds out her hand to Terumichi, who takes leave of them saying he wishes he "could have heard that sound" of Masuo's dead brother under the ground. Kazuomi, who let Terumichi leave because Masuo was to take over the family line, is seen sobbing angrily at the family shrine.

As Masuo and Ritsuko board a rowboat for the last leg of the journey to Terumichi's island, Masuo remarks that Terumichi did not come to their grandmother Shizu's (Nobuko Otowa) funeral. He immediately remembers in flashback Ritsuko's arrival at Kazuomi's funeral a few days before. Though Masuo had become a high-school baseball coach, hoping to avoid taking over the Sakurada family responsibilities, he has no choice but to officiate at Kazuomi's funeral where everyone urges him to assume his grandfather's position. Feeling tremendous pressure and exhaustion, he lies down in a far corner of the room and begins to take on the identity of his suffocating brother as Ritsuko tries to comfort him with passionate kisses. But this Ritsuko is wearing the white kimono of death, and no sounds of the mourners across the room can be heard.

Arriving at the island in response to Terumichi's telegram "Terumichi dead," they find his corpse lying naked in his hut. Ritsuko calmly prepares herself to commit suicide, and Masuo does nothing to stop her. He rushes outside, where suddenly his childhood fantasy baseball game resumes. All the participants disappear after a hit into the underbrush, and Masuo in closeup puts his ear to the pebble beach, blocking the baseball from view and showing the Buddhist rosary in his hand.

Subjectivity is a very important element of the film. We see the action of the present and the five flashback ceremonies, but we are compelled to accept Masuo's narrated interpretation of all the events. Oshima uses camera strategy to make us question him: when he first puts his ear to the ground to listen to his dead brother, he is alone in a vast empty space, but the camera moves around a tree and reveals Ritsuko, Tadashi and Terumichi all watching him. He uses narrative technique to make us question him: Ritsuko denies that the childhood baseball game ever took place, yet for Masuo it is vivid enough to replace reality at the end of the film. And Masuo's narration is constantly undercut by his actions on the screen: he claims everything he did was to escape the clutches of the family, yet he is left with the full responsibility for it; he swears he will give up baseball when his mother dies, yet he becomes a baseball coach. Throughout the film we find his feelings contradicting his passive responses to the people around him, and in the end we recognize how fully trapped he is because of the film's circular structure. Masuo remains alone, listening to the dead, and even his present conversations with Ritsuko have had the questionable atmosphere of unnatural sound—automobiles and people have passed close by them without making any noise. In the end even baseball, which for many in the postwar era was a symbol of hope and democracy,[59] is blotted out by the paraphernalia of death.

Not only Masuo, but each character in the film is a study in defeat. Terumichi, the most vital of the youngest generation, chooses to destroy himself rather than carry on the corrupt Sakurada line, and Ritsuko chooses romantic submersion of her own identity in following him. She, like her mother Setsuko, is defeated by her acceptance of her woman's role, a condition described by the grandmother Shizu at the time of Masuo's mother's death: "The ultimate happiness for a woman is to be buried in the Sakurada family grave." Even Kazuomi, restored to power after the war, meets defeat when Terumichi, heir to his sexual authority and aggression, refuses to stay at home. The failure of Masuo's wedding underscores the fact that no one can succeed Kazuomi. The middle generation too fails to make changes or find new values. The family shows a benign tolerance for Communists like Uncle Isamu, and when Uncle Susumu returns after Maoist indoctrination, he refuses to speak; by the time of his son's death he is wearing a military uniform again. Oshima does not subscribe to the simplistic view that people like Kazuomi have fully rebuilt their feudalistic empires, for there are no ideals upon which to reconstruct them. *The Ceremony* shows the spiritual death of Japan implied in the emperor's renunciation of divinity gradually catching up in the postwar generation's refusal to participate in a crumbling society.

Each year that Oshima selected for a ceremony is a significant one in the postwar history of Japan and reflects on the mood of the film. 1947 was the beginning of the end for hopes of democracy; the Cold War was on, and so was the "Red Purge," while the emperor was kept on. In 1952, the U.S.-Japan Security Treaty had been put into effect, the Korean War was on with Japan as launching station and economic beneficiary, and the Japan Communist Party had severed relations with the radical student left which faltered without leadership. By 1961, the Security Treaty had been renewed despite massive bloody protest, the prime minister claiming it was the will of the "silent majority,"[60] and the decade was drifting off into prosperity and concern with the 1964 Summer Olympics in Tokyo. In 1971, the Security Treaty had again been renewed despite protest, and the Japanese intelligentsia was still reeling in shock over the suicide of new rightist author Yukio Mishima. Though few approved his act, it pointed out the crippling absence of spiritual values for the 1970s; in the aftermath of the defeated student activism of the late 1960s many radical leaders were dropping out and leaving Japan, while the rest began destroying each other with bitter factionalism.

The chronicle is replete with psychological turning points for the nation, but one of the least discussed is the 1956 wedding of Communist Uncle Isamu. As the organized left was deteriorating into the ineffectual "Song Movement," Isamu and his bride sing Party songs, but she is interrupted by Uncle Mamoru (Mutsuhiro Toura) who launches into a drinking song as he serves saké to the gathering. His is a sex song about the fear of castration, mentioning the folk heroine Sada Abe, the subject of Oshima's 1976 *Realm of the Senses*. The dramatic action thus points out the weakness of the Communists' song policy and raises the issue of sexual politics. Kazuomi tries to sing his school song and cannot remember the words; Setsuko finishes this anthem of the elite for him, reminding him of his loss of power and abuse of her. Masuo, called upon to sing rather than volunteering, is, as usual, immediately preempted by Terumichi. But Terumichi's song is about freedom of spirit and brotherhood, and no one else has ever heard it, an indication that his search for ideals will find no sympathizers. Ritsuko ends the singing with the most popular song of the year despite the efforts of the "Song Movement" to bring Party songs to the masses. "The Geisha Waltz" is about a shy woman following her man, which is precisely what Ritsuko ends up doing with her life. Each family member, through his song, ends by revealing not only the direction of his own character, but the confusion in society as a whole.

Moments such as Isamu's wedding and Masuo's mock wedding are full of symbolic complexity that pricks with humor as well. Just as

Isamu's strident bride has her song abruptly squelched, Masuo's "pure Japanese girl" of course does not exist. His impotent attempt to strike back by making love to his grandfather is painfully funny, as is the post-humous reading of Tadashi's manifesto. Masuo, while emerging the only survivor, sees his feelings as well as his intellectual goals subsumed by his physical passivity. Always wearing a slight frown and always feel-ing sorry for himself, he is the Everyman of the postwar world, and as unattractive as he is, Oshima makes us feel with him if not for him.

Inside Outside

Masuo of *The Ceremony* is one of a long line of unattractive personali-ties. Oshima's criminals, fanatics, neurotics and bludgeoned women have, from his very first sullen rather than pitiful child criminal, made his audience think rather than identify or emote. It has even been asserted that people go to see his films not because they like them, but because they are curious about what he will try next.[61] His own statement that he prefers complex structures implies an intellectual detachment and an unwillingness to expose his feelings directly in his work, although he admits he often does let his sentiment override his intellectual concerns. Throughout his work there always emerges a sense of ideological be-trayal, the clear conviction that the political and social realities of post-war Japan are morally wrong. It may well be this attitude of moral rectitude, which has caused him to make films condemning the state as well as the organized left, that inspired director Shohei Imamura to call Oshima a samurai while labeling himself a farmer. The strength of his films, in any case, has been the raising of the political and social issues with the personal twist of criminality and psychological complexity, and the refusal to offer easy solutions. In his insistence on bringing con-temporary problems to the screen, from economic class differences to xenophobia to Communism, he has been the standard-bearer for his age in the "different kind of film."

But changes may be in the offing. The radical Oshima who stated his views clearly in the early 1960s New Wave era, by the late 1960s be-comes a political "mumbler."[62] The reason is the greater importance he currently places on individual psychology, irrationality, and personal depth. A film like *Realm of the Senses*, with its uneasy but total rejection of politics and riveted concentration on two human beings, shows the full development of Oshima's new direction. Sada and her lover Kichizo are without complexes and are concerned only with pleasing each other. For the first time Oshima shows a sexual relationship of equality instead of showing the woman as sexually oppressed. Like all Oshima films, it is disturbing, but there is a more positive note to the uneasiness.

For the last four years, Oshima has been dealing with the problem of film's political inefficacy in a very constructive way. "No matter what political system we live under," he says," the people on the bottom stay there."[63] He had long felt that the oppressed women of Japan had no recourse, but in 1973 he became the host of an extraordinary women's morning television program. He interviews women who come to him with family problems (he is offscreen and the women are shown behind a distorting glass), often abandonment or abuse by their husbands. He patiently draws them out for a full explanation of their woes, tries to suggest new avenues of approach if not solutions, and in extreme cases confronts the offending relative or mate, shaming him into repentance. As the long run of the show indicates, Oshima is phenomenally success-ful. He feels that with this program he at last has a chance to do some-thing to help the people who await the social revolution that never comes, and whom he could not hope to reach with his films. This direct contact with the most pathetic women in Japanese society may even have been part of the inspiration behind *Realm of the Senses*, he says.[64]

Another change apparent with *Realm of the Senses* is that Oshima is moving outside of Japan for the production of his films. The director, whose work has always been intimately tied to Japanese society and psychology, and who told me in 1974 that he could not make films be-cause Japanese society was stagnating, now thinks it possible that he will make films abroad without even using a Japanese cast and dia-logue.[65] He wants only, he says, to be able to be more careful with each film he makes in the future, because he feels he will not make so very many. He has clear ideas of what he wants to do until he reaches the age of 50, but then he feels things may change again, for as he grows older his own grasp of history broadens, "although I don't feel that the age of the samurai is mine yet."[66] He admits he would like to be an international director, and even make films in the U.S. because he likes the chaos there, but as yet he has no answers for Japan. "Modernization may be all right," he says, "but Japan may lose its individuality at the same time."[67] What-ever he does next in the way of feature films, unpredictability will remain one of the delights of his work.

Notes

[1] Masao Matsuda, "Dojidai toshite no Oshima Nagisa" (Nagisa Oshima as My Contemporary), *Sekai no eiga sakka 6: Oshima Nagisa* (Film Directors of the World 6: Nagisa Oshima) (Tokyo: Kinema Jumposha, 1970), p. 40.

[2] Ruth McCormick, "Ritual, the Family and the State: A Critique of Nagisa Oshima's *The Ceremony,*" *Cinéaste* (New York), vol. 6, No. 2, 1972, p. 21.

[3] Joan Mellen, *Voices from the Japanese Cinema* (New York: Liveright, 1975), p. 258.

[4] Ian Cameron, ed., *Second Wave* (New York: Praeger, 1970), p. 98.

[5] Nagisa Oshima, "Nihon eiga 80 nendai e no chobo" (Prospects for Japanese Cinema in the 1980s), *Eiga Hihyo* (Film Criticism, Tokyo), Sept. 1973, p. 19.

[6] Author's conversation with Nagisa Oshima, April 1977.

[7] Oshima, *op. cit.*, p. 19.

[8] Yoshikuni Murayama, "Oshima Nagisa e no jerashii" (Jealousy of Nagisa Oshima), *Sekai no eiga sakka 6, op. cit.*, p. 68.

[9] Masaki Kobayashi quoted in Mellen, *op. cit.*, p. 258.

[10] Oshima conversation, *cit.*

[11] Nagisa Oshima, *Taikenteki sengo eizo ron* (A Theory of the Postwar Film Image Based on Personal Experience) (Tokyo: Asahi Shimbunsha, 1975), p. 137.

[12] "Oshima Nagisa jiden to jisaku o kataru" (Nagisa Oshima Talks about Himself and His Films), *Sekai no eiga sakka 6, op. cit.*, p. 72.

[13] Nagisa Oshima, "Waga eiga, waga hanzai" (My Films, My Crimes), *ibid.*, p. 217.

[14] "Oshima Nagisa jiden to jisaku o kataru," *ibid.*, p. 73.

[15] *Ibid.*, p. 73.

[16] Oshima, *Taikenteki sengo eizo ron, op. cit.*, pp. 54–55.

[17] *Ibid.*, p. 41.

[18] Tadao Sato, *Oshima Nagisa no sekai* (The World of Nagisa Oshima) (Tokyo: Chikuma Shobo, 1973), p. 30.

[19] Oshima, *Taikenteki sengo eizo ron, op. cit.*, pp. 138–39.

[20] *Ibid.*, p. 142.

[21] *Ibid.*, pp. 152–53.

[22] "Oshima Nagisa jiden to jisaku o kataru," *op. cit.*, p. 73.

[23] *Ibid.*, p. 74.

[24] Oshima, *Taikenteki sengo eizo ron, op. cit.*, p. 145.

[25] *Ibid.*, p. 147.

[26] *Ibid.*, p. 137.

[27] "Oshima Nagisa jiden to jisaku o kataru," *op. cit.*, p. 76.

[28] Nagisa Oshima, *Sengo eiga: Hakai to sozo* (Postwar Film: Destruction and Creation) (Tokyo: Sanichi Shobo, 1963), p. 26.

[29] "Oshima Nagisa jiden to jisaku o kataru," *op. cit.*, p. 77.

[30] *Ibid.*, p. 76.

[31] Tadao Sato, *Nihon eiga shiso shi* (History of the Intellectual Currents in Japanese Film) (Tokyo: Sanichi Shobo, 1970), p. 378.

[32] Oshima, *Sengo eiga: Hakai to sozo, op. cit.*, p. 37.

[33] Sato, *Nihon eiga shiso shi, op. cit.*, p. 381.

[34] Oshima, "Nihon eiga 80 nendai e no chobo," *op. cit.*, p. 20.

[35] Sato, *Nihon eiga shiso shi, op. cit.*, p. 382.

[36] *Ibid.*, p. 384.

[37] *Ibid.*, p. 384.

[38] Oshima, "Waga eiga, waga hanzai," *Sekai no eiga sakka 6, op. cit.*, p. 215.

[39] *Ibid.*, p. 215.

[40] *Ibid.*, p. 216.

[41] Oshima conversation, *cit.*
[42] McCormick, *op. cit.*, p. 27.
[43] Oshima, "Waga eiga, waga hanzai," *op. cit.*, p. 216.
[44] Nagisa Oshima interview *Newsweek,*(Asian edition), Nov. 15, 1976.
[45] Oshima conversation, *cit.*
[46] *Ibid.*
[47] *Ibid.*
[48] Cameron, *op. cit.*, p. 65.
[49] Sato, *Oshima Nagisa no sekai, op. cit.*, p. 54.
[50] Oshima conversation, *cit.*
[51] Oshima, "Waga eiga, waga hanzai," *op. cit.*, p. 219.
[52] Oshima conversation, *cit.*
[53] Ian Cameron, "Nagisa Oshima : Interview," *Movie* (London), No. 17, Winter 1969–70, p. 12.
[54] Oshima, "Waga eiga, waga hanzai," *op. cit.*, p. 218.
[55] Oshima conversation, *cit.*
[56] *Ibid.*
[57] *Ibid.*
[58] McCormick, *op. cit.*, p. 27.
[59] Nei Kawarabata, "Gishiki no tame no kuronikuru" (Chronicle for *The Ceremony*), *Sekai no eiga sakka 6, op. cit.*, p. 221.
[60] *Ibid.*, p. 222.
[61] Tadao Sato, "The Idol of the Age : Nagisa Oshima, A Standard Bearer for Denunciation," (Program Notes for Oshima Retrospective at New York Museum of Modern Art, 1971), p. 1.
[62] Sato, *Oshima Nagisa no sekai, op. cit.*, p. 303.
[63] Oshima conversation, *cit.*
[64] *Ibid.*
[65] *Ibid.*
[66] *Ibid.*
[67] *Ibid.*

NAGISA OSHIMA: FILMOGRAPHY

1959 *A Town of Love and Hope (Ai to Kibo no Machi)*
pr: Shochiku (Ofuna); orig. sc: Oshima; 'scope ph: Hiroshi Kusuda; music: Riichiro Manabe; cast: Hiroshi Fujikawa, Yuko Mochizuki, Fumio Watanabe, Kakuko Chino, Yuki Tominaga et al. Social comment film pointing out class distinctions and the origins of criminal tendencies. A poor boy becomes friends with a rich girl. He has a pigeon he sells because he needs money, but it is a homing pigeon, so he can sell it over and over again. The bird becomes the symbol of his friendship for the girl as well, but in the end she has her brother shoot and kill it. (Non-circulating print and negative at Shochiku, Tokyo.)

1960 **Cruel Story of Youth/Naked Youth, a Story of Cruelty (Seishun Zankoku Monogatari)*
pr: Shochiku (Ofuna); orig. sc: Oshima; color 'scope ph: Ko Kawamata; music: Riichiro Manabe; cast: Yusuke Kawazu, Miyuki Kuwano, Yoshiko Kuga, Fumio Watanabe, Shinji Tanaka et al. Youth genre film about rebellious delinquents. The boy and girl set up a badger game blackmail racket, but treat each other just as brutally as their victims. Different from the usual delinquent films in that the young lovers discover they are not free after all. (FC, SH)

*The Sun's Burial (Taiyo no Hakaba)
pr: Shochiku (Ofuna); orig. sc: Oshima and Toshiro Ishido; color 'scope ph: Ko Kawamata; music: Riichiro Manabe; cast: Kayoko Honoo, Isao Sasaki, Masahiko Tsugawa, Koji Nakahara, Yusuke Kawazu et al. Petty crime and a morbid look at life in a slum, made with an undertone of the political dissatisfaction toward the Japan-U.S. Security Treaty. Semidocumentary treatment of a slum girl who lives by selling black-market blood in the daytime and prostitution at night. Her militarist father manages a gang of thieves whose earnings will go toward starting the war over again. The title is an obvious symbol for the disillusionment with present-day Japan. (SH)

Night and Fog in Japan (Nihon no Yoru to Kiri)
pr: Shochiku (Ofuna); orig. sc: Oshima and Toshiro Ishido; color 'scope ph: Ko Kawamata; music: Riichiro Manabe; cast: Fumio Watanabe, Miyuki Kuwano, Masahiko Tsugawa, Akiko Koyama, Mutsuhiro Toura et al. A film of political discourse against the traditional Japanese left, assessment of the tactical errors of the student movement, and a call for action to the new left. The production company's anger over the film, and the assassination of a Socialist Party leader a few days after its release, caused its immediate withdrawal from circulation. Oshima reacted by starting his own production company, Sozosha. *KJ* #10. (FC; negative at Shochiku, Tokyo.)

1961 *The Catch (Shiiku)*
pr: Palace Film Prod./Taiho; orig. story: Kenzaburo Oe; sc: Tsutomu Tamura, Toshio Matsumoto, Toshiro Ishido and Teruaki Tomatsu; 'scope ph: Yoshitsugu Tonegawa; music: Riichiro Manabe; cast: Rentaro Mikuni, Sadako Sawamura, Masako Nakamura, Eiko Oshima, Jun Hamamura et al. A black

American airman is captured in a small village during the last summer of WW II. He is used as a scapegoat for all the psychological ills of the villagers, and they end by killing him, the war having ended without their being able to turn him over to the authorities. The mean behavior of the adults is highlighted by the reactions of the village children. *KJ* #9. (No circulating prints; dupe positive at Sozosha, Tokyo.)

1962   *Shiro Tokisada from Amakusa (Amakusa Shiro Tokisada)*
pr: Toei; orig. sc: Oshima and Toshiro Ishido; 'scope ph: Shintaro Kawasaki; music: Riichiro Manabe; cast: Hashizo Okawa, Satomi Oka, Ryutaro Otomo, Rentaro Mikuni, Sayuri Tachikawa et al. Period drama about the insurrections of Japanese Christians in 1637–38. The rebellion, led by Shiro, was ruthlessly squelched, and only resulted in worse persecution of Christians and the severing of relations with the west. Parable of the student movement. (No circulating prints; negative at Toei, Tokyo.)

1965   *Pleasures of the Flesh (Etsuraku)*
pr: Sozosha/Shochiku; orig. story: Futaro Yamada; sc: Oshima; color 'scope ph: Akira Takada; music: Joji Yuasa; cast: Katsuo Nakamura, Mariko Kaga, Yumiko Nogawa, Masako Yagi, Toshiko Higuchi et al. A poor young man is entrusted with an embezzler's money until the man gets out of prison. He cannot go to the police because the embezzler was witness to a murder the young man committed. He decides to spend all the money on women and then commit suicide, but he discovers this life is empty. Parable of the newly rich Japanese nation, now without ideals. (SH)

  The Diary of Yunbogi (Yunbogi no Nikki)
pr: Sozosha/Shibata Organization; orig. diary: Yunbogi Yi; sc: Oshima; ph: Oshima; music: Takatoshi Naito. Montage documentary of photographs taken by Oshima in Korea. Centers on Japanese prejudice against Koreans and the struggle of poor children in the big cities to make a living. (GR)

1966   *Violence at Noon (Hakuchu no Torima)*
pr: Sozosha/Shochiku; orig. story: Taijun Takeda; sc: Tsutomu Tamura; 'scope ph: Akira Takada; music: Hikaru Hayashi; cast: Saeda Kawaguchi, Akiko Koyama, Kei Sato, Mutsuhiro Toura, Hosei Komatsu et al. The failure of ideals in contemporary Japan centered around the activities of a sex criminal. A village schoolteacher tries to start a collective farm, but it fails. The son of the village headman commits suicide, and his girlfriend tries to die with him. While she is unconscious, she is raped by the teacher's husband who goes on to wander around the country raping and killing women. His wife eventually commits suicide. The only glimmer of hope is in the character of the girl, who is neither dead nor a criminal, but a personification of the mass of the people who will simply go on living. *KJ* #9. (FC, PFA/SH)

1967   *Band of Ninja (Ninja Bugeicho)*
pr: Sozosha/ATG; orig. comic strip: Sampei Shirato; sc: Oshima and Mamoru Sasaki; ph: Akira Takada, using Shirato's drawings; music: Hikaru Hayashi; voices: Shoichi Ozawa, Kei Yamamoto, Akiko Koyama, Kei Sato, Noriko

Matsumoto et al. Period drama centering around resistance to the forces of Nobunaga Oda, unifier of Japan in the sixteenth century. *KJ* #10. (No circulating prints; negative at ATG, Tokyo.)

A Treatise on Japanese Bawdy Song/Sing a Song of Sex (Nihon Shunka-ko)

pr: Sozosha/Shochiku; orig. sc: Tsutomu Tamura, Mamoru Sasaki, Toshio Tajima and Oshima; color 'scope ph: Akira Takada; music: Hikaru Hayashi; cast: Ichiro Araki, Hideko Yoshida, Akiko Koyama, Ichizo Itami, Kazuko Tajima et al. A group of provincial high school students have come to Tokyo for their university entrance examinations. Thoroughly disillusioned with the progressive ideals of the older generation and seeing no hope for the future, they react to the alienation they feel in Tokyo by singing bawdy songs together. However, when a Korean girl student sings a song about prostitutes during the period of Japanese dominion in Korea, their songs lose their effect. They end by strangling, in their collective imagination, a girl from a rich family who has been the object of their sexual fantasy. Clear emergence of Oshima's themes of discontented youth, fantasy, and the Korean problem. (Noncirculating print and negative at Shochiku, Tokyo.)

Japanese Summer: Double Suicide (Muri Shinju Nihon no Natsu)

pr: Sozosha/Shochiku; orig. sc: Tsutomu Tamura, Mamoru Sasaki and Oshima; color 'scope ph: Yasuhiro Yoshioka; music: Hikaru Hayashi; cast: Keiko Sakurai, Kei Sato, Mutsuhiro Toura, Hosei Komatsu, Taiji Tonoyama et al. A study of traditional double suicide with the modern twist of insincerity. A man is looking for someone who is willing to kill him, and a woman is looking for someone who is willing to make love to her. These two meet and voluntarily get involved in a gang war. Just before being shot by the police, they suddenly commit suicide. Unlike the situation in the traditional love suicide, the man does not love the woman, but simply wishes to die. (Non-circulating print and negative at Shochiku, Tokyo.)

1968   ### *Death by Hanging (Koshikei)

pr: Sozosha/ATG; orig. sc: Tsutomu Tamura, Mamoru Sasaki, Michinori Fukao and Oshima; ph: Yasuhiro Yoshioka; music: Hikaru Hayashi; cast: Akiko Koyama, Yundo Yun, Kei Sato, Fumio Watanabe, Toshiro Ishido et al; narration: Oshima. Based on the actual story of a Korean high school student who raped and killed two girls in 1958 and was hanged in 1963 when he reached maturity. In Oshima's film the execution fails and a whole series of comic but gruesome attempts at eliciting confession and reenactment of the crime ensues. Focuses on attitudes toward capital punishment and treatment of Koreans in Japan. *KJ* #3. (GR)

Three Resurrected Drunkards (Kaette Kita Yopparai)

pr: Sozosha/Shochiku; orig. sc: Tsutomu Tamura, Mamoru Sasaki, Masao Adachi and Oshima; color 'scope ph: Yasuhiro Yoshioka; music: Hikaru Hayashi; cast: Kazuhiko Kato, Osamu Kitayama, Norihiko Hashida, Kei Sato, Fumio Watanabe, Mako Midori et al. Funny story of political mixups over who is Korean and who is not, beginning when a Korean army deserter steals the clothes of a Japanese high school student while he swims with two friends. The three students are pursued by police, "deported" to Korea and sent to fight with U.S. troops in Vietman. (Positive and negative at Shochiku, Tokyo.)

1969   *Diary of a Shinjuku Thief (Shinjuku Dorobo Nikki)*
pr: Sozosha/ATG; orig. sc: Tsutomu Tamura, Mamoru Sasaki, Masao Adachi and Oshima; BW and color ph: Yasuhiro Yoshioka and Seizo Sengen; cast: Tadanori Yokoo, Rie Yokoyama, Moichi Tanabe, Tetsu Takahashi, Juro Kara et al. Life in Tokyo's busiest cheap entertainment district, largely in documentary form, held together by the sex problems of a young man who steals books and the girl he gets involved with. *KJ* #8. (GR)

Boy (Shonen)
pr: Sozosha/ATG; orig. sc: Tsutomu Tamura; 'scope BW and color ph: Yasuhiro Yoshioka and Seizo Sengen; music: Hikaru Hayashi; cast: Fumio Watanabe, Akiko Koyama, Tetsuo Abe, Tsuyoshi Kinoshita et al. Study of a different kind of criminality based on actual events. A couple train their small child to run in front of passing cars and pretend to be injured. They then demand immediate financial compensation from the frightened drivers. They are caught, but the boy cannot be made to confess. *KJ* #3. (GR)

1970   *The Man Who Left His Will on Film (Tokyo Senso Sengo Hiwa)*
pr: Sozosha/ATG; orig. idea: Oshima and Tsutomu Tamura; sc: Masataka Hara and Mamoru Sasaki; ph: Toichiro Narushima; music: Toru Takemitsu; cast: Kazuo Goto, Emiko Iwasaki, Sugio Fukuoka, Tomoyo Oshima, Kenichi Fukuda et al. A group of high school students feel that they are participating in revolutionary activity by filming the student demonstrations of the "Tokyo War" of 1969. One boy thinks one of their comrades committed suicide in the midst of the filming, but on screening the film that was in his camera, he finds it is nothing but nondescript street scenes. He gradually discovers that they are scenes that all relate to his own life, and in the end he commits suicide. Themes of the meaning of revolutionary activity, despair and frustration of the young, responsibility for other human beings, and fantasy realization. (NY)

1971   *The Ceremony (Gishiki)*
pr: Sozosha/ATG; orig. sc: Tsutomu Tamura, Mamoru Sasaki and Oshima; color 'scope ph: Toichiro Narushima; music: Toru Takemitsu; cast: Kenzo Kawarazaki, Atsuo Nakamura, Akiko Koyama, Atsuko Kaku, Kei Sato et al. Chronicle of a wealthy provincial family from the end of the war to the present, seen mainly at ceremonial occasions such as weddings and funerals when they are all forced to assemble. The relationships, observed mostly through the eyes of one son born in Manchuria, are discouragingly complex but all dominated by the authoritarian grandfather, against whom various family members react in different ways. Themes of feudalistic vestiges in the contemporary family, militarism, the disillusionment of the young. *KJ* #1. (NY)

1973   *Summer Sister (Natsu no Imoto)*
pr: Sozosha/ATG; orig. sc: Tsutomu Tamura, Mamoru Sasaki and Oshima; color ph: Yasuhiro Yoshioka; music: Toru Takemitsu; cast: Hiromi Kurita,

Shoji Ishibashi, Akiko Koyama, Kei Sato, Hosei Komatsu et al. A girl living in Tokyo receives a letter from a boy in Okinawa who claims to be her long-lost brother. He invites her to come to Okinawa for the summer, and she goes. She meets a young tourist guide on arrival there and falls in love with him, only to find that he is her brother. In the end she concludes that he is an imposter and returns to gather her strength to find her real brother. Themes of confused lineage, as in *The Ceremony*, potential incest, and the present and past status of Okinawa vis-à-vis Japan. Oshima's last film before the dissolution of Sozosha. (No circulating prints; negative at ATG, Tokyo.)

1976 *The Realm of the Senses (Ai no Koriida)*
pr: Oshima Prod./Anatole Doman/Argos Film/Oceanique; orig. sc: Oshima; color ph: Hideo Ito; music: Minoru Miki; cast: Eiko Matsuda, Tatsuya Fuji, Aoi Nakajima, Taiji Tonoyama, Akiko Koyama et al. Controversial hard-core pornography, but with something of an Oshima touch. Based on an actual incident during the militaristic 1930s concerning a maid at a Japanese inn who falls in love with the married owner. The two begin a competition for ecstasy locked away in a small inn room. When he realizes that her greatest pleasure comes from strangling him while making love, he gives permission for her to kill him. She then castrates his corpse and wanders around town with his member growing putrid until the police apprehend her. She becomes a folk heroine. A very close study of individual psychology that eschews politics except to show troops marching as the man skulks by, well-done sets and music, and dialogue that appeals strongly to women. Selected and then pulled because of censorship during the 1976 New York Film Festival.

1978 *The Phantom of Love (Ai no Borei)*
pr: Oshima Prod./Anatole Doman; orig. sc: Oshima; color ph: Yoshio Miyajima; music: Toru Takemitsu; cast: Tatsuya Fuji, Takahiro Tamura, Kazuko Yoshiyuki et al.

MASAHIRO SHINODA

1931—

Shinoda's work has a unique freshness,
a dazzling flamboyance that gives him
a place in Japanese film history.

—Kon Ichikawa

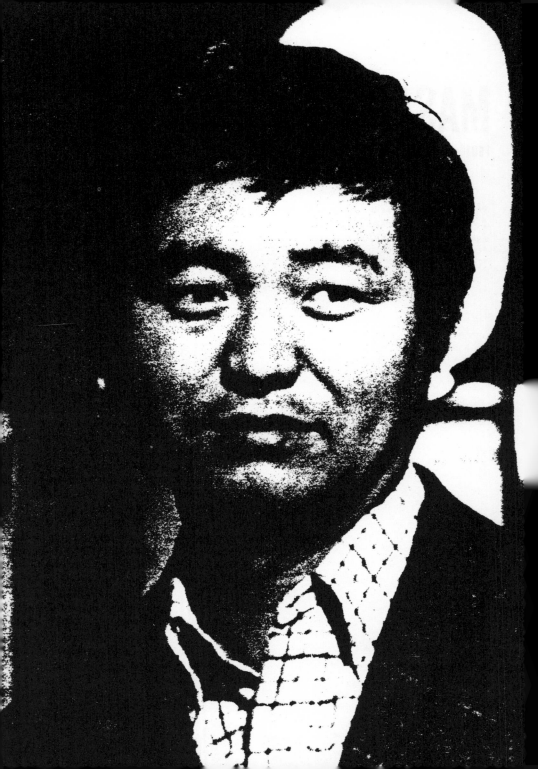

Few human beings possess the energy of a Masahiro Shinoda. Not only has he been producing feature films at a steady rate and with considerable success since 1960, but he has made numerous documentaries and dramatic reconstructions for television, researched and written on his idols Yasujiro Ozu and Kenji Mizoguchi, and expounded at great length on everything from Japanese politics to archaeology to theater for many a captivated listener, including me.

One may not agree with Shinoda's elaborate theories of violence, sex and masochism as constituting the essence of the Japanese character, but his boyish charm and chronic enthusiasm tend to overwhelm any counter arguments. Similarly in his films, these ideas may not be readily acceptable to all, but his ability to express them in a startlingly beautiful form never fails to impress. In his quest for the psychological constants of the Japanese character in the filmic medium, his insistence on his own personal, often eccentric, presentation makes him exemplify the great gains staked out for individualism by the New Wave generation of the 1960s.

A product of the same "Ofuna Nouvelle Vague" as Nagisa Oshima, Shinoda's progress has been slower, more cautious, and directed toward a different kind of expression from that of his colleague. Beginning with contemporary dramas for Shochiku, Shinoda set out with determination and diplomacy to treat subjects he had long loved: sports (*Sapporo Winter Olympic Games*, 1972, and a 1976 television documentary on *Ondekoza*, a traditional folk music and marathon-running ensemble); Japanese theater aesthetics (*Double Suicide*, 1969, and *The Scandalous Adventures of Buraikan*, 1970); and psychological turning points in Japanese history, which he studied in all of his period films. Even in his earlier films for Shochiku, before he went into the period genre and independent production, he was exploring ancient psychology and aesthetics in contemporary settings with works like *Pale Flower* (1963) and *With Beauty and Sorrow* (1965). Instead of pinpointing moments in the contemporary consciousness of the Japanese and showing the nation's moral failures as Oshima has done, Shinoda is, he says, "not interested in the future or in utopian ideals. I would like to be able to take hold of the past and make it stand still so that I can examine it from different angles."[1]

Shinoda's aesthetic concerns and belief in the immutability of the violent human condition are close to Mizoguchi's fatalism cast in exquisite beauty. But in his more theoretical approach he resembles his contemporary and fellow Waseda University graduate, Shohei Imamura. For both of them the visible surface of actions or events serves mainly to provide clues to the psychological currents of the civilization giving rise to them. Shinoda insists, "Reality for its own sake is not what interests me. If my films had to be perfect reconstructions of reality, I would not make them. I begin with reality and see what higher idea comes out of it."[2] It is this analytical impulse that brings a modern self-referentialism into Shinoda's technique, an extension of the Mizoguchi-like detached beauty in the rush of his protagonists to their fate of doom.

First Loves

Shinoda was born on March 9, 1931, into one of the most illustrious families in Gifu Prefecture. His ancestors had been large landowners and village headmen in a small town that is now part of Gifu City, and they had a tradition of literary and artistic association. His great-uncle was the model for the hero of Toson Shimazaki's novel *Yoake-mae* (Before Dawn),[3] and his cousin, Toko Shinoda, who is responsible for much of the striking design of *Double Suicide,* is one of Japan's leading abstract calligraphers. Shinoda's father was an engineer, and his mother's family, also of distinguished lineage, had been in the paper lantern and umbrella business—Shinoda admits that the shot of a mass of open paper umbrellas in his 1964 *Assassination* shows a bit of personal nostalgia for this past.[4] The industrialization of Japan took its toll on the family business; thus his father always encouraged him to pursue a career in science, telling him that the opportunities of the new age lay there.[5]

The obedient boy applied himself to studying physics and mathematics in middle school, as well as to mid-distance running, in which he became champion of a four-prefecture district. But at the end of the Pacific War Shinoda experienced the sense of betrayal so many felt, and he blamed science for having been instrumental in waging the war.[6] He abandoned scientific studies and turned wholeheartedly to literature. Like Kenji Mizoguchi before him, he developed a passion for the atmospheric works of Kyoka Izumi and he recalls that his admiration for Kon Ichikawa started when he saw his 1956 adaptation of Kyoka's *Nihombashi.*[7]

When the time came to enter university, Shinoda had no taste for what he considered the scholasticism of the national universities, and he chose Waseda University, where he could run as well as study. The combination of literary and athletic loves proved problematical, however, because the right-wing athletes strongly disapproved of his marching in demonstrations and carrying placards with his Marxist-Leninist literary friends.[8] His dilemma was solved, unfortunately, by a leg injury that forced him to give up running, but his love for sports would later manifest itself particularly in the cross-country ski racing scenes of *Sapporo Winter Olympic Games* and the running practice sequences of his documentary on the *Ondekoza* troupe.

While many of the master directors of previous generations, such as Mizoguchi, Kurosawa and Ichikawa, came to film from painting, Shinoda and his contemporaries Oshima and Imamura emerged from backgrounds in drama. Shinoda is the only one of the three, however, who studied mainly theater history at university. Waseda has a long tradition of being a major school for drama studies, and Shinoda had the opportunity to study under the very best professors in the field of early Japanese theater, Masakatsu Gunji and Shigetoshi Kawatake, the latter a descendant of the Edo Period Kabuki playwright Mokuami Kawatake. But Shinoda did not study drama simply because these luminaries were accessible.

Ever since the end of the war, Shinoda had felt a passionate need to know Japan and examine why its political and economic peculiarities had led it into the war. This search for the essence of the Japanese national character, the same search he would transfer to film, led him back to the Middle Ages. Beginning with an interest in the belief in vengeful ghosts, he learned that the popular theatrical forms that had given rise to Noh drama had been invented by lowly outcasts who had been taken in by the military leaders of the fourteenth century. From this study of the beginning of Noh he moved to the inception of puppet drama and Kabuki theater in the Edo Period. Shinoda felt the secrets of the art of the Japanese must be somehow connected with the emergence of Noh and Bunraku.[9]

Shinoda developed a special love for the work of the playwright Monzaemon Chikamatsu (1653–1725), which he both adapted and analyzed in *Double Suicide*. Again he found significant the fact that Bunraku and Kabuki were arts of the people and that Chikamatsu himself had given up his samurai rank to become a man of the theater, an outcast profession. Later Shinoda became fascinated with the grotesque and frivolous atmosphere of Kabuki in the late Edo Period, particularly with the work of Mokuami (1816–93), which he felt resembled the spirit of contemporary underground theater.[10] He later translated this for the screen with *The Scandalous Adventures of Buraikan*. Shinoda planned to continue his studies of theater history at Waseda University Graduate School, but the traumatic death of his mother prevented this.

New Wave Diapers

Shinoda said that with the death of his mother, who had supported his studies with extreme difficulty, he could not continue. "Without my patroness," he said, "I was forced to go to work."[11] He knew nothing about film, having seen very few movies, but he rushed to take one of the few company entrance examinations that still remained to be given in the following April.[12] In 1953, the year before Oshima was hired, Shinoda was one of eight selected to become an assistant director at Sho-chiku's Ofuna studios out of some 2,000 applicants.[13] He was relieved to have found a job.

For the next six years Shinoda labored as an assistant under almost all of Shochiku's established directors and earned the reputation of a "great assistant."[14] Although in later years he has extolled Shochiku's director system for cultivating strong personalities, many of whom be-came independent directors,[15] at the time he found that in the produc-tion company, unlike in the university, intelligence meant nothing and he was best off keeping his ideas to himself while doing everything he was told. "The main thing I learned," he said, "was that if I became a director myself, under no circumstances would I use the kind of scripts Shochiku was then using."[16]

His chance came with the decline of the company finances and the desperate decision to gamble on the young. After the critical success of Oshima's 1959 *A Town of Love and Hope*, Shinoda was called in for his interview with president Shiro Kido, during which Shinoda expounded his ideas about Yasujiro Ozu's camera angle "like an aloof reclining deity observing the human world."[17] Kido decided to make him a director, but instead of being allowed to make his own prize-winning scenario, Shino-da was assigned a company script. Always a persuasive talker, however, he wore his superiors down to the point where they gave him permission to use his story about the cold-bloodedness of the pop music promotion business on the condition that he adapt it to the current Neil Sedaka hit song, "One-Way Ticket to the Blues." Shiro Kido was pleased enough with Shinoda's 1960 *One-Way Ticket for Love* to shake his hand after the first screening, but the film was a commercial failure, and Shinoda once more found himself an assistant director.

The "Ofuna Nouvelle Vague" was not a unified movement, and for Shinoda it meant something quite different from what it meant for Oshi-ma. Although Shinoda is anything but proud of his earliest efforts—"I made those when I was still at the diaper stage of filmmaking"[18] (he even told Shochiku not to let me see them)—they reveal how different his approach would be from Oshima's. Shinoda has never been as radical as Oshima, although he has said it is "filmmakers that should bear witness to the politics of their age."[19] For Shinoda, the most significant political event of his life was the end of the Pacific War because, he says, "I was just like Yukio Mishima [1925–70]; I really believed the emperor was a god and that I should die for him."[20] Instead of using his film-making as an agitation technique, Shinoda worked on perfecting his directorial skills and commenting on the spiritual emptiness of postwar Japanese life by assessing tradition in conflict with new American in-fluences. Less threatening to the Shochiku establishment than the volatile Oshima, he would stay on until 1965, when he quit only out of sympathy with the union.

The opportunities Shinoda found in the Ofuna Nouvelle Vague up-heaval set him apart from the stoical severity of Oshima and Yoshida for his "almost reckless sensuality and realism."[21] When he was recalled to directing after the success of Oshima's *Cruel Story of Youth* in 1960, he was told to make "a very gutsy film."[22] Immediately he set about finding an anti-Shochiku kind of scenario, employing the young poet Shuji Terayama (1935–). Terayama had never written a script, but Shinoda had read his poetry and found his wit to be strangely captivat-ing. In the course of writing the script for the 1960 *Dry Lake*, a story about a student fanatic set during the anti-U.S.-Japan Security Treaty demonstrations, they agreed that for Japanese there was no such thing as revolution, only terrorism.[23] In many ways the film predicts the de-terioration of the student movement into factional terrorism in the 1970s. Terayama would later become not only a frequent collaborator with Shinoda, but a playwright and director of his own underground theater troupe, as well as director of such powerful if idiosyncratic films as *Pastoral Hide and Seek* (*Denen ni Shisu*, 1974).

Shinoda also felt a need to bring musical innovation into his films. "During the war we weren't allowed to listen to western music, except that by classical German composers," he explains, "so I became an avid fan of American jazz, rock, and all forms of modern music."[24] For *Dry Lake* he also sought out the as yet unknown composer Toru Takemitsu, who was bedridden with tuberculosis at the time. Having heard Takemit-su's "Hallucination Requiem," Shinoda instinctively knew he wanted to work with him,[25] and much of the distinctive character of his films ever since has been the brooding, twanging music of this now internationally recognized avant-garde composer. Although Shinoda would make more conventional films for two years after the Nouvelle Vague year, he would maintain a deep concern with musical innovation during this "diaper stage."

City Images

With his 1962 *Tears on the Lion's Mane* Shinoda at last came into his own. "For the first time," he has said, "I was able to create the kind of film I wanted."[26] The company had been assigning him melodramas and Shochiku regular staff members, but now he was working with Terayama and Takemitsu again. Ever since *One-Way Ticket for Love*, he had seen American rock music as the antithesis of what Japanese tradition values in song and drama: sentimentality or the "tears" that are part of that film's title. The heavy-beat, strident rock of the early 1960s performed by Japanese seemed utterly "grotesque,"[27] and *Tears on the Lion's Mane* shows the protagonist suppressing his tears by launching into loud song accompanied by his gyrations. The effect is all the more disquieting because he has just learned that the man he was told to rough up, and whom he has accidentally killed, was his girlfriend's father. Unlike the youth rebels of other films, this young man has been acting in accordance with the traditional Japanese code of obligation—to a man he believes once saved his life. The boy thinks he is as wild as a lion in a zoo, but in actuality he finds he is the victim of his own sentimental loyalty to a liar and, like the lion, he is really caged—hence the title of the film. Since making this 1962 film, Shinoda has been analyzing the traditional attitudes that permeate the contemporary Japanese mentality despite the veneer of western thought and appearances.

Tears on the Lion's Mane is set on the Yokohama waterfront, and for his next film as well Shinoda chose the cold modernity of this great port city as backdrop for further probing into traditions lingering in the contemporary consciousness. In his 1963 *Pale Flower* he set out to explore ceremonial behavior, focusing on gangster organizations because "The gang world is the only place where the Japanese ceremonial structure can be fully sustained," and he was interested in an "aesthetic response to ceremony, particularly the *hanafuda* [flower card] game."[28] He secured an introduction into the gangster card games from the police (naturally), and interpreted what he saw in a film that he claims became the model for the *yakuza* (gangster) genre that has been the mainstay of the Toei production company since the mid-1960s.[29]

In *Pale Flower* the themes of Shinoda's mature work appear in a unified expression. Compared with the waterfront boy of *Tears on the Lion's Mane*, Murakami (Ryo Ikebe), the gangster hero of *Pale Flower*, is more obviously fated, more obviously masochistic. He is not being deceived by a false guardian like the boy, but kills "when his turn comes," fully accepting this obligation in exchange for the paternalism of the organization. The familial and ceremonial elements of the gangster milieu are so important that Shinoda muses, "If I ever make another gangster film it would have no violence at all. The boss would be a gentle father figure and the dialogue would all be polite greetings like 'good morning' and 'good evening'—like an Ozu film."[30]

Pale Flower also exemplifies the masochism that Shinoda finds inherent in erotic and aesthetic impulses. Murakami is irresistibly drawn to a beautiful woman, Mariko Kaga, who seeks games with larger and larger gambling stakes, drives her sports car at maniacal speeds, and courts danger as a revitalizing thrill. At a point where she is becoming attracted to drugs, Murakami volunteers to perform the next retaliation murder required by the gang—it is not his "turn" because he has just returned

from serving time—in order to provide her with "a bigger thrill than anything else" she can imagine, that of watching the murder. The thrill for
both of them lies not in the murder itself, however, but in the fact that
Murakami gives up his freedom for it. Smiling as he is led away to jail
again, he has destroyed himself solely for this woman's pleasure. Shinoda
is convinced that "no Japanese can die for freedom, but it is very Japanese to die for beauty and aesthetic purity."[31] In the Yokohama films,
set in a city representing western rationalism, the protagonists throw
themselves away for pure loyalty and a woman's pure pleasure.

From the modernity of Yokohama, Shinoda turned to the city that
symbolizes its antithesis, Kyoto. His brain-twisting explanation of his
appreciation of this city is that "only in Kyoto does Japan's ancient
beauty fail to survive, or rather, one could say it survives, but as a
dead thing."[32] Finding this contrariness in the old capital of Japan, he set
out to translate it into film with a story of human relationships just as
contrary.

The people in *With Beauty and Sorrow* (1965), an adaptation of a
story by Yasunari Kawabata (1899–1972),[33] are warped in a way that
again displays Shinoda's belief in the destiny of erotic masochism. The
beautiful and jealous apprentice (Mariko Kaga, the dangerous woman in
Pale Flower) of a woman painter decides to destroy the married man her
teacher once loved, was abandoned by, and still sees when he comes to
Kyoto. The man becomes fascinated with the apprentice and sleeps with
her, but her revenge plan carries her to the seduction and apparent murder of his son. All along both the teacher and the man are enthralled by
the girl's destructiveness, not quite believing she is capable of such di-
abolical acts. The girl herself, prey to a consuming love for her teacher,
almost drowns along with the boy in the boating accident she causes.
The irrational compulsions driving the characters of what Kawabata
called the best film adaptation of any of his works[34] assume the role of
a fated doom.

In both *Pale Flower* and *With Beauty and Sorrow*, films of contrasting
aesthetics, Shinoda expounds the same theory of eroticism and love.
Love is always heightened by the risk of disaster, and that risk becomes a
certainty as soon as jealousy emerges. The gangster Murakami sees the
Chinese drug pusher as a threat to his relationship with the bewitching
gambler, and the angelic apprentice becomes a demon with jealousy.
The gangster knows that the price he will have to pay for entertaining the
woman is his freedom, and the apprentice knows she may lose her own
life in destroying her rival's son. Masochism and murder for the sake of
ideal, pure, beautiful love as mapped out in the horrifying symbolic acts
of these contemporary dramas carries through all of Shinoda's works,
extending even to his recent period films.

The masochistic gambler personality appears in Shinoda's first period films as well as in his contemporary city works. Hachiro Kiyokawa (Tetsuro Tamba), the hero of the 1964 *Assassination* (which some, including Kon Ichikawa, consider Shinoda's best film),[35] gambles with politics and his own life at the end of the Edo Period, and loses. Behind his assassination is the implication that the Meiji emperor himself was a wily politician. The little man hero of *Samurai Spy* (1965) is likewise a helpless pawn in baffling power struggles of an earlier upheaval surrounding the establishment of the Edo military dictatorship. *Clouds at Sunset* (1967), more modern and yet a kind of period film set around 1937, shows how a political system requiring conscription forces an army deserter to lead an underground and dangerously criminal life. However, those who suffer most from political injustice are the women in all of these films: Kiyokawa's woman is tortured for information on his whereabouts, the hero of *Samurai Spy* meets his woman because she has been set upon by a group of his rivals, and the heroine of *Clouds at Sunset* is publicly ruined by her association with the deserter who sells her to save himself. These long-suffering women bear an uncanny resemblance to many a Kenji Mizoguchi heroine, but it is in the realm of camera technique that Shinoda says he learned a great deal from both Mizo and Ozu.[36]

Mizo, Ozu Plus Alpha

The Ofuna Nouvelle Vague of the early 1960s erupted with new contents relating more directly to the lives of the postwar baby-boom generation. The technical and formal qualities of the new "different kind of film," however, tended to be French imports: hand-held cameras, long traveling takes, telephoto and zoom lenses, jump-cuts and a whole new antinarrative mode of construction. As with most foreign importations, the techniques were quickly adapted to Japanese needs and reinterpreted in a Japanese context.

In Japan as in France, the lining up of heroes and villains enhanced the political overtones of the new aesthetics. Oshima and Yoshishige Yoshida attacked all of the Japanese "master directors," including Kurosawa, Ichikawa, Kinoshita and Ozu, for their reliance on big budgets and their failure to bring real socio-political issues into their films. Shinoda, however, while joining the campaign against Kurosawa for his financial excesses and Hollywood-like camera, traveling with the characters' actions,[37] was able to erect his own idols of camera technique: Kenji Mizoguchi and Yasujiro Ozu.

As an assistant director at the Ofuna studios, Shinoda worked for Ozu on *Twilight in Tokyo* (1958), and he was deeply impressed by the master's attention to detail in the composition of each shot.[38] It was only after working with Ozu that he began a serious and extensive study of the camera and editing style of both Ozu and Mizoguchi. While the French New Wave established itself to a great extent on the political aesthetics André Bazin extracted from postwar Italian neo-realism,[39] Shinoda maintains that the early works of Mizoguchi and Ozu, such as the 1932 *I Was Born, But* . . ., reveal the political and social conditions of the times in precisely the same way neo-realism sought to do.[40] But these Japanese did what they were doing outside any theoretical dictates and fifteen years in advance of the Italians.

Most important for Shinoda in the work of Ozu and Mizoguchi is their assertion of their own "space" as *auteurs*. His concept of a director's space in the cinematography arises from the temporal as well as the compositional elements of the moving photographic image. He marvels, for example, at Ozu's eccentric editing: "It's all built on his own inner sense of time. Three- five- and seven-second takes are the basic rhythm of his films, which turn out to be made up of an incredibly large number of shots, usually a succession of about 2,000 still images."[41] In Mizoguchi's case he admires not only the traveling camera, moving at its own speed and not at that of the characters, but the objectifying withdrawal to long shot when treating violence and eroticism on the screen—perhaps best evidenced in his most recent film, *Banished Orin* (1977), which is also built as a succession of nearly still images like Ozu's late work. The "space" in *Banished Orin* is sometimes peculiarly like Ozu's irrational cutaways: in flashback Orin (Shima Iwashita) is ejected from the blind shamisen-players' troupe, then a shot of crabs edging along the waves at a beach intervenes before the next shot of Orin in the present alone on the shore with her back to the camera. Sometimes it resembles Mizoguchi's pictorial placement of humans in nature more closely: Orin and the man who has just committed murder over her stand under a gnarled tree on the shore as he tells her they must part; he then exits from one side of the frame, she walks out the other side, and only the dark, twisted tree is left like a *sumi* ink painting. Shinoda's camera has become more static like Ozu's in his recent films, but the angle is set closer to Mizoguchi—it is at Shinoda's own eye-level, usually looking down on his protagonists. This Mizoguchi-like detachment has become a consistent feature of Shinoda's work, a kind of icy aestheticism best seen in *Banished Orin*, where Kazuo Miyagawa's camerawork supersedes all messages and all emotion (Shinoda jokes about the fact that in order to maintain the director's eye-level camera angle, the much shorter cinematographer had to stand on a box for most of the shooting).[42]

Having had no formal training in art history or graphic composition, Shinoda became as absorbed in this aspect of filmmaking as he did in bringing modern music and new scripts into the medium. Joining composer Toru Takemitsu and scriptwriter Shuji Terayama as a regular member of Shinoda's staff was cinematographer Masao Kosugi. In the early days at Shochiku, the two trained together. Shinoda recalls Kosugi's unique lighting methods as the opposite of the usual practice: "He'd start with an unlit set, put in one light, and if he didn't like the effect, take it away and start all over from another angle. Every day it took the whole morning to set up the lighting; we could only start filming after noon."[43] Nevertheless Shinoda soon became autocratic on the set in his own way, and he maintains, "It doesn't matter who the cameraman is, I can work with anyone."[44] Since he insists on doing all his own camera setups, presumably he means he can work with anyone who will submit to doing things his way.

Shinoda's way began with experimentation in color and genre in *Killers on Parade* (1961), a crime action film. He considered it a chance to manipulate the expression of the color and the narrative. The barrage of action is very loosely connected, and the use of harsh primary colors is an attempt to present an opposition to the muted tones favored for the creation of a "Japanese atmosphere."[45]

In his later films Shinoda went much farther to break down the Shochiku film stereotype. *Pale Flower* became so much Shinoda's own that the Shochiku scriptwriter refused to accept it, and the ensuing altercation delayed release of the film for nine months. Shinoda suppressed the dialogue and the story and opened the film with the heavy atmosphere of the gambling room. In a montage of over 140 cuts which precedes the dialogue, the impending peril and the personalities are defined by the monotonous cant of the dealer, the furtive and aggressive glances of the game's participants, and detailed, highly restrained motions. "This is a nihilistic film!" fumed scriptwriter Baba, and Shochiku, in confusion, shelved it.[46]

With Beauty and Sorrow attempts to recreate the color and texture of the Heian period (794–1185). The harmonious tones of traditional Japanese architecture and textiles, the somber shadows of graveyards and temples, and the hollow resonance of huge bronze temple bells dominate the film. One has the impression that with this oppressive refinement and stillness Shinoda seeks an aesthetics of death and a society so elegantly turned in on itself that the result is homosexuality. About his own film Shinoda says enthusiastically, "I've never seen such decadence treated in such soft colors in any other film."[47]

With the 1967 *Clouds at Sunset* Shinoda embarked on independent production with his own company, Hyogensha (Expression Company). Since then a crucial feature of all of his works has been the playing of the leading roles by his wife, Shima Iwashita, whom he met when he first began directing at Shochiku. Her performances, particularly in the double roles of courtesan and wife in *Double Suicide*, have been focal points of Shinoda's work, much as Nagisa Oshima has relied on the acting of his wife, Akiko Koyama, in his films. In *Clouds at Sunset* Shinoda had Iwashita represent the traditional self-sacrificing, victimized woman who has all the charm of abject innocence (a theme he would attempt to turn around in another story of a woman's relationship with an army deserter in the film commemorating his tenth anniversary in independent production, *Banished Orin*). At the same time, he experimented with the technical limitations of independent production—*Clouds at Sunset* was made entirely on location in the bleak and impoverished seacoast town that plays its own role in the story. After succeeding in proving to himself and to the major production companies that a location film could be done on a meager budget, he was ready for an aesthetic experiment of the opposite extreme with his next film, *Double Suicide*.

Double Suicide

For his 1969 Hyogensha/ATG production Shinoda sought a totally constructed reality within which to set a story of the destruction that he sees as the inevitable result of eroticism. He selected one of his first loves for adaptation, Chikamatsu's popular 1720 Bunraku puppet play *Shinju Ten no Amijima*.[48] It has been noted that Shinoda, like Mizoguchi, has been able to bring Chikamatsu's work almost unchanged to the screen because both film directors and playwright share the "fatalistic concept of waiting destiny, and the inability of any man to escape it."[49] But unlike Mizoguchi and other directors who have adapted Chikamatsu's work to film, Shinoda made a filmic analysis of the theatrical form of Bunraku. In so doing, he removed himself yet farther from the subject and the emotion, creating a work that is about filmmaking, about early eighteenth-century aesthetics, as well as about Bunraku and the deeply rooted Japanese attitude toward love, marriage and fate.

The film begins backstage in the Bunraku theater with preparations for the presentation of the play during which the lifelessness of the dolls' heads without the blackclothed puppeteers to manipulate them is emphasized. We are quickly made to realize that the puppeteers represent the hand of fate. We hear Shinoda's voice on the telephone discussing the final graveyard scene with scriptwriter Taeko Tomioka, and we are prepared for the circularity of a Mizoguchi film. The film title, read aloud in the sing-song voice of a puppet play narrator, intervenes, and the hero appears as an actor, not a doll. He passes a group of Buddhist pilgrims on a bridge, then stops to look down at the corpses of two lovers by the river who have committed suicide. Through this introduction we are told exactly what to expect, and the rest of the film becomes an aesthetic exercise in a novel presentation of a traditional form. It is a stylization executed with severe discipline; Shinoda has described the experience of making the film as "like drinking ice water."[50]

Jihei (Kichiemon Nakamura), an Osaka paper merchant, has fallen in love with Koharu (Shima Iwashita), a courtesan he cannot afford to keep. But his love is fired by jealousy that arises because of a rich, vulgar merchant, Tahei (Hosei Komatsu), who flaunts his ability to buy Koharu out of indenture. Koharu has also fallen in love with Jihei and even turns away other customers to be with him. The lovers finally begin to see suicide as the only way of realizing their desire to be together.

Jihei's wife, Osan (also played by Shima Iwashita), senses the lovers' intent and does all she can to save her husband's life. She takes over the operation of the paper shop to provide money while he languishes in lovesick, helpless jealousy; she pawns everything of value down to the children's dress clothing; she tries to appeal to Jihei's sense of responsibility for his two children; and finally in desperation she secretly writes to Koharu to beg her to spare her husband's life by breaking off the affair.

Jihei's in-laws try to appeal to his self-esteem, but to no avail. Osan's father surprises her and Jihei in the midst of a terrified attempt to save Koharu by giving up all they own; the enraged old man drags his daughter away, demanding a divorce. Jihei is free to follow the path love has marked out for him. Absolving themselves of worldly responsibilities by cutting their hair to become a Buddhist "monk" and "nun," Jihei and Koharu commit suicide after a night of lovemaking in a graveyard.

Throughout the telling of the story, the veiled, blackclothed stage hands (*kuroko*) of the Bunraku theater, in which they are regarded as invisible, appear. Shinoda, however, calls attention to them by cutting away to sympathetic expressions on their faces through their black gauze veils, stopping the action while one of them wrests a letter away from the actors and holds it up to the camera, and having them lead or aid the actors who submit like dolls. Aiding in the fated destruction, the compassion on their faces speaks for the playwright and the film director. Yet their presence is chilling, as is the extreme stylization of the physical atmosphere.

The world in which the characters live revolves and comes apart like a Kabuki stage, and the walls and floors almost swallow the people with abstract calligraphy, blowups of lavish Edo Period woodblock prints and Bunraku libretti. In combination with the "invisible" stage hands, this world closes in on the protagonists. Jihei literally steps into another world, for example, when Osan is taken away. The stage hands point him the way, and in slow motion he begins to tear his shop apart. A freeze frame catches him in a flurry of white papers. We then see him from above, standing alone and immobilized in anguish. *Kuroko* gather around him, the sets begin to fall away, and the camera follows as he is propelled backward. The *kuroko* lean him against a wall that turns him out of the screen, its shiny aluminum surface dissolving into a rippling water surface. This constructed, intrusive world enhances the idea of fate as well as the idea of theater, which Shinoda further stresses by moving the camera and avoiding montage—the whole film is built of a little over 240 shots.[51]

Double Suicide's application for the present day is part of its detached stylization. By using Shima Iwashita for both the courtesan and the wife, Shinoda stresses the total irrationality of love suggested in the dialogue. When Koharu wonders why Jihei loves her, his only answer is because she is a woman and he is a man. But in the film Osan is the same woman, and Shinoda calls attention to the practice of Japanese married men of seeking romance outside marriage, while the wife fulfills the function of household manager and child-bearer. Yet even as he points out the persistent irrational attitude toward women's roles in Japan and attempts to show pity for the downtrodden, Shinoda believes that love is blind and doomed.

Beauty in Destruction

From the outset of his filmmaking, Shinoda set aesthetic goals for himself. The search for the staff he has gathered has been part of his path toward stylization, and from his goals emerges an eccentric world view. His fatalism, like Mizoguchi's, is always beautiful in the extreme, but the consistent destruction of his protagonists has become an obsession for him. The mysterious lady of *Pale Flower* dies in her thrill-seeking with drugs; the lovely apprentice of *With Beauty and Sorrow* destroys the world of all the people she becomes involved with; Koharu and Jihei want death as the symbol of their love. In other period films, Shinoda selects eras at the edge of destruction: the death of the shamaness Himiko (1974) marks the beginning of hard-boiled political maneuvering; the hero of *Assassination* goes down with the Edo Period; the lusty, primitive innocence in need of familial reassurance represented by Orin, the blind shamisen player, is the end of premodern Japan, submerged in industrialization and militarism.

Shinoda readily admits to his eccentricity: "Whatever is in the process of being destroyed is beautiful," he maintains.[52] This mannered aesthetic, always returning to masochism, sex and violence, infuses all of his films and interacts with his subjects and results in a highly detached stylization. As an assessment of historical events, this aesthetic is perhaps too limited to allow for clear political statement, but this is not, after all, where

Shinoda's strength lies. In pure visual and sound experience his films impress with the lush flamboyance Kon Ichikawa so admires, and his contribution to the generation of the 1960s has been his devotion to beauty.

Notes

1 Author's conversation with Masahiro Shinoda, May 1974.
2 *Ibid.*
3 *Nihon eiga kantoku zenshu* (Dictionary of Japanese Film Directors) (Tokyo: Kinema Jumposha, 1976), p. 198.
4 "Shinoda Masahiro jiden to jisaku o kataru" (Masahiro Shinoda Talks about Himself and His Films), *Sekai no eiga sakka 10: Shinoda Masahiro, Yoshida Yoshishige* (Film Directors of the World 10: Masahiro Shinoda and Yoshishige Yoshida) (Tokyo: Kinema Jumposha, 1971), p. 66.
5 *Ibid.*, p. 67.
6 *Ibid.*, p. 67.
7 *Ibid.*, p. 68.
8 *Ibid.*, p. 68.
9 *Ibid.*, p. 69.
10 *Ibid.*, p. 102.
11 *Ibid.*, p. 70.
12 Author's conversation with Masahiro Shinoda, October 1977.
13 "Shinoda Masahiro jiden to jisaku o kataru," *op. cit.*, p. 71.
14 "Oshima Nagisa jiden to jisaku o kataru" (Nagisa Oshima Talks about Himself and His Films), *Sekai no eiga sakka 6: Oshima Nagisa* (Film Directors of the World 6: Nagisa Oshima) (Tokyo: Kinema Jumposha, 1972), p. 76.
15 Hideo Matsuoka interview with Masahiro Shinoda, *Mainichi Shimbun* newspaper (Tokyo), February 6, 1975.
16 "Shinoda Masahiro jiden to jisaku o kataru," *op. cit.*, p. 72.
17 *Ibid.*, p. 75.
18 Shinoda conversation, 1974, *cit.*
19 Matsuoka and Shinoda, *op. cit.*
20 Shinoda conversation, 1977, *cit.*
21 Shigemi Sato, "Kawaita Mizuumi hyo" (Review of *Youth in Fury*), reprinted from *Eiga Hyoron* (Film Commentary, Tokyo) October 1960, in *Gendai Nihon eiga ron taikei 3: Nihon nuberu bagu* (Survey of Contemporary Japanese Film Theory 3: The Japanese Nouvelle Vague) (Tokyo: Tojusha, 1970), p. 284.
22 "Shinoda Masahiro jiden to jisaku o kataru," *op. cit.*, p. 77.
23 *Ibid.*, p. 78.
24 Shinoda conversation, 1977, *cit.*
25 "Shinoda Masahiro jiden to jisaku o kataru," *op. cit.*, p. 77.
26 *Ibid.*, p. 86.
27 *Ibid.*, p. 86.
28 *Ibid.*, p. 87.
29 Shinoda conversation, 1974, *cit.*
30 *Ibid.*
31 Shinoda conversation, 1977, *cit.*
32 "Shinoda Masahiro jiden to jisaku o kataru," *op. cit.*, p. 92.

33 Translated into English as *Beauty and Sadness* (New York: Alfred Knopf, 1975) by Howard S. Hibbett.
34 "Shinoda Masahiro jiden to jisaku o kataru," *op. cit.*, p. 92.
35 Author's conversation with Kon Ichikawa, October 1977.
36 Matsuoka and Shinoda, *op. cit.*
37 Joan Mellen, *Voices from the Japanese Cinema* (New York: Liveright, 1975), p. 252.
38 Masahiro Shinoda, "Mizoguchi Kenji kara toku hanarete" (Far away from Kenji Mizoguchi), *Kikan Film* (Film Journal, Tokyo), No. 3, 1969, p. 154.
39 *See* André Bazin, *What Is Cinema?*, vol. 1 (Berkeley and Los Angeles: University of California Press).
40 Matsuoka and Shinoda, *op. cit.*
41 Shinoda conversation, 1977, *cit.*
42 *Ibid.*
43 *Ibid.*
44 Shinoda conversation, 1974, *cit.*
45 "Shinoda Masahiro jiden to jisaku o kataru," *op. cit.*, p. 79.
46 *Ibid.*, p. 87.
47 *Ibid.*, p. 92.
48 Translated into English as *The Love Suicide at Amijima* (Cambridge, Mass.: Harvard University Press, 1953) by Donald H. Shively, and as "The Love Suicides at Amijima" in *Major Plays of Chikamatsu* (New York and London: Columbia University Press, 1961) by Donald Keene.
49 Donald Richie, *Japanese Cinema* (New York: Doubleday Anchor Books, 1971), p. 176.
50 Shinoda conversation, 1977, *cit.*
51 *Ibid.*
52 *Ibid.*

MASAHIRO SHINODA: FILMOGRAPHY

1960 *One-Way Ticket for Love* (*Koi no Katamichi Kippu*)
pr: Shochiku (Ofuna); orig. sc: Shinoda; ph: Masao Kosugi; music: Masayoshi Ikeda; cast: Kazuya Kosaka, Noriko Maki, Masaaki Hirao, Yachiyo Otori, Tatsuo Nagai et al. Something of a youth genre film capitalizing on the rise of rock music. The woman promoter responsible for discovering a now famous pop singer takes a liking to a young musician and gets him a job. He falls in love with another girl, however, and asks the promoter to get her a job too. She does, but asks the famous singer to "take care of the girl." The girl's former lover appears and tries to shoot the singer, but is stopped by the musician, who then tries it himself. The singer is only slightly wounded, and the girl ends up waiting for the musician to get out of jail. Shochiku liked the film, but it was a commercial failure, and Shinoda was consequently demoted. (Non-circulating print and negative at Shochiku, Tokyo.)

Dry Lake/ Youth in Fury (*Kawaita Mizuumi*)
pr: Shochiku (Ofuna); orig. story: Eiji Shimba; sc: Shuji Terayama; ph: Masao Kosugi; music: Toru Takemitsu; cast: Shinichiro Mikami, Shima Iwashita, Junichiro Yamashita, Hizuru Takachiho, Kayoko Honoo et al. Portrait of a "little Hitler" type frustrated revolutionary. A boy who leads a far from exemplary, rather aimless and debauched life decides to get involved in meting out justice as he sees it. A member of a student leftist coordinating committee, he dallies with bar madames, hires thugs and seeks revenge for a friend on a member of the Diet. He finally decides that the anti-Security Treaty demonstrations are useless and decides to blow up the whole confusion with dynamite, but is apprehended by the police. (PFA/SH; negative at Shochiku, Tokyo.)

1961 *My Face Red in the Sunset/Killers on Parade* (*Yuhi ni Akai Ore no Kao*)
pr: Shochiku (Ofuna); orig. sc: Shuji Terayama; color ph: Masao Kosugi; music: Naozumi Yamamoto; cast: Yusuke Kawazu, Shima Iwashita, Kayoko Honoo, Ryohei Uchida, Fumio Watanabe et al. Action film about a shady building contractor who tries to destroy the woman journalist who exposed him. He hires a gang of killers, chosen according to their marksmanship, to get the journalist. One of the gunmen, a young amateur, falls in love with the journalist and also becomes the target of the pros. Comic accidental murders and jealousy of the boy's marksmanship on the part of the pros; loosely connected action and harsh colors. A critical failure, which Shinoda attributes to its "eccentricity." (PFA/SH; negative at Shochiku, Tokyo.)

Epitaph to My Love (*Waga Koi no Tabiji*)
pr: Shochiku (Ofuna); orig. story: Ayako Sono; sc: Shuji Terayama and Shinoda; ph: Masao Kosugi; music: Naozumi Yamamoto; cast: Yusuke Kawazu, Shima Iwashita, Yumeji Tsukioka, Fumio Watanabe, Takanobu Hozumi et al. Melodrama made at Shochiku's behest. A journalist in Yokohama falls in love with a coffee-shop waitress. Her father is injured, so the boy approaches his former patroness for money to pay the medical expenses, but he is suddenly called away on business. The girl marries a rich boy while he is away, but is hit

by a car and stricken with amnesia. Her new husband divorces her, and the journalist tries to win her back, but while he is away on business again, she tries to commit suicide. The shock restores her memory, and their love. Terayama had written "a wonderful scenario—like a Rorschach test" but the company didn't like it and Shinoda had to redo it with a more orthodox construction. (PFA/SH; negative at Shochiku, Tokyo.)

Shamisen and Motorcycle/Love Old and New (*Shamisen to Otobai*)
pr: Shochiku (Ofuna); orig. story: Matsutaro Kawaguchi; sc: Takao Yanai; ph: Masao Kosugi; music: Masayoshi Ikeda; cast: Miyuki Kuwano, Yumeji Tsukioka, Masayuki Mori, Yusuke Kawazu, Yuki Tominaga et al. Another melodrama for the company. A girl is injured in a motorcycle accident with her upper-class boyfriend. The doctor who cares for her gets her a job and begins going to her widowed mother's house for singing lessons accompanied by shamisen. The girl feels there is something strange about this and moves out. Finally the older people explain that they had been lovers before the war but were separated by their parents, and the girl herself is actually the doctor's daughter. The boy the girl had been seeing was kept away by his parents, but now he proposes to her. Shinoda felt this was an artificial story, but used it to explore what a real Shimpa drama was like. (No circulating prints; negative at Shochiku, Tokyo.)

1962 *Our Marriage* (*Watakushi-tachi no Kekkon*)
pr: Shochiku (Ofuna); orig. sc: Zenzo Matsuyama and Shinoda; ph: Masao Kosugi; music: Naozumi Yamamoto; cast: Noriko Maki, Chieko Baisho, Eijiro Tono, Sadako Sawamura, Shinichiro Mikami et al. Family drama that touches on pollution before it was really considered a problem. Two sisters whose father can no longer make a living in the now dying seaweed industry go to work in a factory. The younger girl falls in love with a coworker who is in love with her older sister. The older girl decides to marry the son of the seaweed industry union leader in order to get her father's union debts canceled. But a former laborer who is now a rich company president reappears, and the older sister decides to marry him instead. The younger sister is left wondering why the coworker she loves so much should be rejected by her sister. Matsuyama's script was assigned, with the order to make a low-budget film in three weeks. Shinoda did it, but changed the story considerably to show that poverty can destroy human feelings. (PFA/SH; negative at Shochiku, Tokyo.)

Glory on the Summit: Burning Youth (*Yama no Sanka: Moyuru Waka-mono-tachi*)
pr: Shochiku (Ofuna); orig. story: Yorichika Arima; sc: Yoshio Shirasaka; ph: Masao Kosugi; music: Naozumi Yamamoto; cast: So Yamamura, Isuzu Yamada, Takahiro Tamura, Shima Iwashita, Chieko Baisho et al. Youth rebellion in the bourgeoisie. A man who works in the finance ministry has three sons, the oldest of whom has died in a mountaineering accident. The father continues to encourage his sons to be professionally and socially ambitious, and they continue to try to escape parental pressure by mountain-climbing. The second son

loses his leg in a mountain accident and destroys his father's hopes for him. The youngest son decides he too must climb. Shinoda was credited with showing the unreasonableness of contemporary society through the neutral activity of hiking. (No circulating print; negative at Shochiku, Tokyo.)

Tears on the Lion's Mane (*Namida o Shishi no Tategami ni*)
pr: Shochiku (Ofuna); orig. sc: Shuji Terayama, Ichiro Mizunuma and Shinoda; 'scope ph: Masao Kosugi; music: Toru Takemitsu; cast: Takashi Fujiki, Koji Nambara, Kyoko Kishida, Mariko Kaga, So Yamamura et al. The disillusionment of a young tough in the midst of union struggles. A Yokohama dock worker acts as spy and thug for the shipping company because he believes the manager saved his life when he was a baby and was crippled as a result. Told to rough up the worker who is trying to form a union, he accidentally kills the man, and later finds out it was his girlfriend's father. Despondent, he still continues to do as he is told, and begins an affair with the company president's wife. She tells him the manager's story is a lie, and the outraged boy beats the man to death. As he desperately tries to explain to the workers and his girl, the police come to take him away. (Non-circulating print and negative at Shochiku, Tokyo.)

1963 ***Pale Flower (*Kawaita Hana*)**
pr: Shochiku (Ofuna); orig. story: Shintaro Ishihara; sc: Ataru Baba and Shinoda; 'scope ph: Masao Kosugi; music: Toru Takemitsu; cast: Ryo Ikebe, Mariko Kaga, Takashi Fujiki, Chisako Hara, Koji Nakahara et al. The first film about the real world of contemporary gangsters, a study of paternalism, obligation, and the excitement of masochism. A gangster fresh out of prison for an assigned murder meets a mysterious girl at a closed game who wants to gamble for bigger stakes. He introduces her into the big games, attracted by her thrill-seeking. In a gang war, he volunteers to perform revenge murder again, and invites the girl to watch, for excitement she has never seen before. Later, back in prison, a new inmate informs him the girl was made into a drug addict by a junkie assassin who used to be at the games. Concentration on powerful visuals, which resulted in a fight with the scenarist that delayed the film's release by nine months. (AB)

1964 ***Assassination (*Ansatsu*)**
pr: Shochiku (Kyoto); orig. story: Ryotaro Shiba; sc: Nobuo Yamada; 'scope ph: Masao Kosugi; music: Toru Takemitsu; cast: Tetsuro Tamba, Shima Iwashita, Isao Kimura, Eitaro Ozawa, Eiji Okada et al. Personality study of an enigmatic figure in the events leading up to the Meiji Restoration of 1868. Hachiro Kiyokawa, the head of a prominent fencing school, had been a staunch supporter of restoration of the emperor to power. He had been jailed for killing a military government policeman who attacked one of his disciples. But he was released from jail when he sold the military government the idea of his forming a terrorist group to go to Kyoto and wipe out the pro-imperialist forces. Meanwhile his former colleagues try to understand his motives. They feel that it was either the massacre of pro-imperialist friends that he survived several years before, or the torture murder of his mistress, who refused to reveal their where-

abouts, that caused him to become cynical about political ideals. The military government has decided in any case that he is untrustworthy, and sends a master swordsman assassin after him to Kyoto. Just when their leader is informing the supposedly pro-military terrorists that the emperor has given his authorization for them to join those who support him, the assassin arrives to murder him. Almost impossible to understand without a plot outline, due to involved flash-back construction and large cast, but a visually and psychologically powerful film. (AB)

1965 *With Beauty and Sorrow* (*Utsukushisa to Kanashimi to*)
pr: Shochiku (Ofuna); orig. story: Yasunari Kawabata; sc: Nobuo Yamada; color 'scope ph: Masao Kosugi; music: Toru Takemitsu; cast: So Yamamura, Mariko Kaga, Kaoru Yachigusa, Misako Watanabe, Kei Yamamoto et al. A girl who is in love with her painting teacher decides to destroy the middle-aged married man who once got the teacher pregnant and left her, but still has some hold on her affections. The girl seduces the man's son, and he drowns in a boating accident she causes, but which she herself survives. (SH)

Samurai Spy/Sarutobi (*Ibun Sarutobi Sasuke*)
pr: Shochiku (Ofuna); orig. story: Koji Nakata; sc: Yoshiyuki Fukuda; ph: Masao Kosugi; music: Toru Takemitsu; cast: Koji Takahashi, Mutsuhiro Toura, Misako Watanabe, Seiji Miyaguchi, Tetsuro Tamba, Jun Hamamura et al. Period film about spies, counter-spies and double spies that expresses disillusionment with politics. Set after 1600 when the new Edo military government was trying to wipe out the last remnants of opposition and all Japanese Christians. Sarutobi is a low-level spy who is the last to have been in the company of a murdered double spy, and he is consequently pursued by both sides, although he knows nothing. In the course of all the mysterious murders and rescues, he manages to fall in love, and when the whole mess is resolved, he proposes to the girl. Shinoda wanted to show that politics brings no human progress, and little men like Sarutobi just want to live their lives in peace. (AB)

1966 *Punishment Island/Captive's Island* (*Shokei no Shima*)
pr: Nissei Prod./Daiei; orig story: Taijun Takeda; sc: Shintaro Ishihara; ph: Tatsuo Suzuki; music: Toru Takemitsu; cast: Akira Nitta, Rentaro Mikuni, Kei Sato, Shima Iwashita, Hosei Komatsu, Kinzo Shin et al. About the Japanese attitude toward personal experiences of World War II. A boy whose whole family was murdered during the war because his father was an anarchist sets out to seek revenge. He returns to the island where he was sent as a child after the murder. He had been viciously abused in a reform school there, and finally thrown into the sea by the guard. He was rescued by a fisherman and now is a salesman. He begins to fall in love with a girl on the island, and then finds that her father is the man responsible for his father's death and had been sent to head the reform school at the same time he himself had been sent there as an inmate. But the old man has no recollection of all this, and the daughter convinces the boy to spare him. The boy then buries his past. Some critics feel this is Shinoda's best film. (AB)

1967 *Clouds at Sunset (Akanegumo)*
pr: Hyogensha/Shochiku; orig. story: Tsutomu Minakami; sc: Naoyuki Suzuki; color 'scope ph: Masao Kosugi; music: Toru Takemitsu; cast: Shima Iwashita, Tsutomu Yamazaki, Kei Sato, Mayumi Ogawa, Kiyoshi Nonomura et al. Melodrama about a deserter from the Japanese army and the girl he victimizes. She is from a poor family and works at an inn where she meets the man who promises to get her a better job in another town. She goes and meets her sister, who tells her the inn she is going to work at has a very bad reputation. Later the man comes back with an elderly man to whom he is indebted and encourages the girl to sleep with him for money. She does, planning to pay her father's medical bills. Finally the military police come to question her about the man and decide to use her as bait to catch him. The publicity ruins her, but she still believes he is the only person who ever helped her. Filmed entirely on location, in an attempt at real replay of historical events. *KJ* #8. (FC; negative at Shochiku, Tokyo.)

1969 **Double Suicide (Shinju Ten no Amijima)*
pr: Hyogensha/ATG; orig. story: Monzaemon Chikamatsu; sc: Taeko Tomioka; ph: Toichiro Narushima; music: Toru Takemitsu; cast: Shima Iwashita, Kichiemon Nakamura, Hosei Komatsu, Yusuke Takita, Kamatari Fujiwara et al. Period drama that is at the same time an appreciation of a theatrical form, the Bunraku puppet drama. An early eighteenth-century merchant falls in love with a courtesan and lets his business and family go to ruin. His wife's parents finally take her away, and since the merchant has no money to redeem the courtesan, they commit suicide together. Controversial aesthetic interpretation of Bunraku, and novel view of the frustrations of Edo society. *KJ* #1. (AB)

1970 *The Scandalous Adventures of Buraikan (Buraikan)*
pr: Ninjin Club/Toho; orig. sc: Shuji Terayama; color 'scope ph: Kozo Okazaki; music: Masaru Sato; cast: Tatsuya Nakadai, Shima Iwashita, Shoichi Ozawa, Tetsuro Tamba, Fumio Watanabe et al. Attempt to appreciate Kabuki in terms of pop art and underground theater. Set in 1841 when the country was suffering under stringent reforms designed to hold down spending and redistribute wealth into the coffers of the military government. Centers around the activities of a collection of outlaws, derelicts and prostitutes who are all struggling to survive. The motley group is brought together in an attempt to rescue a girl who has been forced to become the mistress of a powerful lord, but the plan is found out. The derelict who survives goes back to trying to drown his mother so that he can marry the prostitute he loves. A grotesquely funny film. (TO)

1971 *Silence (Chinmoku)*
pr: Hyogensha/Mako International/Toho; sc: Shusaku Endo, based on his novel of the same title; color ph: Kazuo Miyagawa; music: Toru Takemitsu; cast: David Lampson, Mako, Shima Iwashita, Eiji Okada, Tetsuro Tamba et al. Period drama set in seventeenth-century Nagasaki during the persecution of Christians. A Portuguese missionary is subjected to severe torture by the military government and finally apostasizes, putting his foot on a religious

painting. He falls in love with a Japanese woman who has apostasized to save her husband's life, and ends as a dissolute. *KJ #2*. (TO)

1972 *Sapporo Winter Olympic Games (Sapporo Orimpikku)*
pr: News Eiga Seisakusha Remmei/Toho; sc: Nobuo Yamada, Aromu Mushiake, Motoo Ogasawara and Taeko Tomioka; ph: News Eiga Seisakusha Remmei camera crew; music: Masaru Sato. Documentary on the 1972 Winter Olympics at Sapporo, Japan. Attempt to capture the human element in both participants' and audience's expressions and antics, but the original 166-minute version also had a tiring emphasis on ceremonial aspects of the games. The shorter version released abroad is consequently better. Shinoda does an interesting interview with Japanese ski jumper Yukio Kasaya. (TO)

1973 *The Petrified Forest (Kaseki no Mori)*
pr: Hyogensha/Toho; orig.story: Shintaro Ishihara; sc: Nobuo Yamada; color ph: Kozo Okazaki; music: Toru Takemitsu; cast: Kenichi Hagiwara, Sayoko Ninomiya, Masako Yagi, Haruko Sugimura et al. Story about a boy and his mother, centering on the agonies he goes through when she has a love affair. Shinoda wanted to study the mother complex of Japanese young people, who appear strong on the outside, but are actually weak. Rather a disaster. (No circulating prints; negative at Toho, Tokyo.)

1974 *Himiko (Himiko)*
pr: Hyogensha/ATG; orig. sc: Taeko Tomioka; color ph: Tatsuo Suzuki; music: Toru Takemitsu; cast: Shima Iwashita, Rentaro Mikuni, Masao Kusakari, Rie Yokoyama, Choichiro Kawarazaki et al. Prehistoric drama about a semi-legendary shaman queen of Japan named Himiko. She rules by direct communication with the gods, giving her commands in a frenzied trance, but is actually manipulated by a ruthless elder. When Himiko falls in love with her brother, who returns from distant travels, the elder has her killed and the boy brutally punished. Himiko is succeeded by another girl who appears to have the entranced gift of prophecy. Insinuations of Korean connections and widespread incest in early Japan, and a clear statement that the truth will not be known until the early imperial tombs are opened. Rich photography with a feeling for the wilds of civilization's dawn. (FC; negative at ATG.)

1975 *Under the Cherry Blossoms (Sakura no Mori no Mankai no Shita)*
pr: Geiensha/Toho; orig. story: Ango Sakaguchi; sc: Taeko Tomioka and Shinoda; color ph: Tatsuo Suzuki; music: Toru Takemitsu; cast: Shima Iwashita, Tomisaburo Wakayama, Hiroko Isayama, Hideo Kanze, Yusuke Takita et al. Eerie story set in the twelfth century giving full play to Shinoda's eroticism, sadism and aestheticism with a supernatural twist. A rough mountain hunter feels he owns all he can see except a cherry grove that seems to make those who wander through it in full bloom go insane. One day he sets upon a group of travelers with an indescribably beautiful noblewoman in the party. He murders her husband and takes her as his wife, carrying her on his back as she commands. On arrival at his home she has him kill all his other women except one servant, and he continues attacking travelers to provide her with the lifestyle of the capital she longs for. Finally she persuades him they must go

to live in the capital, where she has him hunt heads of all sorts of people for her to play with. Finally he tires of nightly murder and wants to go back to the mountains. She tearfully agrees to return, but as they walk through the flowering cherry grove he suddenly sees her as a demonic hag and murders her in terror. (Positive and negative at Toho, Tokyo.)

1977   *Banished Orin* (*Hanare Goze Orin*)

pr: Hyogensha/Toho; orig. story: Tsutomu Minakami; sc: Keiji Hasebe and Shinoda; color ph: Kazuo Miyagawa; music: Toru Takemitsu; cast: Shima Iwashita, Yoshio Harada, Rie Yokoyama, Taiji Tonoyama et al. Early twentieth-century period drama about a blind shamisen player who is banished from her troupe for having engaged in sexual relations with men. She becomes friends with an army deserter, telling him her story in flashbacks. She at last finds happiness with him in an asexual brother-sister relationship, but they are destroyed when she breaks her vow of chastity and he becomes jealous enough to murder. Heavy symbolism accusing Japan of modernizing through a military-industrial fascist alliance; superb four-season photography by Miyagawa.

SELECTED BIBLIOGRAPHY

Western-Language Bibliography

Anderson, Joseph, and Donald Richie. *The Japanese Film: Art and Industry*. New York: Grove Press, 1960.

Burch, Noël. *Theory of Film Practice*. New York and Washington: Praeger, 1973.

Erzatty, Sasha. *Kurosawa*. Paris: Editions Universitaires, 1964,

Estève, Michel (ed.). *Akira Kurosawa. Etudes cinématographiques*, Nos. 30–31, Spring, 1964. Paris: M.J. Minard.

Giuglaris, Shinobu et Marcel. *Le cinéma japonais*. Paris: Editions du Cerf, 1956.

Kinema Jumpo (ed.). *The Complete Works of Akira Kurosawa*. Tokyo: Kinema Jumposha, 1971–72.

Mellen, Joan. *Voices from the Japanese Cinema*. New York: Liveright, 1975.

—*The Waves at Genji's Door: Japan through Its Cinema*. New York: Pantheon Books, 1976.

Mesnil, Michel (ed.). *Kenji Mizoguchi*. Cinéma d'aujourd'hui, No. 31. Paris: Editions Seghers, 1965.

—(ed.). *Akira Kurosawa*. Cinéma d'aujourd'hui, No. 77. Paris: Editions Seghers, 1973.

Richie, Donald. *The Japanese Movie: An Illustrated History*. Tokyo and Palo Alto, California: Kodansha, 1966.

—*The Films of Akira Kurosawa*. Berkeley and Los Angeles: University of California Press, 1965.

—*Japanese Cinema: Film Style and National Character*. New York: Doubleday and Co., Anchor Books, 1971.

—*Ozu: His Life and Films*. Berkeley and Los Angeles: University of California Press, 1974.

—(ed.). *Ikiru* (Kurosawa). London: Lorrimer. New York: Simon and Schuster, 1968.

—(ed.). *Rashomon* (Kurosawa). New York: Grove Press, 1969.

—(ed.). *Seven Samurai* (Kurosawa). London: Lorrimer. New York: Simon and Schuster, 1970.

—(ed.). *Focus on Rashomon*. New Jersey: Prentice-Hall, Inc., 1972.

—and Eric Klestadt (eds.) "Tokyo Story" (Ozu), in Howard S. Hibbett, ed., *Contemporary Japanese Literature*. New York: Knopf, 1977.

Schrader, Paul. *Transcendental Style in Film: Ozu, Bresson, Dreyer*. Berkeley, California: University of California Press, 1972.

Svensson, Arne. *Japan: Screen Guide*. New York: Barnes, 1970.

Tessier, Max. *Yasujiro Ozu. Anthologie du cinéma.* Juillet-Octobre, 1971. Paris: Avant
    Scène du Cinéma.
Tucker, Richard N. *Japan: Film Image.* London: Studio Vista, 1973.
Ve-Ho. *Kenji Mizoguchi.* Paris: Editions Universitaires, 1963.

Journals
Cahiers du cinéma. Paris, 1951–.
Cinéma. Paris, 1954–.
Film Comment. New York, 1950–.
Sight and Sound. London, 1950–.

Japanese-Language Bibliography
Gendai Nihon eiga ron taikei 現代日本映画論大系 (Survey of Contemporary Japanese
    Film Theory). 6 vols. Tokyo: Tojusha, 1971–72.
Ichikawa Kon 市川崑 and Wada Natto 和田夏十. *Seijocho 271 Banchi* 成城町 271 番地.
    Tokyo: Shirakaba Shobo, 1961.
Imamura Shohei no eiga 今村昌平の映画 (The Films of Shohei Imamura). Tokyo: Haga
    Shoten, 1971.
Iwasaki Akira 岩崎昶. *Nihon eiga sakka ron* 日本映画作家論 (Theories on Japanese
    Filmmakers). Tokyo: Chuo Koronsha, 1958.
Kido Shiro 城戸四郎. *Nihon eiga den: Eiga seisakusha no kiroku* 日本映画伝: 映画製作者
    の記録 (The Story of Japanese Film: A Movie Producer's Record). Tokyo: Bungei
    Shunjusha, 1956.
Kishi Matsuo 岸松雄. *Jinbutsu: Nihon eiga shi* 人物: 日本映画史 1 (Personalities:
    Japanese Film History 1). Tokyo: Daviddosha, 1970.
Nihon eiga kantoku zenshu 日本映画監督全集 (Dictionary of Japanese Film Directors).
    Tokyo: Kinema Jumposha, 1976.
Nihon eiga sakuhin zenshu 日本映画作品全集 (Dictionary of Japanese Films). Tokyo:
    Kinema Jumposha, 1971.
Ogawa Toru 小川融. *Gendai Nihon eiga sakka ron* 現代日本映画作家論 (Theories on
    Contemporary Japanese Filmmakers). Tokyo: Sanichi Shobo, 1965.
Oshima Nagisa 大島渚. *Sengo eiga: Hakai to Sozo* 戦後映画: 破壊と創造 (Postwar
    Film: Destruction and Creation). Tokyo: Sanichi Shobo, 1963.
—*Taikenteki sengo eizo ron* 体験的戦後映像論 (A Theory of the Postwar Film Image
    Based on Personal Experience). Tokyo: Asahi Shimbunsha, 1975.
Sato Tadao 佐藤忠男. *Chambara eiga shi* チャンバラ映画史 (History of Swordfight
    Movies). Tokyo: Haga Shoten, 1972.
—*Kurosawa Akira no sekai* 黒沢明の世界 (The World of Akira Kurosawa). Tokyo:
    Sanichi Shobo, 1969.
—*Nihon eiga shiso shi* 日本映画思想史 (History of the Intellectual Currents in Japanese
    Film). Tokyo: Sanichi Shobo, 1970.
—*Oshima Nagisa no sekai* 大島渚の世界 (The World of Nagisa Oshima). Tokyo:
    Chikuma Shobo, 1973.
—*Ozu Yasujiro no Geijutsu* 小津安二郎の芸術 (The Art of Yasujiro Ozu). Tokyo: Asahi
    Shimbunsha, 1971.
Sekai eiga kiroku zenshu 世界映画記録全集 (A Complete Record of World Films).
    Tokyo: Kinema Jumposha, 1973.

Sekai eiga sakuhin: Kiroku zenshu 世界映画作品: 記録全集 (Films of the World: A Complete Record, 1972–74). Tokyo: Kinema Jumposha, 1975. 1975–76 edition, 1977.

Sekai no eiga sakka 世界の映画作家 (Film Directors of the World). 35 vols. Tokyo: Kinema Jumposha, 1969–.

Shindo Kaneto 進藤兼人. *Aru eiga kantoku no shogai* ある映画監督の生涯 (The Life of a Film Director). Tokyo: Iwanami Shoten, 1976.

Takamine Hideko 高峰秀子. *Watashi no tosei nikki* わたしの渡世日記 (My Professional Diary). 2 vols. Tokyo: Asahi Shimbunsha, 1976.

Tayama Rikiya 田山力也. *Nihon eiga sakkatachi: Sosaku no himitsu* 日本映画作家達: 創作の秘密 (Japanese Filmmakers: Secrets of Creation). Tokyo: Daviddosha, 1975.

Yoda Yoshikata 依田義賢. *Mizoguchi Kenji no hito to geijutsu* 溝口健二の人と芸術 (Kenji Mizoguchi: The Man and His Art). Tokyo: Tabata Shoten, 1970.

Journals

Eiga Hyoron 映画評論 (The Filmcrit). Tokyo, 1926–75.

FC (FC). Tokyo: Tokyo National Museum of Modern Art Film Center, 1971–.

Kinema Jumpo キネマ旬報 (Motion Picture Times). Tokyo, 1923–.

INDEX

用心棒
ようじんぼう
黒沢明監督作品
撮影・宮川一夫
製作・田中友幸・菊島隆三
山田五十鈴
加東大介
志村喬
藤原釜足
渡辺篤
沢村いき雄
西村晃
土屋嘉男
清水元
藤田進
山茶花究
東野英治郎
河津清三郎
太刀川寛
ジェリー藤尾
夏木陽介
宝・黒沢プロ作品
宝株式会社配給